Gray Markets

Gray Markets

Prevention, Detection and Litigation

David R. Sugden

Oxford University Press, Inc., publishes works that further Oxford University's objective of excellence in research, scholarship, and education.

Oxford New York
Auckland Cape Town Dar es Salaam Hong Kong Karachi Kuala Lumpur Madrid Melbourne
Mexico City Nairobi New Delhi Shanghai Taipei Toronto

With offices in
Argentina Austria Brazil Chile Czech Republic France Greece Guatemala Hungary Italy
Japan Poland Portugal Singapore South Korea Switzerland Thailand Turkey Ukraine
Vietnam

Copyright © 2009 by Oxford University Press, Inc.

Published by Oxford University Press, Inc.
198 Madison Avenue, New York, New York 10016

Oxford is a registered trademark of Oxford University Press
Oxford University Press is a registered trademark of Oxford University Press, Inc.

All rights reserved. No part of this publication may be reproduced, stored in a retrieval system, or transmitted, in any form or by any means, electronic, mechanical, photocopying, recording, or otherwise, without the prior permission of Oxford University Press, Inc.

_____

Library of Congress Cataloging-in-Publication Data
Sugden, David R.
  Gray markets : prevention, detection and litigation / David R. Sugden.
      p. cm.
  Includes bibliographical references and index.
  ISBN 978-0-19-537129-1 ((pbk.) : alk. paper)
1. Gray market—Law and legislation—United States. 2. Marketing—Law and legislation—United States.
3. Gray market—Law and legislation. 4. Liability (Law) I. Title.
  KF1609.S84 2009
  346.7304´88—dc22   2008049460

_____

1 2 3 4 5 6 7 8 9

Printed in the United States of America on acid-free paper

Note to Readers
This publication is designed to provide accurate and authoritative information in regard to the subject matter covered. It is based upon sources believed to be accurate and reliable and is intended to be current as of the time it was written. It is sold with the understanding that the publisher is not engaged in rendering legal, accounting, or other professional services. If legal advice or other expert assistance is required, the services of a competent professional person should be sought. Also, to confirm that the information has not been affected or changed by recent developments, traditional legal research techniques should be used, including checking primary sources where appropriate.

(Based on the Declaration of Principles jointly adopted by a Committee of the American Bar Association and a Committee of Publishers and Associations.)

You may order this or any other Oxford University Press publication by
visiting the Oxford University Press website at www.oup.com

Contents

ACKNOWLEDGMENTS	xi
ABOUT THE AUTHOR	xiii
PART I: **Introduction: The Gray Market**	1
CHAPTER 1: **Shades of Gray: The Spectrum of Product Diversion**	3
a. The Gray Market	3
b. From Bad to Worse: The Black Market	6
CHAPTER 2: **From iPhones to Viagra: The Affected Industries**	9
a. Airline Industry	10
b. Automotive Industry	11
c. Cigarette Industry	13
d. Cosmetics and Personal Care Products	14
e. Clothing and Apparel	16
f. Food and Drinks	17
g. Watches and Jewelry	18
h. Natural Resources	20
i. Technology	21
j. Pharmaceuticals	22
k. Toys	24
CHAPTER 3: **Black and Gray Market 2.0: From Flea Markets to eBay**	27
a. Globalization	28
b. Internet	32
c. Technology	35
d. Decreased Trade Barriers	37
CHAPTER 4: **The Rippling Effect: Gray Market Consequences**	39
a. Economic Consequences	40
i. Partner Relationships	44
ii. Customer Satisfaction and Brand Goodwill	47
iii. Warranty and Service Costs	49
iv. Research and Development	51

vi   Contents

        b. Social Consequences   52
           i. Consumer Health and Safety   52
           ii. Harm to the Environment   55
           iii. Tax Revenue   56
           iv. Organized Crime   59
        c. Benefits of the Gray Market   60
           i. Discover and Reach New Markets   61
           ii. Overcome Supply Chain Constraints   63
           iii. Reduce Combating Expense   63

PART II: **Prevention: Reducing the Gray Market Potential**   65

CHAPTER 5: **Education: Promoting Gray Market Abstinence**   67
        a. Employees   67
        b. Distribution Partners   70
        c. Consumers   72
        d. Industry Alliances   73
        e. Government Relations   75
        f. Media   76

CHAPTER 6: **Troubleshooting Supply Chain Vulnerabilities**   77
        a. Selecting and Qualifying Partners   78
           i. Background Research   78
           ii. Training and Certification   80
        b. The Partner Contracts   81
           i. Guidelines and Promises   84
           ii. Incentives for Compliance   96
           iii. Penalties for Noncompliance   99
        c. Tightening the Supply Chain   102
           i. Acknowledging Geographic Vulnerabilities   102
           ii. On-Site Security   106
           iii. Transit Security   110
           iv. Product Security   111

CHAPTER 7: **Alternative Gray Market Strategies**   115
        a. Worldwide Pricing   115
        b. Staggered Distribution   116
        c. Internal Distribution   117
        d. IP Insurance   119

PART III: **Detection: Monitoring the Supply Chain**   121

CHAPTER 8: **Red Flags: The Warning Signs of Gray Market Activity**   123
        a. Pricing That Is Too Low   123
        b. Unreasonable Spikes in Orders   125

c. Unusual Orders	126
d. Special Discount Requests	126
e. Warranty Exchange Requests	128
f. Unusual Delivery Requests	129

CHAPTER 9: Methods of Detection — 131

 a. Audits — 131
 b. Internet Monitoring — 133
 c. Brand Protection Purchases — 134
  i. The Uncertain Future of Brand Protection Purchases — 138
 d. Informants — 140
 e. Dumpster Diving — 140

PART IV: Reaction: Legal Strategies After Gray Market Discovery — 143

CHAPTER 10: Initial Strategies — 145

 a. Litigation Alternatives — 145
  i. The International Trade Commission (ITC) — 145
  ii. Arbitration — 148
 b. Civil or Criminal Justice — 151
 c. State or Federal Court — 157
 d. Personal Jurisdiction and Venue — 159

CHAPTER 11: Preliminary Remedies — 165

 a. Search and Seizure — 166
 b. Temporary Restraining Orders and Preliminary Injunctions — 170
 c. Knock 'n Talks — 173
 d. Cease and Desist Correspondence — 174

CHAPTER 12: Civil Discovery — 175

 a. E-Discovery: The Amended FRCP — 176
 b. Forensic Preservation and Examination — 178

CHAPTER 13: Theories of Recovery: Breach of Contract — 183

 a. Introduction to Contract Law — 184
 b. Contract Law's Treatment of the Gray Market — 186
 c. Affirmative Defenses and the Gray Market — 188
 d. Remedies — 189

CHAPTER 14: Theories of Liability: Intentional Interference with Contract (IIWC) — 191

 a. Introduction to IIWC — 191
 b. IIWC's Treatment of the Gray Market — 194
 c. Affirmative Defenses — 197
 d. Remedies — 197

CHAPTER 15: Theories of Liability: Intentional Interference with Prospective Economic Advantage (IIEA) — 199

a. Introduction to IIEA — 199
b. IIEA's Treatment of the Gray Market — 202
c. Affirmative Defenses and the Gray Market — 204
d. Remedies — 205

CHAPTER 16: Theories of Liability: Copyright — 207

a. Introduction to Copyright Law — 208
  i. Copyright Infringement — 209
  ii. Copyright Registration — 211
  iii. International Protection — 212
b. Copyright Law's Treatment of the Gray Market — 213
  i. Performance Rights — 214
  ii. Importation Rights — 216
  iii. Software Licenses and the First Sale Doctrine: An End Run Around the First Sale Doctrine? — 227
  iv. Software Licenses and the First Sale Doctrine: An End Run Around the First Sale Doctrine *Beyond* Software? — 232
c. Affirmative Defenses — 233
  i. Fair Use — 233
  ii. Waiver or Abandonment of Copyright — 235
  iii. Estoppel — 236
  iv. Innocent Intent — 237
d. Remedies — 237
  i. Injunctive Relief — 238
  ii. Impoundment and Destruction — 239
  iii. Damages and Profits — 239
  iv. Attorney Fees — 240
  v. Criminal Penalties — 240

CHAPTER 17: Theories of Liability: Trademark — 241

a. Introduction to Trademark Law — 242
  i. Importance of Trademarks — 242
  ii. Trademark Causes of Action — 244
b. Trademark Law's Treatment of the Gray Market — 246
  i. The Early Cases and the Gray Market — 246
  ii. Tariff Act and the Gray Market — 249
  iii. The Lanham Act and the Gray Market — 254
c. Affirmative Defenses — 282
  i. The First Sale Doctrine — 282
  ii. Not "Gray Market" Goods? — 285
d. Remedies — 286

CHAPTER 18:	**Theories of Liability: State Law**	289
	a. Gray Market Statutes in California	289
	b. Gray Market Statutes in Connecticut	293
	c. Gray Market Statutes in New York	294
	d. Gray Market Statutes in Washington D.C. and Michigan: Gray Market Cigarette Statutes	295
CHAPTER 19:	**Approaches to Gray Market around the Globe**	297
	a. Canada	300
	b. Mexico	301
	c. Europe	302
	d. Russia	304
	e. China	306
	f. India	308
TABLE OF CASES		311
INDEX		327

Acknowledgments

I wish to thank those people who helped the development and writing of this book:

Special gratitude is owed to Oxford University Press for this opportunity. I owe special praise to my editor, Matt Gallaway, who provided great insight and encouragement throughout the writing process. I am also thankful to the rest of the Oxford University Press team for their hard work making this book a reality: Sarah Bloxham, Michelle Lipinski, and Ninell Silberberg.

I would like to thank my partners at Call, Jensen & Ferrell: Wayne Call, Jon Jensen, Scott Ferrell, Mark Eisenhut, Gina Miller, Matt Orr, Ward Lott, Lisa Wegner, and Julie Trotter. I am privileged to work alongside so many bright and talented practitioners. In addition to making the practice of law an absolute delight, they were encouraging and supportive of this project.

Important contributions were also made by the research assistance of Jonathan Lee and Austin Baillio, who both did a tremendous job researching a variety of issues that greatly contributed to this book. Their hard work on these projects was reflected in many late-night and early morning emails.

My *de facto* editor and father-in-law Roger Goodrich is deserving of special thanks. While your remark that this book "is no spy novel" still stings, I am grateful for your effort to wade through these pages with helpful thoughts and suggestions.

I am also especially grateful to my father. Dad, you provided me with firsthand proof that a successful practice does not have to come at the expense of civility. Indeed, you showed me the ability to disagree without being disagreeable. I wish you could have read these pages. While Roger is right—it is no spy novel—I think you would have enjoyed it.

I am most of all thankful to my beautiful wife. Marni, you continue to amaze me. I am thankful for your enthusiasm and support of this book. I am thankful for your late-night trips for coffee and other writing "fuel." Even when we worked late knowing our two little angels would be making personal wake-up calls a few short hours later, your encouragement and optimism never wavered. My gratitude to you extends far beyond this book. I love you very much.

About the Author

David R. Sugden is a partner at Call, Jensen & Ferrell located in Newport Beach, California. Specializing in intellectual property litigation and brand protection, Mr. Sugden has served as lead counsel in copyright and trademark cases throughout the United States, where he has obtained several seven- and eight-figure verdicts and judgments. Mr. Sugden resides in Orange County with his wife of ten years and two young daughters.

PART

I

Introduction: The Gray Market

CHAPTER 1

Shades of Gray

The Spectrum of Product Diversion

"It's not all black and white. And it's the shades of gray that make entrepreneurs great."
—Professor Lloyd Shefsky, Kellogg School of Management[1]

a. The Gray Market	3
b. From Bad to Worse: The Black Market	6

a. The Gray Market

The twenty-first century has been characterized as the dawning of a flat world.[2] Globalization, technology, and the Internet have each contributed to dramatically level the economic playing field. For companies that manufacture and sell products internationally, the world is not exactly flat. It is *tilted*. From cars and cigarettes to pianos and pharmaceuticals, products intended to be sold in foreign countries are finding their way back to the United States through unauthorized distribution channels. This unauthorized economy is called the gray market, and it is growing in size and scope at an alarming rate. Information Technology (IT) manufacturers alone are losing $40 billion in sales every year to the gray market, and the figure is increasing.[3]

With the gray market's prosperity has come familiarity. Its modern expansion has led more brand owners, distribution partners, and end users to become

---

1. Rebecca Knight, *Shades of Grey that Make an Entrepreneur*, Fin. Times (London), August 4, 2008, *available at* http://www.ft.com/cms/s/2/fe5d91ce-5fdc-11dd-805e-000077b07658,dwp_uuid=02e16f4a-46f9-11da-b8e5-00000e2511c8.html.
2. *See e.g.,* Thomas L. Friedman, The World Is Flat (3rd ed. Picador 2007) (2005).
3. *The Grey Market*, KPMG/Anti-Gray Mkt. Alliance, 2003, at 1, *available at* http://www.agmaglobal.org/press_events/press_docs/KPMG_TheGreyMarket_Web.pdf.

acquainted with its existence. Notwithstanding this familiarity, a great deal of confusion remains. For example, courts and commentators are yet to settle on a precise definition of the gray market. Some describe it as a nefarious economy devoid of any legal value: "The term 'gray market' is really just another word for seedy and illegal black-market goods that the police don't have the resources, or the will, to stop from being sold."[4] Others, meanwhile, describe it more as a nuisance—albeit a *legal* nuisance—for brand owners: "Unlike black-market trafficking in stolen or counterfeit goods, [the] gray-market trade is perfectly legal. . . ."[5]

Judges and scholars are equally unsettled. The United States Supreme Court defined gray market goods as "[f]oreign-manufactured goods, bearing a valid United States trademark, that are imported without the consent of the U.S. trademark holder."[6] Black's Law Dictionary borrowed this description for its own definition.[7] Later cases, however, concluded that the definition was impermissibly narrow and abandoned the requirement that the goods be foreign manufactured.[8] The importation requirement has similarly been relaxed in certain contexts,[9] while other cases and statutes have furnished their own meanings, creating even more uncertainty.[10]

Fortunately, for purposes of this book, reconciling the various definitions is unnecessary. In these pages, gray market goods will simply refer to "goods diverted from a brand owners' authorized sale channel."[11] Moreover, whether gray market goods are illegal cannot be resolved by definition. As the name aptly suggests, gray market goods reside in the murky area of law between

---

4. Scott Carney, *iPod Gray Market Booms in India*, WIRED, Aug. 23, 2006, *at* http://www.wired.com/gadgets/mac/news/2006/08/71639.
5. Raji Samghabadi & Dan Goodgame, *Inside the Gray* Market, TIME MAGAZINE, Oct. 28, 1985, *available at* http://www.time.com/time/magazine/article/0,9171,960231,00.html.
6. K Mart Corp. v. Cartier, Inc., 485 U.S. 176, 179 (1988).
7. BLACK'S LAW DICTIONARY 701 (6th ed.1990).
8. *See* Bourdeau Bros., Inc. v. Int'l Trade Comm'n, 444 F.3d 1317, 1323 (Fed. Cir. 2006).
9. Black's Law Dictionary similarly modified its definition to describe the gray market as "as 'a market in which the seller uses legal but sometimes unethical methods to avoid a manufacturer's distribution chain and thereby sell goods (esp. imported goods) at prices lower than those envisioned by the manufacturer.'" BLACK'S LAW DICTIONARY 989 (8th ed.2004).
10. *See e.g.*, 19 C.F.R. § 133.23(a) (2008) ("'Restricted gray market articles' are foreign-made articles bearing a genuine trademark or trade name identical with or substantially indistinguishable from one owned and recorded by a citizen of the United States or a corporation or association created or organized within the United States and imported without the authorization of the U.S. owner."); *see also* Cal. Civ. Code § 1797.8(a) (2008) ("'[G]ray market goods' means consumer goods bearing a trademark and normally accompanied by an express written warranty valid in the United States of America which are imported into the United States through channels other than the manufacturer's authorized United States distributor and which are not accompanied by the manufacturer's express written warranty valid in the United States.").
11. *See e.g.*, DAVID M. HOPKINS ET AL., COUNTERFEITING EXPOSED 10 (2003).

legitimacy and illegality. Determining the permissibility of gray market transactions requires a comprehensive examination of the facts presented in each case. From the brand owner's efforts to control its supply chains to the side-by-side comparison of authorized and unauthorized goods, judges and juries must analyze a panoply of factors to decide the licitness of the challenged activity.

In addition, merely determining whether gray market activity is permitted by law is an incomplete examination of the issue. Although it is obviously a worthy endeavor when a brand owner contemplates litigation, it is imperative for brand owners to exercise a broader perspective. Instead of concentrating on the likelihood of obtaining a judicial remedy, brand owners must direct their focus on the gray market's impact on their most important and valuable asset: the *brand*.

Reduced to its essence, the brand is a contract between a brand owner and its consumers. From recognition and experience, brand familiarity guides consumers' buying decisions. For example, most Americans can order a Coke, lease a Toyota, or buy a pair of Nikes without having to investigate the manufacturing procedures or ingredients of each product. Because of their brand familiarity, consumers trust that they will receive a tasty soda, a reliable automobile, or a comfy pair of shoes. Indeed, Coca-Cola, Toyota, and Nike are among the world's most valuable brands.[12]

Although the brand is a company's most valuable and sustainable asset,[13] it is also the most vulnerable. Developing a strong brand name can take years and cost millions and—like any reputation—be lost in an instant. The defective tire recall by Bridgestone/Firestone in August 2000 is a notorious example. After an investigation revealed that the company's Firestone tires were causing accidents and deaths in Ford Explorers, the company recalled over 6.5 million tires. Ford and Bridgestone/Firestone severed their 95-year relationship[14] amid the controversy, and experts were convinced that the company would not weather the harm to its image. As one commentator concluded, "Firestone is a dead brand driving."[15]

Given this vulnerability, the gray market poses a formidable threat. Proponents of the gray market aver that the only harm is a potential reduction of domestic profit. In reality, when products escape the intended distribution chain, brand owners lose all ability to control the product. From poor

---

12. *The 100 Top Brands*, BUSINESSWEEK, August 6, 2007 at 59–64, *available at* http://www.businessweek.com/pdfs/2007/0732_globalbrands.pdf.
13. RITA CLIFTON ET AL., BRANDS AND BRANDING 2 (2d ed. 2004) (2003) ("The brand is the most important and sustainable asset of any organization whether a product or service based corporation nor a not-for-profit concern—and it should be the central organizing principle...").
14. Mark Gongloff, *How Tire Recall Affects You*, CNNMONEY, May 22, 2001, *at* http://money.cnn.com/2001/05/22/home_auto/tires_consumer/.
15. JACK TROUT, BIG BRANDS BIG TROUBLE 97 (2002).

product presentation to the commingling of counterfeit goods, brand owners face a host of significant risks. Erosion of customer trust can happen quickly if consumers lack the confidence of knowing whether a good bearing a brand owner's trademark is authentic. In some industries like aviation and pharmaceuticals, the potential harm is even more forbidding.

To protect a company's most valuable asset, being proactive is essential. Assuming a brand owner's supply chain will monitor itself or that any infractions can be solved through litigation is no longer a viable business strategy. In today's global marketplace, brand owners must exercise vigilance to establish, protect, and enforce their distribution channels. This book provides a blueprint of business and legal strategies that can be used to protect brands from the gray market. From educating employees to executing a surprise search and seizure warrant, brand owners will learn the available methods to prevent, detect, and react to incursions by the gray market.

b. From Bad to Worse: The Black Market

In isolation, an unauthorized gray market transaction only deprives a brand owner of its intended profit margins. To illustrate, a foreign distributor persuaded to sell products to a gray market importer causes unwanted competition among a brand owner's domestic resellers. Capitalizing on the arbitrage opportunities created by a brand owner's disparate pricing schemes, the gray market importer is often able to sell products at prices below an authorized reseller's wholesale price.

This narrow examination can tempt a brand owner to conclude that the gray marketing of its products is unworthy of significant concern. So long as products are being sold and disseminated in the marketplace, this microanalysis suggests a benefit to the brand owner. The error of this logic, however, is the failure to consider the overall impact that a gray market can have on a brand's value. One of the more significant consequences of an unchecked gray market is the commingling of gray and black market products.

The black market is a related form of brand abuse, but it lacks the legal ambiguity of the gray market. The gray market constitutes the diversion of products, whereas the black market deals in products that are counterfeit—they are *fakes* and they are illegal. Although the black market has always been a threat to brand owners, the same factors contributing to the gray market's recent expansion are similarly contributing to a burgeoning counterfeit economy.

Meanwhile, the sophistication of counterfeiters continues to improve. Far beyond the crude knockoffs of luxury watches and purses, counterfeiters today have the agility and acumen to penetrate any industry with replicas virtually indistinguishable from their authentic counterparts. A brand owner that fails to control the integrity of its distribution channels puts its entire product line in jeopardy. As gray market goods flow in and alongside a brand owner's intended chain of distribution without detection, the integration of counterfeit goods is inevitable. It is estimated that 5–7 percent of all world trade ($250 billion) is in counterfeit goods.[16] Moreover, counterfeit goods are becoming more difficult to detect; their presence is vast, and, in many industries, they can be dangerous. Although some industries are more notorious for having a consistent infiltration of gray and black market goods, the following chapter illustrates that no industries are immune from the hazards of the gray and black market.

---

16. HOPKINS, *supra* note 11, at 145.

CHAPTER 2

From iPhones to Viagra

The Affected Industries

"Diversion [i.e., gray market] is the result of a company shooting itself in the foot. It is a result of how you run your business."
—Richard S. Post[1]

a.	Airline Industry	10
b.	Automotive Industry	11
c.	Cigarette Industry	13
d.	Cosmetics and Personal Care Products	14
e.	Clothing and Apparel	16
f.	Food and Drinks	17
g.	Watches and Jewelry	18
h.	Natural Resources	20
i.	Technology	21
j.	Pharmaceuticals	22
k.	Toys	24

---

1. RICHARD S. POST & PENELOPE N. POST, GLOBAL BRAND INTEGRITY MANAGEMENT xii (2008).

a. Airline Industry

In 1989, a Convair 580 airplane bound for Germany crashed into the sea off Norway killing all 55 people on board. The report from the investigation concluded that the accident was caused by the use of counterfeit bolts in the airplane's tail.[2] Today, the United States Federal Aviation Authority (FAA) estimates that 500,000 counterfeit airline parts are sold each year.[3]

Notwithstanding this volume, the United States Department of Transportation (DOT) concluded in February 2008 that "neither manufacturers nor FAA inspectors have provided effective oversight of suppliers."[4] To reach this conclusion, the DOT worked with personnel from "an international consulting firm and performed supplier control audits at companies that supply parts to Boeing, Bombardier/Learjet, General Electric Aircraft Engines, Rolls-Royce, Pratt & Whitney, and Airbus."[5] Like so many industries with a global supply chain, the airline industry has made itself vulnerable for the same reasons:

> Manufacturers are increasingly using domestic and foreign parts and system suppliers to reduce their manufacturing costs and spread risks among multiple partners. Suppliers provide investment capital and assume responsibility for the design and production of systems and sub-systems supplied to prime manufacturers. For example, Boeing's risk-sharing partners in Japan, Italy, and the United States will build composite structures for the Boeing 787, which will include sub-systems that are already certified, tested, and ready for final assembly.[6]

Although the FAA had worked towards implementing a risk-based oversight system for aviation manufacturers, the system was implemented without taking into account the degree to which manufacturers now use foreign suppliers to make airplanes.[7] For example, the FAA only requires inspectors to

---

2. Willy Stern, *Warning! Bogus Parts Have Turned Up in Commercial Jets. Where's the FAA?*, BUSINESSWEEK, June 10, 1996, *available at* http://www.businessweek.com/1996/24/b34791.htm.
3. *The Negative Consequences of International Intellectual Property Theft: Economic Harm, Threats to the Public Health and Safety, and Links to Organized Crime and Terrorist Organizations*, IACC White Paper, 2005, at 10, *available at* http://www.iacc.org/resources/IACC_WhitePaper.pdf.
4. Memorandum from David A. Dobbs, Principal Assistant Inspector Gen. for Auditing and Evaluation to Acting Fed. Aviation Adm'r., February 26, 2008, at 4, *available at* http://www.pogoarchives.org/m/tr/faa-supplier-20080226.pdf.
5. *Id.* at 1.
6. *Id.* at 2.
7. *Id.* at 3.

conduct four supplier audits—regardless of how many suppliers the manufacturer actually uses. Stating the obvious, the DOT remarked that "[t]his process is not adequate to determine the risk that a manufacturer will produce substandard parts."[8] With respect to the manufacturers, the DOT determined that "three of the five manufacturers [it] reviewed did not have procedures in place to routinely visit all their critical suppliers and sub-tier suppliers." The failures have "allowed substandard parts to enter the aviation supply chain."[9]

These failures to monitor supply chains invite gray and black market interference. The concerns are even greater in developing countries where regulations are more suspect. At cruising altitude, the danger of product diversion is far graver than lost profits.

b. Automotive Industry

The automotive industry is similarly plagued with gray and black market products winding their way in and out of authorized supply channels. In its 2008 study, the Department of Commerce's (DOC) annual industry assessment concluded that counterfeit automobile parts cost the American automotive supplier industry over $12 billion per year and that "counterfeit and gray market automotive components accounted for as much as 3.2 percent of all global counterfeit trade."[10] According to the study, "Ford estimates that counterfeit auto parts cost them $1 billion annually."[11] Beyond economics, there are numerous examples of products of dubious origin causing collisions that have injured or killed drivers and passengers. Given the dangers, the DOC warned automobile companies to consider *all* consequences when partnering with companies in regions well-known for counterfeiting capabilities:

> Because the transfer of knowledge would allow the Chinese to compete against the proprietors and may invite counterfeiting, many companies are reluctant to send advanced technology to China. When considering sourcing from China, U.S. companies are cautioned to not be lured by price and/or low wage rates alone. . . .[12]

---

8. *Id.* at 4.
9. *Id.*
10. DEP'T OF COMMERCE, U.S. AUTO. PARTS INDUS. ANNUAL ASSESSMENT 19 (March 2008), http://trade.gov/static/auto_reports_parts_assessment.pdf.
11. *Id.*
12. *Id.* at 25.

The DOC's admonition is sound. In 2004, General Motors Daewoo Automotive & Technology (GM) discovered that a Chinese carmaker, Chery, was copying GM's car models and distributing them throughout China.[13] The investigation was impaired when GM discovered that Chery's main joint venture partner in China, the Shanghai Automotive Industry Corporation (SAIC) was also a twenty percent shareholder in Chery.[14] The fact that the ultimate owners of Chery and SAIC were the governments of Anhui and Shanghai, respectively, made matters even more complicated.[15] In addition to clones, "American manufacturers have found rip-off version of brand-name filters, brakes, shock absorbers, pumps, batteries and windshields. The fakes are not always benign: bogus brake pads have been found made of compressed sawdust, and low-grade crude oil has masqueraded as transmission fluid."[16]

Even when brand owners deploy measures designed to restrict the production of unauthorized goods, the risk is never completely eliminated. One method brand owners use to control the unauthorized overproduction of goods is to limit the availability of raw materials necessary for assembly. By receiving a finite amount of the needed ingredients, a manufacturing plant cannot produce excess products to sell for its own secret gain. Although capping the access to raw materials is an estimable strategy, it is not sufficient. In the automotive industry particularly, limiting the availability of raw materials can have devastating consequences.

For example, in June 2007 the United States government ordered the recall of 450,000 faulty tires made by a Chinese manufacturer. The recall effort came after a fatal accident was blamed on tires that were missing a needed safety feature.[17] The Chinese manufacturer, the Hangzhou Zhongce Rubber Company, denied any wrongdoing. Hangzhou was China's second largest tire manufacturer and had contracts to supply or collaborate with some of the world's biggest tire makers, including Goodyear and Cooper Tire. According to experts close to the facts, however, the recall involved a "common problem: Chinese manufacturers who win a contract after agreeing to produce a product following certain guidelines or specifications and then, often for

---

13. Richard McGregor, *GM Seeks Resolution on Chery 'Piracy'* Fin. Times (London), June 7, 2004, available at http://search.ft.com/ftArticle?queryText=GM+Seeks+Resolution+on+Chery&y=0&aje=true&x=0&id=040607003877&ct=0&nclick_check=1.
14. *Id.*
15. *Id.*
16. Moisés Naím, Illicit: How Smugglers, Traffickers, And Copycats Are Hijacking The Global Economy 120 (Anchor Books 2006) (2005).
17. David Barboza & Andrew Martin, *Chinese Tire Maker Denies Defective Work, and Sees an Effort to Undercut its Exports*, N.Y. Times, June 27, 2007, at C3 (the safety feature was designed to prevent tire separation).

cost saving reasons, switch to a cheaper ingredient or a process that lowers costs."[18]

c. Cigarette Industry

Although gray or black market cigarettes do not present the same consumer dangers as aviation or automotive parts—cigarettes are *already* dangerous—the cigarette industry is often shadowed by unwieldy gray and black market economies. Although disparate pricing is typically within a brand owner's control, the well-known $206 billion Multi-state Settlement Agreement between the tobacco industry and state attorney generals left tobacco owners little choice but to dramatically raise domestic prices.[19] Meanwhile, many states passed laws that increased the amount of taxes, making the price even higher for smokers.[20] The consequence of these price increases was an interstate and international gray market boom.[21]

Within five years of the tobacco settlement, the price of cigarettes in the United States nearly doubled with taxes making up "approximately sixty percent of the total price of cigarettes."[22] In response, "[h]undreds of web sites ... sprung up to cater to customers ... fed up with high cigarette prices."[23] The Web sites were operated by companies selling gray market cigarettes: "'cigarettes manufactured for sale overseas' that are then 're-imported and sold without the manufacturer's permission.'"[24]

Gray market cigarettes hurt more than the tobacco companies. Federal and state governments lose tax revenue. "Because foreign websites can sell gray market Marlboros, which normally sell for $70 a carton in New York City, for a mere $15 a carton, not only do cigarette manufacturers such as Philip Morris lose a significant portion of their profits, but federal, state, and local governments do not receive any tax revenue from the sale."[25] Anti-smoking organizations also claim that gray market sellers make cigarettes too readily available to minors: "Due to their low prices and insufficient or

---

18. *Id.*
19. Kenneth Howe, *Price Rise Puts Heat on Smokers Run on Cigarette Sales and Internet Vendors*, S.F. CHRON., Nov. 27, 1998, at A1.
20. *Id.*
21. For further discussion on the gray market cigarette economy, see Section b of this chapter.
22. Michael Kwon, *Filtering the Smoke Out of Cigarette Websites*, 30 BROOK J. INT'L L. 1067, 1071 (2005).
23. John Reid Blackwell, *Tobacco Campaign: Major Companies Defend their Turf Against 'Underground' Competitors*, RICHMOND TIMES DISPATCH, Mar. 24, 2003, at D4.
24. Anthony Ciolli, *Gray Market Cigarettes*, 11 DEPAUL J. HEALTH CARE L. 119, 119 (Spring 2008) (citing Kwon, *supra* note 1, at 1072).
25. *Id.* at 120.

non-existent identification methods, anti-smoking organizations have often attacked gray market cigarettes as being too easily accessible to children and too available to low-income individuals who could otherwise not afford them due to high taxes."[26]

This unusual alliance of tobacco companies, governmental officials, and anti-smoking organizations has been successful in lobbying efforts to prohibit the gray marketing of cigarettes. The federal government and most states have enacted statutes outlawing the sale or distribution of reimported cigarettes.[27] In addition to the efforts in the legislature, tobacco companies have had to be diligent in their fight to prevent the continued gray marketing of their products.[28]

d. Cosmetics and Personal Care Products

Although almost any domestic grocery or liquor store is suitable for tobacco companies to promote and sell their products, the marketing of cosmetic products involves an entirely different strategy. There is nothing unusual or inherently problematic with 7-Eleven selling Marlboro cigarettes. To the contrary, American consumers are conditioned to expect a variety of tobacco products available at such establishments.

What would be unusual, however, would be discovering the same 7-Eleven also selling $200 bottles of designer perfume or cologne. Indeed, to maintain the prestige of their products, cosmetic brand owners impose strict limits on where their products can be found. Although brand owners of more pedestrian toiletries are content to promote their products in virtually any retail outlet, the more expensive "perfume [and other cosmetic] companies deliberately limit their products to fancy department stores (instead of discount drug and cosmetic outlets) to make them seem more chic."[29]

This proscription of allowable retail outlets creates an environment vulnerable to the gray market. In addition to the typical reimportation of

---

26. Id.
27. See e.g., 26 U.S.C. § 5754 (2008) (banning importation of previously exported tobacco products); Cal. Rev. § Tax Code § 3016 (2008) (making illegal in California the importation of cigarettes in violation of Section 5754 and the importation by third parties of American-branded cigarettes manufactured abroad); See also Rebecca Deusser, Panagiotakos, Trying to Snuff Out Gray Market Cigarettes, LOWELL SUN, Nov. 29, 2005, at 18.
28. See e.g., R.J. Reynolds Tobacco Co. v. Cigarettes Cheaper!, 462 F.3d 690 (7th Cir. 2006) (lawsuit to prevent retailer from selling reimported cigarettes).
29. Mark Honingsbaum, Dollars and Scents—Gray Market Perfumes—Scams, Hustles, and Boondoggles, WASH. MONTHLY, July 1, 1988, at http://findarticles.com/p/articles/mi_m1316/is_n6_-_7_v20/ai_6495570.

products manufactured for foreign distribution, "fancy department stores" have been reported to habitually "off-load[] a certain amount of fragrance through the back door at wholesale price, [wherein] the retailers can get instant cash and still make a profit by pocketing the promotional and other expenses the manufacturer has paid him [sic] up front."[30]

In the 1980s, there were reports that cosmetic brand owners were complicit participants in the gray marketing of their products. In a competitive and shrinking industry,[31] the gray market provided an opportunity to expand a brand owner's retail base:

> Trapped in a straightjacket of their own creation, the perfume companies find the gray market offers an easy way out. By turning a blind eye to the diversion of perfumes from prime retail outlets to mass discounters, perfume companies can sell their potions widely and keep them prestigious.[32]

In the years and decades that followed, brand owners discovered that it is a naïve endeavor to simultaneously turn a blind eye to product diversion while striving to keep a brand prestigious. With the advent of the Internet, globalization, and other factors discussed in Chapter 3, such disregard is unsound business. The commingling of counterfeit products alone is sufficient to destroy the value of a brand.

One brand owner keenly aware of this reality is Paul Mitchell, maker of personal hair care products. The company has aggressively sought to prevent and punish those trying to copy or divert its products. On one occasion, the brand owner discovered an individual selling fake Paul Mitchell products. To track down the individual and the imitation goods, the company hired a private investigator. After the investigation revealed more than $1 million worth of fake products, the counterfeiter was sentenced to 16 months in prison.[33] In addition to coordinating its investigations with law enforcement, Paul Mitchell has filed more than 30 lawsuits to stop the sale of counterfeit or gray market goods.[34] Paul Mitchell is not a lone victim; to protect the integrity and value of their brands, perfume and personal care product

---

30. *Id.*
31. *Id.* ("Selling scent is a tough business. For a number of reasons—including an aging clientele increasingly reluctant to spend $185 for an ounce of scent—sales of concentrated perfume at prestige outlets slipped from $231 million in 1980 to $208 million in 1985.").
32. *Id.*
33. *Paul Mitchell Wages War on Makers of Fake Products*, CHI. TRIB., June 13, 1999, at 12.
34. HOPKINS, *supra* note 11, at 145; *see also e.g.,* John Paul Mitchell Systems v. Randalls Food Markets, Inc., 17 S.W. 3d 721 (Tex. App. 2000); John Paul Mitchell Systems v. Pete N Larry's Inc., 862 F. Supp. 1020 (W.D.N.Y. 1994).

manufacturers cannot afford to sit idly on the sidelines while their products are diverted or copied without recourse.[35]

e. Clothing and Apparel

Clothing and apparel makers face additional challenges to product diversion because of the seasonal lifespan of their products. To remain competitive in the marketplace, brand owners must offer new styles to customers every few months. When a previous season's collection is not liquidated, there is a temptation to find *any* buyer to off-load the excess inventory. In addition, manufacturing partners will often produce garments that, though not suitable for authorized retail, are not wholly unwearable. To sustain the desirability of their brands, successful apparel manufacturers implement strict controls over how these categories of goods are handled.

Abercrombie & Fitch v. Fashion Shops of Kentucky, Inc.[36] illustrates how a brand owner successfully monitors the authorized retailing of its products. The plaintiff Abercrombie & Fitch (Abercrombie) is a well-known retailer of casual clothing targeted at men and women aged eighteen through college. Abercrombie maintained in the case that "it enjoys an excellent reputation through its high-quality merchandise, highly successful marketing efforts, and its 110-year history in the field."[37]

Abercrombie implemented strict controls over the handling of products that were not worthy for sales in its retail stores. Although the garments were produced by various manufacturers overseas, all merchandise was inspected at its distribution center in New Albany, Ohio. The merchandise that passed inspection was sold in Abercrombie's stores. The merchandise that failed inspection was allowed to be sold by the manufacturers. However, strict restrictions were imposed in a "Sell-Off Compliance Agreement" (Agreement):

> [N]o Abercrombie merchandise can be sold in the United States, and Abercrombie must approve of the final destination for the merchandise. In addition, Abercrombie requires that certain modifications be made: the brand names on all interior labels must be "blacklined" or "cut" through prior to being sold; all marketing that contains brand names (such as price tickets and hangtags) must be removed; and interior

---

35. *See e.g.*, United States v. Eight-Nine (89) Bottles of "Eau de Joy," 797 F.2d 767 (9th Cir. 1986); Parfums Givenchy, Inc. v. Drug Emporium, Inc., 38 F.3d 477 (9 th Cir. 1994).
36. Abercrombie & Fitch v. Fashion Shops of Kentucky, Inc, 363 F. Supp. 2d 952 (S.D. Ohio 2005).
37. *Id.* at 954.

prints and tapes which contain the brand names must be marked through completely with black indelible ink.[38]

With respect to end-of-season merchandise that did not sell at their outlet stores and any damaged merchandise that came from its retail stores, Abercrombie permitted a specific chain of retail stores called "Gabriel Brothers" to carry these goods.[39] Instead of strictly prohibiting the sales of these goods (and run the risk that they would be furtively sold anyway), Abercrombie allowed its partners to sell the products while maintaining control over the dissemination of its branded goods.

Abercrombie then employed measures to supervise compliance. Knowing that merely broadcasting its edicts was insufficient to ensure obedience, Abercrombie employed a team of "[i]nvestigators world-wide to ensure that their manufacturers are not 'selling-off' or manufacturing merchandise without their approval."[40] As discussed in later chapters, Abercrombie's strategies chronicled in the *Fashion Shops* case can effectively prevent and *deter* unwanted gray market activity.

f. Food and Drinks

Makers of food and drinks are—like all brand owners—susceptible to abuse. Because of the consumability and perishability of such goods, however, their makers face additional hazards. Even if certain goods have not been affirmatively adulterated, many foods deteriorate in quality and even may become unsafe if eaten after an expiration or "sell-by" date. When these goods are leaked into unauthorized distribution channels, the brand owner has no ability to prohibit these unwanted sales. Equally troubling is the prospect of ingesting counterfeit fare of unknown origin and ingredients.

In 1999, the Anti-Counterfeiting Group (ACG) reported several instances of counterfeit alcohol being discovered wherein the contents were mortally dangerous. For example, scotch whiskey labeled Blended Royal Crown was discovered to contain large quantities of paint thinner.[41] ACG's report also chronicled the discovery of fake Stolichnaya vodka, which contained ingredients capable of causing blindness.[42] Several well-known brands have been similarly attacked: Johnnie Walker Blue Label, Chivas Regal

---

38. *Id.* at 955.
39. *Id.* at 956.
40. *Id.*
41. Press Release, Blueprint Marketing Services on behalf of the Anti-Counterfeiting Group, Counterfeit Alcohol: It Could Cost You More Than A Hangover (Nov. 19, 1999).
42. *Id.*

Premier Scotch, Black & White, Glen Moray, Laphroaig, Stolichnaya Russian Vodka, Remy Martin and Martell.[43]

Wine and spirits are just the beginning of the spectrum of abused brands. In *Ferrero U.S.A. Inc. v. Ozak Trading, Inc.*,[44] a gray marketer was found importing America's well-known Tic Tac breath mints. However, the Tic Tacs intended for foreign distribution contained different ingredients than their domestic counterparts. The Tic Tacs intended for domestic distribution had 1.5 calories per mint, contained sugar, and were sold in packages labeled with nutritional information that conformed to the Food and Drug Administration (FDA)'s requirements. The Tic Tacs intended for foreign distribution, meanwhile, had 2 calories per mint, a fructose sweetener, and were packaged with labeling under European standards.[45] Although the nonidentical products did not pose any danger to consumers, the court agreed that the differences in products would be confusing to consumers and ultimately injure the brand.[46]

One of the more troubling examples of brand abuse in the food and drink industry is the dangerous counterfeiting of baby formula For example, in 1995, the *New York Times* reported an investigation by the FDA that uncovered over 45,000 pounds of counterfeit infant formula in California.[47] Beyond mints and baby food, products like soda,[48] chocolate,[49] and even beef[50] have been challenged by gray and black marketers. Given the dangers associated with unsupervised food products, diligent supervision over a brand owner's supply chain is imperative.[51]

g. Watches and Jewelry

A gray market or counterfeit designer watch is one of the quintessential products one may think of when asked to contemplate brand abuse. Images of suspect characters discreetly peddling high-end watches from a briefcase or

---

43. J. Dey, *Bad Wine in Old Bottles: Bootleggers Held*, INDIAN EXPRESS, April 5, 1998, at 1.
44. Ferrero U.S.A. Inc. v. Ozak Trading, Inc, 952 F.2d 44 (3d Cir. 1991) (At issue in the opinion was the award of attorney fees. However, the opinion recites and endorses its previous "memorandum opinion" affirming the plaintiff's trademark infringement claim).
45. *Id.* at 46.
46. *Id.*
47. Mariam Burros, *Eating Well; F.D.A. Target: Baby Formula*, N.Y. TIMES, Sept. 6, 1995, at A1.
48. *See e.g.*, Pepsico v. Nostalgia Prod. Corp., 1991 WL 113161 (N.D.Ill.) (materiality based on Mexican "Pepsi" labels that were in Spanish and did not contain a list of ingredients, along with quality control and marketing differences).
49. *See e.g.*, Société Des Produits Nestlé, S.A. v. Casa Helvetia, Inc., 982 F.2d 633 (1st Cir. 1992).
50. Jeff Barnard, *Branding Beef—For Profit*, DENVER POST, Nov. 5, 2000, at L8.
51. *See e.g.*, U.S. v. Hanafy, 302 F.3d 485 (5th Cir. 2002).

car trunk are easy to conjure. Although these illustrations are not wholly inaccurate, globalization and technology have rendered them largely anachronistic. Watches and jewelry are still susceptible to diversion and counterfeiting. However, street vendors are a mere proton in the universe of brand abuse.

The Internet has become the locale for consumers and sellers of jewelry to conduct their business. Today, more than fifty percent of American luxury consumers start their shopping "research" on the Internet.[52] Even while these luxury consumers begin their searches at major portals, "70 percent of the search results are non-authorized, counterfeit or gray market sellers."[53]

Although many perceive adversity, some—not just the counterfeiters and gray marketers—see opportunity. In December 2007, former Yahoo executives Lawrence Kosick and Ned Taylor launched ViaLuxe (www.vialuxe.com) in an effort to "transform the luxury jewelry and watch industry and make online luxury shopping safer . . . [by] helping consumers find, research, and purchase the finest in authorized watch and jewelry brands." According to its Web site:

> Vialuxe is dedicated to helping consumers research, find and buy the finest watch and jewelry products. We are the first and only website to offer consumers a safe and elegant place for luxury goods. We make the process of searching for watches and jewelry safer and easier. All of the retailers on our website are authorized dealers for the brands they carry. Unlike Google or eBay, we only display products from authorized dealers which saves you, the customer, the time and risk associated with using the internet to purchase luxury goods.[54]

Brand owners must be concerned with more than mere rogue Web sites. Gray market brands often find their way into well-known discount centers throughout the country. The 2008 case of *Omega S.A. v. Costco Wholesale Corp.*[55] is a recent example. The plaintiff Omega S.A. (Omega) manufactures watches in Switzerland and sells them globally through a network of authorized distributors and retailers.[56] The defendant Costco Wholesale Corp. (Costco) obtained Omega watches from the gray market for resale in its stores: "Omega first sold the watches to authorized distributors overseas. Unidentified third parties eventually purchased the watches and sold them to

---

52. Nicole Davis, *Former Yahoo Executives Make Buying Authentic Luxury Watches and Jewelry Easier and Safer for Consumers—Enter Vialuxe*, Reuters, Dec. 12, 2007, *available at* http://www.reuters.com/article/pressRelease/idUS159006+12-Dec-2007+PRN20071212.
53. *Id.*
54. http://www.vialuxe.com/About-Us/Information/4231.
55. Omega S.A. v. Costco Wholesale Corp., 541 F.3d 982 (9th Cir. Sept. 3, 2008).
56. *Id.* at 983.

ENE Limited, a New York company, which in turn sold them to Costco. Costco then sold the watches to consumers in California. Although Omega authorized the initial foreign sale of the watches, *it did not authorize their importation into the United States or the sales made by Costco.*"[57] Although the trial court found nothing improper with Costco's acquisition and sale of these gray market goods, the Ninth Circuit Court of Appeals reversed the holding and concluded that Costco had indeed violated Omega's copyrights.[58]

The *Omega* case reveals a challenge facing brand owners in most industries. Gray market products are not just found in underground emporiums or on unprincipled e-commerce Web sites. Gray market products are often found in well-established and well-respected venues that simply purchase products from the cheapest vendor.

h. Natural Resources

The economic pulls of supply and demand coupled with disparate pricing are often sufficient to create an environment ripe for the gray market. Although gray market goods are typically thought of as manufactured products of reasonably high complexity, it is not always the case. Goods as uncomplicated as steel have been subject to gray market economies for years. The United States witnessed a gray market in steel during World War II that continued through the Korean War. With "scare-buying and hoarding" causing steel prices to increase, President Truman addressed the country:

> Every businessman who is trying to profiteer in time of national danger and every person who is trying to get more than his neighbor is doing exactly the thing that any enemy of this country would want him to do.[59]

Indeed, all it takes are demand and price differentials to make an industry vulnerable to the gray market. In March 2008, Malaysia witnessed a similar gray market in steel caused by a strong demand and unreasonably *low* prices due to government price controls: "Many contractors have been forced to procure steel bars from the gray market to keep up with construction schedules, at prices significantly more expensive . . . above government

---

57. *Id.* at 984 (emphasis added).
58. For further discussion of Omega S.A. v. Costco Wholesale Corp., see Chapter 19.
59. Louis Kriesberg, *National Security and Conduct in the Steel Gray Market*, SOCIAL FORCES, Vol. 34, No. 3, 268–77, 268 (March 1956).

control[led] price[s]."[60] Similar circumstances around the world have been accounted for in the timber[61] and water[62] industries.

i. Technology

The IT industry has been the modern poster child for brand abuse. Recent studies have revealed that the IT industry loses up to $5 billion in annual profits to the gray market.[63] It is also subject to the danger of black market products. With so many brand owners manufacturing their goods overseas, factories with suspect regard for intellectual property are becoming more adept at creating counterfeit products. Even if the brand owners can spot the fakes, the unauthorized resellers often cannot.

For example, in *Microsoft v. Compusource Distributors, Inc.*,[64] Microsoft sued a distributor for selling counterfeit software and hardware. After Microsoft discovered this unlawful activity, it issued a cease and desist letter to Compusource demanding that it immediately stop selling counterfeit products. Instead of following Microsoft's edict, Compusource's president testified that he telephoned his Microsoft suppliers to discuss the matter with them. According to the president, the suppliers assured him that the products were legitimate and that the products were simply cheaper because they were bought on the gray market.[65] Regardless of whether the president's or the supplier's belief in the authenticity of the products was genuine, this case shows the risk of counterfeit products flowing through distribution channels into the hands of consumers.

Because technological products are commonly accompanied with warranty and troubleshooting services, brand owners incur additional costs when they support these gray goods. For example, in *Osawa & Co. v. B&H Photo*,[66] the brand owner sought to enjoin the unauthorized importation and sale of its photographic equipment. The plaintiff Osawa & Company (Osawa) sued

---

60. Press Release, Real Estate and House. Developers' Ass'n Malaysia, Comments from Master Builder's Ass'n Malaysia (MBAM) and Real Estate & House. Developers Ass'n (REHDA) on Steel Bar Price Increase (March 8, 2007), *available at* http://www.rehda.com/posts/070308.html.
61. *See e.g.*, Stuart Thompson, *Status of the Environment in Bosnia and Herzegovina: A Current Assessment*, 12 GEO. INT'L ENVTL. L. REV. 247 (1999).
62. *See e.g.*, Apollinaris Co. v. Scherer, 27 F. 18 (C.C.N.Y. 1886).
63. *The Grey Market*, KPMG/Anti-Gray Mkt. Alliance, 2003, at 1, *available at* http://www.agmaglobal.org/press_events/press_docs/KPMG_TheGreyMarket_Web.pdf.
64. Microsoft v. Compusource Distributors, Inc., 115 F. Supp. 2d 800 (E.D. Mich. 2000).
65. *Id.* at 804.
66. Osawa & Co. v. B&H Photo, 589 F. Supp. 1163 (D.C.N.Y. 1984).

a gray marketer when some discount camera dealers in New York imported equipment without its consent or permission.[67]

To show that the gray market sales injured Osawa, the brand owner presented evidence that it was providing warranty services on the gray market goods sold by the defendants. Accordingly, Osawa argued that it had and would continue to suffer damages by way of incurring these additional warranty costs. The court agreed that these damages constituted the requisite harm to issue the injunction. Equally important, the case exemplifies the epiphenomenal costs brand owners incur in a gray market economy.

From video games[68] and satellite services[69] to DVDs[70] and music equipment,[71] brand owners in the technology industries are never afforded a respite from the threats of gray and market activity. Although virtually all industries are vulnerable, technology is an especially chronic target.

j. Pharmaceuticals

When it comes to brand abuse, profitability trumps salubrity. Even in the highly regulated and potentially dangerous industry of pharmaceuticals, there are unfortunately countless examples of individuals placing their own greed above the well-being of patients in genuine need of medicine. One troubling example is the 2006 case of *United States v. Hill*,[72] wherein a doctor pleaded guilty to his conspiratorial participation in an illegal gray market scheme.

The defendant, Dr. Hill, was engaged in the unlicensed wholesale distribution of prescription drugs such as Serostim, Neupogen, and Lupron, which were used primarily for treating cancer and AIDS.[73] Dr. Hill's scheme took advantage of the fact that the drug manufacturer, Tap Pharmaceuticals (Tap), sold the medications to licensed doctors at a much lower cost than wholesale prices when the patients were insured by Medicaid or Medicare.[74] Dr. Hill and his co-conspirators would order these drugs for the ostensible purposes of selling them to their Medicaid and Medicare patients. Instead of being sold to these patients, however, the drugs would be repackaged and re-labeled for

---

67. *Id.* at 1165.
68. *See e.g.,* Red Baron-Franklin Park, Inc. v. Taito Corp., 883 F. 2d 275 (4th Cir. 1989) (video games).
69. *See e.g.,* Bell ExpressVu Ltd. P'ship v. Rex, [2002] 2 S.C.R. 559 (Can.) (satellite services).
70. HOPKINS, *supra* note 11, at 4.
71. VAS Indus. v. NY Sound, 2006 WL 1699537 (S.D.N.Y.).
72. United States v. Hill, 171 Fed.Appx. 815 (11th Cir. 2006) (unpublished).
73. *Id.* at 819.
74. *Id.*

resale in the gray market.⁷⁵ At sentencing, the court revealed its disdain for the illegal and dangerous scheme:

> Dr. Hill being a licensed medical doctor. Drugs that are issued in the name of other people, and we are not talking, by the way, for instance, say, a stronger Aspirin or something else you need a doctor's prescription for, but we are talking about highly regulated drugs that are very very expensive. . . . No effort at maintaining the pedigree which is so important in this area so if there is a need to recall the drugs, that could be done, and the transactions are just huge.⁷⁶

The focus in the *Hill* case was a rogue individual who put patients at risk for his own personal gain. Brand owners must be aware, however, that it is not always the black or gray marketers that are the focus of litigation. Given the solvency of drug companies, legal theories are often asserted to hold them responsible for not sufficiently protecting patients from injurious gray or black market products.

In *Fagan v. AmerisourceBergen Corp.*,⁷⁷ for example, the plaintiff Timothy Fagan alleged that he suffered injuries when an unknown party diluted his prescription medication for anemia. The drug at issue, Epogen, was manufactured by Amgen, which in turn sold it to AmerisourceBergen Corp. (ABC), an authorized distributor for Amgen, which in turn sold the drug to pharmacies.⁷⁸ According to Mr. Fagan, however, ABC also purchased Epogen on the gray market and passed it off as a genuine "Amgen" product. Mr. Fagan sued ABC as well as Amgen, alleging that "Amgen, for its part, negligently allowed its drugs to be sold on the gray market and negligently allowed its authorized distributor, ABC, to pass off gray market Epogen as genuine 'Amgen' Epogen."⁷⁹

Brand owners can be targeted for not only permitting a gray market to exist but also for allowing the commingling of counterfeit drugs in their supply chains. *Lynn v. Serono Inc.*⁸⁰ involved these precise allegations. The plaintiff Kelly Burke contracted AIDS when she received HIV-contaminated

---

75. *Id.*
76. *Id.*
77. Fagan v. AmerisourceBergen Corp, 164 Fed.Appx. 37, 2006 WL 151807 (2d Cir.) (unpublished).
78. *Id.* at 38.
79. *Id.* (The trial court originally dismissed Amgen. However, the Second Circuit remanded the case back to the trial court to articulate whether it really intended on dismissing the gray market claims given that it concluded that the plaintiff had "successfully pled negligence on ABC's part by alleging that ABC "facilitate[ed] the gray market by trading on it." *Citing Fagan.*, 356 F. Supp. 2d 198, 209.
80. No. GIC761598 (Sup. Ct. San Diego filed Jan. 31, 2001).

blood in a transfusion. She was prescribed Serostim as part of her treatment, but received counterfeit Serostim, which caused her to develop a rash. Burke's co-plaintiff, Robert Lynn, an HIV patient who also received counterfeit Serostim recalled that the drug "burned like hell and raised a knot the size of a quarter."[81] Although criminals were directly responsible for injecting counterfeit products into the authorized distribution channels, Burke sued the manufacturers and distributors, claiming that they "should have taken more care to use security markings on the products and should have taken more care in securing the distribution of the product, given the black market abuse in the product."[82] The case, which settled in 2002,[83] exemplifies the risks brand owners face when injuries are caused by gray or black market products. Even when a brand owner has no affirmative role in the alleged wrongdoing, willful inaction can render a brand owner vulnerable to litigation.

The specter of litigation can be especially daunting when drug companies consider the breadth of unauthorized pharmaceutical markets. According to various estimates, there are over $10 billion in lost revenues to counterfeit drugs.[84] In Africa, twenty-five to fifty percent of the pharmaceutical market is counterfeit.[85] Even in a highly regulated industry where diversion itself is prohibited by law,[86] brand owners must be vigilant about the integrity of their sales channels. Such action is necessary to protect patients and the value of brands.

k. Toys

The toy industry falls similarly prey to black and gray marketers. In particular, as it has become more common for toys to be manufactured overseas, , the industry has seen a dramatic increase in infringing activity. The European Union, for example, has seen a drastic increase in the seizure of counterfeit toys: "Last year ... seizures of counterfeit toys were up by 98 percent on 2006 levels."[87] Especially when there are spikes in the demand for certain toys, the potential for black and gray market activity increases.

---

81. Don Oldenburg, *Raising the Alarm on Rise in Counterfeit Drugs*, WASH. POST, Apr. 5, 2005, at C09.
82. HOPKINS, *supra* note 11, at 7071.
83. *Id.*
84. *Id.* at 5.
85. Tope Akinwade, *Lethal 'Cures' Plague Africa*, WORLD PRESS REV. Vol. 51, no. 2, Feb. 2004 available at http://www.worldpress.org/Africa/1749.cfm.
86. *See e.g.*, 21 U.S.C. § 381(d)(1) ("(1) Except as provided in paragraph (2) and section 384 of this title, no drug subject to section 353(b) of this title or composed wholly or partly of insulin which is manufactured in a State and exported may be imported into the United States unless the drug is imported by the manufacturer of the drug.").
87. *EU Concerned by Surge in Import of Counterfeit Drugs, Toys, Cosmetics*, Int'l Herald Trib., May 19, 2008 *available at* http://www.iht.com/articles/ap/2008/05/19/europe/EU-GEN-EU-Fake-Goods.php.

Original Appalachian Artworks, Inc. v. J.F. Reichert, Inc.,[88] for example, involved the once popular Cabbage Patch Kids dolls. The plaintiff Original Appalachian Artworks, Inc. (Original Appalachian) granted an exclusive license to Coleco Industries, Inc. (Coleco) to manufacture, market, and sell full-sized copies of the dolls in the United States. Because of the dramatic popularity of the dolls in the United States, gray marketers sought to take advantage of the arbitrage opportunities. Specifically, the defendant Joseph Reichert (Reichert) purchased and imported various European Cabbage Patch Kids dolls.[89] As covered in Chapter 11, it was not until Original Appalachian sought judicial intervention that the unwanted sales stopped.

---

88. Original Appalachian Artworks, Inc. v. J.F. Reichert, Inc., 658 F. Supp. 458 (E.D. Pa. 1987).
89. *Id.* at 462.

CHAPTER

3

Black and Gray Market 2.0

From Flea Markets to eBay

a. Globalization	28
b. Internet	32
c. Technology	35
d. Decreased Trade Barriers	37

Not long ago, brand owners could take comfort in the intrinsic barriers hampering gray and black marketers. Although most large cities have places known by its dwellers to be a source for cheap goods of dubious origin, consumers had to consciously decide to explore these markets in addition to or in lieu of conventional establishments.

Canal Street in New York's Chinatown is a well-known example. The street is lined with densely packed shops offering watches, purses, and other luxury items at prices that are corruptively low.[1] Until relatively recently, these markets did not pose a significant threat to brand owners. The remote locations of these markets created a sufficient bulwark to market entry. As a result, brand owners knowingly conceded that a small percentage of its would-be buyers bought cheap knock-offs instead.

In fact, many brand owners justified their tolerance of these bazaars on the belief that someone shopping for a $20 Rolex watch is *not even a would-be customer.* This customer is simply looking for a cheap gimmick or perhaps his or her economic reality precludes any possibility of buying a genuine product for several thousand dollars more.

Brand owners were also untroubled because the knock-offs were so obviously inferior to the genuine goods they sought to mimic. Although a *Guccci*

---

1. Moisés Naím, Illicit: How Smugglers, Traffickers, And Copycats Are Hijacking The Global Economy 120 (Anchor Books 2006) (2005). ("The storefronts are the tip of the iceberg. Within the shops are glossy catalogs of particularly valuable fakes—ones hard to produce or particularly desirable at the moment—which runners fetch from hideaways once a deal is struck.").

purse may have looked just like a *Gucci* purse from across a dimly lit cocktail lounge, a casual glance in an unobstructed environment could quickly distinguish the two. Because such a terse inspection could expose these products as feeble imitations, brand owners concluded that no real threat existed.

Regardless of whether this conclusion was previously justified does not warrant further discussion because, to put it mildly, times have changed. Customers looking for bargains found in the black or gray market now have the ability to *virtually* browse anywhere there is an Internet connection. Equally alarming for brand owners is the modern difficulty of spotting illegitimate products. As this chapter later explains, the obstacles that were once sufficient to appease concern for brand owners have been obliterated. As a result, the gray and black market economies have enjoyed an incredible boost extending their reaches from the Canal Streets of the world to every consumer with a laptop and a telephone line.

a. Globalization

In 2005, Arnold Schwarzenegger joined his friend and fellow action star Jackie Chan in Hong Kong to promote a campaign against film piracy in China. The 30-second anti-piracy public service announcement featured both actors in leather jackets zooming down a road on motorcycles, dodging exploding cars and other hazards. "When you buy pirated movies and music, you support criminals!" Mr. Chan says. Mr. Schwarzenegger adds, "Let's terminate it!"[2]

As discussed in Chapter 19, there are countries haplessly devoid of the necessary resources and infrastructure to adequately protect intellectual property. Countless articles and books can be found lamenting the lack of international enforcement to protect American innovation. It is worth remembering, however, that America is an ex-pirate itself:

> [O]ne of the undeniable reasons [Charles] Dickens had gone to America [in 1841] was to work for the acceptance of International Copyright so that his books, among those others to be sure, would no longer be pirated by unscrupulous American publishers. It was a mission in which he entirely, humiliatingly failed, and a copyright agreement between England and the United States was not concluded until 1891.[3]

---

2. *See e.g.*, Ben Sisario, *Fighting Piracy in China*, N.Y. TIMES, Nov. 19, 2005, at B8.
3. Gehard Joseph, *Charles Dickens, International Copyright, and the Discretionary Silence of Martin Chuzzlewit*, 10 CARDOZO ARTS & ENT. L.J. 523 (1992).

As the above illustrates, assaults on innovation are nothing new. What is new is how easy mounting these assaults has become. The speed and simplicity in which people communicate, buy, sell, and ship products across oceans and borders have paved the way for a worldwide outburst of infringement. Although many brand owners were savvy to take advantage of the benefits modern globalization offered, the attendant harm to brand integrity caught most companies completely by surprise.

Of course, globalization is not new either. It is as old as ambition. To globalize merely means to extend to other parts of our planet.[4] From the invention of the wheel several thousand years ago to Google's IPO in 2004, humankind has craved the tools of globalization. As history has shown, there are occasions when an invention or event will jolt globalization forward. Obvious examples include the invention of the steam engine and printing press.

Beginning with the fall of the Berlin Wall in 1989 and the breakup of the Soviet Union two years later, modern globalization has mightily picked up its tempo. Following the collapse of national and economic barriers was the collapse of *communication* barriers. One of the lasting consequences from the Internet boom and subsequent bust was an infrastructure for instant and affordable worldwide communication. Today, when Webvan and Pets.com are mentioned, it is to illustrate the dangers of ruthless investing and imprudent business practices. After all, within two years of their IPOs—which raised $375 million and $82.5 million respectively[5]—both companies were among the many dot-com casualties of the 1990s. However, the infusion of capital into such companies sparked a collateral investment in fiber-optic cable companies. Fiber optics, which are made up of optically pure glass, have two advantages over copper wire. *First*, fiber-optic cables have much more bandwidth. Thus, larger audio or video files can be transmitted at a lower cost. *Second*, data can travel for many miles without impairing the integrity of the signal. Copper wire, meanwhile, begins to suffer degradation within a few feet of transmission. Like train tracks laid for miners in California's gold rush of the 1840s and 1850s, the *virtual* gold rush of the 1990s left us with a worldwide network of fiber optic cables allowing for cheap and efficient communication to most parts of the globe.

By the time the cables were laid, many American businesses were already familiar with the economic advantages of assembling goods in countries with

---

4. *Dictionary.com Unabridged (v 1.1)* (Random House 2008), http://dictionary.reference.com/browse/globalization.
5. *See e.g.*, Andrew Ross Sorkin, *Investing; Just Who Brought Those Duds To Market?* N.Y. TIMES, Apr. 15, 2001, at 31 ("In one blindingly fast riches-to-rags story, Pets.com filed for bankruptcy just nine months after Merrill Lynch took it public."); Harry Blodget, *Irreplaceable Exuberance*, N.Y. TIMES, Aug. 30, 2005, at A19 ("Why do we overpay for thousands of doomed upstarts (Netscape, eToys, Webvan) and underpay for future giants (Microsoft, Google, eBay)?").

cheap labor forces. The apparel and automobile industries had been manufacturing offshore for decades. Laying the fiber optics, however, gave companies the ability to smoothly tap another resource that is cheaper outside of the United States: *knowledge*. From technical support hotlines for our latest gadgets to transcription services for medical doctors, any task requiring reading, writing, or talking could now be done in a cubicle across the room or a cubicle across the globe.

One example of particular interest to this author was highlighted in TIME Magazine's April 2008 article entitled, "Call My Lawyer . . . in India."[6] Chronicling the virtues of saving clients money, the article explained how lawyers in Mumbai, Bangalore, and Gurgaon "do legal grunt work" for a fraction of what large American firms typically charge. By the end of 2008 it is estimated that 29,000 legal jobs will be outsourced and as many as 79,000 by 2015.[7]

Globalization has its enthusiasts and critics. Critics point to the loss of American jobs, the harm to the environment, and the cruel exploitation of workers in developing nations as proof that the path of globalization is paved with immorality. Such aspersions gain traction when companies like Nike[8] are associated with sweatshop conditions in poor countries. The condemnation reached a boiling point in Seattle during the World Trade Organization's Ministerial Conference of 1999. Thousands gathered to protest the abuses ostensibly spawned by globalization. With the use of pepper spray, tear gas, and rubber bullets, police officers sought to quell the protesters who prevented access to the event. Unrest grew to violence, and vandalism and chaos remain the resonating memories from the three-day conference that was supposed to highlight trade negotiations among developed and developing nations.[9]

Globalization's critics argue that the harm caused by multinational corporations is grounded in their economic self interest. Ironically, proponents of globalization assert that economic self interest will force *good behavior*; as the potential harm a business can suffer if exposed to be a bad corporate citizen provides a sufficient incentive to act appropriately. As stated by one commentator, "[g]iven the direct link between brand value and both sales and share price, the potential costs of behaving unethically far outweigh any

---

6. Suzanne Barlyn, *Call My Lawyer... in India*, TIME, Apr. 3, 2008, *available at* http://www.time.com/time/magazine/article/0,9171,1727726,00.html.
7. Id.
8. *See e.g.*, Samuel Freedman, *A 'Fair Trade' Approach to Licensed College Gear*, N.Y. TIMES, Feb. 13, 2008, at B5 ("On campuses across the country since the 1990s, student advocates have particularly pressured administrators and corporations, most visibly Nike, to sell only those licensed items produced without sweatshop labor.").
9. Art Thiel, *Seattle Will Remember When We Blew It with the WTO Gig*, SEATTLE POST-INTELLIGENCER, Dec. 3, 1999, *available at* http://seattlepi.nwsource.com/thiel/thie033.shtml.

benefits, and outweigh the monitoring costs associated with an ethical business."[10] Highlighting Nike's efforts to rehabilitate its reputation, the commentator explained, "Nike, a company once criticized for the employment practices of some of its suppliers in developing countries, now posts results of external audits and interviews with factory workers at www.nikebiz.com."[11]

Advocates of globalization also argue that although the conditions of sweatshops are often dreadful, they can be the best and only economic boost available in poor countries. In *The End of Poverty*, Jeffrey Sachs asserts that "sweatshops are the first rung on the ladder out of extreme poverty."[12] Contrasting the conditions of Malawi, where poverty threatens daily survival, to the inhabitants of Bangladesh, where there is a labor force enduring sweatshop-like conditions, he writes:

> These young women already have a foothold in the modern economy that is a critical, measurable step up from the villages of Malawi (and more relevant for the women, a step up from the villages of Bangladesh where most of them were born).... [C]losing such factories as a result of wages forced above worker productivity would be little more than a ticket for these women back to rural misery.... Virtually every poor country that has developed successfully has gone through these first stages of industrialization.[13]

With respect to the gray and black market, whether one is a proponent or opponent of globalization is an issue of diminishing importance. Like trying to retrieve an e-mail after hitting *send*, trying to stop or slow the inertia of globalization is futile. Efforts to shape the character of globalization, such as mandating safe working conditions, are of course laudable endeavors. Nonetheless, it is worthwhile to accept that modern globalization is a permanent reality.

Because the bell of globalization cannot be un-rung, successful brand owners must learn to capitalize and cope with the rewards and risks of this new economy. To generalize, American businesses have done a fine job capitalizing on the rewards. As described above, evidence of American businesses taking advantage of inexpensive labor and knowledge can be found everywhere. These advantages get passed on to consumers in the form of cheaper goods and services.

---

10. CLIFTON, *supra* note 13, at 34.
11. *Id.*
12. JEFFREY D. SACHS, THE END OF POVERTY 12 (Penguin Books 2006) (2005).
13. *Id.* at 11–12.

Where American companies have fallen short has been with respect to understanding the need to step up efforts to protect their brands and intellectual property. The benefits of global expansion reach far beyond legitimate trade. Illegitimate trade has been equally eager to take advantage of the efficiencies and economies of scale that globalization offers. As a result, threats to brand owners in the form of black or gray market activity have skyrocketed in size and scope since the 1990s. Revenues derived from counterfeiting and piracy have increased by more than four hundred percent since the early 1990s. During the same time period, legitimate trade only increased by fifty percent.[14]

As discussed in Chapter 2, there are few, if any, industries immune from attack. From the luxurious to the mundane and the simple to the complex, there is now a global network of illegitimate traders willing to copy or divert genuine products for their own profits' sake. Given the ease in which these illegitimate products can be bought and sold, it is imperative that brand owners take preventative action. The belief that diverted or counterfeit products are a small reality containable with token opposition is an outdated and provincial mindset. Globalization is the reality and its profound rippling effects mandate that brand owners respond.

b. Internet

> "It is beyond irony that the internet—essentially an American invention and 'supplied' by America—has become such an instrument of challenge to its brands and its institutions."
>
> —Rita Clifton, Author and Brand Expert[15]

Along with its many virtues, the Internet provides an ideal environment for corruption. From pedophiles to terrorists, this low-cost tool of global connectivity allows users to communicate instantly and, as important, anonymously. These same factors have provided a platform for individuals and businesses to seamlessly buy, sell, and trade black and gray market products all over the world. It estimated that $25 billion in counterfeit goods are traded online every year.[16]

---

14. Interpol, *The Impact and Scale of Counterfeiting*, http://www.interpol.com/Public/News/Factsheet51pr21.asp (last visited Oct. 6, 2008).
15. CLIFTON, *supra* note 13, at 5.
16. *Imitating Property is Theft*, THE ECONOMIST, May 15, 2003, *available at* http://www.economist.com/displaystory.cfm?story_id=1780818.

eBay, where black or gray marketers freely buy and sell products, contains numerous examples of the challenges brand owners face. It has been reported that a search on eBay found 340 advertisements selling software at far below the retail price.[17] Adobe has stated that seventy to ninety percent of its software sold on auction sites is pirated.[18] The ubiquitous availability of non-genuine goods has resulted in efforts to hold eBay accountable for the wrongdoing of its users.

The efforts have been largely unsuccessful.[19] For example, in *Hendrickson v. eBay Inc.*,[20] eBay was sued when pirated copies of the movie "Manson" were found being offered for sale. The movie's owner alleged that eBay was liable for copyright infringement because it participated in and facilitated the unlawful sale and distribution of unauthorized copies of the film. The movie owner's legal theory was that eBay was *secondarily* liable because it provided an online forum, tools, and services to the third party sellers of the pirated movie.[21] By analogy, the owner argued that eBay should be liable in the same way traditional swap meet organizers have been held liable for the sales of counterfeit recordings by independent vendors.[22]

Trying to distance itself from the swap meet analogy, eBay characterized itself for the court as a publisher of "electronic classified ads."[23] The court disagreed with the description as being an oversimplification of its business. The court noted that eBay is known first and foremost as an Internet *auction* Web site.[24] Summarizing the facts, the court explained that "eBay's Internet business features elements of both traditional swap meets—where sellers pay for use of space to display their goods—and traditional auction houses—where goods are sold via the highest bid process."[25] Although the court acknowledged that eBay manifests the characteristics of an online swap meet, it refused to find liability pursuant to the "safe harbor" provision of the Digital Millennium Copyright Act (DMCA),[26] which protects Internet service providers from liability for direct, vicarious, and contributory infringement.

---

17. HOPKINS, *supra* note 11, at 120.
18. *Id.*
19. For a discussion of a brand owner's successful lawsuit against eBay in Europe, see page 303.
20. Hendrickson v. eBay Inc., 165 F. Supp. 2d 1082 (C.D. Cal. 2001).
21. *Id.* at 1087.
22. *See e.g.*, Fonovisa, Inc. v. Cherry Auction, Inc., 76 F.3d 259 (9th Cir. 1996) (Court held that the complaint stated causes of action for vicarious and contributory copyright infringement against the operators of a traditional swap meet).
23. *eBay*, 165 F. Supp. 2d at 1083.
24. *Id. citing* Leslie Walker, *EBay Goes Off-Line To Train Its Next Block of Dealers*, WASH. POST, Aug. 9, 2001 at E1 ("eBay, the giant Internet auction house"); Pradnya Joshi & Charles V. Zehren, *Bidders' Remorse Online Auctions Now No. 1 Source of Internet Fraud*, NEWSDAY, Aug. 30, 2000 ("eBay, the world's largest online auction service").
25. *Id.* at 1084.
26. 17 U.S.C. § 512 (2008).

Chapter 16 discusses in more detail the substance of copyright liability. For purposes of this chapter, however, it is sufficient to understand that Web sites like eBay are comfortably shielded from liability for the unlawful activity of their users. As a result, there are many Web sites that provide a convenient platform to buy and sell gray and black market products. Along with eBay, Web sites such as iOffer and craigslist give users the opportunity to shop, buy, sell, and trade everything imaginable.

For those not wanting to cull through the morass of products irrelevant to their business, there are Web sites more narrowly tailored to fit their needs. For example, Alibaba describes itself as "the world's largest marketplace for global trade and the leading provider of online marketing services for importers and exporters."[27] Alibaba allows users to specify their product search by first selecting a specific country and then browsing for various products. If the user selects China, for example, more than forty categories of products will appear. From cars to fashion accessories, users can search for various products offered for sale by Chinese companies and individuals. The selection is huge: there are oftentimes several hundred thousand listings under each category. A recent search of "timepieces, jewelry, eyewear" in China revealed more than 256,853 listings.[28]

There are also industry-specific Web sites. The North America Association of Telecommunication Dealers (NATD) provides a forum where telecom brokers can quickly do business with one another to fit their specific needs. The Association of Service and Computer Dealers International (ASCDI) provides a similar platform for companies in the business of buying and selling computers and other technology business solutions.

The resources for online commerce are boundless and they are especially beneficial to black and gray marketers. Brand owners spend millions of dollars developing, manufacturing, and marketing their products. Without having to incur any of these costs, unauthorized brokers are able to enjoy further savings by inexpensively selling products on these online platforms. Relying on the name recognition that the legitimate brand owner paid dearly to develop, unauthorized brokers can upload their offers with the confidence that a simple word search will lead interested buyers to their listings. Without the overhead of the legitimate brand owner or the higher cost for authorized products, these brokers can easily divert sales away from the brand owner's legitimate channels.

Brand owners are learning how the Internet has provided a surge in gray market activity. In December 2006, USA Today reported how the Internet

---

27. Alibaba.com, http://www.alibaba.com/trade/servlet/page/help/new_to_alibaba/what_is_alibaba (last visited April 14, 2008).
28. *Id.*, http://chinasuppliers.alibaba.com/ (last visited April 14, 2008).

had sparked the gray market's expansion.[29] The article chronicled brand owners' vexation with the practice and explained how some manufacturers will not provide gray market repairs even when customers are willing to pay for them.[30] The money saved not servicing the gray market products does, of course, come at a cost: The consumer—who in many instances has no idea the product was procured from the gray market—will be angry and frustrated at being left with a defective product that the brand owner is unwilling to repair. Although difficult to quantify on a balance sheet, this type of harm to the goodwill of a company can be devastating.

There are efforts on the part of these auction and trading sites to limit illegal activity. eBay's Verified Rights Owner (VeRO) Program allows intellectual property owners to report and request the removal of listings that infringe their rights. eBay's Police Blotter feature also reports noteworthy cases in which eBay has worked alongside law enforcement to catch those abusing eBay in furtherance of their criminal enterprise. Similarly, the NATD and ASCDI have their own code of ethics to which its participants are required to abide. Violations of these codes can result not only in suspension from the trading networks but also in the public humiliation of being listed among the companies who have been found to engage in improper activity.

Nonetheless, brand owners attempting to find and report all infringing activity on the Internet may find themselves engaged in a never-ending game of whac-a-mole. Quite simply, the Internet has created millions of *virtual* back alleys where criminal conduct takes place every day with little or no detection. Given this new marketplace, brand owners must be that much more careful to prevent their products from slipping into the gray market or being duplicated in the black.

c. Technology

The famous 2002 film *Catch Me if You Can* chronicles the exploits of Frank Abagnale Jr., one of the most notorious and successful confidence men in American history. Abagnale's frauds ranged from impersonating pilots to collecting millions in forged checks. Abagnale's shenanigans took place during the 1960s. His low-tech tricks worked in a low-tech world. Surely, Frank Abagnale Jr. could not get away with duping so many people out of so much money today. Has not the last fifty years of electronic and digital innovation made such criminal activity overwhelmingly difficult? As history has

---

29. Michelle Kessler, *Some See Red Over Gray-Market Goods*, USA TODAY, Dec. 11, 2006, at 1B, *available at* http://www.usatoday.com/tech/products/2006-12-10-gray-market_x.htm.
30. *Id.*

taught us, criminals are an enterprising and ambitious lot. In terms of brand abuse, the benefits of modern innovation have ironically tipped the advantage in favor of the crooks.

Today, laser printers, scanners, and computer graphics software allow fraudsters with limited budgets and sophistication to mass produce fake labels, trademarks, and other documentation to falsely convince customers that black or gray market goods are genuine products. Other technologies similarly allow for low-cost replication of CDs and DVDs. These latter technologies hurt many industries beyond music and film. Software as well as hardware products that require software are also duplicated, further depriving revenues to the legitimate brand owner.

Technological progress has also made transporting gray and black products faster and easier. Gray marketers win sales by promising products for less money in less time. Price arbitrage has always allowed gray marketers to promise cheaper goods. The recent advancements in transportation and logistics, however, have made the latter promise much easier to deliver. Advancements in cargo containers, better roll-on and roll-off tools, superior port management, and even modern refrigeration techniques have all played a role in improving worldwide shipping. In addition, companies like UPS, FedEx, and PayPal provide business owners with a litany of tools to make efficient the machine of national and international commerce. From tracking products and confirming delivery to ensuring payment and tracking invoices, the world's smallest business can now seamlessly participate in the global economy. The benefits are obvious. These tools remove what were once barriers to market entry and create a much more level playing field.

Because technological innovation is unbiased, the modern tools of transportation and logistics assist gray and black marketers just as they assist brand owners. In fact, gray marketers often require little or no warehouse space because, rather than keep an inventory, they will fill the vast majority of orders via drop shipments from other sources. Thus, the increased speed in which a transaction can be processed is particularly beneficial for gray marketers.

In this era of fast and easy duplication, the realities of globalization are forcing companies to have a paradoxical business strategy. Although intellectual property is enduring a season of heightened vulnerability, American businesses are essentially forced to share their secrets with outsourced foreign partners to remain viable. A 2004 *Business Week* article explained both the scope and necessity of foreign outsourcing: "Makers of apparel, footwear, electric appliances, and plastics products, which have been shutting U.S. factories for decades, know well the futility of trying to match the China price." In that same article, a business professor articulated the imperative for domestic business to manufacture oversees: "If you still make anything labor intensive, get out now rather than bleed to death. Shaving 5% here and there won't work."³¹

Of course, the requisite savings have consequences. Providing access to technology and company know-how has been devastating to various American businesses. Less than honorable partners will over-manufacture genuine goods, manufacture their own copycat goods, or share secret processes to other individuals or companies. The accounts of American businesses getting burned by foreign deceit are endless. And yet, remaining domestic for all operations is rarely a viable option. Brand owners must therefore be willing to go oversees but prudent enough to go oversees *prepared*.

d. Decreased Trade Barriers

The removal of trade barriers can be both tangible and intangible. Examples of tangible barrier removal include the creation of the Suez and Panama Canals. The Suez Canal in Egypt was completed in 1869 and removed a relatively large land barrier—Africa—thereby shortening the trade time between Europe and Asia. Similarly, the Panama Canal, completed in 1914, joined the Pacific and Atlantic oceans, thereby reducing the trade time between the eastern and western United States as well as Latin America and East Asia, and removing the dangerous circumnavigation of South America.

Although the fall of the Berlin Wall in 1989 was in fact the removal of a *physical* barrier, its significance went far beyond ending the separation of East and West Berlin. Thomas Friedman describes in *The World is Flat* the profound rippling effects of the crumbling barricade:

> The fall of the Berlin Wall on 11/9/89 unleashed forces that ultimately liberated all the captive people of the Soviet Empire. But it actually did so much more. It tipped the balance of power across the world toward those advocating democratic, consensual, fee-market-oriented governance, and away from those advocating authoritarian rule with centrally planned economies.³²

Once the Berlin Wall was removed, the 1990s became a watershed decade of *intangible* barrier removal. Tariffs dropped dramatically. The North American Free Trade Agreement (NAFTA) was passed in 1994 and eliminated

---

31. Pete Engardio & Dexter Roberts, *The China Price*, BUSINESSWEEK, Dec. 2004, *available at* http://www.businessweek.com/magazine/content/04_49/b3911401.htm.
32. THOMAS L. FRIEDMAN, The World Is Flat (3rd ed. Picador 2007) (2005) at 52.

the majority of tariffs on products traded among the newly created North American trade bloc of Canada, the United States, and Mexico.[33] Also, the World Trade Organization (WTO), which was designed to liberalize international trade, was established a year later (with China joining the WTO in 2002).[34]

These events complimented the momentum of globalization, the Internet, and technology to create a liberated world in which to do business. Although the infrastructure to conduct business at rapid speeds was being established, governments around the world took notice and, essentially, got out of the way. Not wanting inefficiencies to leave them behind, developed nations loosened their controls over goods to reduce any delays or congestion at borders and ports.

Although these various forces caused quick and rapid change in the marketplace, political and judicial systems could simply not keep up. As goods are ubiquitously developed, manufactured, bought, sold, and shipped among many countries, legal principles such as jurisdiction and venue have proven to be ill-equipped to consistently bring about a just result. When having a physical office is no longer the *sine qua non* to conduct business, determining the location of a company's *principal place of business* for purposes of examining jurisdiction over a defendant is quickly becoming an irrelevant and antiquated relic of legal analysis.

The benefactors of this virtual asylum are, unsurprisingly, those individuals and companies that profit from infringing brand owner's rights. This machinating lot is typically savvy enough to simultaneously take advantage of the efficiencies of the open economy while shielding itself from a court's jurisdiction. The result for brand owners is too often the frustrating predicament of trying to seek justice against a defendant whose relationship with the forum state is attenuated enough to be just beyond its jurisdictional reach.

The challenge of obtaining relief in the judicial system underscores the necessity for brand owners to take the requisite steps to *prevent* brand abuse as opposed to merely *reacting* to brand abuse. The modern global economy has proven to be an ideal environment for illegitimate trade. To succeed, brand owners must similarly take advantage of the benefits offered in this new marketplace while simultaneously taking the appropriate steps to maintain the integrity of their brands.

---

33. North American Free Trade Agreement, U.S.-Can.-Mex., Dec 17, 1992, 32 I.L.M. 289 (1993), *available at* http://www.nafta-sec-alena.org/DefaultSite/index_e.aspx?DetailID=78.
34. WTO, *Understanding the WTO: Basics—The GATT years: from Havana to Marrakesh*, http://www.wto.org/english/thewto_e/whatis_e/tif_e/fact4_e.htm.

CHAPTER 4

The Rippling Effect
Gray Market Consequences

"[S]keptics would argue that since smuggling has always been more a nuisance than a scourge, it is a threat we can learn to live with as we have always done."
—Moisés Naím[1]

a.	Economic Consequences	40
	i. Partner Relationships	44
	ii. Customer Satisfaction and Brand Goodwill	47
	iii. Warranty and Service Costs	49
	iv. Research and Development	51
b.	Social Consequences	52
	i. Consumer Health and Safety	52
	ii. Harm to the Environment	55
	iii. Tax Revenue	56
	iv. Organized Crime	59
c.	Benefits of the Gray Market	60
	i. Discover and Reach New Markets	61
	ii. Overcome Supply Chain Constraints	63
	iii. Reduce Combating Expense	63

---

1. Moisés Naím, Illicit: How Smugglers, Traffickers, And Copycats Are Hijacking The Global Economy 120 (Anchor Books 2006) (2005).

a. Economic Consequences

From an economic perspective, it is commonly asserted that a gray market does not adversely affect brand owners. When products intended for overseas distribution resurface in the United States to compete with domestic distribution, gray market proponents will characterize this circumstance as a win-win for all involved: the brand owner, the gray marketer, and the customer. The benefit to the latter stakeholders is easy to ascertain. The gray marketer *wins* because it is able to profit from the arbitrage created by the brand owner's disparate prices. The customer *wins* because he or she enjoys the benefits (i.e., lower prices) of price wars between authorized and unauthorized resellers.

Finally, the brand owner *wins* because a sale brings revenue regardless of whether it occurs in Macau or Manhattan. Gray market advocates contend that sales in developing countries that result in American importation essentially subsidize foreign distributors so that they can remain viable and spread international brand appeal and awareness. If these foreign distributors were strictly required to limit their sales to resellers in their poverty-stricken territory—the argument goes—the foreign distributors could not keep their doors open.[2]

The shortcoming of this argument is its microanalysis. Examining a single transaction fails to consider the long-term consequences of *multiple* transactions. It is in this analysis that the more untoward consequences of an unabated gray market can be found. John Kilts, the first outside CEO at Gillette in seventy years, quickly learned these lessons when he joined the company in 2001.[3] Before taking the post, Kilts and a team conducted an exhaustive investigation into the causes of Gillette's recent history of mediocrity. The problem did not stem from poor products; Mach3 razors, Duracell batteries, and Oral-B tooth brushes were among the many products in Gillette's arsenal of popular brands. And yet, the company was failing. It had "missed its earnings for fourteen consecutive quarters. Sales and earnings had been flat for five years. Two-thirds of Gillette's products were losing market share."[4]

To accurately perform a root cause analysis of Gillette's underperformance, Kilts and his team conducted a comprehensive examination of the

---

2. *See e.g.*, U.S. v. Braunstein, 281 F.3d 982 (9th Cir. 2002) (Describing a Mexican distributors sales to a gray marketer as "particularly important because [the gray marketer] could afford to buy large quantities of product from [the Mexican distributor]. [A]fter the currency devaluation, 'most of the distributors in Mexico were virtually bankrupt,' so that 'they really had no credit or cash to purchase any product.'").
3. Thomas J. Neff & James M. Citrin, You're In Charge—Now What? 23 (2005).
4. *Id.*

company. Instead of simply relying on company insiders, the team "visited stores, inspected warehouses and dropped in at manufacturing plants. [Kilts] spoke with suppliers, pored over consumer feedback reports, picked the brains of board members, and chatted with retail customers."[5] It was during this objective examination that Kilts "discovered Gillette's *dirty little secret.*"[6] The dirty little secret was Gillette's unofficial policy of unloading its inventory at bargain prices in order to meet quarterly goals:

> To hit their sales numbers each quarter, Gillette's salespeople habitually resorted to a business practice known as trade loading: offer a cut-rate deal, rearrange product packaging, do anything to make a sale to a retailer to stock inventory. While trade loading isn't illegal, it is not a sustainable strategy because you are in essence borrowing from the future to pay for the present and devaluing your products in the process. Major retail customers, the chain stores selling Gillette products, knew the company was desperate to make its numbers and came to learn that all they had to do was wait until the last week of the quarter to order so that they could cut the best deal possible.[7]

The pressures to trade load are the same pressures that cause companies to "dump" or "divert" products into the gray market. In addition to slashing prices for retail outlets, it is not uncommon for sales teams to find *any* buyer even if the sales team knows that it will be competing with that gray market *buyer* the following quarter when it is trying to make legitimate sales. Kilts prepared a pamphlet entitled "Escaping the Circle of Doom," wherein he explained the dangers created when companies like Gillette make overly aggressive growth and sales projections. Rather than miss targets, businesses will make "bad decisions" to meet the unrealistic targets. Bad decisions beget bad decisions and the "circle of doom" continues to spiral downward.

When companies fail to contain the gray market, they end up having to compete with their own products in the marketplace. In *Alan's of Atlanta, Inc. v. Minolta Corp.*,[8] the well-known camera manufacturer Minolta Corporation (Minolta) was sued by a retailer for various antitrust violations in its policy of giving certain "key dealers" extremely favorable pricing. The plaintiff retailer argued that Minolta's policy, which included providing free cameras, equipment, advertising, promotions, and other benefits, constituted an illegal price discrimination scheme in violation of various antitrust statutes.[9]

---

5. *Id.*
6. *Id.* (emphasis added).
7. *Id.*
8. Alan's of Atlanta, Inc. v. Minolta Corp, 903 F.2d 1414 (11th Cir. 1990).
9. Specifically, the plaintiff argued that Minolta violated Sections 2(a), 2(d), 2(e), and 2(f) of the Clayton Act, as amended by the Robinson-Patman Act, 15 U.S.C. §§13(a), (d), (e), and (f).

Minolta and its representatives defended the legality of the pricing scheme because, among other reasons, it was necessary to compete against gray market pricing.

Although the court denied Minolta's motion for summary judgment, the court agreed that the gray market defense could "prove particularly persuasive [because i]n the United States there were clearly gray market camera equipment sellers, the identity, prices, and practices of which were rather obfuscated."[10] Indeed, the trial court concluded that Minolta's pricing scheme was a "reasonable response" to the gray market threat and was thus excusable.[11] The case is emblematic of the long-term problems caused by gray market complicity. Although the short-term rewards might seem to justify a gray market sale or two, brand owners may soon find that their biggest competitors are themselves.

The Ninth Circuit Court case of *United States v. Braunstein*[12] is another example of the obstacles a brand owner can face when insufficient efforts have been made to stop unwanted gray market activity. Even when the economic harm is discovered, the inertia of previously condoned activity can undermine the efforts to stop unwanted gray market. The case involved a criminal action brought against a gray marketer named David Braunstein (Braunstein) who bought Apple computers from Apple Latin America Company (ALAC) for resale in the United States. ALAC was a subsidiary of Apple Computer Company (Apple) and was responsible for the sale of Apple products to Mexico, Central America, South America, and the Caribbean.[13]

The arrangement between Braunstein and ALAC was, on its face, suspicious. It was estimated that Braunstein purchased approximately one million dollars per month from ALAC. Notwithstanding the large volume, Braunstein always paid ALAC up front and in cash. Moreover, there were no written agreements defining the relationship between Braunstein and ALAC, nor any documents memorializing the substance of any particular transaction. The problem, of course, had to do with the fact that Braunstein was importing the products into the United States. Specifically, Braunstein sold most of his ALAC inventory to a businessman in Arizona who resold the products throughout the United States.[14] As the court noted, this harmed Apple:

> ALAC's deals with Braunstein benefited ALAC in the short term by increasing the sales volume of products for which there were few, if any, other buyers. But the deals hurt Apple in the long-term by undercutting

---

10. Alan's of Atlanta, 903 F.2d at 1417.
11. *Id.* at 1421–22.
12. United States v. Braunstein, 281 F.3d 982 (9th Cir. 2002).
13. *Id.* at 984.
14. *Id.* at 985–86.

its ability to generate profitable sales in the United States. ALAC's business dealings effectively put ALAC's own distributors (whose sales area was limited to Latin America and the Caribbean) into direct competition with Apple's United States distributors. Moreover, Braunstein and Kaplan were selling their Apple inventory within the United States at a much cheaper price than the other United States distributors were offering, which hurt the sales of those distributors and caused confusion and resentment in the market.[15]

Concerned with the "systemic underselling of Apple's United States distributors by ALAC distributors,"[16] Apple hired an international private investigation firm to look into ALAC's business practices. The reports generated by the private investigator as well as those generated by the federal government provide an enlightening account of what motivated the participants and how the gray market wreaked havoc on Apple's intended distribution channels.

For example, the pressure on ALAC and its sales employees to generate revenue created a tempting environment to sell Apple products outside their authorized channels. According to one report created by investigators for the federal government, "ALAC 'was under pressure to generate high sales volume,' and deals such as the one with Braunstein facilitated that goal. Some of that pressure [also] appears to stem from the fact that ALAC employees worked on commission."[17] This temptation was compounded by the fact that business was slow in Latin America: "[A]fter the currency devaluation, 'most of the distributors in Mexico were virtually bankrupt,' so that 'they really had no credit or cash to purchase any product.'"[18]

Apple's private investigators reached similar conclusions. The pressures on ALAC to generate sales resulted in ALAC selling products that would directly compete with those companies that sold Apple products in the United States. The problem was made worse by the fact that Apple had not appropriately policed its distribution channels: "There was no accountability or penalties related to the [gray] market. ALAC was under pressure to generate high sales volume, and delivered most of its product F[ree] O[n] B[oard] Miami. Once the product left the [ALAC] warehouse there was little if any effort to ensure it was exported as claimed by the customer."[19]

The case against Braunstein for his allegedly fraudulent gray market activity was ultimately dismissed by the federal government. Apple was required to produce its entire private investigator report wherein it was revealed that

---

15. *Id.* at 985.
16. *Id.*
17. *Id.*
18. *Id.*
19. *Id.* at 986.

Apple was aware of the gray market and, making matters worse, condoned its existence.[20] Because of Apple's implicit participation with Braunstein's gray market scheme, the federal government's case for fraud fell apart. More problematic for Apple, however, was the fact that its own subsidiaries were complicit in a scheme that pitted the company against itself.

Once a brand owner becomes aware that it must contend with black or gray market challenges, it must also realize that inaction will only exacerbate the problem. Not only will the infringing players become emboldened by their conduct going unchecked, but any efforts by the brand owner to promote its brand will similarly promote and benefit the unauthorized market.[21] Given this threat, brand owners must carefully consider the consequences of over-investing in marketing and under-investing in brand protection. Procter & Gamble took a close look at these issues when it learned that fifty percent of its consumer products were counterfeit. By cutting its marketing budgets, the company was able to use the surplus funds to increase brand protection activities and, within two years, the counterfeiting rate was cut in half.[22]

The economic repercussions of an unbridled gray market can be profound. The following pages identify some of the more specific consequences brand owners may face.

i. Partner Relationships

In today's global marketplace, brand owners have channel partners throughout the world and throughout their chains of distribution. Manufacturing, distributing, and reselling partners are now regular participants in the brand owners' efforts to disseminate products to consumers around the world. Like every relationship—business or otherwise—breakdowns are inevitable when there is a lack of trust. When a gray market emerges causing unwanted competition with a brand owner's authorized sales, relationships with these channel parties can be irreparably impaired.

---

20. *Id.* Investigators interviewing various personnel revealed that ALAC knew of Braunstein's intent to import the products into the United States. One ALAC employee stated the following: "The leaders of Apple Latin America at the time . . . knew they could 'quietly' dump the PowerBooks (which were already excess inventory for Apple USA) with Braunstein, and be heroes. Accordingly, Apple Latin America did not care where Braunstein sold the computers, or even if he sold them." *Id.* at 988.
21. Richard S. Post & Penelope N. Post, Global Brand Integrity Management 163 (2008). ("When your products end up in the gray market, they compete directly with your products, and you end up competing with yourself. Why compete with your own products? Every advertising dollar you spend is helping unauthorized sales as much as yours.").
22. *See id.*

Consider, for example, the honorable reseller. This reseller's operation is dedicated to the brand it is authorized to sell. It will promote the brand above competing products and restrict its sales pursuant to any price or geographic limitations imposed by the brand owner. Especially if the product has technical components, the reseller will make a significant investment to ensure that its employees are qualified to sell, install, and—when necessary—repair the product. The reseller's loyalty and investment is premised on the trust it places in the brand owner. The reseller trusts that the brand owner will continue to create desirable products. Equally important, the reseller trusts that the brand owner will protect the integrity of its sales channels.

Problems emerge when the reseller finds itself losing sales to the gray market. Although competition is inevitable, the anticipated competition comes from the brand owner's *competitors*. What makes the reseller's attenuating business more troublesome is the fact that it is losing sales to end users buying the *same* products at prices that would cripple the reseller's profit margins. Troubled that another reseller is selling goods for less than the reseller's wholesale price, the reseller contacts the brand owner seeking its assistance to reclaim the integrity of its sales channel.

How the brand owner responds will significantly impact the future health of the parties' relationship. Should the brand owner quickly address and solve the problem, the reseller's dedication to the brand owner and its products will be solidified. Grateful that the brand owner was unwilling to acquiesce to unauthorized sales, the reseller will have a reassured confidence that its continued loyalty to the brand owner will be sufficiently lucrative.

On the other hand, if the brand owner does not adequately address the emergence of a gray market, the reseller will inevitably question the efficacy of its reselling arrangement. Unable to compete with unauthorized resellers that procure their products from foreign sources, the reseller may simply change brands. In this instance, the reseller would simply stop buying and selling the brand owner's products and endeavor to market a competitor's product that has adequate controls over the sale channels. An even more problematic option for the reseller would be for the reseller to simply become a participant in the gray market. Realizing that the brand owner is ostensibly uninterested in its enforcement, the reseller will remain an "authorized" reseller; however, this "authorized" reseller will procure products from the gray market when the economics prove the unauthorized transaction to be more advantageous.

Ignoring a gray market economy is akin to kindling the gray market economy. Motivated by pragmatism as much as capitalism, resellers quickly understand that they are left with little choice when a brand owner fails to take heed of the problem. Because continuing to offer goods at above-market prices is not a sustainable business model, the brand owner is left with a reseller that no longer sells its products or a reseller that sells its products that were obtained from the gray market. In other words, an unchecked gray market begets an even larger gray market until the inertia of the problem dilutes the overall value of the brand.

It would be imprudent for brand owners to underestimate the magnitude of the gray market's temptations. According to a KPMG study, 71 percent of authorized partners believe it is *necessary* to source products from the gray market in order to survive and 41 percent admitted to *regularly* sourcing product from the gray market.[23] In addition to the obvious price advantages found in the gray market, product availability is oftentimes an added benefit. If a brand owner fails to properly thwart a developing gray market, the gray market will continue to mushroom, resulting in the creation of a shadow inventory that the brand owner can neither control nor track. In addition to making it more difficult for brand owners to forecast manufacturing needs, this shadow inventory provides authorized partners with an easy alternative to procure goods. In the event the brand owner or its authorized distributor do not have the goods immediately available, authorized resellers can turn to the gray market. Because deals are won and lost based on price *and speed*, the gray market inventory is oftentimes too appealing to ignore.

An examination of these issues inevitably leads to the conclusion that brand owners must take action to ensure that their authorized channel partners are loyal allies. If a few breaches in a brand owner's supply chain are ignored, it will not be long before the brand owner's distribution channels are a porous milieu where gray and black markets thrive. Breaches must be addressed and authorized partners must believe they are valued by the brand owner to encourage brand loyalty.

Notwithstanding these imperatives, brand owners are commonly failing to take the necessary steps to secure a strong allegiance with its channel partners. For example, Ford Motor Company uses reverse online auctions to essentially guarantee it is getting the lowest price for components.[24] In addition to Ford running the risk that it will end up purchasing gray or counterfeit components, this process also sends a message to its suppliers: Your relationship with this brand owner will end the moment another supplier can deliver a lower price.[25] It is this type of pressure that leads channel partners to believe it is "necessary" to procure products from the gray market to survive. Because the rippling effect of impaired partner relationships is a burgeoning gray market, brand owners must do much more to foster these relationships. Chapter 5 identifies the steps brand owners can take to best garner channel partner fidelity.

---

23. *The Grey Market*, KPMG/Anti-Gray Mkt. Alliance, 2003, at 4, *available at* http://www.agmaglobal.org/press_events/press_docs/KPMG_TheGreyMarket_Web.pdf.
24. Jeffrey K Liker & Thomas Y. Choi, *Building Deep Supplier Relationships*, in Harv. Bus. Rev. on Supply Chain Mgmt., 2006, at 27.
25. Id.

ii. Customer Satisfaction and Brand Goodwill

In 2001, Dennis Tuckish of Pompano Beach, Florida, wanted to purchase Chrysler's popular "PT Cruiser."[26] The PT Cruiser was in high demand in 2001 and, unbeknownst to Mr. Tuckish, various dealers purchased a large inventory of PT Cruisers from Canada through the gray market.[27] Taking advantage of the currency exchange rate, these dealers would import the cars and sell them as "new" to unsuspecting customers. Although the cars may not have necessarily been titled to a previous owner, the cars were by no means "new." In order to sell Canadian PT Cruisers in the United States, the odometers needed to be converted from kilometers to miles. In addition to this procedure potentially damaging the car, it created an opportunity for tampering wherein the reseller could shave thousands of miles off of the vehicles, thus increasing their market price.[28]

Mr. Tuckish purchased one of these gray market PT Cruisers and almost immediately had problems with his car. Although it was represented to him as new, he suffered problems such as power loss and engine surge. After several attempts to repair the vehicle, Mr. Tuckish filed a request for arbitration with the Florida's Motor Vehicle Arbitration Board (the Board) against Daimler-Chrysler in a "Lemon Law" proceeding.[29] The Board determined that Daimler-Chrysler was not liable because, it was determined by the Board, Mr. Tuckish purchased a "used" car. Accordingly, any claims would have to be brought against the dealer.[30]

Although Mr. Tuckish accepted the Board's ruling and pursued his rights against the dealership,[31] it is reasonable to assume that he is probably not driving a Daimler-Chrysler today. Although Daimler-Chrysler prevailed in its arbitration against Mr. Tuckish, it suffered an adverse judgment of customer satisfaction. When dissatisfied customers accumulate, a brand's future success becomes perilous. Brand development turns on two types of purchases: the initial purchase and the repeat purchase.[32] The initial purchase is the result of the customer somehow becoming aware of the product. Whether this awareness comes from advertising, word of mouth, or other public relations efforts, *communication* is the most important ingredient. On the other hand, the *repeat* purchase is typically in response to the actual experience the customer enjoyed from the initial purchase. Given Mr. Tuckish's experience,

---

26. *See* Tuckish v. Pompano Motor Co., 337 F. Supp. 2d 1313 (S.D. Fla. 2004).
27. *See id.* at 1315.
28. *Id.*
29. *Id.* at 1316.
30. *See id.*
31. *See id.* at 1313.
32. THORSTEN H. NILSON, COMPETITIVE BRANDING 63 (1996).

no amount of creative advertising would likely convince him to buy another Daimler-Chrysler.

Mr. Tuckish's experience is not unique. If customers purchase what they believe to be "new" products, there is inevitable disappointment when they learn that they instead purchased a gray or black market good. This disappointment is compounded further if the brand owner, like Daimler-Chrysler, refuses to take any measures to remedy the customer's predicament. Refusing to replace, repair, or support a gray or black market product is an ostensibly sensible strategy. Why would a brand owner spend money troubleshooting a transaction from which it had received little or no revenue? The justification to *not* assist the customer, however, ignores the double-edged sword of customer dissatisfaction.

In the era of e-mail, blogs, and YouTube, an unsatisfied customer is a potent threat to any brand. AOL learned this lesson the hard way when Vincent Ferrari of the Bronx publicized his grueling efforts to cancel his online service. Determined not to lose a paying customer, the AOL representative essentially filibustered Mr. Ferrari's requests for cancellation. The call lasted over twenty minutes, Mr. Ferrari used the word "cancel" twenty-one times and at one point tried to make the point as clear as possible: "When I say, 'Cancel the account,' I don't mean, 'Figure out how to help me keep it.' I mean, 'Cancel the account.'"[33]

After enduring such nonsense, Mr. Ferrari expressed customer frustration in a medium more appropriate for the twenty-first century. Rather than adhere to the conventional method of submitting a letter of dissatisfaction, he posted the call as an audio file on his blog. As the *New York Times* explained, "[s]hortly thereafter, those five minutes became the online equivalent of a top-of-the-charts single."[34] Indeed, the article, which in itself publicized the call, chronicled the popularity of Mr. Ferrari's call. Postings on his blog came from other AOL customers echoing his frustration based on their own experiences; there were over 300,000 visits to his blog; and Mr. Ferrari was invited to appear on NBC's "Today" show to complete the media trifecta (print, online, and television) in which he could share his ordeal.[35]

AOL suffered national embarrassment by the online postings of *one* customer. As that episode makes clear, considering how to respond to a customer's complaint requires a great deal more than merely looking at the alleged problem's "price." As discussed in the next section, brand owners are commonly faced with the dilemma of whether or not to honor warranties on gray market products. Although not honoring the warranties of illegitimate products

---

33. Randall Stross, *Digital Domain: AOL Said, "If You Leave Me I'll Do Something Crazy,"* N.Y. TIMES, July 2, 2006, at 33.
34. *Id.*
35. *Id.*

can save money for the brand owner in the short-term, refusing to honor warranties on such products can dramatically impair the perceived value of the brand.[36] Particularly when wide-spread publication of the brand owner's treatment of the customer could be embarrassing, brand owners must consider the intangible cost of diminished customer satisfaction.

iii. Warranty and Service Costs

One of the ways brand owners seek to combat the gray market is to refuse warranty claims when the product was sourced from the gray market. Even when the end user has no idea that it did not purchase an authorized product, brand owners will refuse to honor repair or replacement requests. Brand owners will justify this strategy by citing cost concerns. Warranting all products regardless of source would invariably be more expensive. To cover these increased costs, brand owners would have to increase the price of its goods. To protect consumers from price increases, the argument goes, brand owners will limit the application of its warranties to authorized products only.

This practice of not honoring warranties is particularly prevalent in the electronics industry. Sony and many others will not warranty products purchased through the gray market.[37] Some other brand owners are even more aggressive. The United States division of Nikon will only service products purchased through an authorized reseller. It refuses to service gray market repairs even if a customer is willing to pay for them.[38] Computer maker Lenovo similarly refuses to service gray market goods.[39] Other companies like Garmin, which manufactures global positioning systems (GPS), will analyze whether to provide services on a case-by-case basis.[40]

Although these strategies have intuitive appeal, they are problematic, as seen in the previous discussion, which chronicled a car buyer that inadvertently purchased a gray market "PT Cruiser." Even though the customer purchased the vehicle from a third-party dealership, he first turned to the manufacturer Daimler-Chrysler for relief when problems were discovered. The customer's reaction is representative of the general opinion and expectation that consumers have towards brand owners. In a recent study, it was found that customers typically blame brand owners for any defects in quality control.[41]

---

36. HOPKINS, *supra* note 11, at 39.
37. Michelle Kessler, *Some See Red Over Gray-Market Goods*, USA TODAY, Dec. 11, 2006, at 1B, *available at* http://www.usatoday.com/tech/products/2006-12-10-gray-market_x.htm.
38. *Id.*
39. *Id.*
40. *Id.*
41. *The Grey Market*, KPMG/Anti-Gray Mkt. Alliance, 2003, at 3, *available at* http://www.agmaglobal.org/press_events/press_docs/KPMG_TheGreyMarket_Web.pdf.

Even if the problem was caused by a product outside of the authorized distribution chain, consumers consider such problems within a brand owner's zone of accountability.

This presents brand owners with a Hobson's choice. On the one hand, refusing to warrant products sold outside its chain of distribution certainly avoids an unwanted increase in company overhead. On the other hand, such a policy does not account for the repercussions of customers bewildered to learn that the troubleshooting hotline featured in the documentation accompanying their purchase is not available.

Mindful of the hazards that can threaten a business when its consumers are unhappy, many brand owners have simply elected to service gray market goods. The rationale behind this policy was well articulated in *Osawa & Co. v. B&H Photo*.[42] At issue in the case was a brand owner's effort to enjoin the unauthorized importation and sale of various photographic equipment. The plaintiff Osawa & Company (Osawa) was the registered owner of the Mamiya United States trademarks as well as the exclusive United States distributor of Mamiya products. Osawa initiated litigation when it discovered some discount camera dealers in New York City that allegedly imported various equipment without Osawa's consent or permission.[43]

Osawa requested that the court issue an injunction against the gray market importation. In that effort, Osawa presented evidence to show how the unauthorized gray market importations caused it irreparable harm. Among the theories of harm was the fact that Osawa was providing warranty services on the gray market goods sold by the defendants. Accordingly, Osawa argued that it had suffered and would continue to suffer damages by way of incurring these additional warranty costs. The defendants argued that this could not support Osawa's damages theory because it was "self-inflicted."[44] According to the defendants, Osawa had no obligation to honor its warranty on gray market goods and could simply refuse the service. Because Osawa was electing on its own to honor such warranties, the costs could not constitute "irreparable harm" to obtain a preliminary injunction. The district court rejected the defendants' arguments and concluded that Osawa's decision to honor warranties on gray market goods did indeed constitute damages. The court's reasoning articulates with precision the challenges faced by brand owners deciding whether to pay for warranty and service costs on gray market products:

> Plaintiff gives warranty service on defendants' grey market sales not out of stupidity or neglect but because plaintiff's management perceives

---

42. Osawa & Co. v. B&H Photo, 589 F. Supp. 1163 (D.C.N.Y. 1984).
43. *Id.* at 1165.
44. *Id.* at 1167.

that dissatisfied purchasers of Mamiya cameras will damage the reputation of the Mamiya mark, which is the most significant asset on which plaintiff's business is founded. The customers do not know the cameras they purchased are from the grey market because defendants do not tell them. Thus, as to warranty repairs, not only are defendants operating free of a significant cost that plaintiff bears, but their sales increase plaintiff's cost.[45]

When products are sold on the gray market, warranty and service claims on these products will come at a significant cost. If the brand owner elects to service products it never sold, the increased cost is easily ascertainable. If the brand owner elects not to service these products, the increased cost is found in the more intangible category of customer dissatisfaction. Under either circumstance, the brand owner suffers.

iv. Research and Development

From English philosopher John Locke to the United States Supreme Court, it has been acknowledged that the creators of innovation deserve protection. In *Mazer v. Stein*,[46] the United States provided a pragmatic justification behind this policy:

> The economic philosophy behind the clause empowering Congress to grant patents and copyrights is the conviction that *encouragement* of individual effort by personal gain is the best way to advance public welfare through the talents of authors and inventors. . . . Sacrificial days devoted to such creative activities *deserve* rewards commensurate with the services rendered.[47]

The cost of inventing a new product can be substantial. Especially in industries like pharmaceuticals, research and development (R&D) costs can be in the hundreds of millions, or even billions, of dollars.[48] Brand owners will therefore price their goods to cover these expenses as well as fund future efforts to create even better products. Ensuring that individuals and companies collect their R&D costs ultimately benefits consumers. Although the prices may be higher than consumers would prefer, the macro investment in

---

45. *Id.* at 1167–68.
46. Mazer v. Stein, 347 U.S. 201 (1954).
47. *Id.* at 219 (emphasis added).
48. HOPKINS, *supra* note 11, at 152.

the pioneering industry inevitably leads to the innovation of products that make our lives safer, more convenient, and more enjoyable.

When a brand owner's products are counterfeited or traded on the gray market, it threatens the business model that is designed to recoup R&D costs. Because gray marketers and black marketers do not have *any* R&D costs, they are basically making a profit once their selling price exceeds the cost of goods. Although brand owners can increase their prices to more aggressively recoup their R&D investment, this may only make the gray and black market problem worse as the larger price disparity will make the unauthorized products that much more appealing to prospective purchasers.[49]

Rather than abandon R&D efforts, or naively increase prices hoping to recoup a return on their inventing costs, brand owners must focus on the problem and not the mere *symptoms* of the problem. Until and unless brand owners make a correct diagnosis and realize that the threat stems from the black or gray market, harm to the brand and balance sheet will likely continue.

b. Social Consequences

The effects of a flourishing gray market extend far beyond the emolument of the brand owner. Although the economic consequences of the gray market provide plenty of reasons for a brand owner to aggressively combat such commerce, the social consequences can be even more daunting. From dangers to consumers to indirectly contributing to the enrichment of society's lowest elements, controlling the channels of distribution is as much a moral responsibility as it is a fiscal one.

i. Consumer Health and Safety

Any product with at least some modicum of popularity will face competition from genuine products procured from the gray market and counterfeit imitations procured from the black. If the product's brand owner fails to control the authorized channels of distribution, it will not have a ability to quickly ascertain whether a bargain basement price constitutes an unauthorized—albeit genuine—import or a dangerously defective knock-off. This can leave brand owners in the unenviable position of being impotent to obtain legal relief against gray marketers while facing their own liability for the wrongdoing of product pirates.

---

49. *Id.* at 153.

An example of this predicament can be found in the gray and black marketing of baby formula. In 1995, the *New York Times* reported an investigation by the FDA that uncovered over 45,000 pounds of counterfeit infant formula in California.[50] The article chronicled the scheme's evolution from gray market product diversion to outright black market counterfeiting:

> The scam was made possible by a vast increase in the number of so-called diverters—wholesalers who buy goods from retailers that are selling products at extremely low prices—and other sources.... Legitimate diverters may buy from stores or wholesalers, but the shady ones may buy off the backs of trucks selling supplies that were meant to be discarded because of some defect.[51]

The "legitimate formula" that was seized fell into two categories: *First*, formula that was "actually damaged or outdated and was scheduled to be destroyed by companies hired by manufacturers [but i]nstead, those companies sold the formula to diverters."[52] *Second*, formula that was "destined for overseas [but] was diverted to domestic retailers."[53] For years, the scheme only involved this first category "legitimate" formula. The scheme was still dangerous; in addition to the risks attendant to reselling outdated or defective formula, the gray marketers would miscode the formula, thereby impairing the ability to recall or track the distribution of legitimate formula. Although the criminals would make fake boxes and labels to sell the products, they did not begin making counterfeit formula until much later.[54]

The discovery of the counterfeit formula was not made until parents with sick children began complaining to the manufacturers about the smell and appearance of the imposter formula. Retailers and wholesalers of the counterfeit formula then found themselves defending a class action filed by parents who alleged that "their infants became ill with maladies like irritable bowel syndrome, vomiting and diarrhea."[55] Although the article did not mention whether any litigation was pending against the manufacturer, as explained below, brand owners can just as easily find themselves facing negligence lawsuits alleging that their inability to control their distribution channels allowed for the dangerous commingling of gray and black market products.

When brand owners discover this kind of abuse, relying on the justice system to curb such activity is not enough. For example, in *United States. v. Hanafy*,[56] a defendant was criminally charged with an almost identical gray

---

50. Marian Burros, Eating Well; *F.D.A. Target Baby Formula*, N.Y. TIMES, Sept. 6, 1995 at A1.
51. *Id.*
52. *Id.*
53. *Id.*
54. *Id.*
55. *Id.*
56. United States v. Hanafy, 302 F.3d 485 (5th Cir. 2002).

market scheme as identified in the 1995 *New York Times* article. The defendants sold infant formula that had been purchased, obtained through welfare programs, or stolen by various third parties not associated with the defendants.[57] The defendants then consolidated the cans of formula into cardboard containers or shipping trays.[58] To give buyers the appearance that the trays of formula came directly from the manufacturer, the defendants used the manufacturer's trademarks on the cardboard containers and shipping trays.[59] The government charged the defendants with violating a variety of criminal statutes including selling misbranded goods as well as counterfeiting trademarks. The jury convicted the defendants and, on a motion for retrial, the district court reversed the convictions.[60]

On appeal, the Fifth Circuit Court examined whether the defendants' conduct did indeed amount to criminal liability. The court first considered the issue of whether the defendants illegally used counterfeit trademarks. Although the infant formula had a checkered history, it was never contended that the formula was counterfeit or adulterated in any way. Because the formula was "genuine," the court reasoned that there was no way for the formula to be considered counterfeit.[61] Turning to the cardboard boxes and shipping trays, the court again concluded that the defendants were not guilty of any crime. Because the shipping trays were truthfully marked with the contents they contained, the court could not find that the defendants had illegally used counterfeit marks.[62]

The court reached a similar conclusion in its analysis of whether the defendants had illegally misbranded food articles. Even though there was witness testimony from wholesalers that they would not have bought the formula had they known it had been repackaged, the court affirmed the district court's

---

57. *Id.* at 486.
58. *Id.*
59. *Id.*
60. *Id.* at 486–87.
61. *Id.* The court stated that there were two "exceptions" to the use of a mark on allegedly counterfeit goods: "One is an exception for 'gray goods.' 'Gray goods' are goods that are authentic and that have been obtained from overseas and imported into the United States. The second exception is the 'authorized use' or 'overrun' exception. Under this exception, a counterfeit mark 'does not include any mark or designation used in connection with the goods or services of which the manufacturer or producer was, at the time of the manufacture or production in question authorized to use the mark or designation for the type of goods or services so manufactured or produced, by the holder of the right to use such mark or designation." *Id.* at 488, *citing* 18 U.S.C. § 2320(e)(1). Characterizing these examples as "exceptions" to the use of mark on counterfeit goods is not accurate. These "exceptions" do not warrant criminal liability because they do not involve counterfeit products—they are genuine products purchased or produced without the manufacturer's consent.
62. *Id.* The Court acknowledged that its holding would not rely on the reasoning of cases examining similar facts in the civil context. Because the Court was reviewing a criminal case, its interpretation of the corresponding criminal statute would be done so narrowly. *Id.* at 489.

holding that merely identifying the contents of the shipping trays with the same information that is already on the cans of formula did not rise to the level of criminal culpability.[63]

U.S. v. Hanafy illustrates the limited relief that a brand owner can find in the criminal court system. The dangers of gray market formula and its subsequent commingling with black market formula were well documented in the *New York Times*' 1995 article and yet, several years later, the Fifth Circuit Court of Appeals was unwilling to sanction criminal defendants doing essentially the same thing because the formula was "unadulterated."

Of course, the integrity of a product can be severely compromised without manifest tampering. As discussed in Chapter 2, the dangerous gray marketing of pharmaceuticals is an example. Although ten percent of all drugs sold worldwide are believed to be counterfeit,[64] genuine pharmaceuticals that have been diverted from an authorized supply chain can also become unreliable or unsafe. Merck & Co. is one of the world's leading pharmaceutical companies and is currently addressing this epidemic.[65] Authentic and "unadulterated" Merck products can become dangerous when they are, for example, stored at room temperatures, marketed past their expiration dates, or repackaged in a way that compromise sterility or misrepresent their purpose or dosage.[66] Outside of the United States, it is common for expired products that resellers should have destroyed to turn up at bazaars and flea markets.[67] Gray market dangers are not limited to infant formula or pharmaceuticals. Sadly, there are legion accounts of ostensible gray market products causing unthinkable harm to unwary buyers.

ii. Harm to the Environment

Another unintended consequence of the gray market economy can be damage to the environment. The Association of Leaders in Equipment Distributors (AED) is an international trade association that represents companies involved in the distribution, rental, and support of equipment used in construction, mining, forestry, power generation, agriculture and industrial applications. AED's Washington D.C. office focuses on the advocacy of policy

---

63. *Id.* at 490.
64. *Counterfeit Medicines*, WORLD HEALTH ORGANIZATION (WHO), February 14 2006, *available at* http://www.who.int/mediacentre/factsheets/fs275/en/print.html.
65. *No Trade in Fakes Supply Chain Tool Kit*, U.S. CHAMBER OF COM. & COALITION AGAINST COUNTERFEITING AND PIRACY (CACP), 2006, at 9, *available at* http://www.verical.com/resources/docs/FinalSupplyChainToolKit1.5.07.pdf.
66. *Id.*
67. *Id.*

and legislation that is favorable to the equipment industry.[68] Among the policy issues it promotes is the prevention of gray market equipment imports. From an economic perspective, AED states that the "importation of equipment that does not comply with EPA emission rules ('gray market equipment') puts authorized equipment distributors at a competitive disadvantage."[69] From an environmental perspective, noncompliant equipment has the potential to pollute without consequence.

The Clean Air Act[70] and applicable Environmental Protection Agency (EPA) regulations[71] prohibit the importation into the United States of non-road equipment that does not comply with the Clean Air Act emissions standards. The law further provides that manufacturers affix an official EPA "tag" to each engine before importation.[72] According to the EPA, the agency's enforcement activities on the gray market front have prevented tens of thousands of pieces of equipment from being imported and resulted in hundreds of enforcement cases against violators. AED strives to ensure that the EPA and U.S. Customs Service zealously enforce their regulations.

AED is not without its critics. In 2002, the Independent Equipment Dealers Association (IEDA) urged the EPA to loosen its gray market enforcement program. The EPA rejected IEDA's requests, and IEDA appealed the decision to the D.C. Court of Appeals. In June of 2004, the court dismissed IEDA's appeal on jurisdictional grounds.[73]

The effort to prevent imports of noncompliant equipment is indeed a worthy endeavor. However, our borders and customs are imperfect. In fact, they are porous. The availability of illegal drugs is conclusive evidence of America's inability to successfully discern legitimate from illegitimate imports. In addition to the unwanted competition from gray market products, their importation can also allow for the operation of machines and vehicles that would otherwise be prohibited.

iii. Tax Revenue

How a government loses tax revenue to a black market economy is obvious: Criminals typically do not pay taxes on the compensation of their crimes.

---

68. Ass'n of Leaders in Equip. Distrib. (AED), AED Wash. Office—About Us, http://www.aednet.org/government/about_washington.cfm (last visited Oct. 8, 2008).
69. Ass'n of Leaders in Equip. Distrib. (AED), Preventing Gray Mkt. Equip. Imp., http://www.aednet.org/government/washington-policy-issues-detail.cfm?id=40 (last visited Oct. 8, 2008).
70. *See* 42 U.S.C. § 7547 (2008).
71. 40 C.F.R. §§ 89–91. (2008).
72. Violators of the statute and regulations may be penalized by civil fines of up to $27,500 for each violation or by administrative fines of up to $200,000.
73. *See* Indep. Equip. Dealers Ass'n v. E.P.A., 372 F.3d 420 (C.A.D.C. 2004).

For the same reason Al Capone never claimed income from the revenue enjoyed from his illegal bootlegging of liquor during the Prohibition Era of the 1920s and 1930s,[74] black marketers today are unwilling to advise the IRS of their earnings from selling stolen or counterfeit goods.

Given the size of the black market economy, the lost tax earnings are significant. For example, it is estimated that at least $1 billion was spent in Los Angeles County in 2005 for counterfeit goods.[75] To illustrate the enormity of this industry, "$2 billion is the equivalent to the average annual sales of about 39 Wal-Marts, 49 Home Depots, or 54 Target Stores."[76] Los Angeles, though a large city, is not an anomaly. Trade in counterfeits has grown at eight times the speed of legitimate trade.[77] State and local governments lose more than mere sales tax revenue. Additional tax revenue sources are cut back when lost business revenues are reflected in lower spending and fewer jobs.[78] Governments are further burdened with the added police, court, and prison costs associated with combating counterfeiting and related activity.[79]

The tax revenue losses from the unauthorized trade of genuine products are less apparent but by no means insignificant. For purposes of illustration, an oversimplification of microeconomics' theory of supply and demand predicts that a product's price will equalize the quantity demanded by consumers and the quantity supplied by producers. This economic equilibrium breaks down, however, if distortions are present in the marketplace. For example, a fifty percent tax on an item that costs $1.50 to the consumer is worth only $1.00 to the producer. This market distortion in the form of a tax creates a wedge between the value to the consumer and the return to the producer. Sometimes these market distortions are insignificant enough that neither the consumer nor producer feel compelled to adjust their behavior. In other instances, these market distortions can wreak havoc on a competitive marketplace.

An examination of the tobacco industry illustrates some of the impacts significant market distortions can have on an industry. In 1999, smokers in the United States witnessed a significant price increase imposed by the tobacco companies, though some states added an additional price jump in form of

---

74. Fed. Bureau of Investigation, *Solving Scareface How the Law Finally Caught Up with Al Capone*, March 28, 2005, http://www.fbi.gov/libref/historic/famcases/capone/capone.htm (last visited Oct. 8, 2008).
75. Gregory Freeman et al., *A False Bargain: The Los Angeles County Economic Consequences of Counterfeit Products*, http://www.laedc.org/consulting/projects/2007_piracy-study.pdf.
76. Id.
77. NAÍM, *supra* note 1 at 112.
78. Gregory Freeman et al., *A False Bargain: The Los Angeles County Economic Consequences of Counterfeit Products*, http://www.laedc.org/consulting/projects/2007_piracy-study.pdf.
79. Id.

sales tax.[80] The tobacco companies raised their prices in the United States because they began to pay $206 billion to settle the smoking-related health lawsuits filed by various states.[81] In California, meanwhile, voters passed an initiative that imposed an additional tax of fifty cents per cigarette pack.[82]

Prior to the price increases effective dates, there were indicators that smokers would look for ways to avoid the added costs. The stockpiling efforts in late 1998 were the first sign that smokers were keenly aware that their habit faced a fiscal impact the following year. With the price and tax increases looming, stores such as Costco were reporting double-digit sales increases as smokers were buying large quantities of cigarettes that were not yet impacted by the price increases.[83]

Meanwhile, law enforcement officials were concerned that smokers would turn to the Internet for gray market cigarettes or elsewhere for smuggled cigarettes once the price increases took effect.[84] Such concerns were valid. Just a few years earlier, Canada experienced a gray market and smuggling epidemic when its cigarettes were more expensive than in the United States.[85] Specifically, in 1994, Canada's higher sales tax on cigarettes and alcohol created such a lucrative opportunity for smugglers that commentators compared it to the illegal trafficking of alcohol during Prohibition.[86]

Canada's smuggling epidemic became so pervasive that Canada's Prime Minister Jean Chrétien was compelled to reduce federal cigarette taxes by as much as $10 per carton. Axiomatically, cutting the taxes would impact Canada's revenue and the move was not made without criticism. Manitoba's Finance Minister was particularly critical: "Smugglers should be dealt with through tough law enforcement" and not market competition. "To be dealing with this issue on a tax reduction basis makes no sense."[87] However, the price disparity between Canadian and American cigarettes was significant enough that the tax cut was considered necessary to combat the vibrant smuggling economy. When Quebec was the only province to similarly cut provincial taxes on cigarettes, neighboring provinces witnessed the creation of a "new 'gray market' as tens of thousands of smokers . . . crush[ed] across the border to snap up legal cheap smokes."[88]

---

80. Kenneth Howe, *Price Rise Puts Heat on Smokers Run on Cigarette Sales and Internet Vendors*, S.F. CHRON., Nov. 27, 1998, at A1.
81. *Id.*
82. *Id.*
83. *Id.*
84. *Id.*
85. Colin Nickerson, *Smuggling Surge Roils Canada in Illegal Cigarette, Alcohol Trade Spurs Crackdown, Violent Response*, BOSTON GLOBE, Feb. 16, 1994, at 1.
86. *Id.*
87. *Id.*
88. *Id.*

The price increases in the United States resulted in the same problems. Within eight months of the price increases, an "exploding gray market" emerged.[89] *Forbes* Magazine summarized the impact of raising cigarette prices to pay its litigation settlements:

> While the settlement lucre has made the nation's trial lawyers and state capitals ironic partners in Philip Morris' business, a secondary effect of the big price hikes it spawned is quietly reshaping the cigarettes industry: an exploding gray market. 'Repatriate product' are cigarettes made in the U.S. and shipped overseas, usually at wholesale prices substantially below those in the U.S., to penetrate markets where U.S. brands aren't as established; $275 for a 50-carton case in some instances, versus $900 in the U.S. (We're not talking about smuggling here; both prices include state and federal taxes.) Exploiting the opportunities for arbitrage, the gray marketers help the foreign distributors unload their excess smokes back to the U.S., where they distribute them to convenience stores and chains as big as Cigarettes Cheaper![90]

Not only can raising taxes create an opportunity for a gray market or smuggling economy, but tax revenues may even *decrease*. According to *Forbes*: "The Brits jacked taxes up to 80% of the price of a pack—only to see the first rise in smoking in the country in the 1990s and tax revenues fall as bootleggers resell cheaper smokes from other countries."[91] Reluctant to allow for similar opportunities, the specter of such economies can deprive governments of tax revenues from products that are particularly susceptible to smuggling or gray market commerce.

iv. Organized Crime

Although trading counterfeit products is a crime with potentially dangerous consequences in itself, the troubling reality is that the profits are often used to fund even more sinister pursuits. There are many examples where counterfeiting activity has been directly linked to support organized crime and terrorism. There is evidence that the practice described pages earlier of smuggling of cigarettes from low-tax states to high-tax states has been used to support such terrorist organizations as al Qaeda and Hezbollah.[92] In addition,

---

89. Seth Lubove, *Brand Power: Philip Morris Inc. Remains Profitable Despite Unpopular Image and Legal Troubles*, FORBES, Aug. 9, 1999, at 98.
90. *Id.*
91. *Id.*
92. Sari Horwitz, *Cigarette Smuggling Linked to Terrorism*, WASH. POST, June 8, 2004, at A1.

"[t]he Russian mob has become a force in video piracy, and Chinese triads have become heavily involved in counterfeit software. The former leader of the Vietnamese gang Born to Kill boasted of making $13 million off counterfeit watches before he was jailed for murder."[93] Terrorists have also funded their activities with unlawful gray market activity as well. Mahmud Abouhalima and the other 1993 World Trade Center bombing conspirators helped finance their plot by re-labeling expired baby formula and reselling it.[94]

A brand owner that fails to control the distribution of its products risks losing more than mere brand value. So long as there is the potential that the proceeds from illegal brand abuse will be used for more catastrophic harm, it is imperative that brand owners take responsibility to monitor their distribution channels.

c. Benefits of the Gray Market

Many brand owners and consumers contend that the gray market and its consequences are insufficient to warrant serious attention. Neither the probability nor the severity of harm justifies a significant dedication of resources to combat its existence. In fact, proponents of the gray market argue that its existence provides an overall *benefit* to brand owners and consumers.

This perspective has been championed by commentators familiar with the European Union's (EU) large and growing gray market of pharmaceutical trade. The gray market thrives because EU countries' governments control drug prices based on the local cost of living. As a result, the same drug may cost half the price in Spain and Greece compared to the U.K. or Germany.[95] Gray marketers are able to take advantage of these price differences "by exporting drugs from low-cost countries to expensive ones in Northern Europe, generating total sales of as much as 5 billion euros a year in Europe."[96] In addition to price discrimination, the gray market has been able to thrive because of "manufacturers' weak vertical control over the drug supply chain."[97]

Proponents of this gray market pharmaceutical trade in Europe justify their support on the premise that gray market trading leads to increased price

---

93. William Green & Katherine Bruce, *Riskless Crime?* FORBES, Aug. 11, 1997, at 101–102.
94. *Terrorist Links to Diversion and Counterfeiting*, AUTHENTICATION NEWS, Oct. 2001, at 9.
95. Matthew Newman, *European Union Should Liberalize Drug Market, EU Judge Says*, BLOOMBERG.COM, Apr. 18, 2005, http://www.bloomberg.com/apps/news?pid=10000085&sid=a.xcsl64Y1d0&refer=europe (last visited Oct. 8, 2008).
96. *Id.*
97. Panos Kanavos & Joan Costa-Font, *Pharmaceutical Trade in Europe: Stakeholder and Competition Effects*, 20 ECON. POL'Y 751, 754 (Oct. 2005).

competition in destination countries, thereby reducing the overall cost of pharmaceutical prices. Believing that the price arbitrage benefits healthcare payers and patients, many EU countries have introduced legislation to encourage the use of parallel-imported medicines.[98]

In addition to the dangers of counterfeit drugs commingling with gray market products in unauthorized distribution channels, recent empirical evidence casts doubt on the premise that the increased price competition reduces the price of pharmaceuticals for consumers. Dr. Panos Kanavos, a lecturer in international health policy at the London School of Economics and Political Science, prepared an in-depth study of Europe's gray market pharmaceutical trade and concluded that the assumed benefits were virtually non-existent.[99] Dr. Kanavos' study concluded that "the gains from parallel trade accrue mostly to the distribution chain rather than to health insurance and consumers."[100] In addition, the availability for price arbitrage "does not produce statistically significant competition effects in destination countries given that parallel traded drugs are priced just under originally sourced drugs."[101]

Because maintaining brand and channel integrity requires a considerable effort, believing that the gray market is minimally problematic is an enticing strategy. As shown by Dr. Kanavos' study, however, further scrutiny of certain posits may prove that this enticing strategy is exceedingly ingenuous. The following pages take a closer examination of some of the other assumed benefits of a thriving gray market.

i. Discover and Reach New Markets

A common ambition among brand owners is global popularity and consumption of their goods. In addition to developed nations, developing economies in South America, Africa, and Asia represent *billions* of potential consumers. Brands like Coca-Cola and McDonalds are keenly aware of this reality and their brands are ubiquitously marketed and sold throughout the world.

Of course, penetrating these markets is not without expense and risk. Especially in emerging economies where the necessary infrastructure to seamlessly market, sell, and deliver products is incomplete or even nonexistent, the challenges are even greater. Brand owners must devote significant financial and personnel resources to simply create the *opportunity* for business.

---

98. *Id.* at 792.
99. *Id.*
100. *Id.*
101. *Id.*

Compounding the risk, of course, is the fact that there is never any guarantee that domestic popularity will translate into international popularity.

Given the novelty of being in a new market, brand owners will typically sell their products at much lower prices. Especially when the standard of living is significantly lower, price discrimination is necessary to promote an adequate volume of sales.

Another strategy that brand owners will employ—by design or negligence—is the tacit approval of unauthorized exportation of their products. In addition to employing a disparate pricing strategy, brand owners will hedge their investment in a foreign market by permitting the gray market to essentially subsidize its existence. Deemphasizing the impact that such unauthorized exports may have on their domestic sales, brand owners permit the exports to take place to ensure there is enough revenue generation to justify and sustain its foreign investment.

As summarized in more detail in Chapter 4, *United States v. Braunstein*,[102] *supra*, exemplifies this approach. A gray marketer's purchases from an authorized distributor of Apple products in Latin America were particularly important and *permitted* because "most all of the distributors in Mexico were virtually bankrupt," so that "they really had no credit or cash to purchase any product."[103] Without any available buyers, allowing gray market sales helped sustain the Latin American distributor. However, the overall harm to the Apple brand was much more profound.[104]

Sometimes the mere volume of sales that ostensibly take place in foreign markets implies that a brand owner is complicit with the gray marketing of its products. During the 1980s, for example, large quantities of perfume were sold in Saudi Arabia and the United Arab Emirates. The volume of exports was so large that it created the inference that the manufacturers were not concerned with unauthorized exports. One president of a perfume manufacturer remarked that "[e]ven if every camel roaming the desert would be lavishly perfumed, there would still be an excess of fragrance in the region."[105]

It may indeed be necessary for brand owners to provide continued capital to its foreign outposts to secure their long-term viability. Allowing this *de facto* subsidization to occur via the gray market is a form-over-substance strategy devoid of long-term consideration. Although the unauthorized exports provide an injection of revenue for a brand owner's new foreign branch, the goods ultimately compete with domestic sales and put the integrity of the brand at risk.

---

102. United States v. Braunstein, 281 F.3d 982 (9th Cir. 2002).
103. *Id.* at 985.
104. *Id.*
105. Mark Honingsbaum, *Dollars and Scents—Gray Market Perfumes—Scams, Hustles, and Boondoggles*, WASH. MONTHLY, July 1, 1988, at http://findarticles.com/p/articles/mi_m1316/is_n6_-_7_v20/ai_6495570

ii. Overcome Supply Chain Constraints

Proponents of the gray market assert that it fills holes or accommodates overflows created in a brand owner's authorized distribution channel. When partners need to rid themselves of excess inventory to make room for new product, the gray market is where buyers willing to acquire the overabundance can be located. Similarly, when neither a brand owner nor an authorized partner has a certain product immediately available, the gray market can serve as an alternative source to procure products.

Although these stop-gap measures can in themselves serve a useful purpose, brand owners will face imposing complications if such activity continues unabated. Channel partners will not need to exercise prudence when making sales orders because they will always have the option of selling their excess inventory. As this cycle continues, an underground inventory of products emerges, making it almost impossible for brand owners to forecast their manufacturing needs with any reasonable degree of certainty. Shortfalls or surpluses thus become inevitable, ironically evolving the gray marketers from culprits for this shadow economy to its integral participants. Until and unless the brand owner affirmatively takes control of its authorized sales channels, the cycle will continue to spiral.

Recognizing this issue, some brand owners have taken over the responsibility of inventory and forecasting for its resellers:

> . . . Saturn understood that the retailers weren't necessarily good at inventory planning and forecasting. So the company asked retailers to let it take over the job of inventory management, and in return it offered to share their risk. If you're out of stock, Saturn will get the part to you from another retailer overnight. Saturn even measures its own employees on how well the retailers serve their customers, their end users.[106]

iii. Reduce Combating Expense

Permitting the gray market and avoiding the "costs" of brand protection has intuitive appeal. Security, investigation, and litigation to enforce the integrity of supply channels are expensive. Especially if a brand owner measures the cost of certain strategies to the immediate recovery, a perception can develop that the remedies do not justify the expenses. The shortcoming of this analysis, however, is the myopic evaluation of costs. In many instances, the cost of litigation can exceed the amount of money damages collected. Instead of

---

106. Scott Beth et al., *Supply Chain Challenges: Building Relationships*, in Harv. Bus. Rev. on Supply Chain Mgmt., 2006, at 75.

looking at these expenses in comparison to the direct recovery, brand owners should consider the costs as part of their overall investment in the brand.

An analogy can be found in a brand owner's marketing strategy. Brand owners rarely compare the cost of one billboard or commercial to the sales directly tied to the advertisement. Instead, brand owners will consider the overall marketing campaign to determine whether it is successfully generating *brand recognition*. A similar approach should be taken when considering the expenses incurred to ensure *brand protection*. Rather than consider the efficacy of one security measure or one contract revision, a brand owner should consider the total impact of its strategies that are cumulatively designed to secure the integrity of its distribution channels.

PART

II

Prevention: Reducing The Gray Market Potential

There is no one strategy that can guarantee the eradication of a gray market. Brand owners must not look for one panacean approach that will solve all brand protection challenges. Although some efforts may indeed be more effective than others, it is the totality of a brand owner's efforts that determine the efficacy of preventing gray market abuse. From education to litigation, brand owners must possess both versatility and perseverance to continually invest in the protection of their brands. This part examines the strategies available to brand owners to prevent, or at least minimize, gray market activity.

As an initial matter, it is better to be proactive than reactive. Preventing a problem is invariably preferable to responding to a problem. In the context of brand abuse, this self-evident principle is especially fitting. In today's global marketplace, an unmonitored gray market can devastate a brand's esteem. Waiting for the problem to surface may be too late.

Preventative efforts are also necessary in the event a brand owner is compelled to petition the courts to vindicate harm inflicted by the gray market. For example, there are occasions when a brand owner's authorized goods are identical in physical appearance to unauthorized gray market goods. As chronicled in latter chapters,[1] brand owners must typically show a judge or jury that its authorized goods are nonetheless "materially different" from gray market goods. When the goods are physically identical, one method of proving that goods are "materially different" is to show that a brand owner adheres to certain quality control procedures to safeguard the character of its goods.[2] For this theory to succeed, however, a brand owner must show that it has actually *adhered to* its quality control procedures.[3] If a brand owner has not sufficiently required that its own employees and distribution partners

---

1 For further discussion on the analysis of "material differences" in gray market products, see Chapter 17.
2 *See e.g.*, Dan-Foam v. Brand Name Beds, LLC, 500 F. Supp. 2d 296 (S.D.N.Y. 2007).

protect the goods, courts will consider any efforts to prevent gray market sales to be nothing more than a legally ineffective attempt to enforce price controls.

From the informal education of employees and channel partners to the formal negotiation and execution of distribution agreements, the following pages reveal the proactive steps to prevent and protect brand owners from the gray market.

---

3 *See e.g.*, Warner-Lambert Co. v. Northside Dev. Corp., 86 F.3d 3 (2d Cir. 1996).

CHAPTER 5

Education

Promoting Gray Market Abstinence

a.	Employees	67
b.	Distribution Partners	70
c.	Consumers	72
d.	Industry Alliances	73
e.	Government Relations	75
f.	Media	76

a. Employees

Beyond extolling the prohibition of gray market activity, brand owners must strive to imbue the virtues and necessity of brand integrity. Instead of merely communicating what is *not* permitted, brand owners must build an understanding throughout the company that protecting the brand benefits the vitality of the company. Brand owners must further convey the message that failing to comprehensively exercise brand security leads to a self-inflicted wound with potentially dire consequences.

To sufficiently communicate the importance of brand integrity, brand owners must reach every corporate level. When examining the gray market, there can be a temptation to conclude that it is merely a "sales issue" and that it can be competently addressed by advising the relevant sales employees of the types of transactions that are not permitted. According to one study, 61 percent of brand owners polled placed gray market responsibility on their sales and marketing departments. In addition to the effort being incomplete, it is akin to tasking an adolescent to be the sole manager of his or her curfew.

The short-sightedness of this effort is compounded when brand owners simultaneously place ambitious sales goals on their sales departments. The tension between reaching revenue goals and policing gray market activity typically results in gray market enforcement becoming a distant priority behind the more rewarding—commission-related—activity.

If a business hopes to adequately protect its brand from the gray market, every level of operation, especially senior management, must be in agreement that brand protection is a priority. There must be agreement that "[t]he brand is the most important and sustainable asset of any organization—whether a product- or service-based corporation or a not-for-profit concern—and it should be the central organizing principle behind every decision and every action."[1] The most successful brands manifestly adhere to this principle. Coca-Cola is the world's most valuable brand.[2] Notwithstanding its triumph, Coca-Cola continues to heavily invest in its brand recognition. Commercials, billboards, and celebrity spokespersons continually remind consumers of its thirst quenching virtues. Recognizing that brand value trumps the value of tangible assets, the Ford Motor Company reduced its physical assets in favor of spending more than $12 billion to acquire brand names such as Jaguar, Aston Martin, Volvo and Land Rover.[3]

In addition to acquisition and marketing efforts, the vigor of brands requires an equally faithful devotion to their protection. If a brand owner's executives are reluctant to consider the gray market to be anything more than a "sales department" issue, *In re Adams Golf, Inc. Securities Litigation*[4] is a compelling example of the potential consequences an inadequately unchecked gray market can have on a business. The case involved Adams Golf, Inc. (Adams Golf), which was a designer and manufacturer of its own custom-fit golf clubs. Among its products was a high-end golf club, called Tight Lies. Thanks in large part to the popularity of Tight Lies, Adams Golf offered its shares to the public and, in its Initial Public Offering (IPO), sold 5,575,000 shares of common stock at $16 per share.[5]

In its registration statement and prospectus, Adams Golf touted the virtues and values of its authorized distribution chain. Specifically, Adams Golf represented to potential shareholders that it only sold its products through authorized distributors. Specifically, Adams Golf assured investors of the following:

> To preserve the integrity of its image and reputation, the Company limits its distribution to retailers that market premium quality golf equipment and provide a high level of customer service and technical expertise. . . . The Company believes its selective retail distribution helps its retailers to maintain profitable margins and maximize sales of Adams' products.[6]

---

1. CLIFTON, *supra* note 13, at 2.
2. *Id.* at 29 (The brand value of Coca-Cola in 2001 was $69 billion).
3. *Id.*
4. *In re* Adams Golf, Inc. Securities Litigation, 381 F.3d 267 (3d Cir. 2004).
5. *Id.* at 270.
6. *Id.* at 271.

As part of this limited distribution network, Adams Golf also represented that it "d[id] not sell its products through price sensitive general discount warehouses, department stores or membership clubs."[7] Adams Golf's assurances of a tightly controlled chain of distribution, unfortunately, proved to be untrue. Shortly prior to its IPO, Adams Golf became aware that its Tight Lies were being sold by Costco, a discount warehouse. Adams Golf disclosed this discovery and further admitted that there were other "sales by other unauthorized discount retailers and international gray market distributors."[8]

Five months after the IPO, Adams Golf divulged additional information revealing that its gray market problem was worse than originally known or disclosed. Anticipating disappointing revenues, Adams Golf stated that sales would "continue to suffer as a result of the 'gray market distribution of its products to a membership warehouse club.'"[9] To make matters worse, the company admitted that it "d[id] not believe that the gray marketing of its product c[ould] be totally eliminated."[10]

Not only was the gray marketing of its products a problem in itself for Adams Golf, it also faced a shareholder class action for its contradictory statements pertaining to its authorized distribution channels. Specifically, the plaintiffs alleged that Adams Golf enjoyed "a rise in sales as products were diverted to the unauthorized distributors."[11] As a result "[t]he short-term income generated by sales to the gray market also skewed the Company's overall financial appearance, creating the false impression of heightened sales and profitability at the time of the IPO. . . ."[12] The long-term consequences, however, resulted in unauthorized distributors selling cheaper products, authorized dealers lowering prices and reducing their orders, and "an overall drop in revenue."[13]

Adams Golf sought to dismiss the case, arguing that the gray market issue was unimportant to a reasonable investor. The Third Circuit Court refused to dismiss the case at the pleading stage, finding that "Costco's inventory of Tight Lies golf clubs may be found to be immaterial, but that is for the fact finder to determine in light of the record."[14] The case was originally filed in 2001. As of September 2008, the case was still being litigated without there yet being a trial on the merits for the "fact finder" to decide Adams Golf's fate.[15]

---

7. *Id.*
8. *Id.*
9. *Id.* at 272.
10. *Id.*
11. *Id.*
12. *Id.* at 271–72.
13. *Id.* at 272.
14. *Id.* at 277.
15. *See* Plaintiffs' Response to Summary Statement in Support of Adams Golf Defendants' Motion for Summary Judgment, *In re Adams Golf, Inc.*, No. 199CV00371 (D. Del. 2008).

Not only did Adams Golf's gray market interfere with its substantive business, but the company has had to contend with seven years of securities litigation. Indeed, the gray market is not just a "sales" problem.

Given the company-wide importance of the issue, brand owners at every level must be taught the value of brand integrity and the consequences of gray market activity. Upper-level management must understand the increased potential of gray market leakage if overly ambitious revenue thresholds are imposed on its sales force. Similarly, if a brand owner elects to have differential pricing throughout the globe, it must adequately prevent the unwanted reimportation of lower priced goods.

Once upper management is in agreement that preventing the gray market is a necessary endeavor, educating the rest of the company is easier. When gray market prevention is a collective priority, there is a shared willingness to dedicate the necessary resources to brand protection. In addition, brand owners become more willing to consider novel compensation approaches to prevent gray market temptations and reward gray market detection. As articulated in *Brand Integrity*, "[t]ying compensation and rewards to plans for protecting products and brands based on company-specific standards sets the stage for success."[16] Instead of rewarding employees solely on their efforts to push sales without an enforced emphasis on *to whom* or *from whom* the products originate, brand owners must have the discipline and foresight to realize that the long-term harm will outweigh any short-term gains.

b. Distribution Partners

> I was always being asked what it was I actually did for a living.... I would tell people, "I buy and sell sports fashion business." Unless they pressed me, I left it at that. What I actually did is look for big brand names like Adidas or Lacoste or Nike and sell them into a country where they already have a distributor. It's called parallel trading. Many years ago when I started out, the big names turned a blind eye to the parallel market.
>
> It was convenient and good business to have one official and several unofficial distributors channeling your goods into a country where the demand was growing and the official distributor was going along just a little too slowly. When the official guy kicked up a fuss, the brand [owner] turned around and blamed the lying cheating little toe-rag who had misled them. "We were told it was going to Nigeria," they would protest, or "these goods were sent to Poland, we have no idea how or what or...." After the dust settled and sales needed a boosting the whole

---

16. Richard S. Post & Penelope N. Post, Global Brand Integrity Management 60 (2008).

process began again, followed by more threats and recriminations. It was always convenient to have a scapegoat handy. "That two-faced swine, we'll never supply him again," they would say. But they did.[17]

In *Lying Bastards*, former gray marketer Ricky George chronicled his ability to capitalize on the reality that brand owners and their authorized distributors and resellers paid mere lip service to the enforcement of their authorized sales channels. It was only when an authorized distributor or reseller found itself competing with Mr. George's more affordable imports that the brand owner purported to do anything. At least from Mr. George's perspective, the brand owners' lamentations about the breaching distributor and unauthorized imports were pure window dressing. To appease the distributor, the brand owner would give the impression that it would do everything in its power to prevent the unwanted competition from happening again. Under the brand owner's macro analysis, however, any affirmative steps of prevention were not worth the effort.

This laissez-faire approach to channel management is no longer a viable business strategy. From the potential dangers of counterfeits commingling with gray market goods to the specter of shareholder litigation, a brand cannot maintain any prestige and simultaneously coexist with a shadow gray market inventory. In addition, gray market activity begets gray market activity. Once channel partners learn that gray market transactions can take place without detection or consequence, such unauthorized sales will spiral beyond control of the brand owner.

Not only must brand owners educate their employees and management on the importance of abating gray market activity, brand owners must have very similar communications with their third-party channel partners. As an initial matter, channel partners must be made aware that gray market activity will not be tolerated. The brand owner must distinguish itself from other brands that may tolerate a certain volume of gray market activity which remains below the radar.

The brand owner must then educate its channel partners on the brand-wide harm that will occur if partners engage in transactions not permitted in the partner agreements. Beyond breaching the contract, channel partners must understand that the short-term benefits of a gray market will eventually harm the brand, lower prices and margins, and threaten the overall value of the brand. Although the channel partner will not have the same vested interest in the brand's viability as the brand owner itself, the partner will have an interest in its profitability. Bolstered by the confidence that the brand owner will not tolerate competitors underselling its partners with gray market goods, partners will be more motivated to be part of the collective effort to maintain virtuous distribution channels.

---

17. RICKY GEORGE, LYING BASTARDS: CONFESSIONS OF A GRAY MARKET TRADER, 5–6 (2004).

In addition to encouraging channel obedience through motivation, brand owners must also emphasize the harsh consequences that await those channel partners that stray from their contractual obligations. Both during and after the time the partner agreements are executed, brand owners must emphasize the relevant gray market prohibitions and remedies. If the brand owner has either terminated its relationship with or successfully litigated its rights against violating partners, highlighting the fates of these former partners can bolster the deterring value of the prohibition admonitions.

c. Consumers

There is a delicate balance between publicly acknowledging brand abuse and educating customers on the potential harm of purchasing products from unauthorized sources. In recent years, however, the omnipresent publicity of foreign counterfeits has resulted in less stigma attached to counterfeiting and gray market disclosures. There is an implicit expectation that if the brand has value, someone somewhere will seek to profit from its popularity. So long as brand owners take sufficient action to police and stop such activity, customers will typically remain loyal to the brand.

For example, various luxury brands such as Cartier, Chanel, Coach, and Gucci have faced black and gray market challenges for years. It is no secret that various street corners and e-commerce Web sites offer counterfeit imitations of these labels at discount prices. These brands have managed to remain popular in part because they remain dedicated to policing their brands. To illustrate, each of these companies post on their Web site various tips for spotting counterfeit goods.[18] By arming consumers with the relevant data to discern authentic goods from counterfeit imitations, brand owners can promote the selection of genuine products.

Persuading consumers to avoid gray market products is more difficult. Because gray market products may or may not be counterfeit, brand owners cannot disseminate information to help consumers ascertain whether or not the products came from the gray market. What brand owners often do, therefore, is articulate the vulnerability of products sold through unauthorized channels and the lack of warranty or technical support available to gray market products. For example, Yamaha Corporation of America (Yamaha) has the following gray market policy statement on its Web site:

> **Yamaha Authorized Warranties For The United States Market.**
> Yamaha Corporation of America ("Yamaha") is the exclusive authorized U.S. importer and distributor of Yamaha® musical instruments.

---

18. David M. Hopkins, Counterfeiting Exposed 10 (2003) at 51.

Only Yamaha® products designed and manufactured for the United States meet applicable product safety standards. Only Yamaha Authorized Dealers can provide new Yamaha products with warranty coverage valid in the United States. Only Yamaha Authorized Dealers are trained to provide you with service and support before, during and after your purchase. Many retailers attempt to trade on the valuable reputation of the Yamaha name—before you buy from them, Yamaha would like you to know the potential risks of doing so.

Safety Issues. Yamaha's electronic products operate on normal alternating current. The importation, distribution and use of such products not designed for the United States can result in (a) damage to the product; (b) damage to household wiring; (c) fire; (d) loss of insurance coverage and, in some jurisdictions (e) violation of municipal ordinances. Further, any attempt to modify such products to enable them to operate on normal U.S. voltage and current may increase the above risks, and is also likely to void any non-U.S. warranty coverage as may have existed for the product.

Warranty Policies. Yamaha provides warranty coverage for new Yamaha® products originally sold by Yamaha Authorized Dealers located in the United States. Check our Dealer Locator for a list of U.S. Authorized Dealers. Yamaha products purchased from retailers other than Yamaha Authorized Dealers (whether via the Internet, or otherwise) will NOT be covered by Yamaha's warranties, and U.S. service centers will not repair such products under warranty.[19]

d. Industry Alliances

It is not unusual for current or former foes to unite when threatened by a common enemy. When differences are set aside to collectively battle a shared opponent, victory is more attainable. These types of alliances are commonly seen in war, politics, and business. In the context of the gray market, competitors in the marketplace share a common enemy, and coordinating efforts and resources can result in cumulative benefits.

The Alliance for Gray Market and Counterfeit Abatement (AGMA), a nonprofit organization that was incorporated in 2001, is an example of such a coordinated effort. AGMA, as its name suggests, is an alliance dedicated to address the global impact of gray marketing.[20] AGMA is comprised of leading technology companies; its founding members are 3Com, Cisco Systems,

---

19. Yamaha Corp. of America, Warranty/Safety/Information, http://www.yamaha.com/warranty_safety.asp (last visited Oct. 8, 2008).
20. Alliance for Gray Market and Counterfeit Abatement (AGMA), Who We Are, http://www.agmaglobal.org/ (last visited Oct. 8, 2008).

Hewlett-Packard and Nortel.[21] Although these companies are not allies in the marketplace, the organization was formed in order to create mutually beneficial initiatives to combat gray market in the aggregate. Some of AGMA's initiatives include educational initiatives, a hotline and e-mail link for reporting gray market and counterfeit activities, benchmark studies, formulation of nonbinding best practices, and public policy advocacy in areas such as law enforcement and customs.[22]

Industry groups such as AGMA can be a beneficial supplement to a brand owner's efforts to stop gray market activity and other brand abuse. The benefits of shared information and strategies are an inevitable benefit to brand owners. In addition, brand owners can promote their membership in such organizations to emphasize to employees, partners, and customers that combating the gray market is a high priority.

Various associations span a wide range of topics and industries to protect Intellectual Property (IP). Topics range from data and insight on the IP situations in various foreign countries to specific and effective IP protection strategies, educational seminars, public awareness, law enforcement coordination, and even legislative lobbying.[23] Below are some organizations a brand owner may wish to consider:[24]

Intellectual Property Owners Association (IPO)	www.ipo.org
International Trademark Association (INTA)	www.inta.org
American Intellectual Property Law Association (AIPLA)	www.aipla.org
Copyright Society of America	www.csa.org
Automotive Aftermarket Suppliers Association (AASA)	www.aasa.org
Electronic Retailers Association (ERA)	www.retailing.org
Alliance for Gray Market and Counterfeit Abatement (AGMA)	www.agma.org
Coalition Against Counterfeiting and Piracy (CACP)	www.cacp.org
Global Anti-Counterfeiting Group (GACG)	www.gacg.org
Quality Brands Protection Committee (QBPC)	www.qbpc.org.cn

---

21. *Id.*
22. *Id.*
23. *Id.*
24. Bradley J. Olson, Michael R. Graham, John Maltbie, and Ron Epperson, *The 10 Things Every Practitioner Should Know About Anti-Counterfeiting and Anti-Piracy Protection*, 7 J High Tech L 106, fn. 41 (2007).

Such associations are often supported by governments, because they represent such large segments of the economy. Aside from the economy of scale created in such alliances, industry associations can lend a brand owner additional credibility when interfacing with government officials for enforcement assistance.

Of course, industry membership will not in itself stop brand abuse. Brand owners must undertake their own efforts to prevent, detect, and fight the gray market. The same way joining a running club does not in itself make one ready for a marathon, industry alliances do not render a brand owner immune from brand attacks. In addition to the membership, the brand owner—like the jogger in the running club—will need to work hard to ensure the vigor of its brand.

e. Government Relations

An essential element of brand protection is having a strong relationship with the relevant government offices and agencies. From ensuring that customs will make its best efforts to prevent the importation of illegal goods to coordinating with the U.S. Marshals to conduct an efficient search and seizure, brand owners must provide enough information and assistance so that the government's resources are useful allies in their preventative and enforcement efforts.

Various government agencies offer their own, similar resources as well, with no membership requirements. For instance, the United States Department of Justice operates an IP protection hotline (for both domestic and foreign operations) staffed by attorneys at 1-866-999-HALT.[25] They also run a Website at www.stopfakes.gov with additional IP protection resources.

With respect to a brand owner's effort to promote the prevention of the gray market, positive government relations are important. Trademark owners have on occasion made lobbying efforts to promote legislation aimed at stopping gray market activity.[26] Similar to membership in industry groups with the shared mission of abating brand abuse, petitioning the government on various brand abuse issues is an implicit communication to both allies and potential foes that stopping brand abuse is a high priority.

---

25. Bradley J. Olson, Michael R. Graham, John Maltbie, and Ron Epperson, *The 10 Things Every Practitioner Should Know About Anti-Counterfeiting and Anti-Piracy Protection*, 7 J HIGH TECH L (2007).
26. *See e.g.*, Indep. Equip. Dealers Ass'n v. EPA, 372 F.3d 420 (2004) (discussing lobbying efforts of OEM of non-road engines to get EPA to support the idea of labeling products that were valid for importation so that identical gray market products that lacked label would therefore not be importable).

f. Media

Brand owners should not be reluctant to promote their efforts to combat the gray market and other brand abuses in the various media outlets. Efforts to protect the integrity of a brand owner's brand should not be a stealthy endeavor. If potential infringers perceive a particular brand owner as a difficult target, they will move on to other—less challenging—targets. One method for brand owners to educate potential infringers that they are indeed difficult targets is to disseminate through various media outlets whatever successes and victories they have obtained in their brand protection efforts. By showing trial verdicts and successful preliminary injunction orders, the brand owner is able to, once again, educate its employees, partners, and customers that brand protection is a critical element of its business.

CHAPTER 6

Troubleshooting Supply Chain Vulnerabilities

a. Selecting and Qualifying Partners   78
   i. Background Research   78
   ii. Training and Certification   80
b. The Partner Contracts   81
   i. Guidelines and Promises   84
     (a) Gray Market Prohibitions   84
     (b) Records and Audit Rights   86
     (c) Security Audits   90
     (d) Quality Control Guidelines   90
     (e) Venue Selection   91
     (f) Choice of Law   92
     (g) Damages   93
     (h) Attorney Fees   95
   ii. Incentives for Compliance   96
     (a) Territorial Exclusivities   96
     (b) Technical Support and Training   97
     (c) Return Policies and Warranty Support   97
     (d) Delivery Terms   98
     (e) Price Protection   98
   iii. Penalties for Noncompliance   99
     (a) Probation or Suspension   99
     (b) Monetary Penalties   100
     (c) Termination   101
c. Tightening the Supply Chain   102
   i. Acknowledging Geographic Vulnerabilities   102
   ii. On-Site Security   106
   iii. Transit Security   110
   iv. Product Security   111

a. Selecting and Qualifying Partners

Brand owners need a great deal more than well-written contracts and top-of-the-line software applications to create reliable distribution channels. Although these items are necessary, they are by no means sufficient. The fate of a brand owner's distribution channel lies with the *people*. This clichéd truism is echoed when describing virtually every business endeavor, and its repetition is especially germane here. Notwithstanding the law's strong presumption in favor of employee mobility, America's courts are brimful of cases where companies are accusing competitors of luring away employees—or, put another way—*poaching their talent*.

These disputes are fought among a town's smallest businesses to the world's largest corporations. In January 1999, for example, Wal-Mart sued Amazon, alleging that the online bookstore lured away its employees. When the case settled, Amazon denied any wrongdoing, at the same time acknowledging its motivation: "Amazon.com ... [is] only interested in hiring the most qualified and talented individuals. This agreement allows us to continue to do so."[1]

Especially in a brand owner's quest to create reliable distribution channels, the quality of partners is paramount. In addition to being substantively competent to fulfill their specific role in the channel, brand owners must sufficiently vet prospective partners to ferret out those that should not be trusted. Once partners are selected, brand owners must then make certain that the partners are properly equipped to promote the brand with superb customer and quality service.

i. Background Research

Most brand owners require prospective partners to provide a great deal of information during the selection process. In order to analyze the suitability of the contemplated relationship, applying partners are often required to answer questionnaires, fill out forms, and provide other information and documentation. In most cases, brand owners will then evaluate the data that was provided and render a decision. This practice is incomplete and is an invitation for challenges in the future.

Like a bank lending money without checking a borrower's credit, brand owners must do more to verify the veracity of an applicant's submittals. Instead of simply examining how the anticipated partner relationship will *benefit* the brand owner, an examination of the potential *risks* is equally indispensable. Accordingly, brand owners must ascertain, for example,

---

1. *The Media Business; Wal-Mart Agrees to Settle Lawsuit Against Amazon*, N.Y. Times, Apr. 6, 1999, at C6.

whether the applicant is or has been an authorized partner for another brand owner. To the extent the applicant has prior partner experience, brand owners should query both the applicant and partnered brand owner about the condition of the relationship.

In addition to asking the applicant to list any allegations, lawsuits, or administrative claims that have ever been charged against it, the brand owner should compare the applicant's responses with an independent search for all criminal, civil, and administrative filings involving the applicant and its principals. Of course, any history of criminal or civil litigation is cause for additional due diligence. Especially if the lawsuits involve allegations of payment delinquency, fraud, or intellectual property infringement, the brand owner should be especially concerned.

Brand owners should also conduct their own investigation with respect to various trade associates that rate or govern the members of their industries. For example, the North America Association of Telecommunication Dealers (NATD) provides an online forum where telecom brokers can do business. The NATD has its own code of ethics to which its participants are required to abide. Violators of the ethics code are posted online to warn other members to proceed cautiously if transacting business with these companies.

Brand owners' due diligence must extend beyond the corporate entity that is making the formal partnership application. The ease with which corporate entities can be created and dissolved allows corrupt individuals to vanish and reemerge under successive corporate names in the hope that the unwary will be ignorant of their depraved history. Brand owners must therefore perform an independent search with broader parameters. In addition to finding out when and by whom the official applicant filed its articles of incorporation, brand owners should also find any other corporate filings by similar names or filings by other individuals associated or employed by the official applicant To the extent other entities are found, the same search for criminal, civil, and administrative claims should be made.

The brand owner's due diligence must then focus on the applicant partner's employees. Brand owners should consider doing similar background checks on the key personnel. The number of individuals and the positions of these "key personnel" will vary depending on factors such as company size or prospective role in the distribution channel; however, the search should be comprehensive enough to provide the brand owner with the confidence that the applicant's employees are a respectable lot. Because the brand owner cannot reasonably conduct a background search on every employee, it must ascertain what the applicant does when it hires employees. Especially when brand owners run the risk of products or trade secrets being stolen or leaked from a distribution partner, its partners must make an adequate showing that they have strict policies to prevent the inadvertent hiring of a pilfering workforce.

It is imperative for the brand owner to visit the prospective partner's place of business and tour the facility. In addition to scheduled visits, representatives of the brand owner must plan a few *unannounced* visits during the application process as well. The obvious advantage of such unannounced visits is the ability to see a truer picture of how the applicant runs its operation. Although the floor may be polished and the security cameras running during the sanctioned tour, the brand owner will want to know whether the same devotion is shown when visitors are not expected.

Finally, the brand owner should have a practice of culling, saving, and organizing its due diligence efforts. In addition to saving records and files of accepted applicants, brand owners should maintain a database of rejected applicants, terminated partners, and other known infringers. By creating and maintaining such a database, the brand owner will have another source to cross-check when new applications are submitted.

ii. Training and Certification

Assuming that an applicant partner possessed the requisite competence and unblemished history to become a brand owner's channel partner, the brand owner must then make sure that the channel partner is sufficiently equipped to promote the brand in a positive way. Beyond having the warehouse space and available sales representatives, brand owners must ensure that the distribution partner has the requisite knowledge and skill to ensure that all sales transactions are accompanied with the necessary customer service. The level of training is typically dictated by the complexity of the product.

Dan-Foam v. Brand Name Beds, LLC,[2] is a good example of a brand owner providing its resellers with relatively extensive training for a seemingly simple product. The plaintiff Tempur-Pedic, Inc. (Tempur-Pedic) manufactured and distributed mattresses, pillows, and other foam-based bed products. Tempur-Pedic sold its products through an authorized seller network and, to ensure the quality of its products, it trained its staff on the proper use and care of the products. In addition, Tempur-Pedic would periodically visit authorized retailers after initial training to "ensure that retailers in each sales territory incorporate[d] the Tempur-Pedic training and [were] actually providing correct information to customers."[3] In addition to providing training for interaction with customers, Tempur-Pedic also taught retailers and shippers the proper delivery and handling of the products. Because the products were sensitive to heat and cold and could be damaged if not handled properly, the brand owner required that the products be delivered in a very strict manner:

> In order to prevent this permanent damage from occurring, "[a]uthorized delivery personnel know upon arriving to a customer's home, where the mattress needs to be folded in order to fit around a corner or up a

---

2. Dan-Foam v. Brand Name Beds, LLC, 500 F. Supp. 2d 296 (S.D.N.Y. 2007).
3. *Id.* at 301.

staircase, that they should wait a few hours before finishing the delivery so that the mattress can soften and can thus be *briefly* folded with the top side of the mattress inwards."[4]

In addition to the fact that this training was necessary to maintain the quality of the product, the brand owner's articulated policy and actual adherence to the policy proved to be relevant in the court's analysis of whether a gray marketer's unauthorized sales infringed Tepur-Pedic's trademarks.[5]

In more complicated industries, it is common for brand owners to require even more formalized training before a distribution partner is permitted to sell or service certain goods. Although the channel partner may be allowed to sell certain types of goods, the brand owner will require that the partner obtain the requisite "certification" before the partner is entitled to deal in certain goods. The brand owner will then provide specific training, essentially in a classroom setting, to teach and test the channel partner to *certify* its competence to promote certain products.

Although certification programs are not necessarily uncommon, actual enforcement is. Brand owners are often much too careless about their certification requirements. Especially when a channel partner has proven its mettle to successfully promote and sell other branded goods, there is a temptation to afford it the flexibility of selling a larger panoply of goods. The risk in this practice is two-fold. Most directly, there is a risk to the end customer. In the event the product is not delivered, installed, or serviced correctly, the brand owner's goodwill suffers. An additional risk is more intangible: By the brand owner turning a blind eye to its partner's lack of certification, the brand owner sends a subtle message to its partner that adherence to the partner agreement is not absolute. Once this message is communicated, it will not be unreasonable for a partner to assume that the brand owner will be similarly undisciplined when it comes to protecting intellectual rights. To prevent such an unwanted inference, a brand owner must be as martinet about its training requirements as it is in its protection of brand abuse.

b. The Partner Contracts

> "*Trust is essential, of course. But before trust comes smart contracting.*"
>
> —Chris Gopal, Vice President of Global Supply Chain Management, Unisys[6]

---

4. *Id.*
5. For further discussion on *Dan-Foam*, see Chapter 17.
6. *Supply Chain Challenges: Building Relationships, in* Harv. Bus. Rev. on Supply Chain Mgmt., 2006, at 75.

In a study analyzing gray market issues in the IT industry, 87 percent of original equipment manufacturers (OEMs) required that their products be sold by authorized distributors.[7] However, the survey also concluded that there were "widely varying contractual requirements for managing the reselling activities of these trading partners."[8] Moving from bad to worse, "only half of the OEMs require[d] controls on the flow of products *from* their distributors."[9] The failure of brand owners to adequately articulate their partners' prohibitions and authorizations can be self destructive. It is a frustrating letdown for a brand owner to discover a rogue distributor or reseller engaging in gray market transactions only to later discover that the delinquent partner has not actually breached an express provision of its contract.

Faltings et al. v. International Business Machines Corp.[10] is an illuminating example. Peter Faltings and James Corcoran of New Jersey wanted to open a computer store and sell IBM computers. A large chain of computer stores signed them up to a franchise agreement. In order to sell IBM computers, however, IBM required that Faltings and Corcoran's corporation, Security Software, sign a separate reseller agreement.[11]

Rather than sell IBM computers to store customers that would use the products, the vast majority of IBM computers sold by Faltings and Corcoran were to unauthorized resellers. A few years after the parties signed their agreement, IBM became suspicious that Security Software might be selling products on the gray market. IBM therefore conducted an audit that confirmed its concern: In one year alone, Security Software sold approximately $12 million into the gray market. Nearly eighty percent of its sales had been to unauthorized resellers. With these discoveries, IBM terminated the parties' contract.[12]

The above facts would ordinarily foreshadow a lawsuit brought by the brand owner. The inevitable next step would be IBM suing Security Software to recoup the unjust enrichment it enjoyed by abusing the terms of the reseller agreement. In direct contrast to the anticipated course of action, *IBM was sued by Security Software*. The reason for this surprising twist was borne from the contract's ambiguity: "IBM claims the Agreement specifically forbade Security Software to sell to resellers; Faltings and Corcoran say the Agreement contained no such restriction."[13]

Because the agreement was ostensibly open to interpretation, IBM did not even terminate the agreement for cause. After the audits uncovered Security

---

7. *The Grey Market*, KPMG/Anti-Gray Mkt. Alliance, 2003, at 5, *available at* http://www.agmaglobal.org/press_events/press_docs/KPMG_TheGreyMarket_Web.pdf
8. *Id.*
9. *Id.* (emphasis added).
10. Faltings et al. v. International Business Machines Corp., 854 F.2d 1316, 1988 WL 83316 (4th Cir. 1988) (Unpublished).
11. *Id.* at *1.
12. *Id.*
13. *Id.*

Software's bountiful gray market business, IBM simply "notified Security Software that it was terminating its Retail Dealer Agreement on three months' written notice."[14] Not only was IBM precluded from collecting any damages, it soon found itself defending Security Software's lawsuit for wrongful termination of the reseller agreement. Although IBM ultimately prevailed in the case, it was not before incurring the expense of protracted litigation that involved a jury trial and appeal.

IBM's failure to expressly prohibit gray market transactions[15] was an expensive misstep. Rather than recouping damages from a gray market distributor disguised as an authorized reseller, IBM had to *spend* thousands (perhaps millions) defending its right to terminate the gray marketer's contract.

In the event brand owners decide to seek redress by way of litigation, failing to properly memorialize gray market prohibitions makes litigation much more difficult. In *Sebastian International, Inc. v. Consumer Contacts Ltd.*,[16] the brand owner entered into an "oral contract" with a distributor in South Africa that allegedly prohibited any sales outside of South Africa.[17] Specifically, Sebastian International manufactured and sold personal care beauty supplies. It was vexed to learn that the South African distributor was shipping over $200,000 worth of products to the United States for gray market resale. Without a written contract that contained any gray market, venue selection, or choice of law provisions, there was no apparent way for Sebastian International to seek justice against the distributor in the United States.

Sebastian International had to settle for the consolation prize of litigating against the gray market reseller that purchased the South African products. Without any contractual relationship between the parties, Sebastian International also had to settle for a more difficult theory of recovery. Instead of being able to allege a simple breach of contract cause of action, Sebastian International had to rely on copyright infringement and its more complex applications to the gray market. The theory ultimately backfired and the first line of the opinion demonstrates the court's impression of the strategy:

> This case comes to us in the guise of an alleged copyright infringement but, in reality, is an attempt by a domestic manufacturer to prevent the importation of its own products by the "gray market."[18]

---

14. *Id.*
15. The jury ultimately concluded that the agreement did preclude gray market sales. The goal of brand owners, however, must be to draft contracts that are sufficiently clear that their interpretation does not become the task for a jury. Instead, the contracts should be unequivocal so that judges may decide their meaning as a matter of law.
16. Sebastian Int'l, Inc. v. Consumer Contacts Ltd., 847 F.2d 1093 (3d Cir. 1988).
17. *Id.* at 1094.
18. *Id.* at 1094.

Although the failure of a contract to unambiguously spell out the consequences of every foreseeable circumstance is understandable, the failure to memorialize the most basic terms of a substantial business transaction is more difficult to fathom. *Johnson & Johnson Products, Inc. v. Dal International Trading Co.*,[19] for example, involved the sale of almost one million toothbrushes where "[n]o written contract was entered."[20] Making matters even more complicated, the buyer was in Poland and allegedly assured Johnson & Johnson that "it intended to distribute the products in Poland only."[21] The Polish buyer failed to adhere to this alleged oral contract and eighty dozen toothbrushes found their way back to the United States.[22]

Without any written agreement, Johnson & Johnson was forced to allege that (1) the Polish buyer defrauded Johnson & Johnson when it misrepresented its intention to only sell the toothbrushes in Poland, and (2) the retailer that ultimately came into possession of the toothbrushes did not have valid title to the toothbrushes because it had a duty to investigate whether the toothbrushes were procured by fraud. The theory failed, leaving Johnson & Johnson without any ability to stop the continued sales of its gray market toothbrushes.

Not only is a written agreement with distribution partners imperative, there are a variety of provisions that a brand owner must include, or at least consider, with respect to the gray market. The following pages discuss the contractual provisions that most effectively give brand owners the ability to articulate and, if necessary, litigate forbidden gray market activity.

i. Guidelines and Promises

(a) Gray Market Prohibitions

Brand owners' contracts must contain express provisions prohibiting gray market activity. Such provisions make litigation against any infringing partners a great deal simpler. In addition, the contracts may also be used to debunk arguments that a brand owner has consented to gray market imports. The contracts must therefore provide that authorized distributors must only sell to authorized resellers and that authorized resellers must only sell to end users. When brand owners offer their products for different prices around the world, territorial restrictions are necessary as well.

---

19. Johnson Products, Inc. v. Dal International Trading Co., 798 F.2d 100 (3d Cir. 1986).
20. *Id.* at 101.
21. *Id.*
22. *Id.* at 101–02.

In *Original Appalachian Artworks, Inc. v. Granada Electronics, Inc.*,[23] a gray market importer defended claims of trademark infringement by arguing that the brand owner had essentially consented to the gray market importation of toy Cabbage Patch Kids dolls. The trademark holder, Original Appalachian, had granted a restrictive license to a Spanish company allowing for the manufacture and sale of the dolls. The license's restriction provided that the dolls could only be sold in Spain and could only be sold to those who would agree not to use or resell the licensed products outside of Spain.[24]

The dolls manufactured for Spanish distribution were materially different from the dolls intended to be sold in the United States. When Original Appalachian discovered that its Spanish dolls were being resold in the United States, it commenced litigation against the company responsible for the unauthorized imports. The importer raised several defenses to justify its conduct. Among its contentions, the importer argued that Original Appalachian "consented to the importation of the [dolls]."[25] The court rejected the argument; the fact that the goods passed through U.S. Customs was not tantamount to consenting to their importation. In a concurring opinion, one of the justices bolstered the rationale with an endorsement of Original Appalachian's licensing agreement:

> This argument is not persuasive when, as in this case, it is not clear that OAA could not have prevented by contract the importation of these Cabbage Patch dolls by third-party distributors, such as [the defendant]. As a practical matter OAA appears to have tried. Under its license agreement [the Spanish licensee] agreed not to sell outside its Spanish-licensed territory, and further agreed to sell only to purchasers who also agreed not to sell outside that territory. Without any effective means of further controlling the distribution of its product, for example, by means of an equitable servitude on the dolls, OAA should not be held responsible for the dolls' importation.[26]

Once a brand owner has crafted its contracts, it must ensure that they are signed by all channel partners. The consequences of ignoring this formality can significantly impede brand protection efforts. An instructive example is *Dan-Foam v. Brand Name Beds, LLC.*,[27] *supra*. In *Dan-Foam*, the defendant

---

23. Original Appalachian Artworks, Inc. v. Granada Electronics, Inc., 816 F.2d 68 (2d Cir. 1987).
24. *Id.* at 70.
25. *Id.* at 73.
26. *Id.* at 75–76 *citing* 3A R. CALLMANN UNFAIR COMPETITION, TRADEMARKS AND MONOPOLIES § 16.16, at 83 (L. Altman 4th ed. 1983) ("[Equitable] servitudes have not been the basis of any holding barring parallel imports of genuine trademarked goods.").
27. Dan-Foam v. Brand Name Beds, LLC, 500 F. Supp. 2d 296 (S.D.N.Y. 2007).

Brand Name Beds, LLC (BNB) sold Tempur-Pedic products on the Internet that it had procured from the gray market. Tempur-Pedic asserted BNB was not required to adhere to Tempur-Pedic's quality control requirements. Accordingly, Tempur-Pedic argued, the mattresses sold by BNB were materially different from those sold by its authorized resellers.

Problematic for Tempur-Pedic's case, however, was the fact that only some of Tempur-Pedic's authorized resellers had actually signed reseller agreements with Tempur-Pedic. Beginning in 2006, Tempur-Pedic implemented a program requiring all authorized resellers to execute new written agreements prohibiting sales to anyone other than end-users of the products. BNB asserted that it purchased its products from authorized resellers that had not yet signed any agreements with Tempur-Pedic. Thus, BNB argued, the resellers who sold BNB branded goods were not in breach of any contract with Tempur-Pedic.[28]

Factual disputes over how many resellers had in fact *not* signed the reseller agreement[29] prevented the court from deciding BNB's motion for summary judgment. Nonetheless, the case illustrates the vulnerability brand owners may encounter when their authorized resellers have not all signed their partner agreements.

(b) Records and Audit Rights

In addition to gray market prohibitions, a brand owner must also ensure that its partners maintain adequate records. To the extent breaches in a brand owner's distribution chain are discovered, it is important for a brand owner to have the ability to immediately investigate its partners' sales activity in order to find the leaks. Therefore, brand owners must require that their partners maintain records that reveal what products were sold and to whom they were sold. Partner agreements should contain clauses similar to the following example:

> Reseller shall maintain true and accurate records, in accordance with generally accepted accounting principles (GAAP) and industry standards of all products sold by Reseller. Each month, Reseller shall prepare point of sale (POS) reports and any other reports reasonably required by Brand Owner. The POS reports shall identify, at a minimum, the following: (1) Reseller's end of month product inventory; and

---

28. *Id.* at 301–303.
29. *Id.* at 302, n. 47 ("BNB asserts that "[m]any of the retailers in Plaintiffs' national network of 'authorized' dealers have not entered into" this Retailer Agreement. Tempur-Pedic disputes this by asserting that "[a] majority of Tempur-Pedic's 2,000+ authorized retailers have signed written agreements, some since 2004 . . . and all retailers nationally are being transitioned to [the] new form of written agreement as a result of efforts undertaken by the company starting in 2006.").

(2) Reseller's product sales from the previous month. The product sales information shall include the following information for each sales transaction: (1) end users' name and address; (2) the product code(s) and (if applicable) serial number(s) of the product(s) sold; and (3) the date of the transaction.

In addition to the above, brand owners must grant themselves the right to audit their partners' books and records. For the same reason most people make a good faith effort to pay all requisite taxes, distribution partners are more likely to comply with their contractual obligations when they are cognizant that their conduct may be subject to review.[30]

Having the contractual right to conduct such an audit provides brand owners with the most efficient method to collect and review the documents they need in a gray market investigation. Although a brand owner hopes to have an informal and workable relationship with its distribution partners, the reality is that the relationship is governed by the parties' written agreement. Thus, any informal request from a brand owner to review a partner's books and records may simply be turned down. If such an informal request is denied, a brand owner is left to collect the documents through the costly and time-consuming method of civil discovery. To take away the partner's discretion to turn down such requests, brand owners can include an audit clause similar to the following:

> Brand owner shall have the unfettered right, upon three business days' notice, to examine all of Reseller's books and records that mention or reference in any way Brand Owners' products. Failure or refusal by Reseller to grant Brand Owner full access to these books and records shall constitute a material breach of this Agreement.

Of course, brand owners must do more than merely negotiate for the contractual right of mandating record keeping and audit rights. Brand owners must actively enforce their agreements. *United States v. Braunstein*,[31] *supra*, illustrates some of the harmful consequences of ignoring enforcement efforts after partner agreements have been signed.

Prior to the government even beginning its investigation of Braunstein, Apple was concerned that its Latin American distributors, ALAC, were engaging in gray marketing. To help the examination of its business practices, Apple hired Kroll Associates (Kroll). Kroll conducted an investigation and concluded that "'a potentially significant gray market problem existed' at ALAC and that '[t]here also appear to be a number of issues internal to ALAC

---

30. *See e.g., The Grey Market*, KPMG/Anti-Gray Mkt. Alliance, 2003, at 3, *available at* http://www.agmaglobal.org/press_events/press_docs/KPMG_TheGreyMarket_Web.pdf.
31. Braunstein, 281 F.3d at 982.

which were contributing to the gray market problem.'"[32] Kroll based this conclusion on several reasons including ALAC's failure to enforce compliance with its agreements:

> ALAC does not obtain any of the reporting required under the terms of the signed agreements (which are currently expired) with its customers.[33]

Not only had ALAC failed to require its distributors to maintain things like POS reports, it had also let the agreements expire. This delinquency would ultimately prove fatal to the government's case against Braunstein.

In 1997, the United States Attorney's Office began investigating Braunstein and his dealings with ALAC. It was estimated that Braunstein purchased approximately one million dollars worth of products per month from ALAC. Notwithstanding the large volume, Braunstein always paid ALAC up front and in cash. Moreover, there were no written agreements defining the relationship between Braunstein and ALAC, nor any documents memorializing the substance of any particular transaction. Immediately after purchase, Braunstein imported the products into the United States.[34]

When Braunstein learned that he was subject to a criminal investigation with respect to his importing business, his attorney wrote a lengthy letter to the prosecuting attorney asserting that his client had done nothing wrong. The letter's thesis was that ALAC had full knowledge that the bulk of his client's purchases were being resold to resellers in the United States. Even if ALAC's employees had told the prosecutors that Braunstein was only authorized to resell the Apple products in Latin America, Braunstein's attorney assured the prosecutor that Apple's own financial documents would "disprove these contentions."[35]

The United States Attorney's Office continued its prosecution of Braunstein. During the grand jury proceeding, ALAC representatives testified that "Braunstein was only authorized to sell Apple products within Latin America."[36] The grand jury returned an indictment charging Braunstein with several crimes including wire fraud, interstate transportation of goods obtained by fraud, and money laundering. The district court summarized the indictment as follows:

> The Government alleges that [Braunstein] entered into a conspiracy... to defraud Apple Computer by inducing Apple to sell them Apple

---

32. *Id.* at 985–86.
33. *Id.* at 986.
34. *Id.* at 985.
35. *Id.* at 987.
36. *Id.* at 989.

products at prices substantially below what they could be purchased [for] in the United States. Defendant would purchase computers through his Mexican business entities ostensibly for sale in Mexico. However, instead of distributing and selling the products in Mexico, Defendant would instead sell the products in the United States . . . to other Apple reseller[s] and wholesalers in the United States at prices substantially below Apple's listed wholesale price for such items.[37]

After the indictment, Braunstein's lawyer subpoenaed a variety of documents from Apple to bolster its defense that Apple *knew* that Braunstein was importing products into the United States for domestic resale. Among the documents requested was the Kroll report examining Apple's gray market problem.

Apple sought to quash the subpoena, but the court ordered its production. The court reasoned that the report was relevant to Braunstein's defense: "It is the defendant's contention that he [engaged in gray market transactions] with the knowledge of Apple Latin America, and that accordingly, his conduct could not be unlawful since it would negate intent and indeed if it was consistent with Apple's distribution practice, it would simply be a commercial transaction. . . ."[38]

Apple continued to fight its obligation to turn over the Kroll report and other documents relevant to its knowledge that a gray market existed. Finally, less than one month before trial, Apple turned over the subpoenaed documents to Braunstein's lawyer. The Kroll report was produced as well as other documents revealing that Apple was fully apprised of the gray market's existence. *Less than one week later, the United States Attorney dismissed the indictment.*[39] Not only was the case dismissed, the Ninth Circuit Court held that Braunstein should be entitled to a reimbursement of his fees and costs because, with the revelation of the Apple documents, the government's case against him was "frivolous."[40]

In a matter of one week, Apple's knowledge and implicit toleration of the gray market changed a criminal fraud case to a *frivolous* prosecution. The result would likely have been no different had it been a civil case brought by Apple. Brand owners cannot have it both ways: They cannot succeed in efforts to redress gray market activity if there is a history of turning a blind eye to it.

---

37. *Id.* at 989–90.
38. *Id.* at 990.
39. *Id.*
40. *Id.* at 997.

(c) Security Audits

It is essential that brand owners undertake sufficient measures to maximize the security and safety of their products. Especially when brand owners rely on third-party businesses to distribute and sell their products, brands become vulnerable to attack in a variety of ways. From old fashioned thievery to collusive divulgement of trade secrets, distribution partners can often be the brand owner's best protector or its enemy within. Instead of leaving this dichotomy to chance, brand owners must obtain and exercise the right to routinely audit the security of its partners.

Section c discusses The various strategies brand owners must undertake to best protect their brands are discussed later in this Chapter. Once the requisite methods are determined, brand owners must ensure that its partners understand their respective roles and duties. The typical method for communicating such obligations is through partner agreements. To the extent the best security practices evolve during the life of a partner contract, brand owners must have procedures in place to routinely modify or supplement their agreements and ensure that all partners are consistently guided by the same set of rules.

In the partner agreements, brand owners must similarly afford themselves the right to routinely inspect and audit the practices of its partners to verify compliance with its security protocols. Audits can range from an informal inspection of a facility and its employee workstations to virtual audits that use network-based applications to monitor communications or product movement.

Contracts that give brand owners the right to conduct security audits will not guarantee obedience from distribution partners. Actually conducting the audits and enforcing infractions are the next steps. Herb Armstrong, director of information technology for the Navy's Mine Warfare Training Center, explained the importance of enacting and testing compliance: "We put our policies in place, trained all our personnel, then crack the whip. Usually the first time you chop off someone's head, people start to take notice."[41]

(d) Quality Control Guidelines

To maintain the popularity of a brand, brand owners must maintain the quality of their goods. This self-evident reality requires a great deal more than manufacturing great products. Brand owners must ensure that their products remain in impeccable condition from their creation in the factory to their ultimate acquisition by an end user. Depending on the product, the requisite quality control measures can range from the simple to the sophisticated.

---

41. Daniel Tynan, *Closed Door Policy*, FEDTECH, August 2007, http://fedtechmagazine.com/article.asp?item_id=352 (last visited Oct. 9, 2008).

Goods that are relatively fragile may require packaging, shipping, and installation guidelines to reduce the possibility of damage through the supply chain journey.[42] Goods that are perishable, such as food or pharmaceuticals, may have much stricter guidelines with respect to temperatures and timelines during storage and transportation. Depending on what is needed, brand owners must make certain that the quality control standards are clearly articulated in the agreement.

In addition to the benefit of having a clear pronouncement of a partner's obligations, having the quality control requirements spelled out in the written agreements can provide an added benefit should a brand owner find itself needing to litigate its rights against a gray marketer. Brand owners are often tasked with proving that their authorized products are "materially different" from unauthorized gray market goods. The challenge of proving a material difference can be challenging when there are no manifestations of physical differences. As explained in Chapter 17, however, the law does not always require the differences to be physical. For example, a brand owner can show that its authorized products are materially different if they, unlike their gray market counterparts, are subject to legitimate, substantial, and nonpretextual quality control procedures and that nonconforming sales will diminish the value of the mark.[43]

Accordingly, brand owners' partner agreements must include a full articulation of any packaging, storing, transporting, and installing requirements necessary to maintain the quality of their goods.

(e) Venue Selection

Brand owners must be sufficiently sophisticated to craft their agreements with an eye towards litigation. In addition to stating a partner's obligations and prohibitions, the agreements should be designed to make any necessary lawsuit as expedient and cost effective as reasonably possible.

A case pending in a remote location is one of the ways a lawsuit can quickly become expensive and inconvenient. The effort and cost of having witnesses and lawyers travel back and forth from a brand owner's locale to the epicenter of the case can sometimes sufficiently deter litigants from commencing or even defending lawsuits.

In today's global marketplace, brand owners face the prospect of litigating all over the world. With partners throughout the globe, brand

---

42. *See e.g.,* Dan-Foam A/S v. brand Named Beds, LLC, 2007 WL 1346609 (S.D.N.Y. 2007) (discussing brand owner's transportation and installation guidelines to maintain the quality of its mattresses); *see also* Zino Davidoff SA v. CVS Corp., 2007 WL 1933932 (S.D.N.Y. 2007) (plaintiff's only "quality control measure" with respect to packaging were batch codes and unit production codes).
43. *See e.g.,* Warner-Lambert Co. v. Northside Dev. Corp., 86 F.3d 3, 7 (2nd Cir. 1996).

owners must preemptively seek the ability to control the location of its litigation battlegrounds by including forum selection clauses in its partner agreements.

Specifically, a brand owner and partner can, by their agreement, designate a forum in which any litigation shall take place.[44] Forum selection clauses are *presumed valid*. Thus, enforcement will be ordered unless it clearly would be "unreasonable and unjust, or the clause [is] invalid for such reasons as fraud or overreaching."[45] Given this presumption of validity, brand owners should designate the city or county that is most convenient for litigation.

The presumption of validity can be overcome. For example, partners may convince a court not to enforce a venue selection clause if the burden is so high that it in effect deprives that party of his day in court.[46] To meet this threshold, a party must meet a "heavy burden of proof."[47] For example, the financial difficulty a party may have in litigating in the designated forum such as travel expenses for party and witnesses is *not* itself a sufficient ground to deny enforcement of a valid forum selection clause.[48] Instead, a party would likely need to show that traveling to a distant forum would result in a combination of financial and physical hardship.[49] Such a showing is unlikely when, in the context of partner relationships, the lawsuit is between two commercial entities.

Without such financial *and* physical hardship, a partner wishing to avoid the enforceability of a forum selection clause would likely need to show that the forum was selected in bad faith or that consent to the forum selection clause was obtained by fraud or overreaching.[50] So long as the selected forum bears a rational relationship to brand owner's place of business, brand owners should have such clauses routinely enforced.

(f) Choice of Law

Even in the most industrialized countries, the penalties for infringing intellectual property remain quite modest.[51] Similar to preemptively selecting the venue in which any litigation will take place, brand owners may select the law

---

44. Carnival Cruise Lines, Inc. v. Shute, 499 U.S. 585, 595 (1991).
45. M/S Bremen v. Aapata Off-Shore Co., 407 U.S. 1, 15 (1972).
46. *Id.* at 18.
47. *Id.* at 19.
48. P & S Business Machines, Inc. v. Canon USA, Inc., 331 F.3d 804, 807 (11th Cir. 2003); Effron v. Sun Line Cruises, Inc., 67 F.3d 7, 10 (2nd Cir. 1995) (U.S. citizen forced to litigate in Greece).
49. Murphy v. Schneider Nat'l, Inc., 362 F.3d 1133, 1142 (9th Cir. 2004).
50. Carnival Cruise Lines, Inc., 499 U.S. at 594–95.
51. HOPKINS, *supra* note 11, at 7 (Without any penalties there is "little if any deterrent against counterfeiting. Until 1984, there was not even a U.S. federal criminal statute prohibiting product counterfeiting.").

that will govern any partner disputes. Parties to a contract may agree as to the law which will govern their transaction, even as to issues going to the validity of the contract.[52] Courts will respect the law to which the parties agreed to be bound.[53]

Absent fraud or violation of public policy, clauses selecting the law are generally determinative so long as the state selected has sufficient contacts with the transaction.[54] Because a brand owner will typically name its home state or town as the forum of choice for any litigation, selecting that state's laws to be the rules governing the dispute will provide the needed nexus to enforce the provision. Because many of the rights in gray market cases are decided by applying federal law, the enforceability of such choice of law provisions is rarely contended.

(g) Damages

One of the challenges brand owners commonly face when litigating issues related to the harm to its intellectual property is quantifying the damages. Especially in gray market cases where there may be no material differences between authorized and unauthorized sales, a defendant could make a relatively persuasive argument that the brand owner should not recover any damages. The gray market partner may argue that it imported genuine products from a foreign distributor. Thus, although the price at which it obtained the goods is less expensive, the brand owner still receives revenue for the transaction. To reduce or eliminate these challenges, brand owners should include liquidated damages clauses in their agreements.

A liquidated damages clause allows for the parties to designate, during the formation of their contract, the amount of damages or the method to calculate damages in the event of a breach. In general, liquidated damages clauses will be upheld if (1) damages flowing from a breach are difficult to ascertain, and (2) the provision fixing the damages is a reasonable measure of the anticipated probable harm.[55] If the amount fixed is grossly disproportionate to the probable loss, the provision will not be enforced.[56]

For example, in *BDO Seidman v. Hirshberg*,[57] the accounting firm BDO had a liquidated damages provision in its manager contracts, which required that managers who left BDO were required to compensate the firm if he or she served any former BDO client within 18 months of departure. The measure of damages under this provision provided that the amount of

---

52. Gen. Elec. Co. v. Deutz Ag, 270 F.3d 144, 155 (3d Cir. 2001).
53. *Id.*
54. Int'l Minerals & Res., Pappas, 96 F.3d 586, 592 (2nd Cir. 1996).
55. BDO Seidman v. Hirshberg, 712 N.E.2d 1220, 1227 (N.Y. 1999).
56. *Id.*
57. BDO Seidman v. Hirshberg, 93 N.Y.2d 382 (1999).

"compensation" owed by former managers was equal to 1 ½ times the fees charged to each lost client over the last full year the client was served by the firm.[58] The clause was challenged by the defendant after he left the firm and performed services for over one hundred former clients. These clients were billed $138,000 during the prior year. Accordingly, BDO demanded that the defendant reimburse the firm $207,000.00. The defendant refused and challenged the enforceability of the liquidated damages provision.[59]

When analyzing the enforceability of the liquidated damages clause, New York's Court of Appeals agreed that the measure of damages was sufficiently difficult to ascertain to satisfy the first requirement of enforcing a liquidated damages provision.[60] It would be impossible to look back and posit with any certainty how long a former client would have stayed a BDO client but for the former manager leaving and making his or her services available as an alternative source.[61] Although these damages could not be reconstructed with any accuracy, the court was uncomfortable agreeing that the 1½ multiplier bore a rational nexus to the probable harm: "[T]he averment regarding the basis of the liquidated damages *by no means conclusively demonstrates the absence of gross disproportionality.*"[62] Because there was not sufficient evidence to show that the provision was reasonable, the court remanded the case back to the trial court for "further development of the record on the liquidated damages formula."[63]

Brand owners face a similar challenge. When a partner decides to buy or sell gray market products instead of adhering to its contractual obligations, damages are difficult to quantify with certainty. Such transactions can impair the goodwill of a brand owner if customers become disillusioned to learn that the product may be materially different from an authorized good or that the brand owner will not honor the warranty on the product.

Although this type of harm can be devastating to a brand owner, gray marketers can often argue that such damage theories are too amorphous to be awarded or, in the alternative, that any damages should be extremely modest. To avoid the lengthy and often costly conflict over the amount of recoverable damages, brand owners can include liquidated damages provisions that state with precision how damages for gray market transactions should be calculated. For example, if an authorized reseller sells to gray

---

58. *Id.* at 861.
59. *Id.* The defendant also argued, albeit unsuccessfully, that the liquidated damages clause should be invalid because it was essentially an illegal non-compete clause. *See id.* at 388–95.
60. *Id.* at 396 ("The damages here are sufficiently difficult to ascertain to satisfy the first requirement of a valid liquidated damages provision.").
61. *See id.* at 396.
62. *Id.* at 396–97.
63. *Id.* at 397.

market resellers in lieu of end users, a liquidated damages provision may state the following:

> The pricing the reseller receives is based on the reseller's promise to sell only to end users. In the event Brand Owner discovers that reseller knowingly sold to an unauthorized reseller, the contract price is cancelled and the normal retail price will apply to all products sold to unauthorized resellers.

Having such a clause can not only make it easier for a judge or jury to calculate a brand owner's damages, it can also streamline settlement negotiations. A brand owner that exercises its audit rights and discovers forbidden transactions should be able to quickly and objectively reach an agreement on the amount of owed compensation.

(h) Attorney Fees

The general rule in this country, known as the American Rule, states that attorney's fees incurred by the successful party in an action are not recoverable in the absence of a statute or an enforceable contract.[64] Because of this rule, litigation can often be a Pyrrhic victory where the judgment bounty only slightly exceeds the cost of battle. Brand owners with a keen eye towards economics may even be tempted to forego litigation believing it is simply too cost-prohibitive to endure such brand protection efforts.

An effective strategy to reduce the cost of litigation is to include an attorney fees provision in all partner agreements providing that the prevailing party of any dispute related to the agreement shall be entitled to recover its costs and attorney fees. Not only does this provide the brand owner with the opportunity to recover its fees should it be successful, it puts added pressure on the breaching partner. The breaching partner will risk not only paying money to its own attorneys, it will face the added risk of having to reimburse the brand owner for the *brand owner's* fees and costs as well.

The enforceability of attorney fees clauses are governed by state law. For example, some states like California will interpret a *unilateral* fee provision as a *mutual* fee provision.[65] Thus, even if the agreement provides that only the brand owner would be entitled to fees if it was the prevailing party,

---

64. Fleischmann Distilling Corp. v. Maier Brewing Co., 386 U.S. 714, 717 (1967); *see also* Alyeska Pipeline Serv. Co. v. Wilderness Soc'y, 421 U.S. 240, 247–62 (1975) (discussing the history and development of the American Rule).
65. Cal. Civ. Code § 1717(a) (2008) ("In any action on a contract, where the contract specifically provides that attorney's fees and costs, which are incurred to enforce that contract, shall be awarded either to one of the parties or to the prevailing party, then the party who is determined to be the party prevailing on the contract, whether he or she is the party specified in

California law will interpret the contract to mean that the prevailing party—whether it is the brand owner or the partner—shall be entitled to recover attorney fees and costs.

ii. Incentives for Compliance

For a brand owner to have successful partnership relationships, its agreements must contain more than a litany of prohibitions. In addition to the documents identifying the various *sticks*, the contracts must include a sufficient number of *carrots*. By articulating the mutual benefits to the brand owner and its partners, partner contracts can identify the various incentives for partners to abide by their obligations.

(a) Territorial Exclusivities

One of the incentives brand owners can offer channel partners is territorial exclusivity. A territorial exclusivity is a clause in a contract that grants a channel partner a geographic region within which it will be the sole entity selling the brand owner's goods. At their core, territorial exclusivities benefit brand owners by preventing intrabrand competition, which can drive down the prices of goods. Insulating channel partners from such competition provides some assurances that their anticipated margins will be sustainable.

This advantage to the channel partner spawns two favorable consequences. *First*, the channel partner will have an incentive to invest in the promotion of the brand. Knowing that it will not face unwanted competition from other resellers, the partner will be more inclined to invest in marketing and promotional campaigns because it will have the confidence that such efforts will inure to its benefit—no another authorized or unauthorized reseller in the territory. *Second*, the channel partner will be less likely to yield to gray market temptations. The price protection the channel partner will enjoy by being the sole reseller will ameliorate any economic pressures to supplement the business with gray market activity. In addition, loyalty begets loyalty: efforts by brand owners to protect unwanted competition engender a more prosperous relationship in which partners are less likely to jeopardize their bond by engaging in conduct injurious to the brand owner.

Of course, brand owners must do more than merely include territorial exclusivities in their partner contracts. Not only will failing to abide by the provisions put a strain on the partner relationships, but also if brand owners

---

the contract or not, shall be entitled to reasonable attorney's fees in addition to other costs.").

fail to take sufficient steps to protect the territory from unwanted gray market competition, they can be held liable for attendant harm.

For example, in *Alleghany Pharmacal Corp. v. Parbel of Florida, Inc.*,[66] a brand owner was held liable when it "refused to participate in efforts to stop the gray market import into the United States" of its products. The defendant had licensed to the plaintiff its trademark for use in the United States. The plaintiff faced unwanted competition, however, when an independent British manufacturer produced products that found their way to the United States via the gray market. Given the court's conclusion that the defendant had not done enough to prevent the gray market, it awarded the plaintiff over $1 million as proven lost future profits attributable to the breach of contract.[67]

(b) Technical Support and Training

One of the ways distribution partners can promote a particular brand is by promoting their particular expertise in a product. Especially with more technological goods, consumers are more likely to purchase from a retailer that has acquired a level of mastery with respect to the installation, maintenance, or repair of the product. Towards that end, brand owners must ensure that their partners are qualified and trained to become partners in the first place. As new products evolve and new products are released, brand owners must provide partners with the necessary training to provide customers with top service. Moreover, partners that endeavor to fulfill the various training opportunities should be rewarded. In addition to being afforded the opportunity to sell certain products where training is mandatory, brand owners should have a recognition policy in place wherein partners can use their qualifications to market their expertise and promote the brand.

(c) Return Policies and Warranty Support

Brand owners with liberal return and warranty policies engender positive goodwill for the brand in several ways. As an initial matter, promoting such policies communicates to customers that the brand owner is willing to stand behind the quality of its goods. Such representations also communicate to customers that making a financial investment in the product is much less riskier than an all-sales-are-final transaction. In addition to engendering goodwill at the moment of purchase, consumers' faith in a brand can be reinforced if any problems or defects are efficiently remedied. By exercising these policies through their authorized partners, brand owners also reduce the risk of the unwanted diversion of products. Products that the brand owner refuses

---

66. Alleghany Pharmacal Corp. v. Parbel of Florida, Inc., 226 A.D.2d 104 (N.Y. 1996).
67. *Id.* at 105.

to accept or return are unlikely to sit idle in a partners' warehouse if there is a willing buyer. As a result, the secondary market can become flooded with products in need of repair or replacement. Not only can these products compete with a brand owner's authorized distribution channels, they can further impair the goodwill of a brand if they are delivered to customers with any prior defects still in disrepair.

(d) Delivery Terms

It is often suggested that it is quicker to procure products from the gray market than through authorized channels.[68] As a result, authorized resellers can feel compelled to procure products from the gray market in order to win an account if the brand owner does not or cannot ensure expedited delivery of their goods. There are two fundamental methods by which brand owners can minimize this type of gray market temptation.

First, the brand owner's overall methods to curb the gray market will reduce the easy availability of gray market goods. In other words, if a large shadow inventory of gray market goods is ubiquitously and openly traded among unauthorized channels, the ability to prevent authorized resellers and distributors from dipping into this market is more difficult. By cleansing the market of such goods, partners will be less disposed to stray from the authorized channels for the pragmatic reason that it may not, after all, be more efficient than the authorized distribution chain.

Second, brand owners can make the efficient delivery of products a top priority. By sharing the value that delivery times are matters of high importance, brand owners can embolden the health of their partner relationships. Automobile maker Saturn is a good example: "Saturn will get the part to you from another retailer overnight. Saturn even measures its own employees on how well the retailers serve their customers, their end users."[69] Of course, the realities of the manufacturing cycles will limit how instantly a good can be delivered. To the extent brand owners have standard lead times for the delivery of products, these figures should be included in the partner agreement. These figures allow partners to properly forecast their inventory needs and provide customers and potential customers with reliable data for the anticipated delivery of sought goods.

(e) Price Protection

As discussed here, many brand owners will offer additional discounts for authorized resellers if the reseller is competing for a particularly large account.

---

68. *The Grey Market*, KPMG/Anti-Gray Mkt. Alliance, 2003, at 4, *available at* http://www.agmaglobal.org/press_events/press_docs/KPMG_TheGreyMarket_Web.pdf.
69. Scott Beth et al., *Supply Chain Challenges: Building Relationships*, in Harv. Bus. Rev. on Supply Chain Mgmt., 2006, at 75.

Because the volume of these prospective transactions is so lucrative, brand owners will cut their margins to ensure the sale is not lost to one of their competitors. Special discounts may also be provided when the end user is an educational, governmental, or non-profit entity. These special discounts are counterproductive if resellers misrepresent the true identify of their end user in order to dishonestly qualify for the exceptionally lower cost. Although this abuse needs to be monitored in a variety of ways, brand owners should also monitor the marketplace sufficiently in order to set realistic discounts. If a brand owner's wholesale price does not afford the reseller with a sufficient margin, the reseller will face Morton's Fork of either foregoing a sale or misrepresenting the details of the transaction to be profitable. To relieve partners of this dilemma, brand owners' discounts should provide sufficient price protection to succeed without deceit.

iii. Penalties for Noncompliance

The strength of a brand depends in large part on the strength of the partner relationships: "[P]artnerships are the supply chain's lifeblood."[70] As discussed in prior pages, a brand owner must work diligently to establish a platform to minimize risk. Because a supply chain will not thrive on its own, brand owners must take several preemptive measures. From vetting potential partners to aligning brand owner and partner incentives, brand owners can lay the blueprint for partnership prosperity.

Brand owners must also establish strategies to deal with partners that are caught breaching their partnership obligations. Although there is a simplistic appeal of incorporating a strict "no tolerance" policy for brand abuse, it is neither realistic nor pragmatic. On the other hand, brand owners cannot ignore partner infractions; a neglected gray market quickly becomes a burgeoning gray market. Instead, brand owners must establish a system where the penalty aptly fits the infraction. Like a judge sentencing a criminal, there may be mitigating or aggravating circumstances that impact the suitability of the punishment.

(a) Probation or Suspension

Not every partner found engaging in gray market activity deserves to have its contract terminated. The partner may have a storied history of being a profitable and honorable reseller or distributor that made a regrettable exception to its established fidelity. A reseller may have made a good faith mistake believing it was selling to an end user when in fact it was selling to a gray marketer. A rogue employee for a partner that was effectively disciplined may

---

70. Jeffrey K Liker & Thomas Y. Choi, *Building Deep Supplier Relationships*, in HARV. BUS. REV. ON SUPPLY CHAIN MGMT., 2006, at 25.

have been the sole cause for a partner straying from its obligations. There are many conceivable circumstances where full termination would not be warranted. Thus, a brand owner must have the flexibility to tailor its discipline.

One possible strategy is establishing a probationary system in which the brand owner affords a partner to remain in good standing while being on notice that any further infractions will result in its termination. Another strategy is the implementation of suspensions. By limiting the ability to purchase certain products or make purchases during certain seasons, a brand owner can levy a penalty designed to deter future malfeasance. For example, in *3 Lab, Inc. v. Kim*,[71] the case involved an authorized distributor for Estée Lauder. When Estée Lauder received a "tip" that the distributor was selling gray market products in violation of its distribution agreement, the company conducted an investigation and suspended the contract for three to four months.[72]

(b) Monetary Penalties

Brand owners provide authorized resellers and distributors with preferred pricing for their products. The discounts are designed to enable the partners to remain profitable in a competitive market. As mentioned above, the discounts are typically even greater when the distributor or reseller is selling to certain customers. Brand owners typically pass on greater discounts when the ultimate end user is an educational, governmental, or non-profit entity. Brand owners will also allow greater discounts when a partner is competing against a rival brand for an unusually large sales opportunity.

Unless strictly enforced, these discount policies are vulnerable to abuse. Resellers may misrepresent the true identity of the end user to the brand owner in order to increase their own margins. Promising that the sale is to a school or charitable organization, the reseller may take advantage of the greater discounts and sell to a for-profit business or, even worse, an unauthorized reseller. When such deception occurs, one strategy some brand owners employ is to simply fine the reseller in an amount that erases the discount that was perpetuated by the dishonesty by sending a revised invoice. The revised invoice can state the reason for the amended amount, for example, as follows:

> The contract price for 100 units of widgets was $20.00 based on ABC Reseller's representation that the end user for the widgets was Washington High School. ACME Brand Owner has investigated and verified that Washington High School was not the end user and discovered that ABC

---

71. 3 Lab, Inc. v. Kim, 2007 WL 2177513 (D.N.J. 2007).
72. *Id.* at *3.

Reseller sold the widgets to ProfitCo. The $20.00 unit price was premised on the representation that the end user was an educational institution entitled to Tier 1 preferred pricing. Because the end user is ProfitCo, the normal Tier 2 price of $40.00 applies. Please find enclosed a revised invoice for $20,000.00.

(c) Termination

Brand owners typically reserve the right to terminate their partner agreements with or without cause. Although the above methodologies discuss options short of termination, there are many circumstances when this more drastic measure is the best strategy. Given the importance of keeping branded products away from unauthorized channels, terminating a partner may be necessary for sufficient channel protection. Even when termination appears to make perfect sense, brand owners must anticipate a certain level of pushback from various company representatives. Especially when the partner was a source of significant revenue and *commission* for various employees there will be a campaign of reluctance to levy the death penalty.

In addition to seeking input from employees that directly dealt with the delinquent partner, management for the brand owner must look at the larger picture to determine whether maintaining the partner relationship is in the company's best interests. A distributor or reseller that sold a large volume of product to gray marketers would have generated significant revenue for the brand owner given its large volume of purchases. By leaking so many of these same goods to the gray marketer, however, the partner also inflicted a great deal of harm to the brand.

The brand owner's employees that were enriched by the partners' purchases will have an economic incentive to oppose termination. Because of this conflicted interest, these benefactors should not adjudicate the fate of the breaching partner. Instead, the decision should be made by a disinterested person or group not impacted by the termination or survival of the partner.

In the event the brand owner terminates a partner, it must do a great deal more than issue a termination letter. Brand owners must have a post-termination policy in place to protect and preserve all property that was given or licensed to the partner. From remaining inventory to confidential trade secrets, brand owners must make certain that it does not unnecessarily arm a terminated—*and potentially disgruntled*—partner to inflict even more harm. Similar to escorting a terminated employee off-site after collecting all company effects, brand owners must coordinate the termination with its collection of all necessary property and information. In the days, weeks, and even months following the termination, the brand owner must continue to monitor its former partner to verify that it is not engaging in any prohibited conduct.

c. Tightening the Supply Chain

Once a brand owner has its employees hired, its channel partners vetted and selected, and its contracts properly drafted and executed, there is a temptation to assume that all will be well. Although taking the foregoing steps lays the critical foundation for an upstanding supply chain, brand owners must dedicate themselves to continually monitor their status. There are simply too many vulnerabilities in a distribution channel to assume that it will enforce itself.

Conversely, an absentee brand owner compounds any temptations channel partners or employees may have to stray from their responsibilities because such neglect implies that any infidelity will be uncaught and unpunished. Like a parked patrol car slowing down traffic, a brand owner must manifest the perception of omnipresence to its employees and partners. The following pages identify specific areas where brand owners should focus their monitoring resources.

i. Acknowledging Geographic Vulnerabilities

Crises are inevitable in business. Especially when a business transcends borders, disruptions can spawn from catastrophic events like political upheavals and natural disasters to the more provincial issues like cultural or lingual misunderstandings. Understanding the inevitability of obstacles is necessary to manage expectations. It would be naïve to anticipate a global supply chain without any hitches. It would be equally credulous to treat the fate of supply challenges with resigned acceptance. Brand owners must instead take every measure reasonably possible to ensure that keeping their supply chain hermetic with both preemptive and responsive strategies.

When considering supply chain management strategies, brand owners must consider the geographic locations where their products are most susceptible to abuse. Whenever a brand owner's product will pass through a region or country where intellectual property rights are not respected or enforced, brand owners must be especially cautious. These areas are also typically populated with a citizenry that has a desire for the goods being manufactured but cannot afford the brand owner's retail price. Given the politics and demographics, brand owners in these regions must make special efforts to *prevent* brand abuse because taking action *after* an abuse has occurred will be much more difficult.

In *Global Brand Integrity Management*, there is an illustrious recap of a meeting between the authors and a senior official in the Ministry of Foreign Affairs of Vietnam about a software piracy issue.[73] After efforts were made to

---

73. Richard S. Post & Penelope N. Post, Global Brand Integrity Management xii (2008).

communicate the importance and benefits of the Vietnamese government undertaking efforts to stop software piracy, the official demurred: "Those software companies are making too much money. It costs them almost nothing to produce the programs, and they sell them for hundreds of dollars. Our people cannot afford them. We need these programs to develop our country, and I [and the rest of the government] will look the other way until we no longer need them."[74] Vietnam is not an anomaly. There are many countries that similarly have little interest or appreciation of rewarding and encouraging the cost of innovation.

China is widely recognized as the most notorious source of counterfeit and gray market goods. There are many reasons why China has become the poster child for intellectual property infringement. Two significant factors are China's access to the intellectual property of multinational corporations and China's lack of an effective justice system to prevent, punish, or deter such unlawful activity. Because China boasts an immensely large population with a surfeit of capable workers, brand owners have been quick to establish partnerships with Chinese companies to manufacture their goods.

There is an obvious benefit when a product can be made overseas for a fraction of what it would cost domestically. In order to educate these partners to effectively produce a brand owner's goods, however, the brand owner must essentially turn over the blueprints to its business. Although brand owners would never provide a competitor with the trade secrets to their success, turning over this information to a manufacturing partner is a prerequisite to having goods produced. Once equipped with a brand owner's know-how, ingredients, and processes, a brand owner's *partner* can instantly become its *competitor*. It can become a competitor by overproducing the requested volume and selling the unauthorized goods to various distributors and resellers. The partner can also share the brand owner's trade secrets to friends or relatives with similar facilities so that they can manufacture imitation products.

These hypothetical illustrations have become a reality for countless businesses that have chosen to manufacture their products in China. Counterfeiting and IP theft cause billions of dollars in losses for various industries.[75] Pharmaceutical manufacturer Pfizer estimates that it loses as much business to counterfeiters as it does to legitimate competitors, and that China is the primary source of the counterfeits.[76] Because so many of these products make their way into other countries, including the United States, the production of counterfeit goods and unauthorized goods in China inevitably affects a brand owner's market share.

---

74. Id.
75. *Redefining Intellectual Property Value: The Case of China*, PricewaterhouseCoopers, Oct. 2005, at 25, *available at* http://www.pwc.com/techforecast/pdfs/IPR-web_x.pdf.
76. Id.

When doing business in these vulnerable countries, therefore, brand owners must take even more steps to protect their brands. Surprisingly, however, some of the most sophisticated brand owners fail to follow this imperative. *Johnson & Johnson Products, Inc. v. Dal Trading International Trading, Co.,*[77] *supra*, is a worthy example of this common shortcoming. The controversy began because Johnson & Johnson (J&J) agreed to sell 80,000 dozen toothbrushes and certain baby products to Dal International Trading Company (Dal) *without a written contract*. Dal was a company located and doing business in Poland and, according to J&J, Dal agreed that it would only sell the J&J products in Poland.[78] It is unclear from the case why J&J did not have Dal execute a written agreement; however, this failure ultimately hurt J&J's brand and its lawsuit.

Failing to adhere to this allegedly oral contract, Dal caused or allowed the goods to be diverted from their intended destination of Poland and instead rerouted to the United States. Through a relatively circuitous route, the J&J products ended up in the hands of Quality King Manufacturing, Inc. (Quality King). Quality King was an independent distributor of various health and beauty aids. By the time the goods arrived at Quality King's warehouse, J&J's shipping labels had been stripped from most of the cartons to disguise the identity of the various supply sources.[79] Quality King was, in typical gray market fashion, the benefactor of price arbitrage. The J&J goods it purchased were priced for the Polish market at a level lower than the wholesale price in the United States for the same products. Accordingly, Quality King had the ability to set its prices below those being charged domestically by J&J.[80]

J&J sued and requested that the trial court issue a preliminary injunction to prevent Quality King from selling the imported gray goods. J&J argued that Dal committed a fraud when it represented to J&J that it would only sell the products in Poland. With respect to Quality King, J&J argued that it did not properly obtain title to the goods in question because it *should have known* by the price and circumstances of the transaction that Dal had committed a fraud to obtain and sell the goods. In other words, because Quality King was not a "good faith purchaser," and therefore only acquired Dal's *voidable* title in the gray market goods.[81]

Although the district court issued J&J's requested preliminary injunction, the Third Circuit Court of Appeals reversed. The Third Circuit Court concluded that although Quality King probably knew that J&J would not *approve* of Dal's unauthorized importation of goods, this was not tantamount to

---

77. Johnson & Johnson Products, 798 F.2d at 100.
78. *Id.* at 101.
79. *Id.* at 102.
80. *Id.*
81. *Id.*

Quality King knowing that Dal had allegedly committed a fraud. In fact, the court was not even satisfied that J&J had established that Dal had committed a fraud: "If, at the time of contracting with J&J Ltd., Dal had intended to restrict the distribution of goods to Poland and only later decided to distribute the goods elsewhere, no fraudulent inducement to contract would have existed."[82]

Johnson & Johnson is relevant because it shows the difficult consequences a brand owner faces when it fails to properly memorialize the details behind a transaction. A clearer contract with Dal may have prevented its breach. Even if it would not have prevented its breach, J&J may have had stronger grounds to engage Dal in litigation for fraud or breach of contract. For example, venue selection or choice of law provisions may have provided J&J with the opportunity to obtain an enforceable judgment against Dal domestically. Having a written contract with Dal would have also expanded the available causes of action against Quality King. With a written contract in place, J&J may have been able to prevent the Quality King transaction by issuing a cease and desist letter enclosing the parties' written contract and threatening an intentional interference with contract cause of action. Without any written document, however, J&J was left with its argument that Dal committed a fraud and Quality King knew *or should have known* about the fraud. These latter theories are much harder to prove and, accordingly, J&J's preliminary injunction against Quality King was vacated.[83]

As brand owners consider partnering with operations in other parts of the globe, they must consider more than the ostensible savings in production costs. Production costs are meaningless if the partner cannot operate in a reliable environment or if the partner decides to become a competitor of the brand owner. In addition to the balance sheet analysis, brand owners must investigate the viability of the proposed location. Below is a list of factors that are worth considering when examining potential partners in various locales:

- *Crime:* If a proposed manufacturing plant is located in a criminally dangerous region, it is unlikely that any amount of cost savings would justify its selection. A brand owner's employees could be put at risk and the manufacturing facility could be vulnerable to theft and vandalism.
- *Business Corruption:* Every transaction where money changes hands is susceptible to immorality. It would be unreasonable to believe a brand owner could find a region, country, or city without any element of depravity. Nonetheless, there are areas where corruption is so pervasive it is considered an accepted byproduct of commerce. Brand owners must be especially cautious when doing business in these latter milieus.

---

82. *Id.* at 103, fn. 2.
83. *Id.* at 106.

- *Justice System*—There are scores of lamentations about the inefficiency of the American justice system. It is not uncommon for litigation to last several years before the merits of a dispute are actually tried before a judge or jury. Although most courthouses contend with a caseload more voluminous than desired, and although its execution is far from perfect, the American justice system is among the most efficient and trustworthy systems in the world. Many countries' systems are either nonexistent or wholly unpredictable, rendering the enforcement of a simple business contract an unrealizable ambition. The efficacy of a country's justice system should be considered when examining partnership locations as well as when drafting contracts that memorialize a parties' relationship. Venue selection clauses and choice of law provisions may need careful attention to ensure that a brand owner will have the opportunity to effectively vindicate its rights should its partner breach any material obligations.
- *Political System*—It requires no more than a perfunctory survey of the world's current affairs to correctly conclude that chaos and unrest are, in many parts, more common than uncommon. Wars are fought, leaders are exiled, and borders are redrawn only to lay the backdrop for another violent coup a few years or decades later. Before dedicating any resources to manufacturing or distribution partnerships, brand owners must take a close look at the region to determine whether its underpinnings foreshadow harmony, bedlam, or something in between.
- *Available Security*—Even in the world's safest neighborhoods, its dwellers typically lock their doors at night. When manufacturing goods in places where legal obedience is much less certain, measures must be taken to best safeguard the facility and the products it generates. Specific security measures to consider are discussed in more detail below.
- *Health & Safety*—A cheap workforce is alluring to any brand owner. So long as the employees are competent, spending less on labor means lower prices or higher margins. Although this factor is not directly relevant to the infringement of intellectual property, a location that lacks an operational infrastructure to serve the basic needs of the community is unlikely to generate a reliable and productive pool of workers.

ii. On-Site Security

Locations where goods are manufactured and stored must be kept secure from both external and internal corruption. Fortunately, security technology can be very effective. Home and business security is a vibrant and competitive market,[84] which has spawned the development of innovative products and

---

84. Kevin G. Demarrais, *Does Poor Security Ring a Bell for You? Don't Waste Money on a Faulty System*, THE RECORD, June 29, 2007, at B1.

strategies. Brand owners are benefactors of this competition because the companies that develop and administer home and business security typically provide the same services at manufacturing or distribution facilities.

Beyond merely monitoring doors and windows, today's modern systems monitor the relevant indoor space in the event an intruder accesses the facility through an alternative method.[85] The traditional method of video surveillance (CCTV) is still considered a popular and effective strategy.[86] Security experts maintain that installing a workable surveillance system is just the first step. Many contingencies can hamper or disable a security system.[87] For example, a box or crate may block the line of a motion detection device. A power outage may likewise impair reliability of a security system.[88] Beyond the installation, certain employees at the facility must be assigned the responsibility of vigilantly ensuring the system is in working condition.[89]

The same principle applies to CCTV. CCTV is a useful method to conduct facility surveillance.[90] Improper installation or improper use, however, can render the entire system useless.[91] Common pitfalls include the following: poor camera placement, on-premise lighting impairing the quality of video capture, delinquent saving and archiving of video footage, and failure to promptly review footage to confirm eye-witnessed events.[92] Technology continues to evolve, making user errors easier to ameliorate. For example, remote online monitoring and hard-drive-based archival of footage now make the permanent saving of video data a much less burdensome endeavor.[93]

In addition to conventional CCTV systems, there are "intelligent" versions that can highlight notable occurrences for their operators, such as the detection of unusual motion or the sudden impairment of a camera.[94] Some systems even allow operators to define particular areas within a camera's view and thus program responses when something is detected within these more sensitive areas.[95] Although these more robust systems were once burdensome

---

85. *Id.*
86. *Watchgoods That Never Sleep*, WEEKEND MAIL, Jan. 19, 2008.
87. Demarrais, *supra* note 84 (quoting security consultant Jeffrey Zwirn) ("When I look into a failure, there is always a reason, and it's not because a burglar beat the system").
88. *Id.* In one warehouse burglary in Louisiana, thieves cut security cables and made their entrance when no one had responded. Michelle Hunter, *5 Nabbed in Electronics Warehouse Burglary; Stolen goods were valued at about $200,000*, TIMES-PICAYUNE, Apr. 5, 2007.
89. *Watchgoods, supra* note 86.
90. In some countries, CCTV has lead to 50%–70% decreases in crimes. *Id.*
91. *Id. See also* Lisa Terry, *Locking Out Loss*, MULTICHANNEL MERCHANT, May 1, 2007, at 79 (quoting security consultant Barry Brandman) ("after the novelty wears of, not many have the patience to use the cameras").
92. *Watchgoods, supra* note 86.
93. Pete Tenereillo, *I Spy With My Networked Eye—It's not a matter of if enterprise IT managers will be responsible for video surveillance, but when. Are you—and your network—ready?*, NETWORK COMPUTING, Aug. 7, 2006, at 1715.
94. *Id.*
95. *Id.*

on a business' regular network, modern devices and programs are able to easily integrate themselves with most businesses' existing networks.[96]

Traditional security and surveillance is less effective for monitoring the more discreet activities of an inside workforce. When a brand owner must prevent its products from being counterfeited or gray marketed as much as it needs to prevent the theft of genuine goods, measures beyond conventional security are required. To protect these threats to brand integrity, monitoring employees and inventory is necessary.

The scope of security that a brand owner imposes on employees and inventory depends on several factors. If cost and efficiency were not necessary considerations, every brand owner would impose a level of scrutiny that is usually only found at highly classified government and military operations. Multiple layers to verify and re-verify an employee's authorization to enter and exit facilities would be in place. People, purses, wallets, cars, and other items would be routinely screened to ensure that no inventory, information, or other property was being improperly taken off-site. Of course, the economic and pragmatic realities of business preclude most companies from implementing such drastic approaches. Instead, brand owners must apply a set of measures that most effectively balance the tension between protecting their property and maintaining an efficient operation.

In addition to economics, this balancing exercise must consider the likelihood of a security breach as well as the potential of harm should such a breach occur. For example, food and pharmaceutical companies must exercise a great deal more care than, for example, a factory manufacturing tennis balls. Indeed, food and drug companies are required by statute to maintain records showing their products' full chain of custody.[97] Product and component tracking provides for the immediate identification of missing or undersized shipments as well as the name of the last person who touched it.[98] Even though these measures are imposed by law, these companies have concluded that such tracking measures ultimately pay for themselves in the form of brand security, cheaper insurance, and operational efficiency.[99]

---

96. Id.
97. See e.g., Public Health Security and Bioterrorism Preparedness and Response Act of 2002, Pub. L. No. 107-188, 116 Stat. 594 (2002); see also John D. Schultz, Paying for Protection; Air and ocean cargo security may be getting most of the attention lately, but truckers, railroads, and warehouses are paying plenty to keep domestic supply chains safe, LOGISTICS MANAGEMENT, May 1, 2006, at 43.
98. Terry, supra note 91, at 79.
99. Id. See also Maida Napolitano, How does your warehouse stack up? Our first annual survey of warehousing and distribution-center practices reveals that this industry is undergoing dynamic changes, LOGISTICS MANAGEMENT, Nov. 1, 2006, at 55. Tracking technology is used by the vast majority of warehouses with same-day shipping, with far less use of the technology reported for slower warehouses. Terry, supra note 91, at 79.

Many brand owners today track products with database software similar to the programs used by UPS or FedEx, thereby allowing companies and consumers to follow packages en route. In certain instances, more advanced programs will even track a product's component parts; this feature can be particularly helpful if a brand owner's components—but not necessarily the entire product—are vulnerable to gray market pouching.[100] Even more advanced programs that can track chemicals and other materials present in a product are anticipated in the near future.[101]

With respect to the procedure, products are typically tracked with barcodes on products or batches of products.[102] Scanning devices read the barcodes as the goods enter and exit each step of the distribution chain. One of the more sophisticated measures to track products is radio-frequency identification (RFID) wherein a small computer chip affixed to an item allows the item's route to be tracked wirelessly with various radio devices.[103] With RFID, items may even be tracked passively; even if no one is actively scanning the item, its presence in the facility can be monitored continuously and its movement can be instantly known.[104] The advantages of RFID are seen as far reaching. Some even predict RFID at the consumer checkout stand, complete with automatic billing to RFID credit cards.[105] However, RFID has also spawned a throng of critics, including those in the legislature, who fear its overuse and abuse in invading consumer privacy because of its versatile tracking capabilities.[106] However, the technology is largely free from controversy insofar as its use remains "behind the scenes" until products reach store shelves.[107]

Another method to prevent the production of unauthorized or counterfeit products is to monitor the raw materials or components that are the building blocks of a brand owner's product. Enforced procedures with respect to

---

100. Jean Thilmany, *Supply Chains Respond to Scandals With Product-Tracking Strategies*, MANUFACTURING BUSINESS TECHNOLOGY, Nov. 1, 2007, at 32.
101. *Id.*
102. Joy Orlek, *New Cargo Permits Offer Agents Massive Security Benefits*, FT Now, March 30, 2007. Bar-coding is still widely used (80% of warehouses with same-day shipping), as of 2006. Terry, *supra* note 91, at 79.
103. Steve Painter, *Chip-Tracked Items Spur Bright Visions and Some Dark Ones*, ARKANSAS DEMOCRAT GAZETTE, June 3, 2007, at 75. Wal-Mart heavily uses RFID along its entire chain of distribution. *Id.* RFID is used by 61% of same-day-shipping warehouses. Terry, *supra* note 91, at 79.
104. Painter, *supra* note 103.
105. *Id. See also* Grant Buckler, *Wireless systems let machines speak to each other; Remote links aid product tracking, fleet monitoring, meter reading*, THE GLOBE AND MAIL, Mar. 8, 2007, at B11.
106. Painter, *supra* note 103, at 75.
107. One particular RFID device even allows consumers to disable its functionality at will. Ann Bednarz, *IBM's 'Clipped' RFID Tag Ready for Market; Privacy-protecting Design from IBM Lets Consumers Tear the RFID Tag's Antenna to Reduce Its Read Range*, NETWORK WORLD FUSION, Nov. 9, 2006.

shipping, receiving, returned goods, product destruction, and product recycling are important ways to ensure that brand owners do not create an environment where there is a surplus of materials to easily create an unwanted ghost inventory.

In addition to physical materials, brand owners must exercise reasonable efforts to protect the *information* that is too sensitive to be disclosed. These items can be anything from a customer list to the trade secret that is essentially the blueprint to a company's success. Procedures with respect to the classification, control, and concealment of this proprietary information must be established and properly adhered to in order to protect unwanted competition from an individual or company enjoying the unfair advantage of having a brand owner's secret documents.

iii. Transit Security

When a product is manufactured and ready to begin its journey through a brand owner's authorized supply chain, it remains vulnerable to attack. From hijacked vehicles[108] to collusive diversion, the journey from the factory to the end user presents the most perilous stage of brand security. Authorized distributors and resellers will be constantly invited to enjoy the profits available in the lucrative gray market. In addition to properly vetting all members of the authorized supply chain, brand owners must continue to protect products from the hands of unauthorized participants.

With respect to products being diverted through theft during transit, these crimes are becoming more common. In Europe, a study found that truck drivers generally did not report such incidents to authorities.[109] Even when such crimes are reported, the non-violent nature of most heists will yield only a superficial investigation.[110] Meanwhile, criminally enterprising individuals see the lucrative bounty onboard, the lack of preventative security, and the unlikelihood of being caught as the trifecta of opportunity. Not surprisingly then, Europe and the United States have been witness to a striking increase in freight theft.[111]

The drivers may be "involved either actively or passively" in the crimes.[112] This reality underscores the importance of thorough background checks. In addition to investigating the backgrounds of partners and their employees, brand owners must be equally conscientious of those responsible for caring

---

108. James Falkner, *More Attacks on Europe's Truckers*, INT'L FREIGHTING WKLY., Mar. 3, 2008.
109. Id.
110. William Hoffman, *Cargo Theft Rising*, J. OF COM., Dec. 17, 2007.
111. See Falkner, *supra* note 108; id.
112. Id.

for their goods during transit. By partnering with a transit company known for appropriately screening its drivers and providing armored vehicles when necessary, a brand owner may spend more money on transportation costs to ultimately save a fortune. Through the ability to consistently guarantee the timely delivery of their products, brand owners can increase strength of their brand while simultaneously preventing and deterring criminals from trying purloin their goods.

Taking these measures will not guarantee that brand owners will be immune from all threats. Especially when the goods are particularly desirable, attempts at thievery are inevitable. By taking the steps reasonably necessary to prevent unwanted supply leakage, brand owners will typically have the benefit of thwarting both attempted crimes and *contemplated* crimes. Criminals want easy targets. If a brand owner manifests itself as being a worthy adversary, criminals will most likely turn to less discriminating prey.

iv. Product Security

Consumers do not want to pay brand-name prices for a counterfeit product that does not work or, even worse, is potentially dangerous. Consumers will similarly be vexed should they find that a brand owner will not honor a product's warranty because it was procured on the gray market. As previously articulated, such customer dissatisfaction is ultimately deleterious to the brand owner.

In addition to taking measures to prevent the likelihood that gray or black market products make their way onto stores' shelves, brand owners are also working towards arming consumers with the necessary tools to authenticate genuine products on their own.[113] The ultimate goal is to empower consumers with convenient programs that can be used with cell phones[114] or in-store kiosks that read a particular serial number[115] to instantly receive key product information. Information that can be provided includes a manufacturer's certification of authenticity and the item's assembly and shipping history.[116] In addition to combating counterfeiting, these programs will facilitate product recalls and other communications related to the product.[117]

---

113. *Id.* (quoting brand protection manager Jack Walsh) ("The consumer aspect is there to be taken advantage of, but no one has done it yet").
114. *See* Buckler, *supra* note 105, at B11.
115. Edward Boyle, *Coding: A Digital Signature*, Paper, Film & Foil Converter, July 1, 2007, at note 41.
116. *Id.*
117. Zino Davidoff SA v. CVS Corp., 2007 WL 1933932 (2007) (UPC codes allow for ability to pinpoint where and when breach in distribution chain occurred).

Other methods to distinguish genuine products from imitation products include specific authentication marks that are difficult to duplicate.[118] Brand owners can choose from a wide variety of difficult-to-copy security features to affix to their goods. Examples include labels that change color when scanned by certain verification tools.[119] Another technology that helps retailers ensure the authenticity of products is a system in which certain product labels can only be seen with a special lens:

> Using a proprietary, handheld plastic verifier lens, the technology indicates whether a document is genuine. When the verifier lens is held over a document or image, a multi-color hidden word, symbol, or image is displayed. In addition, if the document is copied, the prism image itself is not duplicated.[120]

No matter what method brand owners employ to prevent product imitations, counterfeiters inevitably catch up. History has shown that counterfeiters have the ambition and skill to continually improve the quality of fakes. Holographic imaging—a three-dimensional representation of an object, logo, or feature on a flat film—was once believed to be the panacea that could distinguish genuine products from impostors. Today, holographic technology has become much cheaper and much easier to duplicate. Seeing a holographic image no longer evokes the same confidence that the product's origin is a trustworthy source.

Another method to mark products or packaging is intaglio printing. This unique type of incised printing is common in currency and, given its unique texture, difficult to copy. A similar technology is "color shifting" technology. This system provides for ink used on a sign or label to change color when viewed at different angles. These technologies[121] are aimed at making it more difficult for products to be unlawfully copied or mimicked.

Moving beyond such technologies, nanotechnology—the use of microscopic circuitry and robotics for product authentication—is anticipated to be the next strategy among brand owners to distinguish their products from imitations. What has not been yet been established, however, is its current market viability.[122]

---

118. Lynn G. Crutchfield, *Brand Security & Product Authentication Special Report, Part 4*, PAPER, FILM & FOIL CONVERTER, July 1, 2006.
119. Dave Wicker, *Brand Security & Product Authentication Special Report, Part 2*, PAPER, FILM & FOIL CONVERTER, July 1, 2006.
120. *Id.*
121. *See e.g.*, Benjamin Jones, *Winemakers in Spain Take Protective Steps*, N.Y. TIMES, Nov. 24 2000, at C5 (Rioja winemakers added a small metallic strip to the labels of some of their wines to distinguish genuine bottles).
122. Press Release, University of Maine, University of Maine Alum to Speak on Nanotechnology Applications (Apr. 27, 2006).

In addition to these markings providing the ability to differentiate bogus products, such efforts can also engender consumer goodwill. Brand credibility improves when there is a perception that spurious products can be easily identified. Especially when a fake product could be dangerous, consumers need the confidence to know that hazardous clones are filtered from the marketplace. Even in instances in which consumers are not particularly keen about verifying the genuineness of a product, brand erosion will still occur if a black or gray market is allowed to thrive without opposition. To illustrate, consumers are less likely to be enraged to discover that they are watching a pirated DVD as they would be to discover that they fed their children counterfeit baby food. In terms of brand management, however, both hypothetical situations warrant a quick response.

The manufacturer of baby food must react immediately for obvious reasons. If the public infers that quality control problems exist, thereby making it impossible for the food maker or the consumer to ascertain what is and what is not a genuine product, the brand faces imminent extinction. The reasons the DVD manufacturer must likewise provide swift response are entirely different. Because a pirated DVD does not have safety or performance issues, the risk to the brand owner is that consumers will grow accustomed to the price of bootlegged products. Unless brand owners can effectively communicate the harm and consequences of watching these contraband products, consumers will become unwilling to pay brand-name prices when an illegal copy works just as well. Although ensuring that all albums or movies contain the generic copyright infringement admonition is worthwhile,[123] it is far from being an effective means to prevent such unlawful copying.

Mindful of this truth, DVD manufacturers created a specific region-encoding system several years ago. This system provided that a DVD distributed in Europe would not play on a DVD player distributed in North America and vice versa.[124] Although designed with noble intentions, the strategy ultimately failed. Although it stalled DVDs' inter-region transfers, pirates soon figured out how to disable the region restrictions.[125] In addition, "region-free" DVD players that played all DVDs, regardless of region, hit the marketplace as well.[126] Meanwhile, bona fide consumers were sometimes frustrated when legitimately purchased DVDs would not interface with the legitimately purchased DVD player.

---

123. Red Baron-Franklin Park, Inc. v. Taito Corp., 883 F. 2d 275 (4th Cir. 1989) (for video game units sold abroad, there was a notice stating that the game was for use in "Japan only" and that operation outside the territory may violate international copyright and trademark laws).
124. Ken Fisher, *Japan and US to share region encoding on Blu-ray*, ARS TECHNICA, Dec. 28, 2005, http://arstechnica.com/news.ars/post/20051228-5857.html.
125. *Id.*
126. *See* Region Free DVD Player Guide, http://buyersguide.bargainoffers.com/region_free_dvd_guide.shtml.

In terms of preventing unauthorized sales, codes and other tracking methods are necessary to determine whether certain shipments are being improperly diverted. Indeed, gray goods are often made with all of the signs attendant to a genuine product. In terms of preventing an unauthorized gray market at the consumer level, brand owners will often put limitations on the number of goods each consumer may purchase. When selling its new and popular iPhone, Apple Computer imposed restrictions on the number of units each consumer could purchase.[127] A static analysis of Apple's practice may seem counterproductive. After all, why would a brand owner ever want to *limit* the number of sales? There cannot be a justifiable reason for Apple to place a "cap" on the sales of its own products. However, a dynamic analysis of this practice is necessary to determine its wisdom: Limiting the number of iPhones per customer prevented any gray marketers garnering its own inventory to resell the products on the secondary market. In addition to exploring the latest technological measures that are currently baffling counterfeiters, brand owners should also keep in mind the simple, low-tech strategies that may be helpful as well.

---

127. *Apple Limits Sale of iPhones: Two Per Person and No Cash*, NY TIMES, Oct. 27, 2007, at C2.

CHAPTER 7

Alternative Gray Market Strategies

a. Worldwide Pricing	115
b. Staggered Distribution	116
c. Internal Distribution	117
d. IP Insurance	119

a. Worldwide Pricing

Because the gray market is created in large part because of disparate pricing schemes, one proposed strategy suggests to eradicate the gray market by selling goods at a fixed price regardless of the intended country of distribution. Courts reluctant to prohibit gray market practices have shared this opinion:

> If [the plaintiff] chooses to sell abroad at lower prices than those it could obtain for the identical product here, that is its business. In doing so, however, it cannot look to the United States trademark law to insulate the American market or to vitiate the effects of international trade. This country's trademark law does not offer [the plaintiff] a vehicle for establishing a worldwide discriminatory pricing scheme....[1]

The proposal that globally fixed prices will eradicate the gray market has two fundamental flaws. As an initial matter, it ignores the *de facto* price discrimination that will remain depending on the national or state taxes levied on the products. As chronicled in Chapter 4, the different tax schemes among Canadian provinces led to a fierce economy of gray market cigarettes. Second, disparate pricing schemes are a mandated reality of business. It is naïve to

---

1. NEC Electronics v. CAL Circuit Abco, 810 F.2d 1506 (9th Cir. 1987).

suggest that brand owners can solve the problem by having their laptops sell for the same price in Manhattan as they do in Jakarta. If brand owners were forced to employ such fixed prices, the global distribution of products would dry up as the prices would simply be out of reach of too many consumers.

For example, certain HIV anti-retroviral drugs can cost up to $15,000 per year in the United States.[2] The prices are designed to cover costs and continue R&D efforts. Through various humanitarian and charitable efforts, these same drugs are made available in Africa for a fraction of the cost. If pharmaceutical companies were forced to charge the same price to its American and African patients, its business model would not survive. The companies would have to either discontinue further R&D efforts or be resigned to the reality that its medicines would remain beyond the reach of needy patients in impoverished countries. Given the unwelcome consequences of either scenario, brand owners often have no choice but to employ disparate pricing schemes.

b. Staggered Distribution

In certain industries, staggering the distribution of products is common. According to the Motion Pictures Associate of America, for example, "[i]t is simply impossible with present technologies to supply film prints of a movie to all of the theaters around the world at the same time."[3] Therefore, film studios typically release their films in theaters in the United States and then overseas in a staggered sequence. After a film has debuted in a theater, it is released to the pay-per-view, video, and television market. To prevent interference with the revenue generated by the theatrical market, studios will also stagger the release of DVDs to only those countries where the film's theatrical run is complete. In fact, *supra*, DVDs are sometimes regionally coded to prevent them from even functioning in countries not yet authorized for distribution.[4]

The claim that it is "impossible" to have a theatrical release seems a little dubious. The decision to stagger products is often motivated by a brand owner's concern that enforcement of intellectual property rights is difficult or impractical. For example, Apple delayed the release of its popular iPhone in India by more than a year and a half following its release in the United States. Although the company did not articulate the basis for the delay, *The Telegraph*

---

2. HUNG FAN ET AL., AIDS: SCIENCE AND SOCIETY 91 (2007).
3. Motion Picture Association of America (MPAA) Frequently Asked Questions, http://www.mpaa.org/DVD_FAQ.asp (last visited Oct. 12, 2008).
4. *Id.*

of Calcutta surmised that it was Apple's concern over brand abuse that led the company to its decision: "India is one of the fastest growing mobile phone markets but there are still some doubts about the uptake of a product like the iPhone. Apple has reason to be apprehensive: official sales of the iPod are dwarfed by indistinguishable look-alikes in the gray market."[5]

For products like the iPhone, with which there is a high degree of hype prior to a domestic release, staggering the distribution of products is a prudent strategy. Limited distribution prevents gray marketers from capitalizing on the frenzied appetite for such products. Staggered distribution is, however, a stop-gap measure only. After the initial excitement of such goods has waned and the market has reached its equilibrium, the potential for arbitrage will remain. In other words, staggering distribution of products can be *part* of a brand owner's strategy; however, it cannot be the *only* strategy.

c. Internal Distribution

The economic advantages of outsourcing distribution responsibilities are accompanied by the unfortunate disadvantages of brand abuse. Every time a brand owner relies on a third-party company for brand promotion and distribution, there is an increased risk of breaches in the distribution channel. Most brand owners accept these hazards as simply doing business in a global economy, and exercise their best efforts to control the integrity of their channels with thorough due diligence, sound contracts, and steadfast monitoring of their channel partners.

One strategy brand owners can employ is to not outsource anything, although this method strays from the conventional wisdom. One brand owner that has implemented this strategy with remarkable success is Spanish brand owner Zara. With over six-hundred-fifty stores in over fifty countries,[6] Zara has one of the fastest supply chains in its industry. Although most apparel designers operate on a seasonal cycle in which it takes nine to twelve months for goods to go from design to a store's shelves,[7] Zara views the industry much differently. As the president of Zara's parent company Inditex

---

5. Jayati Ghose, *iPhone puts India on Hold*, THE TELEGRAPH (Calcutta, India), June 28, 2007, *available at* http://www.telegraphindia.com/1070628/asp/frontpage/story_7986060.asp# (The author's use of the term "gray market" in this context implies that its author actual meant *black* market).
6. Kasra Ferdows, Michael A. Lewis & Jose A.D. Machuca, *Rapid Fire Fulfillment*, *in* HARV. BUS. REV. ON SUPPLY CHAIN MGMT., 2006, at 50.
7. Devangshu Dutta, *Retail @ the Speed of Fashion*, 2002, http://www.3isite.com/articles/ImagesFashion_Zara_Part_I.pdf.

observed, "[t]his business is all about reducing response time. In fashion, stock is like food. It goes bad quick."[8]

Given this ephemeral perspective, Zara's supply chain can "design, produce, and deliver a new garment and put it on display in stores worldwide in a mere 15 days."[9] Zara's lightning quick supply chain is even more noteworthy because it "manages all design, warehousing, distribution, and logistic functions itself."[10] Zara's president Amancio Ortega summarizes his supply chain philosophy this way: "[Y]ou need to have five fingers touching the factory and five fingers touching the customer."[11] Zara's supply chain speed also allows the company to maintain a consistent panoply of goods for its consumers' selection: Zara's two hundred designers create approximately forty thousand new designs each year, from which ten thousand are selected for production.[12]

Controlling its distribution in-house and having no lag time between inspiration and consumer consumption of its garments also reduces the likelihood that its garments will be pouched by competitors cloning their designs. This latter advantage is somewhat ironic because Zara is chronically chastised for being a brand abuser itself. Although there are no current copyright protections for fashion designs, the Council of Fashion Designers of America is promoting the Design Piracy Prohibition Act,[13] which would create some limited protections in such works. In their advocacy for the law, Zara is often cited as one of the primary justifications: "Copycats have always been a thorn in the side of fashion designers, but never more so than today—with fast-fashion retailers including Forever 21, H&M and Zara churning out lower-priced versions of runway looks."[14]

Beyond brand protection, Zara has proven the viability of its supply chain model. In 2008, Inditex overtook well-known brand owner Gap, Inc. with worldwide sales[15] and higher net margins.[16] The ability of other brand owners adopting Zara's in-house model is typically limited by the constant tension between channel control and channel costs. Given the need for brand owners to adapt to changing market conditions, most are unwilling to invest heavily in production facilities. Even in Zara's industries, competitors like Gap and

---

8. *Id.*
9. Ferdows, *supra* note 6, at 51.
10. *Id.* at 52.
11. *Id.* at 51.
12. *Id.* at 54–55.
13. H.R. 5055, 109th Congress (2d Sess. 2006).
14. Emili Vesilind, *Under the Label: The New Pirates*, L.A. Times, Nov. 11, 2007, at P6.
15. Emma Soames, *How Zara Took Over the High Street*, The Telegraph (United Kingdom), Aug. 13, 2008, *available at* http://www.telegraph.co.uk/fashion/main.jhtml?xml=/fashion/2008/08/13/efzara113.xml
16. Ferdows *supra* note 6, at 51.

H&M do not own any production facilities.[17] In other industries, the need for fluidity is even more acute. For example, during the genesis of ink-jet technology, Hewlett-Packard (HP) elected to have its R&D and manufacturing divisions in Vancouver, Washington.[18] A decade later, after the technology had proven its reliability, HP outsourced its entire production of ink-jet technology to manufacturing vendors.[19]

This type of production agility can be impaired when brand owners are too anchored down with their own production assets. Although elements of Zara's supply strategy are worthy of emulation, the economic conditions will prevent most brand owners from being able to whole-heartedly adopt its model.

d. IP Insurance

IP insurance is a fairly new and small segment of the insurance market, but it does exist and has "been growing steadily" in recent years.[20] Most notably, policies can include coverage for information theft that occurs overseas.[21] Options are limited, however, and the majority of policies are for companies *accused* of intellectual property theft, rather than those victimized by it.[22] Also, coverage seems to mainly be targeted at breaches in computer security instead of willful employee leaks.[23] Despite the option of purchasing insurance, industry insiders still recommend thorough exercise of registration procedures and robust internal measures to prevent infringement.[24]

---

17. *Id.* at 60.
18. Hau L. Lee, *The Triple-A Supply Chain, in* Harv. Bus. Rev. on Supply Chain Mgmt., 2006, at 98.
19. *Id.* at 98.
20. *See* Gloria Gonzales, *Securing intellectual property; Few insurance options to cover ideas stolen overseas*, Bus. Ins., Feb. 20, 2006, fn. 59 (quoting Aaron Latto of St. Paul Travelers Co.).
21. *Id.*
22. *Id.*
23. *See id.*
24. *Id.*

PART III

Detection: Monitoring the Supply Chain

CHAPTER 8

Red Flags

The Warning Signs of Gray Market Activity

a.	Pricing That Is Too Low	123
b.	Unreasonable Spikes in Orders	125
c.	Unusual Orders	126
d.	Special Discount Requests	126
e.	Warranty Exchange Requests	128
f.	Unusual Delivery Requests	129

Secrecy is paramount for product diversion to succeed. The channel partner guilty of initiating the product leakage must be sufficiently discreet to hide the activity from the brand owner. The parties receiving the leaked goods must take sufficient steps to disguise the products' origin. From removing product codes that could provide the whereabouts of the distribution breach to creating intentionally circuitous chains of custody, gray marketers cooperate to prevent brand owners from discovering the existence of the problem or the location of its genesis.

To counteract these efforts, brand owners must assiduously police the buying and selling of their goods. Because of the covert nature of the gray market, brand owners must know what to look for in order for its policing strategy to work. The following pages identify some of the particular warning signs that should warn brand owners to look further at a particular company or transaction.

a. Pricing That Is Too Low

One of the easiest methods to detect gray or black market activity is for a brand owner to monitor the prices of its products. Advertisements that channel partners are selling goods for below cost may be symptomatic of improper sales. Although channel partners may on occasion need to slash prices to rid themselves of excess inventory, partners are in the business of *making* money. Resellers or distributors should not be offering such bargains with regularity. In 2001, a reporter for the *New York Times* lampooned his brother for his credulous purchasing behavior:

> My brother Dan is an otherwise smart person who for reasons I cannot begin to understand does not always follow my advice. I submit as evidence a transcript of a recent conversation:
>
> . . .
>
> Dan: . . . I called to tell you to let your readers know about a great deal I just got on a Sony camcorder. It lists for $1,799 but I found it online for $969.
>
> Me (suspiciously): You got a price like that from an authorized dealer?
>
> Dan: I don't know. It's a European model.
>
> Me: Oh my God, that's a gray-market camera! It might not even plug into anything in this country! Don't buy it.
>
> Dan: I already did. This is a bad connection (sound of brother blowing air into the phone), you're breaking up (sound of brother tapping a finger against the receiver). Bye.
>
> I included this sad snippet of dialogue because it illustrates a problem far more troubling and far more pervasive than even sibling rivalry: the pitfalls of buying consumer electronics online.[1]

It is not only consumers like Dan that need to be suspicious of too-good-to-be-true prices. Brand owners must be equally circumspect of such deals. To the extent such products are being advertised, brand owners should conduct further investigation to find out exactly what is being sold. Low prices may mean the goods are used, gray, or counterfeit. In the pharmaceutical industry, for example, "[t]he Big Three (pharmaceutical distributors) have trading divisions that scout the secondary wholesale market for discounted medicine."[2]

When unreasonably discounted products are discovered, it is often necessary for brand owners to make brand protection purchases.[3] Unless the brand owner disguises its identity from the entity advertising these low-priced

---

1. Michelle Slatalia, *Online Shopper; When a Low Price Raises a Red Flag*, N.Y. TIMES, Oct. 4, 2001, at G4.
2. Katherine Eban, *Bad Medicine*, VANITY FAIR, May 2005, *available at* http://www.dangerousdoses.com/pdf/badmedicine.pdf.
3. For further discussion on brand protection purchases, see Chapter 9.

goods, it runs the risk of not getting an accurate picture of the suspected sales—if the party selling the products knows that the purchaser is the brand owner, it will ensure that the goods sold are not infringing products.

b. Unreasonable Spikes in Orders

In Major League Baseball, the 1990s and first few years of this millennium were marked by an unusual spike in home run productivity. Because home runs are among the most exciting parts of a ball game, popularity of the nation's pastime skyrocketed as players chased and broke various home run records that had been untouched since the 1960s. More fans tuned into and attended games, thereby increasing earning expectations for the team owners. As a result, revenues and muscles continued to swell until it was exposed that a large but largely unknowable number of players had relied on illegal steroids and other performance enhancing drugs. In March 2006, the Commissioner of Baseball Alan H. ("Bud") Selig requested that former Senator George J. Mitchell investigate the allegation that several players had used illegal steroids and performance enhancing drugs. Senator Mitchell's 400-page report issued the following year reads like an indictment against Major League Baseball's inability to police itself.[4]

Although baseball's failure to immediately investigate the cause for its players ballooning size and production is not forgivable, it is understandable. The Steroid Era, to which it is now referred, provided a benefit to everyone: fans enjoy seeing home runs, players were hitting and throwing balls harder, further, and faster, and owners were the benefactors of the gripping popularity of the game. None of the stakeholders in the game had any short-term incentives to stop what was happening. Had these same stakeholders had the foresight to consider what would happen once the cheating rings were exposed, they may have acted differently. The Steroid Era is now considered one of baseball's darkest times and several of the famous players of this period are now considered *infamous* representatives of a shameful and embarrassing racket.

Looking back, almost everyone in baseball shares at least some culpability. In hindsight, what is most remarkable is that no one in baseball's authority asked whether what was going on was simply too good to be true. Middle infielders that had never hit more than five or ten home runs were now

---

4. *See* George J. Mitchell, Report to the Commissioner of Baseball of an Independent Investigation into the Illegal Use of Steroids and other Performance Enhancing Substances by Players in Major League Baseball, (2007), *available at* http:// mlb.mlb.com/mlb/news/mitchell/index.jsp (describing Major League Baseball's drug policy).

consistently hitting over thirty or forty home runs and there was unwillingness to investigate the improbable spike in productivity.

Brand owners must not be tempted to make the same mistakes in reviewing the productivity of its authorized distributors and resellers. Of course, it is possible for an authorized reseller to dramatically increase its earnings in a short period time. The increased revenue will benefit the brand owner as well. Like baseball's team owners, there is a temptation not to disrupt this stream of revenue. However, brand owners must remain mindful of the attendant harm that can occur if this ostensibly productive reseller is not selling to end users. Indeed, "[c]orrupt wholesalers [or other gray marketers] often solicit those who qualify for discounts to buy more [goods] than they need and sell the rest of kickbacks."[5] If months or even years go by while a reseller pours goods into the gray market, the harm to the brand can be quite profound if the brand owner remains idle. When brand owners detect such spikes, due diligence is necessary to verify the legitimacy of the partners' sales.

c. Unusual Orders

Unusual orders can often be a sign that a channel partner is supplementing its business by procuring products from the gray market. Like a shopper that buys hamburger patties and mustard every two weeks from the same grocer—but not hamburger buns—certain orders can tip retailers off that its customers are getting other necessary goods elsewhere. Brand owners must have policies in place to follow up on suspicious orders.

The industry will obviously dictate what types of orders are worthy of a follow-up investigation. In the technology industry, for example, it would be unusual for a reseller to order from a distributor one thousand central processing units (CPUs) but not a single computer monitor. Although it may be a rare occasion that the end user does not in fact need any monitors or the reseller may have previously purchased monitors for its inventory, the nature of the order should trigger the brand owner to do some further due diligence. A likely possibility is that the reseller did not purchase the monitors from an authorized distributor because it was already able to procure the goods from a gray or black marketer.

d. Special Discount Requests

As mentioned in Chapter 6 *supra*, many brand owners will offer additional discounts for authorized resellers if the reseller is competing for a particularly

---

5. *Id.*

large account. Because the volume of these prospective transactions is so lucrative, brand owners are willing to cut their margins even further to ensure the sale is not lost to one of its customers. Special discounts may also be provided when the end user is a nonprofit entity; additional discounts are thus common when the end user is an educational, governmental, or non-profit entity.

Although most brand owners will require the reseller to provide information to justify the requested discount, brand owners—or the sales representatives earning a commission on the transaction—will not verify the probity of information submitted. Failing to verify that the requested discount is legitimate can lead to severe abuse. Brand owners must monitor the type and frequency with which such discounts are requested. Such an abuse was chronicled in *Hewlett-Packard Co. v. Capital City Micro, Inc.*[6] The plaintiff, HP, manufactured various computer products and sold its goods through authorized distributors and resellers. HP's domestic resellers were allowed to purchase goods from authorized distributors and sell only to end users in the United States.[7]

HP had a pricing program called the "Big Deal" program, which allowed authorized resellers to provide competitive pricing to "qualified, large-volume end users."[8] To obtain the "Big Deal" discount, HP's resellers were required to provide specific information regarding the identity of the specific end user and the number of items to be purchased.[9] If HP approved the request, the reseller could then file a claim with HP for reimbursement of the difference between the price paid by the reseller and the discounted price reflected in the "Big Deal" quote.[10]

The defendant Capital City Micro, Inc. (Capital City) requested a "Big Deal" discount on a monthly basis for one year. Capital City represented to HP that it would purchase fifteen hundred laptop computers for a specific end user, P & E, an Anheuser-Busch beer distributor. HP agreed to Capital City's "Big Deal" proposal. As a result, Capital City ordered the laptops and submitted invoices to HP reflecting the alleged sales to P & E.[11]

Six months later, HP discovered that the products sold to Capital City intended for P & E had actually been improperly sold in Saudi Arabia. When HP confronted Capital City with the discrepancy, it was unable to furnish an adequate explanation. Accordingly, HP submitted an invoice for over $2 million representing Capital City's unearned discount on its "Big Deal" purchases.[12]

---

6. Hewlett-Packard Co. v. Capital City Micro, Inc, 2006 WL 149034 (M.D.Tenn. 2006) (Unpublished).
7. *Id.* at *1.
8. *Id.* at *2.
9. *Id.*
10. *Id.*
11. *Id.*
12. *Id.* (HP alleged that a similar scheme was done by Capital City with respect to Compaq, before HP and Compaq merged).

During the course of discovery, it was uncovered that Capital City had used P & E as a phantom end user for Toshiba computers as well. In fact, in a class action settlement involving Toshiba end users, P & E was entitled to a portion of the settlement. Knowing that Capital City was not a true end user, P & E's president refused to sign the class action claim form. A claim form was ultimately submitted and the presidents of Capital City and P & E split over $2.8 million. In their dealings with HP, however, Capital City and P & E repeatedly assured HP that P & E was the end user.[13]

It is unclear how HP discovered that various products were being re-routed to Saudi Arabia. However, the case illustrates how far disingenuous partners may be willing to go in order to defraud a brand owner out of its legitimate pricing scheme. In addition to requesting information from the channel partner and repeated "reassurances," brand owners should have a follow-up policy with the alleged end users to ensure that the products they allegedly purchased is actually be used.

e. Warranty Exchange Requests

Another method in which gray marketers will defraud brand owners is through bogus warranty claims. Many brand owners will offer service contracts for various products, which allow for the repair or replacement of broken or worn out parts. Brand abuse can occur when purchasers will use the service contracts for purposes of fraudulently obtaining replacement parts for *free* to sell on the secondary market.

Nortel Networks, Inc. v. SMC Electronics, LLC,[14] involved such claims of warranty fraud. Brand owner Nortel Networks, Inc. (Nortel) manufactured and sold various networking equipment through authorized channels. The product at issue in the case was its Ethernet Routing Switch 8600 (ERS 8600).

Because of the importance of minimizing a network's downtime, the ERS 8600 allowed for many of its components to be "hot swappable." Hot swapping (also known as hot plugging) is the ability to remove and replace components of a machine while it is still operating. This convenient feature allows a business to have its network components replaced without suffering any network disruption or outages. In order for Nortel's customers to take advantage of the ERS 8600's "hot swappable" capabilities, Nortel offered its customers Professional Service Agreements (PSA)'s wherein customers could receive service support as well as the ability to return and replace various components.

---

13. *Id.* at *3.
14. Nortel Networks, Inc. v. SMC Electronics, LLC, Case No. 06-CV-00787-RJC (W.D. Okl. 2006).

To make sure an end user's network did not suffer any unwanted uptime disruption, Nortel allowed its customer to first request and receive a replacement component before having to send the defective part back to Nortel. Once the replacement had taken place, the customer was obligated to return the allegedly defective component to Nortel.

The case began when Nortel discovered that SMC essentially became a gray market distributor by misusing Nortel's PSA. Specifically, SMC purchased a PSA ostensibly for its own ERS 8600. After its purchase, however, SMC began ordering various replacement parts in very large volumes pursuant to the terms of its PSA.

A short time later, Nortel was contacted by Children's Hospital of Philadelphia (CHOP) because the thirty-five pieces of Network Hardware it had recently acquired were not working. Because there was no record that CHOP was a Nortel customer, Nortel conducted some further investigation. In its investigation, it discovered that CHOP's parts were "replacement" parts that were sent to SMC. Indeed, SMC was using its PSA to fraudulently obtain components from Nortel and reselling the parts on the gray market. Before a trial on the merits, SMC stipulated to a judgment of $10 million.[15]

The case illustrates the unintended consequences of policies designed to improve service and customer satisfaction. When products like the ERS 8600 require the replacement of products before the end user *returns* the broken or worn out product, brand owners must have policies in place to monitor the legitimacy, volume, and frequency of such requests. If the requests reveal anything questionable, further investigation is required.

f. Unusual Delivery Requests

A dark alley is the quintessential locale for transactions of dubious legality. Although the buying and selling of gray market goods will rarely take place in dark alleys, how and where goods are delivered is relevant to a brand owner's or partner's analysis of whether the transaction is worthy of suspicion. For example, the insistence that goods be delivered or picked up at remote locations is an obvious red flag. P.O. boxes in lieu of physical office locations are another potential indicator that the transaction is not what was represented. Deliveries that lack a return address are an obvious cause for concern. Although there can be instances in which the businesses have legitimate needs to protect the identity of the ultimate end user or supplier, the motivations may not be benign. Any efforts to obfuscate the identity, location, origin, or destination of products should be investigated further as the motivation for secrecy may be to hide illicit activity.

---

15. *Id.*

CHAPTER 9

Methods of Detection

"Trust, but verify."
—Ronald W. Reagan (1911–2004)

a.	Audits	131
b.	Internet Monitoring	133
c.	Brand Protection Purchases	134
	i. The Uncertain Future of Brand Protection Purchases	138
d.	Informants	140
e.	Dumpster Diving	140

Whether or not warning signs of gray market activity exist, protecting brand integrity requires businesses to monitor the marketplace for possible supply chain leaks. In order to detect gray market activity, the methods often require clandestine strategies by the brand owner or its agents. The fact that covertness is required does not mean, however, that brand owners should be laconic about the existence of their detection efforts. Like announcing the presence of undercover air marshals on airlines to deter terrorism,[1] brand owners should likewise make it notoriously known in the industry that they are doing the necessary legwork to ferret out any unlawful activity. The following describes some of the available methods to ascertain whether various players in a distribution channel are not adhering to their duties and obligations.

a. Audits

As discussed in Chapter 6, brand owners should ensure that their authorized distributor and reseller contracts provide an unfettered right to audit the

---

1. President George W. Bush, Remarks at the Georgia World Congress Center (Nov. 8, 2001) ("We have posted the National Guard in America's airports and placed undercover air marshals on many flights.") (excerpts available at N.Y. TIMES, Nov. 9, 2001, at B6).

books and records of its channel partners. Although the mere presence of these clauses will have a deterring value, exercising these contractual rights with regularity is a much more effective method of promoting gray market abstinence and is also necessary to detect improper activity.[2]

It should first be noted that exercising audit rights does not have to be a costly or overly burdensome endeavor. A full blown audit is rarely necessary. Random spot checks can often be sufficient to reveal, at the very least, suspicious activity. For example, brand owners often require that their authorized resellers provide monthly point-of-sale (POS) reports identifying the customers that purchased products in the previous month. Requiring such reports is useful because they require the authorized reseller to expressly affirm that its customers are end users within any applicable territory restrictions and not unauthorized gray marketers. In reality, brand owners have neither the resources nor the interest in verifying every POS entry. That does not mean, however, that no verifying efforts should take place. Telephone calls to a random sampling of customers identified in POS reports can quickly and easily establish the reliability of a reseller's representations.

Resellers that are selling products on the gray market may be mindful of the risk of providing false customer information, and may simply omit all gray market transactions from their POS reports. Resellers may also be acquiring their products from gray market importers rather than authorized distributors designated by the brand owner. To safeguard against these transactions slipping below the radar, brand owners must similarly make periodic cross-references of an authorized reseller's revenues to the volume of product the reseller purchased from authorized distributors. Imbalances of any significance are a strong indication of gray market activity and should be investigated.

"It is difficult to get a man to understand something when his salary depends on his not understanding it."[3] It is likewise difficult to get a man to find something when his finding it will reduce his salary. Although gray market activity damages a business, it may not necessarily damage the pocket book of certain employees. For example, a brand owner's sales employees are generally compensated in an amount tied to the revenues of the authorized resellers they support. A sales employee will typically earn commissions on an authorized reseller's sales regardless of whether the purchaser is a legitimate end user or an unauthorized gray marketer. Thus, that same sales employee may jeopardize his or her personal income by reporting any reseller

---

2. *See e.g.*, *The Grey Market*, KPMG/Anti-Gray Mkt. Alliance, 2003, at 3, *available at* http://www.agmaglobal.org/press_events/press_docs/KPMG_TheGreyMarket_Web.pdf (listing routine compliance audits among various methods to improve contract compliance of authorized channel partners).
3. UPTON SINCLAIR, I, CANDIDATE FOR GOVERNOR AND HOW I GOT LICKED (Farrar & Rinehart 1935).

infractions to the brand owner. Given these conflicting incentives, brand owners must recognize that the employees that economically *benefit* from gray market activity should not be the same employees in charge of *reporting* gray market activity. Unfortunately, most companies have mistakenly delegated gray market responsibility to employees with these conflicted interests.[4] To preserve the integrity of gray market audits, the income of auditing employees should not correspond with the success of the resellers they are overseeing.

Finally, in the event that spot checks uncover suspicious activity that may lead to litigation, brand owners should engage a third party to conduct a formal audit of the targeted reseller. If a brand owner waits until after initiating litigation, any audit or inspection of documents must be done pursuant to the discovery rules of litigation wherein attorneys for the reseller can impair the scope and efficiency of an audit while simultaneously increasing the attendant costs. By relying on the audit clause of the parties' contract, resellers cannot reasonably refuse to cooperate without breaching the agreement. In addition, by having an objective third party auditor complete the audit, the brand owner will better be able to stave off attacks from the reseller that the evidence gathered is somehow not reliable or trustworthy.

b. Internet Monitoring

With the Internet becoming the venue of choice for so many illegitimate enterprises,[5] brand owners protecting their brands must be alert to the threat the Internet has on the stability of their business. Gray market and counterfeit goods are routinely bought and sold on various trading boards, auction sites, business-to-business (B2B) trading networks, and E-commerce Web sites.

At a minimum, brand owners must periodically monitor the Internet for the sale of their products on the black and gray market as well as for the unauthorized use of their trademarks. The challenge of manually searching the Internet for unlawful activity is simply the massive volume of information that must sifted through to locate any relevant material. Merely googling[6]

---

4. *See e.g., The Grey Market*, KPMG/Anti-Gray Mkt. Alliance, 2003, at 3, *available at* http://www.agmaglobal.org/press_events/press_docs/KPMG_TheGreyMarket_Web.pdf (in a survey of original equipment manufacturers, 61% placed the responsibility of gray market issues in sales and marketing departments).
5. For further discussion on the Internet's impact on the gray market, see Chapter 3.
6. The verb "google" has indeed made it into our lexicon. *Webster's New Millennium Dictionary of English, Preview Edition (v 0.9.7)*, http://dictionary.reference.com/browse/google (defining google as the verb "to search for information about a specific person through the Google search engine.").

the brand name is insufficient. Brand owners must be familiar with the locations on the Internet where abuses of their brands are most likely to be found. For example, if a brand owner manufactures telecommunications equipment, it must search industry specific trading networks such as the NATD.[7] In addition, brand owners must also search the more obvious Internet dwellings of corruption discussed in Chapter 6.

Because of the difficulty in manually monitoring the Internet, there are several companies that offer monitoring services to detect brand abuse. MarkMonitor,[8] for example, which is based in San Francisco, with regional offices in London, New York, and Washington D.C., offers solutions to help brand owners protect their sales channels from a variety of online harms. MarkMonitor offers customers its Online Channel Protection (OCP) software, which automatically and continuously gathers relevant information to expose unauthorized resellers of their branded products. The OCP software will also help brand owners identify the worst offenders based on criteria such as sales volume, price variance, usage of trademarked images, location of the web server, and Web site traffic. The OCP software can be managed internally by the brand owner or externally by MarkMonitor employees. When the brand owner determines which gray marketers to pursue, MarkMonitor can investigate the identities of the selected offenders and coordinate the issuance of warning letters, cease and desist letters, and delisting requests to various auction and B2B exchanges.

c. Brand Protection Purchases

A brand protection—or pretext—purchase typically occurs when a brand owner hires investigators to pose as consumers to ascertain how the alleged infringer represents itself to the consuming public.[9] Similar to undercover agents in criminal cases or discrimination testers in civil rights cases,[10] pretext purchasers are often the best tools available to detect violations of

---

7. North American Association of Telecommunications Dealers ("NATD"), Member Benefits, http://www.natd.com/public/pages/natdbenefits.asp (Members of the NATD are entitled to use its online trading network where dealers can buy and sell telecommunications equipment.).
8. MarkMonitor, Online Channel Protection, http://www.markmonitor.com/products/online_channel_protection.php (last visited Oct. 12, 2008).
9. International Trademark Association ("INTA"), *Pretext Investigations in U.S. Trademark Infringement Cases*, Oct. 11, 2007, http://inta.org/index.php?option=com_content&task=view&id=1749&Itemid=153&getcontent=3.
10. *See e.g.,* Richardson v. Howard, 712 F.2d 319, 321-22 (7th Cir. 1990) (observing that the evidence provided by testers is frequently indispensable and that the requirement of deception is a relatively small price to pay to defeat racial discrimination).

the law. No authorized reseller will admit to a manufacturer that it is buying and selling products on the gray market. To observe an authorized reseller's true behavior, the reseller must believe it is communicating with a *legitimate customer*.

In the context of trademark or copyright infringement, the law is generally supportive of pretext purchases. In *Gidatex v. Campaniello Imports, Ltd.*,[11] the court upheld the legality of pretext purchases. The plaintiff Gidatex owned the federally registered trademark "Saporiti Italia" to be used in connection with its furniture accessories. The defendant Campaniello was a former authorized sales agent of Gidatex. After Gidatex terminated the agency relationship, it alleged that Campaniello continued to unlawfully use the Saporiti Italia marks. Specifically, Gidatex alleged that Campaniello engaged in a "bait and switch" tactic wherein it would lure customers into its showrooms with Saporiti Italia advertisements, but then sell furniture produced by other manufacturers.[12]

To prove its "bait and switch" theory, Gidatex's attorney hired two private investigators to pose as interior designers visiting Campaniello's showrooms and secretly tape-record conversations with Campaniello's salespeople.[13] The private investigators paid several visits to Campaniello's showrooms, both before and during litigation, and recorded conversations with salespeople.[14]

Prior to trial, Campaniello filed a motion to exclude all evidence pertaining to the pretext visits on the grounds that Gidatex's attorney violated the Codes of Professional Responsibility established by the American Bar Association (ABA) and the New York State Bar Association (NYSBA) by causing the investigators to communicate with a party known to be represented by counsel. The ABA's disciplinary rule 7-104 provides that "a lawyer shall not ... communicate or cause another to communicate on the subject of the representation with a party the lawyers knows to be represented by a lawyer in the matter unless the lawyer has the prior consent of the lawyer representing such other party or is authorized by law to do so."[15]

---

11. Gidatex v. Campaniello Imports, Ltd., 82 F. Supp. 2d 119 (S.D.N.Y. 1999).
12. *Id.* at 119.
13. Many states have *per se* rules prohibiting and even criminalizing recoding conversations without the other party's consent. *See e.g.*, CAL. PENAL CODE § 632(a) (2007) ("Every person who, intentionally and without the consent of all parties to a confidential communication, by means of any electronic amplifying or recording device, eavesdrops upon or records the confidential communication, whether the communication is carried on among the parties in the presence of one another or by means of a telegraph, telephone, or other device, except a radio, shall be punished by a fine not exceeding two thousand five hundred dollars ($2,500), or imprisonment in the county jail not exceeding one year, or in the state prison, or by both that fine and imprisonment.")
14. *Id.* at 120–21.
15. MODEL CODE OF PROF'L RESPONSIBILITY DR 7-104(A)(1)(2007); *see also* N.Y. COMP. CODES R. & REGS. TIT. 22, § 1200.35 (2007). Most states have similar prohibitions on *ex parte*

Rejecting Campaniello's arguments, the court reasoned that the ethical rules should not govern situations in which an undercover agent is posing as a member of the general public to legitimately investigate unfair business practices.[16] As an initial matter, the ethical rules were intended to preserve the attorney-client relationship. Because the investigators were merely impersonating interested customers, there was no risk that the salespeople would disclose information protected by the attorney-client privilege. In addition, the court noted that disallowing such investigative methods could allow targets to freely engage in unfair business practices that are harmful to both trademark owners and consumers.[17]

A similar ruling can be found in *Apple Corp. v. Int'l Collectors Soc'y*.[18] In *Apple*, the plaintiffs owned and controlled various trademarks and copyrights associated with the legendary rock-n-roll band, The Beatles. The plaintiffs commenced litigation when they discovered that the defendants were selling postage stamps bearing images of The Beatles without any authorization. Several months after initiating litigation, the plaintiffs filed a motion for a temporary restraining order and preliminary injunction[19] barring the defendants from selling any stamps containing any likeness of The Beatles.

Prior to the hearing on the preliminary injunction, the parties entered into a consent order wherein the defendants were prohibited from selling any stamps bearing the image of The Beatles.[20] Several months later, the parties purported to resolve the entire lawsuit with a similar consent order, which, with limited exceptions, permanently prohibited the defendants from selling stamps or other products bearing or referring to the name The Beatles or John Lennon.[21] Shortly thereafter, the plaintiffs' attorney instructed various individuals and investigators to pose as customers in order to verify defendants' compliance with the consent order.[22] Upon discovering numerous violations, the plaintiffs reinitiated litigation and used the pretext communications to prove defendants' indiscretions.

In opposition to the contempt motion, the defendants sought to dissolve the consent order. The defendants alleged that the plaintiffs breached the implied covenant of good faith and fair dealing by, among other things, using

---

communications with parties known to be represented by counsel. *See e.g.*, CAL. RULE OF PROF. CONDUCT 2-100(A) (2007) ("[A] member shall not communicate directly or indirectly about the subject of the representation with a party the member knows to be represented by another lawyer in the matter, unless the member has the consent of the other lawyer.")

16. *Gidatex*, 82 F. Supp. 2d at 122.
17. *Id.*
18. Apple Corp. v. Int'l Collectors Soc'y, 15 F. Supp. 2d 456 (D.N.J. 1998).
19. For further discussion on the use of temporary restraining orders and preliminary injunctions, see Chapter 11.
20. *Id.* at 458–59.
21. *Id.* at 460.
22. *Id.* at 461–64.

individuals and investigators to improperly "test" their compliance with the consent order. The defendants argued that through the use of "intimidation, misrepresentation, and unethical conduct," the plaintiffs' investigators provoked the defendants' breach of the consent order. The court rejected this argument. It found no evidence of intimidation. With respect to misrepresentation, the court concluded that the misrepresentation was necessary to discover the defendants' violations of the consent order and did not constitute unethical behavior.[23]

Similar to *Gidatex, supra*, the defendants also argued that the plaintiffs' conduct violated various ethical rules governing the conduct of attorneys. The court similarly concluded that no violations occurred. Relying on analogous authority, the court noted that the limited use of deception to learn about ongoing wrongdoing in the criminal or civil rights context has not been condemned on ethical grounds by the courts.[24]

In *Midwest Motor Sports v. Arctic Sales, Inc.*,[25] however, the court excluded tape recordings obtained by a private investigator on ethical grounds. The case arose out of a dispute between Arctic Cat, a snowmobile manufacturer, and two dealers, Elliot and A-Tech. Elliot sued Arctic Cat when it terminated its franchise and established A-Tech as a new franchisee in the same city. During discovery, Arctic Cat's attorney hired a private investigator to visit Elliot and A-Tech and secretly record conversations with each dealer's employees.[26]

During his deposition, the investigator admitted that he had been instructed by Arctic Cat's attorney to record anything a "representative might say about the lawsuit."[27] He further admitted talking with the president and owner of one of the dealers. The court concluded that the conduct of Arctic Cat's investigator violated the ABA's Model Rules of Professional Conduct, which had been adopted by South Dakota.[28] Given that it would have been unethical for Arctic Cat's attorney to communicate with the president about matters relevant to the lawsuit, it was likewise improper for the attorney's agent to do the same.[29]

Arctic Cat's attorneys tried to shield themselves from culpability by arguing that they instructed the investigator to only speak with low-level

---

23. *Id.* at 471.
24. *Id.* at 475.
25. Midwest Motor Sports v. Arctic Sales, Inc., 347 F.3d 693 (8th Cir. 2003).
26. *Id.* at 695.
27. *Id.* at 696.
28. *See* MODEL RULES OF PROF'L CONDUCT R. 4.2 (2002) ("In representing a client, a lawyer shall not communicate about the subject of the representation with a person the lawyer knows to be represented by another lawyer in the matter, unless the lawyer has the consent of the other lawyer or is authorized to do so by law or a court order.")
29. *Id.* at 697–98.

sales people. The court was not persuaded by this attempt at "passing the buck" to the investigator.[30] Even if such instructions were given, lawyers cannot escape responsibility for the wrongdoing they supervise by asserting that it was their agents, not themselves, who committed the wrong.[31]

The holding of *Arctic Cat* is not irreconcilable with *Gidatex* and *Apple*. The investigator in *Arctic Cat* sought to obtain admissions about the dealer's sales volumes and practices, which was a "critical portion" of the parties' million-dollar damages analyses.[32] In the latter cases, however, the investigators were simply posing as interested customers to ascertain the representations being made or products being sold in the sales process. Brand owners and their counsel must therefore ensure that its investigators only elicit information that would typically be disclosed in an ordinary sales transaction. Once investigators cross the line and explore information that would otherwise be privileged or not ordinarily disclosed, the pretext communications are no longer proper.

i. The Uncertain Future of Brand Protection Purchases

The use of "pretexting" has come under recent scrutiny in the wake of the HP scandal wherein private investigators illegally used false pretenses to obtain personal information of various HP board members. The controversy began when one of HP's board members, Patricia Dunn, wanted to find out which of her fellow directors was leaking information to the media. Ms. Dunn authorized a team of independent electronic-security experts to obtain the personal phone records of her fellow board members. Although the phone records revealed a pattern of calls made to media outlets, thereby exposing the divulging director, the tactics used by Ms. Dunn's team were quickly denounced as unethical and illegal.[33]

What caused so much controversy was the method in which Ms. Dunn's investigators obtained personal telephone records. Describing the practice as "pretexting," it was discovered that the investigators would call telephone companies and falsely identify themselves as various HP directors in order to obtain copies of each members' personal account. Because the deception led phone company employees to disclose private information, Ms. Dunn and

---

30. *Id.* at 698.
31. *Id.*
32. *Id.*
33. David A. Kaplan, *Intrigue in High Places*, NEWSWEEK, Sept. 5, 2006, *available at* http://www.newsweek.com/id/45735 ("The entire episode—beyond its impact on the boardroom of a $100 billion company, Dunn's ability to continue as chairwoman and the possibility of civil lawsuits claiming privacy invasions and fraudulent misrepresentations—raises questions about corporate surveillance in a digital age.").

those involved were all criminally charged with illegally gathering phone records of her fellow board members.[34]

The pretexting in the Hewlett-Packard case is fundamentally different from a pretext purchase used to discover trademark or copyright infringement. Nonetheless, the outrage over Ms. Dunn's spying endeavors have caused lawmakers to propose statutory prohibitions against pretexting that could impair a brand owner's ability to conduct a legitimate pretext purchase. For example, in California the legislature has considered this issue in Senate Bill 328, which would prohibit the use of "pretexting" to obtain personal information about any individual.[35] Although the bill is intended to protect one's privacy from illegal techniques used to gather personal information, there is concern that it may ban all private use of pretext investigations, including pretext purchases.

In response to such statutory proposals, industry groups advocating the rights of trademark and copyright owners have responded. The International Trademark Association (INTA) is a non-profit membership association dedicated to the protection of trademarks and related intellectual property.[36] On December 23, 2007, INTA's Board of Directors approved a resolution articulating its position with respect to pretext investigations in trademark infringement cases. Specifically, INTA is "concerned about the proposed S.B. 328 ('the Bill'), currently being considered by the California legislature, which if made law will effectively prohibit all private uses of pretext investigations, including trademark pretext investigations."[37] INTA endorses ethical and legal pretexting as an essential tool in investigating and combating infringement and counterfeiting and it urges governments not to prohibit private uses of pretext investigations with respect to infringement and counterfeiting.[38]

The music and movie industries have similarly lobbied state legislators to preserve their right to engage in pretext purchases to pursue counterfeiters. Pretext purchases are necessary, the Recording Industry Association of America and the Motion Picture Association of America contend, in order to crack various piracy rings.[39] Until specific statutory prohibitions are

---

34. Damon Darlin, *Ex-Chairwoman Among 5 Charged In Hewlett Case*, N.Y. TIMES, October 5, 2006, at A1.
35. S.B. 328 Leg., Reg. Sess. (2007).
36. International Trademark Association ("INTA"), About INTA, http://www.inta.org/index.php?option=com_content&task=view&id=14&Itemid=37&getcontent=4.
37. International Trademark Association ("INTA"), *Pretext Investigations in U.S. Trademark Infringement Cases*, Oct. 11, 2007, http://inta.org/index.php?option=com_content&task=view&id=1749&Itemid=153&getcontent=3.
38. *Id.*
39. Marc Lifsher, *License to Lie Sought in Piracy Battle*, L.A. TIMES, Apr. 4, 2007, at B1.

established, brand owners must rely on case law to determine what, if any, limits exist with respect to the legality of pretext purchases.

d. Informants

Although technology and the Internet make it easier for gray and black marketers to create anonymity, they cannot be profitable in total isolation. They must market their products and correspond with customers, distributors, and employees. Their conduct may fall below the radar of a brand owner, but there is always a pool of individuals that know or at least suspect such activity. In order for brand owners to avail themselves of these knowledgeable resources, they must make themselves extremely accessible.

Several companies' Web sites advertise hotlines for people to call and report suspected fraudulent activity. For example, Microsoft Corporation has a toll-free Anti-Piracy Hotline[40] and e-mail address for customers or resellers to report suspected infringement. Although the callers are asked to provide their contact information in case additional information is needed, callers are permitted to remain completely anonymous. Nortel Networks, Cisco, and others offer similar services on their Web sites to report gray market or other improper transactions.[41]

e. Dumpster Diving

Another method of secretly detecting suspected gray and black market activity is through dumpster diving. The practice, as the name suggests, is the unglamorous inspection of a target's trash. Given the potential privacy and constitutional issues implicated in such a search, brand owners and their counsel must be familiar with the United States Supreme Court's holding in *California v. Greenwood*,[42] wherein the Court upheld the constitutionality of dumpster diving when certain conditions exist.

Although *Greenwood* was a criminal narcotics case, its analysis with respect to the constitutionality of dumpster diving is equally apposite in the gray market context. The case began when an investigator for the Laguna

---

40. The telephone number is, aptly, 1-800-RU-LEGIT. Microsoft, Reporting Software Piracy, http://www.microsoft.com/piracy/reporting/default.aspx.
41. *See e.g.*, Nortel Networks, Report Gray Market Activity, http://www.nortel.com/prd/greymarket/enterprise/index.html; Cisco Systems, Protecting Against Gray Market and Counterfeit Goods, http://blogs.cisco.com/news/comments/protecting_against_gray_market_and_counterfeit_goods/ (last visited Oct. 12, 2008).
42. California v. Greenwood, 486 U.S. 35 (1988).

Beach Police Department received information that a truck full of narcotics was on its way to Billy Greenwood's home. The investigator conducted surveillance of Mr. Greenwood's home and saw several vehicles make brief stops during the late night and early morning hours. The investigator followed one of the vehicles to a residence that had previously been under investigation as a narcotics-trafficking location.[43]

The investigator then asked the neighborhood's regular trash collector to provide her with the trash bags that had been left on the curb in front of Mr. Greenwood's home. The trash collector obliged and the investigator found items indicative of narcotics use.[44] Reciting the information the investigator extracted from Mr. Greenwood's trash in an affidavit, the investigator was able to obtain a search warrant, which when executed uncovered quantities of narcotics leading to Mr. Greenwood's arrest.[45]

The trial court and court of appeals dismissed the criminal charges on the grounds that a warrantless trash search violated the Fourth Amendment's prohibition against unreasonable searches and seizures. The United States Supreme Court reversed the prior courts' dismissals. In its analysis, the Court first articulated the standard by which the constitutionality of the trash search would be measured: "The warrantless search and seizure of the garbage bags left at the curb outside the Greenwood house would violate the Fourth Amendment only if respondents manifested a subjective expectation of privacy in their garbage that society accepts as objectively reasonable."[46] In other words, trash can be searched unless Mr. Greenwood believed he had a privacy interest in the trash and that his expectation was reasonable. Under the facts of the case, the Court concluded that Mr. Greenwood could not have had a reasonable expectation of privacy.

To briefly illustrate, the Court noted that " . . . it is common knowledge that plastic garbage bags left on or at the side of a public street are readily accessible to animals, children, scavengers, snoops, and other members of the public."[47] In addition, Mr. Greenwood had placed his trash on the curb for the express purpose of conveying it to a third party, the trash collector, who might have sorted through the trash or allowed others to do so.[48] There can be no reasonable expectation of privacy, the Court concluded, when someone deposits their trash in an area particularly suited for public inspection for the express purpose of having strangers take it.[49]

Of course, *Greenwood* does not stand for the proposition that all dumpster diving is lawful. The trash must essentially be left in an area where it can

---

43. *Id.* at 37.
44. *Id.* at 37–38.
45. *Id.* at 38.
46. *Id.* at 40.
47. *Id.*
48. *Id.*
49. *Id.*

readily be accessed by the public. Brand owners must be mindful of these limitations and must also ensure that any private investigators they hire similarly abide by these limitations. Failure to do so can result in devastating sanctions.

In *Stephen Slesinger, Inc. v. Walt Disney Co.*,[50] rogue private investigators caused a party to lose a case that had been litigated for over thirteen years. Stephen Slesinger, Inc. (SSI) first sued the Walt Disney Company (Disney) in 1991, alleging that Disney failed to pay certain royalties under its licensing agreement, which granted Disney the right to exploit the story rights of the *Winnie the Pooh* series of children's stories owned by SSI. A year or so after initiating its lawsuit, SSI hired a private investigator to assist in prosecuting its lawsuit by obtaining various Disney documents. Without providing any direction or supervision over the investigator's activities, SSI simply instructed the investigators to "obey the law."[51]

Over the next two years, the private investigator obtained thousands of Disney documents by breaking into Disney office buildings and secure trash receptacles. He also trespassed onto the secure facility of a company that Disney had contracted with to destroy its confidential documents.[52] The documents were then passed on to SSI's attorneys and principals, who reviewed them. The private investigator's activities were kept secret from Disney until 2002. In 2004, following an evidentiary hearing over SSI's use of the illicitly-obtained information, the trial court issued a terminating sanction dismissing SSI's entire lawsuit.[53]

The Court of Appeals affirmed the trial court's ruling. The court concluded that the record revealed a " . . . portrait of litigation misconduct run riot, involving SSI's employment of an investigator . . . to take documents from Disney facilities and trash receptacles. . . ."[54] SSI argued that dismissing its case was improper because SSI and its counsel had instructed the private investigator to obey the law. The court rejected this argument because a litigant is vicariously liable for its investigator's intentional misconduct committed within the course and scope of employment.[55] Thus, it was irrelevant whether the investigator's conduct was in excess of authority or contrary to instructions. Holding otherwise, the court reasoned, would permit a party to reap the benefits of its investigator's misconduct by simply claiming that it had instructed the investigator to engage in lawful conduct.[56]

The harsh lesson to be learned from Disney is obvious for brand owners: Instruct, supervise, and verify that its private investigators adhere to all limitations of a legal investigation.

---

50. Stephen Slesinger, Inc. v. Walt Disney Co., 155 Cal.App. 4th 736 (2007).
51. *Id.* at 740.
52. *Id.* at 740.
53. *Id.*
54. *Id.* at 741.
55. *Id.* at 769.
56. *Id.*

PART IV

Reaction: Legal Strategies After Gray Market Discovery

"If there were no bad people there would be no good lawyers."
—Charles Dickens[1]

---

1. CHARLES DICKENS, THE OLD CURIOSITY SHOP (1841).

CHAPTER
10

Initial Strategies

a. Litigation Alternatives	145
i. The International Trade Commission (ITC)	145
ii. Arbitration	148
b. Civil or Criminal Justice	151
c. State or Federal Court	157
d. Personal Jurisdiction and Venue	159

In the event a brand owner makes the unfortunate discovery that its products are being bought and sold by an illegal gray marketer, it is faced with a host of options. Should it initiate a criminal prosecution? Should it initiate civil litigation? Both? And, where should the litigation take place? Before the substance of any lawsuit can be considered by a judge or jury, a brand owner and its counsel have important procedural decisions to best determine how the brand owner's IP rights should be vindicated. From analyzing whether criminal or civil justice is the best course of action to considering where a gray market case can be filed, this chapter discusses the initial strategy considerations that must be considered prior to filing any pleadings.

a. Litigation Alternatives

i. The International Trade Commission (ITC)

In cases where brand owners wish to prevent the importation of gray market products into the United States, one strategy is initiating a proceeding before the United States International Trade Commission (ITC). The ITC is an independent, quasi-judicial federal agency with broad investigative responsibilities on matters of trade. Among its authorities is the right to conduct investigations involving claims of patent and trademark infringement.

The authority to conduct such investigations and issue rulings can be found in Section 337 of the Tariff Act of 1930.[1]

ITC investigations begin by one or more complainants filing a complaint alleging *unfair acts* in the importation of products into the United States by one or more respondents. The most common forms of unfair acts are patent and trademark infringement; however, activities such as copyright infringement, misappropriation of trade secrets, common law trademark infringement, trade dress infringement, and other business torts can also constitute an unfair act under Section 337. After the complaint is filed, the ITC then assigns an administrative law judge (ALJ) to preside over the case. Similar to conventional litigation, the parties will engage in discovery, submit pre-hearing briefs, and conduct a hearing[2] wherein the ALJ will issue its initial determination of whether there has been a violation of Section 337. The ITC reviews the ALJ's initial determination,[3] issues its final determination, and, if a violation is found, issues the proper remedy. ITC rulings can be appealed to the United States Court of Appeals for the Federal Circuit Court.[4]

There are advantages and disadvantages in Section 337 investigations. For example, unlike a civil lawsuit, a brand owner is not entitled to an award of money damages in a Section 337 proceeding. However, the claimant may, in an ITC proceeding, be entitled to injunctive relief that is otherwise unavailable in conventional litigation.

To illustrate, the ITC can issue a cease and desist order against any domestic respondents to bar the sale of infringing products that are presently in inventory in the United States.[5] Cease and desist orders are enforced by the ITC. In addition, the ITC can issue an exclusion directing that U.S. Customs bar the importation of additional infringing products by the named respondents. In some cases, the ITC will issue a general exclusion order to prevent the entry of all infringing products, regardless of their source. To obtain a general exclusion order, a brand owner must provide evidence that reasonably shows that foreign manufacturers other than the respondents will attempt to import the infringing products into the United States. Finally, if an

---

1. *See* 19 U.S.C. § 1337 (2007).
2. ITC proceedings are governed by the Administrative Procedures Act ("APA") (5 U.S.C. §§ 551–59, 701–06, 1305, 3105, 3344, 5372, 7521), the Commission Rules (19 CFR §§ 210.1–.20), and the ground rules of the administrative law judge assigned to the case. In practice, ITC proceedings are similar to bench trials in district courts and, with some exceptions, generally follow the Federal Rules of Civil Procedure and Evidence.
3. *See* 19 U.S.C. § 1337(c) (2008).
4. The ITC is also required to send its final determination to the President for review. *See* 19 U.S.C. § 1337(j)(2). Although the President rarely exercises this power, an ITC determination is occasionally disapproved. *See e.g.*, Duracell, Inc. v. U.S. Intern. Trade Com'n, 778 F.2d 1578 (Fed. Cir. 1985) (President Reagan disapproved determination of the ITC to bar the importation of certain gray market alkaline batteries).
5. *See* 19 U.S.C. § 1337(f).

entity has previously tried to import an excluded article into the United States and the product was denied entry by the U.S. Customs Service, the ITC may order the seizure and forfeiture of subsequent shipments.[6]

ITC investigations generally move faster than litigation in district courts. ITC investigations are typically completed within fifteen months from the commencement of the case. Another advantage to ITC proceedings is that a claimant does not have to establish the commission's jurisdiction over the respondent. Unlike establishing personal jurisdiction in a district court action, *infra*, the importation of one offending product is sufficient to confer ITC jurisdiction.[7]

Finally, it should be noted that brand owners do not need to decide whether to commence conventional litigation *or* an ITC investigation. The remedies available in an ITC proceeding are "in addition to" all other remedies available under the law. It is not uncommon, therefore, for brand owners to litigate their rights in both venues simultaneously. Although defendants have the ability to stay a district court proceeding during the pendency of an ITC investigation,[8] the discovery record in a Section 337 investigation can be used in the district court.[9]

In many instances, brand owners have relied on Section 337 investigations to prevent the importation of gray market goods. In *Bourdeau Bros., Inc. v. Int'l Trade Comm'n*,[10] Deere & Co. (Deere) initiated a Section 337 to exclude the importation of various forage harvesters that had been manufactured solely for sale in Europe. Deere argued that its European version forage harvesters were materially different from its forage harvesters manufactured and

---

6. *See* 19 U.S.C. § 1337(e). The U.S. Customs procedures for implementing ITC exclusion and seizure orders are set forth at 19 C.F.R. § 12.39.
7. *See e.g.*, Sealed Air Corp. v. U.S. Intern. Trade Com'n, 645 F.2d 976, 985 (C.C.P.A. 1981) (The ALJ's and ITC's finding of personal jurisdiction against respondent was unnecessary because "[a]n exclusion order operates against goods, not parties.")
8. *See* 28 U.S.C. § 1659(a) ("In a civil action involving parties that are also parties to a proceeding before the United States International Trade Commission under section 337 of the Tariff Act of 1930, at the request of a party to the civil action that is also a respondent in the proceeding before the Commission, the district court shall stay, until the determination of the Commission becomes final, proceedings in the civil action with respect to any claim that involves the same issues involved in the proceeding before the Commission, but only if such request is made within—(1) 30 days after the party is named as a respondent in the proceeding before the Commission, or (2) 30 days after the district court action is filed, whichever is later.").
9. *See* 28 U.S.C. § 1659(b) ("Notwithstanding section 337(n)(1) of the Tariff Act of 1930, after dissolution of a stay under subsection (a), the record of the proceeding before the United States International Trade Commission shall be transmitted to the district court and shall be admissible in the civil action, subject to such protective order as the district court determines necessary, to the extent permitted under the Federal Rules of Evidence and the Federal Rules of Civil Procedure.").
10. Bourdeau Bros., Inc. v. Int'l Trade Comm'n, 444 F.3d 1317 (2006).

authorized for sale in the United States. Accordingly, Deere alleged that these "gray market" European forage harvesters infringed its trademarks and therefore violated Section 337.[11]

The ALJ and ITC agreed with Deere and issued a general exclusion order with respect to the European forage harvesters as well as cease and desist orders to Bourdeau Brothers, Inc. (Bourdeau).[12] Although the court vacated and remanded the case back to the ITC for further proceedings,[13] the court endorsed the suitability of Section 337 to bar the importation of gray market products: "Many of the goods that are forbidden from importation under section 337 are what are referred to as 'gray market goods': products that were 'produced by the owner of the United States trademark or with its consent, but not authorized for the sale in the United States.'"[14]

ii. Arbitration

Courts are busy[15] and litigation is becoming prohibitively expensive and time-consuming. It can take many months or years after a case is filed before the merits are ever tried before a judge or jury. Appeals to reverse or affirm the judgment last even longer.[16] For this reason, arbitration has become a very popular alternative to litigants seeking a more efficient method to resolve their commercial disputes. Arbitration is one of the many alternative dispute resolution (ADR) processes wherein parties can have their cases decided by a private arbitrator without having to avail themselves of the government judicial process. The arbitrator, who is typically an attorney or retired judge, decides both issues of law and fact and imposes a decision that is tantamount to a judgment in federal or state court.

One of the potential benefits *or risks* of arbitration is the efficiency and finality of the arbitrator's ruling. In conventional litigation, obtaining a final

---

11. *Id.* at 1319–20.
12. Cease and desist orders were issued to others who did not appeal the ITC's determination. *Id.* at 1320.
13. For further discussion of the court's analysis in *Bourdeau Bros.*, 444 F.3d at 1317 and trademark law as it relates to the gray market, see Chapter 17.
14. *Id.* at 1320 *citing* Gamut Trading Co. v. U.S. Int'l Trade Com'n, 200 F.3d 775, 777 (Fed. Cir. 1999).
15. There were over 16.6 million civil cases filed in the state court system in 2005. R. LaFountain, R. Schauffler, S. Strickland, W. Raftery & C. Bromage, *Examining the Work of State Courts, 2006: A National Perspective from the Court Statistics Project* (National Center for State Courts 2007), *available at* http://www.ncsconline.org/D_Research/CSP/2006_files/Introduction.pdf.
16. *See e.g.*, Waco Intern., Inc. v. KHK Scaffolding Houston Inc., 278 F.3d 523, 531 (5th Cir. 2002) (There is no support for the proposition that two years of litigation is sufficient to warrant the award of pre-judgment interest.).

judgment can take several years. Arbitration is typically a much faster track to adjudicate the merits of the parties' disputes; in addition, arbitration awards are rarely disturbed by the courts.

The Federal Arbitration Act (FAA)[17] provides four possible grounds for vacating an arbitration award: (1) fraud or corruption in the proceedings; (2) bias on the part of the arbitrator; (3) refusal by the arbitrator to consider relevant evidence or other arbitrator misbehavior; and (4) failure by the arbitrator to exercise power properly.[18] As implied by the FAA, a party seeking to overturn an arbitration award can only do so under exceptional circumstances, and the party seeking to overturn an arbitration award is under a heavy burden to prove that the standards for such relief have been met.[19] Indeed, any "colorable justification" for the award will be sufficient to uphold the award.[20]

One of the reasons brand owners and their counsel may be reluctant to avail themselves to the speedier and less expensive forum of arbitration is the belief that arbitrators only have the authority to award monetary relief. One of the most important remedies in intellectual property litigation is the ability to stop a defendant—both during and after litigation—from continuing its unlawful conduct. Arbitration should be avoided, the reasoning goes, because an arbitrator does not have the authority to order a preliminary injunction or other interim relief. Although there may indeed be strategic justifications to avoid arbitration, brand owners and counsel should be aware that preliminary remedies may indeed be within an arbitrator's scope of authority.

In *Blue Bell, Inc. v. Western Glove Works Ltd.*,[21] the Southern District of New York examined the scope of an arbitrator's authority in a case between a brand owner and one of its licensees. Although the arbitrator's award disappointed the brand owner, the court's holding illustrates the authority of an arbitrator to issue equitable relief. The plaintiff Blue Bell manufactured and licensed Wrangler and Lee jeans. The plaintiff entered into a written license agreement with the defendant Western Glove wherein Western Glove could manufacture and sell Wrangler jeans. In return, Western Glove was obligated to pay royalties to Blue Bell. In addition, Western Glove was not allowed to use any Blue Bell information to manufacture any non-Wrangler products.

---

17. 9 U.S.C. §§ 1-307 (2008).
18. 9 U.S.C. §§ 10(a)–(d).
19. *See e.g.*, John T. Brady & Co. v. Form-Eze Systems, Inc., 623 F.2d 261, 264 (2d Cir. 1980).
20. *See e.g.*, Matter of Andros Compania Maritima, S.A. (March Rich & Co.), 579 F.2d 691, 703 (2d Cir. 1978).
21. Blue Bell, Inc. v. Western Glove Works Ltd., 816 F. Supp. 236 (S.D.N.Y. 1993) (In trademark infringement case, pre-judgment interest was not recoverable because "[t]here is no support for the claim proposition that two years of litigation is of such length that failure to award pre-judgment interest would constitute an abuse of discretion.").

The license agreement also provided that Western Glove could purchase other Blue Bell products at a discount from its wholesale price.[22]

Blue Bell alleged that Western Glove, in violation of the license agreement, manufactured and sold "knock-off" Wrangler jeans. The license agreement contained an arbitration clause and the parties litigated the merits of the case there.[23] After a five-day hearing, the arbitrator issued a ruling permanently enjoining Western Glove from manufacturing any "knock-off" Wrangler jeans and ordered it to pay Blue Bell monetary damages. However, so long as Western Glove complied with the arbitrator's orders, the arbitrator ruled that it will have "cured" any material breach with Blue Bell, thereby keeping the parties' license agreement intact.[24]

Although neither party opposed the permanent injunction ordered by the arbitrator, Blue Bell objected to the portion of the arbitrator's order that allowed Western Glove to maintain its license agreement. Blue Bell argued that this portion of the award had to be reversed. Blue Bell did not, however, directly attack the equitable nature of the arbitrator's award. Instead, because Western Glove's conduct caused irreparable harm to Blue Bell's trademarks, Blue Bell argued that the arbitrator's ruling was made "in manifest disregard of applicable New York and federal law."[25]

The court rejected this argument. With respect to the arbitrator's power to make the ruling he did, the court explained the contractual foundation to an arbitrator's jurisdiction:

> Arbitral jurisdiction is entirely consensual . . . The arbitrator's powers are derived from the parties' contract. Hence, in the classic sense, an arbitrator is not entitled to do anything unauthorized by the parties: arbiter nihil extra compromissum facere potest. An arbitral award rendered within the framework of the common agreement of the parties is itself part of the contract and hence binding upon them.[26]

---

22. *Id.* at 237.
23. Without any discussion or explanation, the opinion noted that Blue Bell originally sought and obtained a Temporary Restraining Order (TRO) in district court shortly after serving a demand for arbitration. There was likely a need to obtain a TRO to *immediately* stop further sales of counterfeit Wrangler jeans. Because the selection of an arbitrator(s) can take several days or weeks, it may have been necessary to obtain preliminary relief in the district court. *See e.g.*, REVISED UNIFORM ARBITRATION ACT ("RUAA"), § 8(a) (2000) ("Before an arbitrator is appointed and is authorized and able to act, the court, upon [motion] of a party to an arbitration proceeding and for good cause shown, may enter an order for provisional remedies to protect the effectiveness of the arbitration proceeding to the same extent and under the same conditions as if the controversy were the subject of a civil action.").
24. Blue Bell, 816 F. Supp. at 239.
25. *Id.* at 240.
26. *Id.* at 240, *citing* W. Michael Reisman, *The Breakdown of the Control Mechanism in ICSID Arbitration*, 1989 DUKE L.J. 739, 745 (1989).

Given that the parties had agreed to the scope of the arbitrator's powers and because the arbitrator's ruling was not manifestly in disregard of the law, the court confirmed the award.[27]

Specific arbitration rules are in accord. For example, the American Arbitration Association's (AAA) Commercial Rules expressly provide arbitrators with the power to grant provisional remedies: "The arbitrator may take whatever interim measures he or she deems necessary including injunctive relief and measures for the protection or conservation of property and disposition of perishable goods."[28] Accordingly, brand owners may wish to include an arbitration clause in their agreements to ensure that they have the ability to arbitrate disputes with its distribution partners.

Even in the absence of a contract clause mandating arbitration, brand owners may wish to seek or request that defendant gray marketers agree to arbitrate the case instead of conventional litigation. Although the parties will obviously have diametrically opposed goals with respect to the substantive outcome of the dispute, the parties may have an aligned interest in seeking arbitration. Arbitration will appeal to the brand owner because the process is less expensive, less time-consuming, and any judgment rendered is final. The defendant gray marketer may likewise prefer the speed and cost of arbitration. Especially when the brand owner is in an economically dominant position to unilaterally drive up the costs of litigation, the defendant gray marketer may jump at the opportunity to limit the costs attendant to the dispute. In addition, the defendant gray marker can avoid the potential for a runaway jury verdict. Arbitrators are typically attorneys or retired judges; thus, they are less likely to issue damage awards rooted in emotion or anger and more likely to issue damage awards that bear a legal nexus to the harm suffered by the brand owner.

b. Civil or Criminal Justice

What was once considered only harmful to a specific brand owner is now understood to be harmful to the United States. The federal government has taken notice and responded. On September 29, 1999, the National Intellectual Property Law Enforcement Coordination Council (NIPLECC) was established.[29] NIPLECC's mission is "to coordinate domestic and international

---

27. *Id.* at 243.
28. American Arbitration Association (AAA), Commercial Rules, R-34(a), *available at* http://www.adr.org/commercial_arbitration.
29. Treasury/Postal Appropriations Act, Pub. L. No. 106–58, 113 Stat. 430 (1999) (codified as amended 15 U.S.C. § 1128 (2004)).

intellectual property law enforcement among federal and foreign entities."[30] According to its own 2006 annual report, NIPLECC has institutionalized an unprecedented level of coordination within the federal government and delivered a worldwide message that "the United States takes the issue of intellectual property very seriously, we are leveraging our resources to address it and we have high expectations of all of our global trading partners."[31]

To assist brand owners in their fight against IP infringers, the federal government now offers brand owners a number of resources. Brand owners can now find an increasing number of law enforcement resources willing to fight IP crime at the federal level. For example, the Federal Bureau of Investigation (FBI) and Immigration and Customs Enforcement have established special cybercrime operation centers to support IP investigations in field offices nationwide and attaché offices overseas.[32] From 2003 through 2005, the number of open IP investigations of the FBI rose by 22 percent; between 2004 and 2005, the number of defendants charged by the FBI with IP offenses increased by 98 percent.[33] In addition, the Justice Department has established twenty-five Computer Hacking and Intellectual Property (CHIP) units and designated a CHIP coordinator in every U.S. Attorney's Office, increasing the number of IP trained prosecutors to more than two-hundred-thirty nationwide.[34]

There are advantages as well as disadvantages in having the federal government prosecute cases where a specific brand owner's IP rights have been infringed. One plain advantage for the brand owner is economical: Brand owners can potentially save large sums of money by having federal investigators and attorneys pursue their case rather than investigators and civil attorneys that must be retained at their own expense.

The corresponding disadvantage that brand owners must recognize, however, is that the federal investigators and attorneys are in charge of the case, not the brand owner. Although the brand owner is the alleged "victim" of the crime, the obligations imposed on the federal government with respect to victims are different than the obligations civil attorneys have to their clients.

---

30. 15 U.S.C. § 1128(b) (2008). NIPLECC includes the Office of the U.S. Trade Representative; the Department of Commerce—including the U.S. Patent and Trademark Office and the International Trade Administration; the Department of Homeland Security, which includes the U.S. Customs and Border Protection and U.S. Immigration and Customs Enforcement; the Department of Justice; and the State Department. The U.S. Copyright Office serves in an advisory capacity. NIPLECC ANN. REP., pg. 2 (2006).
31. National Intellectual Property Law Enforcement Coordination Counsel ("IPLECC"), Report to the President and Congress on Coordination of Intellectual Property Enforcement and Protection, Sept. 2006 at 2–3, *available at* http://www.commerce.gov/opa/press/Secretary_Gutierrez/2006_Releases/September/2006%20IP%20report.pdf.
32. *Id.* at 6–7.
33. *Id.* at 7, fn. 6.
34. *Id.* at 7.

In the criminal context, the prosecuting attorney is required to advise victims of case events such as the filing of charges and the schedule of court proceedings.[35] The scope of meetings between victims and federal officials is expressly limited; although a victim has a "reasonable right" to confer with the case's federal prosecutor,[36] the right to confer shall not be construed to impair prosecutorial discretion.[37] As articulated by the Department of Justice, "[b]ecause victims are not clients . . . such consultations may be limited to gathering information from victims and conveying only nonsensitive data and public information."[38]

It is also necessary to consider the level of interest federal prosecutors may have for a particular case. In cases where gray market products are commingled with black market products, especially if the black market products pose a health or safety risk to consumers, federal prosecutors will likely have a keen interest in pursuing the case.[39] In pure gray market cases, however, there is a reluctance to criminalize such conduct.

In *United States v. Hanafy*,[40] *supra*, the district court examined whether a statute that criminalized the trafficking of goods with counterfeit marks was applicable in a gray market context.[41] The defendants purchased and sold gray market infant formula. In an effort to resemble the manufacturers' shipping boxes, the defendants obtained cardboard containers with the manufacturers' trademarks and sold the repackaged and shrink-wrapped tray to unsuspecting purchasers.[42] The defendants were indicted on various charges and found guilty of, among other charges, trafficking goods with counterfeit marks pursuant to 18 U.S.C. § 2320. After the defendants' convictions, they appealed the jury's verdict by asserting that their conduct did not, as a matter of law, violate Section 2320.[43] As explained below, the trial court agreed.

---

35. 42 U.S.C. § 106–7(c)(3)(C), (D).
36. 18 U.S.C. § 3771(a)(5).
37. 18 U.S.C. § 3771(d)(6).
38. Alberto Gonzalez, U.S. Dep't of Justice, Attorney General Guidelines for Victim and Witness Assistance 29–30 (2005).
39. *See e.g.*, *Pharmaceutical Supply Chain Security: Hearing on Before Subcomm. On Criminal Justice, Drug Policy and Human Rights, Comm. On Government Reform*, 2006 Leg., 109th Sess. 2 (2006) (statement of Kevin Delli-Colli, Deputy Assistant Director Financial & Trade Investigations Div.) ("Since 2003 [through 2006], ICE [U.S. Immigration and Customs Enforcement] has initiated 178 criminal investigations of pharmaceutical smuggling [resulting in] millions of dosage units of counterfeit, adulterated, misbranded and unapproved pharmaceuticals have been seized.").
40. United States v. Hanafy, 124 F. Supp. 2d at 1016 (N.D. Tex. 2000).
41. Although the goods at issue were not imported and therefore not pure gray market goods, *Hanafy* is nonetheless illustrative of how criminal statutes apply in the gray market context.
42. *Id.* at 1018.
43. *Id.* at 1019.

Section 2320 punishes one who "intentionally traffics or attempts to traffic goods or services and knowingly uses a counterfeit mark on or in connection with such goods or services."[44] A counterfeit mark is defined as a "spurious mark (i) that is used in connection with trafficking goods or services; (ii) that is identical with, or substantially indistinguishable from, a mark registered for those goods or services . . . ; and (iii) the use of which is likely to cause confusion, to cause mistake, or to deceive."[45]

Although it was undisputed that affixing a *genuine* mark to a *counterfeit* product was unlawful, the defendants argued that their conduct did not violate Section 2320. Because the defendants had merely affixed an unauthorized mark to a *genuine* good, the defendants asserted that criminal culpability was inappropriate.

Noting that the definition of the term "counterfeit mark" in the Lanham Act is nearly identical to the definition in Section 2320, the government argued that Congress clearly intended to criminalize the same conduct for which an individual may be civilly liable.[46] Because such conduct could violate the Lanham Act,[47] the government reasoned that such conduct should similarly violate Section 2320.[48] The district court, however, was reluctant to rely on the Lanham Act as Section 2320 precedent. Unlike the Lanham Act, which dealt with civil liability, Section 2320 is a criminal statute and must be interpreted narrowly.[49]

In addition to the principles of statutory construction, the district court examined the legislative history and concluded that Section 2320 was not intended to criminalize mere gray market activity.[50] Given Congress' intent

---

44. 18 U.S.C.§ 2023(a).
45. *Id.* § 2320(e)(1)(A)
46. Hanafy, 124 F. Supp. 2d at 1022; *see also* U.S. v. Petrosian, 126 F.3d 1232, 1234 (9th Cir. 1997) (The similar definitions of "counterfeit mark" in the Lanham Act and Section 2320 suggests that Congress intended to criminalize all of the conduct for which an individual may be civilly liable.).
47. For further discussion on the substantive analysis of liability under the Lanham Act, see Chapter 17.
48. *See e.g.,* Prestonettes, Inc. v. Coty, 264 U.S. 359, 368–69 (1924) (one who purchases a genuine product in bulk and divides it into smaller portions for sale to consumers may do so as long as the products are marked as having been repackaged); *see also* Monsanto Co. v. Haskel Trading, Inc., 13 F. Supp. 2d 349, 356–58 (E.D.N.Y. 1998) (finding that the defendants violated the Lanham Act when they repackaged small packages of NutraSweet into boxes for resale).
49. Hanafy, 124 F. Supp. 2d at 1023; *see also* U.S. v. Giles, 213 F.3d 1247, 1250 (19th Cir. 2000) (Unlike the Lanham Act, Section 2023 must be construed narrowly); U.S. v. Cisneros, 203 F.3d 333, 342 (5th Cir. 2000) (Section 2320 must be construed more narrowly than the Lanham Act).
50. Joint Statement on Trademark Counterfeiting Legislation, 130 Cong. Rec. 31673 (1984) ("The sponsors are also aware of the existence of 'parallel imports' or 'gray matters' goods. . . . Neither of these types of *goods* are [sic.] counterfeit within the meaning of this legislation.").

and the principles of statutory construction, the district court acquitted the defendants of their Section 2320 conviction.[51] On appeal, the Fifth Circuit Court endorsed and affirmed the district court's ruling agreeing that reliance on the Lanham Act was of little value in the criminal context.[52] Thus, unless a brand owner is aware that an infringing gray marketer is engaging in additional conduct that would constitute a crime, a civil proceeding is a more favorable vehicle to obtain relief.

In the event a gray marketer is also engaging in criminal conduct such as counterfeiting or money laundering, a brand owner may also consider pursuing both criminal and civil remedies simultaneously. One of the benefits of having a criminal investigation taking place while a brand owner is pursuing its rights civilly is the defendant's reluctance to waive his or her Fifth Amendment rights. The Fifth Amendment provides that no person "shall be compelled in any criminal case to be a witness against himself[.]"[53] The purpose of the Fifth Amendment is to ensure that no one is compelled, when acting as a witness in *any investigation*, to give testimony that might tend to show that he himself had committed a crime.[54] Therefore, the privilege applies not only in criminal proceedings but in any other proceeding, civil or criminal, formal or informal, in which the answers might incriminate him or her in future criminal proceedings.[55] A defendant, fearful that answers in a civil deposition or trial may be used against him or her in a future criminal case, may simply "plead the Fifth" when cross-examined about any substantive topic relevant to the criminal investigation.

Although juries in criminal cases are precluded from drawing an adverse inference by a defendant asserting his Fifth Amendment privilege, the same rule does not apply in civil proceedings.[56] Brand owners can highlight the invocation of the Fifth Amendment privilege for the jury's consideration.

Cognizant of the strategic dilemma created for alleged infringers facing both civil and criminal liability, defendants will commonly request that the civil court postpone its case until any criminal proceedings are resolved. An alleged infringer would much prefer to stagger the proceedings such that the criminal case goes first wherein the Fifth Amendment privilege can be asserted, followed by the civil case (assuming there is an acquittal)[57]

---

51. Hanafy, 124 F. Supp. 2d at 1025.
52. U.S. v. Hanafy, 302 F.3d 485, 488–89 (5th Cir. 2002).
53. U.S. Const. amend. V.
54. *See* Lefkowitz v. Turley, 414 U.S. 70, 77 (1973).
55. *Id.*
56. *See e.g.*, National Acceptance Co. v. Bathalter, 705 F.2d 924, 930–32 (7th Cir. 1983) (A factfinder may draw an adverse inference from the invocation of the Fifth Amendment).
57. In the event the defendant was found guilty, a civil trial would likely be unnecessary or the number of issues to be tried would be reduced. A criminal conviction or guilty plea acts as a bar and collaterally estops the retrial of issues in a civil trial when those same issues were

wherein the defendant can provide full testimony without concern that any Fifth Amendment rights are being waived.[58]

Although the power to stay proceedings is incidental to the power inherent in every court,[59] requests for stays are not automatically granted. The Constitution does not ordinarily require a stay of civil proceedings pending the outcome of criminal proceedings.[60] Indeed, "a complete stay of a pending civil action until the outcome of related criminal proceedings is an extraordinary remedy."[61]

There are five factors that a court will consider when deciding a motion to stay: (1) the private interests of the plaintiffs in proceeding expeditiously with the civil litigation as balanced against the prejudice to the plaintiffs if delayed; (2) the private interests of and burden on the defendants; (3) the interests of the courts; (4) the interests of persons not parties to the civil litigation; and (5) the public interest.[62]

Although these are the factors considered, there is no general rule that delineates the criteria for determining when a civil case will impermissibly interfere with an on-going criminal proceeding.[63] Accordingly, such determination must be made on a case-by-case basis.[64] In light of these principles, there are typically three hurdles that a defendant must overcome in order to have the case stayed: (1) the defendant must make a clear showing, by direct or indirect proof, that the issues in the civil action are "related" as well as "substantially similar" to the issues in the criminal investigation; (2) the defendant must make a clear showing of hardship or inequity if required to go forward with the civil case while the criminal investigation is pending; and

---

    actually litigated in the criminal trial. *See e.g.*, Emich Motors v. General Motors, 340 U.S. 558, 568 (1951) ("[A] prior conviction may work an estoppel in favor of the government in a subsequent civil proceeding...").

58. With the criminal proceedings already concluded, the Fifth Amendment privilege would not apply because the alleged infringer could not be criminally tried a second time. *See* U.S. Const. amend. V (No personal shall "be subject for the same offense to be twice put in jeopardy of life or limb..."); *see also*, Green v. United States, 355 U.S. 184, 187–88 (1957) ("The underlying idea, one that is deeply ingrained in at least the Anglo-American system of jurisprudence, is that the State with all its resources and power should not be allowed to make repeated attempts to convict an individual for an alleged offense, thereby subjecting him to embarrassment, expense and ordeal and compelling him to live in a continuing state of anxiety and insecurity, as well as enhancing the possibility that even though innocent he may be found guilty.").
59. Landis v. N. Am. Co., 299 U.S. 248, 257 (1936).
60. SEC v. Dresser, 628 F.2d 1368, 1374–75 (D.C. Cir. 1980).
61. Weil v. Markowitz, 829 F.2d 166, 174 n. 17 (D.C. Cir. 1987).
62. Estes-El v. Long Island Jewish Med. Ctr., 916 F. Supp. 268, 270 (S.D.N.Y. 1995) (quoting Volmar Distribs., Inc. v. New York Post Co., 152 F.R.D. 36, 39 (S.D.N.Y. 1993)).
63. C3, Inc. v. United States, 4 Cl.Ct 790, 791 (1984).
64. *Id.*

(3) the defendant must establish that the duration of the requested stay is not immoderate or unreasonable.[65]

Beyond these five factors and the three-pronged test, courts have indicated other considerations that they take into account in granting a motion to stay: (1) the duplication of effort and litigation costs;[66] (2) whether the government's success in the prosecution of the criminal case would lead to the possibility that the court will be relieved of a substantial amount of work in the civil case;[67] and (3) whether discovery could adversely affect the government's position in any future related criminal proceedings.[68] In addition to presenting facts to show that the above factors tip in their favor, brand owners opposing efforts to stay civil proceedings can also argue that the longer the civil proceeding is delayed the harder it will be to enforce a possible judgment and recover any of the defendant's assets.[69]

c. State or Federal Court

A fundamental element of civil procedure is subject matter jurisdiction. This concept determines the judicial system in which a case can be tried.[70] There are two judicial systems: federal and state. In the event a brand owner intends to commence civil litigation, it or its attorney must decide which system is most available and best suited to hear its claims.

In the state court system, each state defines which types of cases it can hear in its constitutions and statutes.[71] Most states have enacted broad subject matter jurisdiction so that they can hear any type of case that can be brought.[72] Federal courts are courts of limited jurisdiction.[73] The federal courts can only hear certain types of cases as outlined in Article III, Section 2 of the Constitution. This includes claims "arising under" the Constitution and those based on diversity of the parties.[74] Federal courts have also been deemed,

---

65. St. Paul Fire And Marine Insurance Co. v. United States, 24 Cl.Ct. 513, 515 (1991).
66. Volmar, 152 F.R.D. at 39.
67. Golden Quality Ice Cream Co., Inc. v. Deerfield Specialty, 87 F.R.D. 53, 57 (D.C.Pa. 1980).
68. Souza v. Schiltgen, 1996 WL 241824 (N.D.Cal.). However, courts have also held that any discovery prejudice can be remedied by requiring that the government not be required to provide discovery in the civil case or that the plaintiff in the civil case not provide discovery to the government. See e.g., Horn v. District of Columbia, 210 F.R.D. 13, 16 (2002).
69. In re Who's Who Worldwide Registry, Inc., 197 B.R. 193, 197 (1996).
70. BLACK'S LAW DICTIONARY (3rd Pocket ed. 1996).
71. GLANNON, CIVIL PROCEDURE EXAMPLES & EXPLANATIONS 60 (Aspen 2006).
72. Id.
73. Id. at 61.
74. U.S. Const. art III, § 2.

through statute, to have exclusive original jurisdiction over copyright claims and original (but not exclusive) jurisdiction over trademark claims.[75]

Although federal courts are deemed to have jurisdiction over copyright and trademark claims, there are still instances wherein brand owners can choose to litigate their claims in state court. As an initial matter, federal courts' original jurisdiction over trademark cases is concurrent with state courts' jurisdiction. Accordingly, brand owners can decide whether state or federal court is the preferable forum. Even in the context of copyright law, the case can be decided by state court if the copyright claim is based on contract or equitable principles.[76] Assuming the brand owner has a choice, there are several distinctions between the two judicial systems that should be considered.

Although the vast majority of civil lawsuits are resolved short of trial, it is important to consider the differences between jury trials in state and federal court. Most notably, the verdict of the jury must be unanimous in federal court.[77] The unanimity rule applies to all claims and on each affirmative defense.[78] Unlike state courts, which typically require only three-fourths of the jurors to agree upon the verdict,[79] the unanimity rule can increase the possibility of a hung jury.[80] The number of jurors in each system is also different as well. State courts typically require a jury of twelve, and federal courts may select any number of jurors between a minimum of six and a maximum of twelve.[81]

In general, federal judges enjoy a better perception of impartiality and competence. Unlike many of their state court brethren, federal judges are not elected. Federal judges are appointed by the President with the advice and consent of the Senate and hold their office for life.[82] In addition, federal judges typically have more resources available to fulfill their duties. In addition to one or two law clerks who assist with legal research and writing, federal judges can delegate various duties to magistrate judges. Magistrate judges are appointed judges who aid in serving both civil and criminal cases. Magistrates tend to hear pretrial motions and conduct discovery and settlement conferences.[83]

---

75. 28 U.S.C. § 1338 (2000).
76. *See e.g.,* Forry, Inc. v. Neundorfer, Inc., 837 F.2d 259 (6th Cir. 1988).
77. FED. R. CIV. P. 48.
78. Jazzabi v. Allstate Ins. Co., 278 F.3d 979, 984 (9th Cir. 2002).
79. *See e.g.,* CAL. CONST. ART. I, § 16; CAL. CIV. PROC. CODE § 618.
80. The likelihood of a hung jury in a federal civil trial is still extremely low. From 1980 through 1997, hung jury rates ranged from 1.2% to 2.0% of all civil jury trials. *See* Paul L. Hannaford-Agor et al., *Are Hung Juries a Problem?* Nat'l Inst. of Just., Sept. 30, 2002, at 22, *available at* http://www.ncsconline.org/WC/Publications/Res_Juries_HungJuriesProblemPub.pdf.
81. FED. R. CIV. P. 48.
82. U.S. Const. art III, § 1.
83. SCHWARZER, TASHIMA & WAGSTAFFE, CAL. PRAC. GUIDE: FED. CIV. PRO. BEFORE TRIAL 1–2 (The Rutter Group 2007).

Another potential advantage of litigating in federal court is the imposition of the rules of discovery. In an aim to increase the efficiency and decrease the costs of discovery, the Federal Rules of Civil Procedure impose on parties obligations as well as limits on the process. For example, parties are obligated to make various disclosures at the outset of a case.[84] Before deposition or written discovery can even begin, the parties are required to disclose the identity of individuals and documents that they may rely on during the case.[85] As the case progresses, the parties are required to continually supplement their disclosures. Once discovery begins, there is a presumptive limit of ten depositions for each side of the litigation.[86] Interrogatories are limited as well. Only twenty-five interrogatories may be served on any party unless the district court says otherwise.[87] Depending on the amount of discovery a party seeks or is subject to, these discovery limits may be an advantage or disadvantage.

It is generally recommended that brand owners litigate their gray market cases in federal court. Although every case is unique and there may exist particular reasons a state court venue is preferred, the vast majority of copyright and trademark case law is generated by federal courts. Given the added resources and control over discovery, federal courts have a greater familiarity with the legal issues present in gray market cases.[88]

d. Personal Jurisdiction and Venue

The global nature of the gray market economy makes it very likely that any domestically infringing activity will take place far from the brand owner's principal place of business. For example, a brand owner with its main place of business in Los Angeles may discover that an infringing business that is selling products on the Internet has just one office in New York. It would obviously be more convenient for the Los Angeles brand owner to litigate the matter in a California court. Whether the brand owner can indeed litigate in its home town and force the alleged infringer to defend a case on the other side of the country turns on the issue of personal jurisdiction and venue.

---

84. FED. R. CIV. P. 26(a).
85. *Id.*
86. FED. R. CIV. P. 30(a)(2)(A)(i). Also, the deposition is limited to one day of seven hours unless otherwise stipulated by the parties or ordered by the court. FED. R. CIV. P. 30(d)(1).
87. FED. R. CIV. P. 33(a)(1).
88. Even if brand owners elect to file their case in state court, the defendant may elect to remove the case to federal court if such jurisdiction exists. *See* FED. R. CIV. P. 81(c); 28 U.S.C. 1441.

An examination of personal jurisdiction analyzes whether a particular court can exercise jurisdiction over a particular defendant.[89] In the example above, prior to commencing litigation in Southern California, the Los Angeles brand owner would be well-advised to examine whether a Southern California court could properly exercise jurisdiction over the New York defendant.

One of the easiest ways to establish personal jurisdiction over an out-of-state defendant is to contractually agree to jurisdiction in advance of any dispute or lawsuit. As discussed in Chapter 6, brand owners may wish to include forum selection clauses with their channel partners to ensure that any disputes will be resolved in the brand owner's home city or state.[90]

The next easiest way to establish jurisdiction is to actually serve the defendant in the forum state.[91] The service must, however, take place in the forum state. For example, in *Prince of Peace Enterprises v. Top Quality Food Market, LLC*,[92] the plaintiff tried to establish personal jurisdiction by invoking the "so-called 'bulge' jurisdiction."[93] Under Rule 4(k)(1)(B) of the Federal Rules of Civil Procedure, service of process is sufficient to establish jurisdiction over a defendant "who is a party joined under Rule 14 or Rule 19 and is served at a place within a judicial district of the United States and not more than 100 miles from the place from which the summons issues. . . ."[94] The plaintiff, which alleged that the defendants were improperly selling gray market over-the-counter herbal supplements, asserted that jurisdiction was established because the defendants were served in neighboring New Jersey—within 100 miles of the district court in New York. The court was not persuaded with the plaintiff's logic and dismissed the case for plaintiff's flawed interpretation of Rule 4. Because the "bulge service provision" only applied to third parties impleaded and additional parties added to an action or counterclaim, the plaintiff failed to show that the court had personal jurisdiction over the defendant.[95]

---

89. *See e.g.*, Burnham v. Sup. Ct., 495 U.S. 604, 609–610 (1990) (Personal jurisdiction refers to the court's power to render judgment that either commands defendant's personal obedience or imposes obligations on the defendant that will be enforced by other courts).
90. *See e.g.*, National Equip. Rental, Ltd. v. Szukhent, 375 U.S. 311, 316 (1964) ("Parties to a contract may agree in advance to submit to the jurisdiction of a given court.").
91. *See id.* (A defendant served while voluntarily present within the forum state is subject to personal jurisdiction "without regard to whether the defendant was only briefly in the State or whether the cause of action was related to his activities there."). A defendant may also consent to personal jurisdiction by designating a local agent for service of process. *See, e.g.*, Knowlton v. Allied Van Lines, 900 F.2d 1196, 1199 (8th Cir. 1990) (such designation constitutes consent to jurisdiction); *but see* Leonard v. USA Petroleum Corp., 829 F. Supp. 882, 888–91 (S.D. Tx. 1993) (such designation does not constitute consent to jurisdiction).
92. Prince of Peace Enterprises v. Top Quality Food Market, LLC, 2007 WL 704171 (S.D.N.Y.).
93. *Id.* at 2.
94. Fed. R. Civ. P. 4(k)(1)(b).
95. Prince of Peace, 2007 WL 704171 at *2.

In the event that there is no enforceable selection clause, and service in the forum state cannot be accomplished, the defendant must have sufficient "minimum contacts" with the forum state such that "maintenance of the lawsuit does not offend traditional notions of fair play and substantial justice."[96] The analysis of whether minimum contacts are established is not a strict mechanical test; instead, it is an analysis of each case's specific facts to determine whether or not it, in essence, would be fair or unfair to continue the lawsuit in the forum state.

There are two approaches to examining the minimum contacts doctrine. The first approach asks whether the defendant has engaged in "substantial, continuous and systematic" activities within the forum state. If yes, "general" or "unlimited" jurisdiction exists, and the defendant will be subject to personal jurisdiction on any causes of action filed in the forum court.[97] The second approach pertains to cases where "general" or "unlimited" jurisdiction does not exist. In these cases, courts will examine whether the claims sued upon arise out of the defendant's forum-related activities and whether the defendant purposefully directed those activities toward forum residents or purposefully availed itself of the privilege of conducting activities in the forum state. If yes, "specific" or "limited" jurisdiction exists such that the defendant can be sued on claims that are related to its forum-related contacts. In gray market cases, it is typically an analysis of whether "specific" or "limited" jurisdiction exists.[98] In other words, it is typically an analysis of whether the alleged infringer has purposefully availed itself toward the forum state and availed itself of the forum state's privileges such that it would not be unfair to demand that it defend itself in that same state.[99]

A complete analysis of personal jurisdiction is beyond the scope of this book.[100] However, the following illustrates how courts have interpreted factual situations that would be relevant to brand owners or alleged infringers contesting the issue of personal jurisdiction.

For example, if an alleged gray marketer merely advertises in the forum state, several courts have held that such conduct is insufficient "purposeful availment" to support personal jurisdiction in the state where

---

96. Int'l Shoe Co. v. Wash., 326 U.S. 310, 316 (1945).
97. See e.g., Perkins v. Benguet Consol. Mining Co., 342 U.S. 437, 445 (1952).
98. See e.g., Hanson v. Denckla, 357 U.S. 235, 253–54 (1958).
99. Regardless of whether general or specific jurisdiction may exist, courts still require a finding that exercising jurisdiction passes a "reasonableness" test. See e.g., Amoco Egypt Oil Co. v. Leonis Navigation Co., Inc., 1 F.3d 848, 851, fn. 2 (9th Cir. 1993); Burger King Corp. v. Rudzewicz, 471 U.S. 462, 477 (1985).
100. For a thorough examination of personal jurisdiction, please see SCHWARZER, TASHIMA & WAGSTAFFE, CAL. PRAC. GUIDE: FED. CIV. PRO. BEFORE TRIAL 3:76–3:398 (The Rutter Group 2007).

the advertisement appears.[101] However, actual sales of products in the forum state will typically be sufficient to warrant personal jurisdiction. Even if the alleged gray marketer has no office, plant, or personnel in the forum state, it is usually sufficient if the defendant "placed its products in the stream of interstate commerce with the expectation that they will be sold to consumers in the forum state."[102]

The ease with which the Internet allows parties to conduct business across state borders has not dramatically altered the legal principles to be examined. "Despite the Internet's lack of territorial boundaries, the courts have attempted to apply traditional concepts of personal jurisdiction . . . such as whether the defendant intentionally reached beyond its own state to engage in business with residents of the forum state."[103] For example, e-mail communications may subject a nonresident to local personal jurisdiction to the same extent as communications by telephone or mail.[104] Similarly, selling goods and services via the Internet may subject nonresidents to local jurisdictions in actions arising out of such actions.[105] However, a "passive" Web site that merely provides information or advertisements is not sufficient to establish jurisdiction.[106]

In the context of gray market cases, courts follow the traditional analysis of whether personal jurisdiction exists over alleged gray marketers. For example in *Philip Morris USA Inc. v. Veles Ltd.*,[107] the plaintiff Philip Morris was the U.S. owner of trademarks of various cigarettes such as Marlboro, Parliament, and Virginia Slims. The defendants operated online cigarette stores wherein, according to Philip Morris, the defendants were using its trademarks without authorization to advertise and sell gray market cigarettes into the U.S.[108] The defendants were foreign corporations of unknown citizenship. Philip Morris discovered their physical address by looking at the

---

101. *See e.g.,* Federated Rural Elec. Ins. Corp. v. Kootenai Elec. Co-op, 17 F.3d 1302, 1305 (10th Cir. 1994) ("[M]ere placement of advertisements in nationally distributed papers or journals does not rise to the level of purposeful contact with a forum required by the Constitution in order to exercise personal jurisdiction over the advertiser.").
102. World-Wide Volkswagen Corp. v. Woodson, 444 U.S. 286, 297–98 (1980).
103. Edberg v. Neoge Corp., 17 F. Supp. 2d 104, 114 (D.C. 1998).
104. *See e.g.,* Phoenix Mining & Mineral, L.L.C. v. Treasury Oil Corp., 2007 WL 951866 at *5 (S.D. Tex. 2007) (e-mails sent by nonresident defendant to plaintiff in Texas held sufficient to establish personal jurisdiction).
105. *See* EDIAS Software Int'l, L.L.C. v. BASIS Int'l, Ltd., 947 F. Supp. 413, 417 (D. Az. 1996) (also suggesting that "substantial, ongoing" communications could support general jurisdiction, as well as limited jurisdiction).
106. Panavision Int'l v. Toeppen, 141 F.3d 1316, 1320 (9th Cir. 1998) ("No court has ever held that an Internet advertisement alone is sufficient to subject a party to jurisdiction in another state.").
107. Morris USA Inc. v. Veles Ltd, 2007 WL 725412 (S.D.N.Y.).
108. *Id.* at *1.

address provided to register the Web sites' domain names. The defendants did not advertise their physical location, and they conducted their entire business electronically; they took customer orders through their Web sites and confirmed orders and gave shipping notices by e-mail.[109]

After Philip Morris commenced litigation in the Southern District of New York, the defendants filed a motion to dismiss Philip Morris' complaint for lack of personal jurisdiction. Without disputing or denying Philip Morris' allegations, the defendants argued that the case should be dismissed because the allegations were insufficient to confer personal jurisdiction.[110] According to Philip Morris' complaint, the defendants should be subject to personal jurisdiction because defendants advertised and sold products in the Southern District of New York and defendants' wrongful actions have harmed Philip Morris in the court's forum.[111]

Defendants averred that these allegations were insufficient to confer jurisdiction and therefore did not offer any facts to disprove their alleged contacts with New York. The court disagreed with the defendants' logic and held that jurisdiction was proper: "In this trademark action, defendants are accused of misleading consumers with trademark infringement activity on their Web sites, which they use to transact for the sale of cigarettes bearing plaintiff's trademark into New York. The transactions into New York relate to the wrong alleged in the consumer confusion caused by the unauthorized use of plaintiff's trademarks to induce buyers to make web purchases, and the shipment of gray market goods here."[112] With respect to the defendants' contention that plaintiff had not sufficiently proven personal jurisdiction, the court added the following: "[T]he burden on the plaintiff is not to prove personal jurisdiction by a preponderance of the evidence but merely to make out a prima facie case."[113]

Assuming personal jurisdiction is available, the next issue to be considered is the proper *venue*. Although several states or districts may have jurisdiction over the action, the venue rules are designed to give defendants some control over the place of trial.[114] Similar to the above discussion of personal jurisdiction, a full examination of the venue rules is beyond the scope of this book. The following is a discussion of issues that can arise for brand owners and alleged infringers examining venue issues in the gray market context.

---

109. *Id.*
110. *Id.* at *4.
111. *Id.*
112. *Id.* at *5.
113. *Id.*
114. *See* Denver & Rio Grande W. R.R. Co. v. Bhd. of R.R. Trainmen, 387 U.S. 556, 560 (1967).

Similar to personal jurisdiction, parties may contractually agree to the proper venue.[115] If there is no such agreement, parties are guided by the general federal venue statute, 28 U.S.C. § 1391. Section 1391(a) governs venue in diversity cases and Section 1391(b) governs venue in cases arising under federal law. Venue is proper in diversity and federal question cases under the following scenarios: (1) if all defendants reside in the same state, a district court where any defendant resides; or (2) a district court in which a "substantial part of the events or omissions" on which the claim is based occurred.[116] If no such facts exist and diversity is the basis for jurisdiction, venue is proper in a district court in which any defendant is subject to personal jurisdiction at the time the action is commenced.[117] If federal question is the basis for jurisdiction and the two above scenarios cannot be met, venue is then proper in any district court in which any defendant "may be found."[118] This "may be found" option does not even require that the defendant be "found" at the time the action is commenced. Thus, venue could be premised on service made while the defendant was physically located in the state but not when the lawsuit was actually filed.[119] Finally, it should be noted that civil actions arising under copyright laws may similarly be brought "in the district in which the defendant or his agent resides or may be found."[120] This requirement has been interpreted to mean that a defendant is amenable to personal jurisdiction in a particular forum based on realistic "contacts" with that forum. The alleged infringer's amenability to personal jurisdiction must relate, however, to the federal district in which the action was filed, rather than to the state in which the district court is located.[121]

---

115. *See* Carnival Cruise Lines, Inc. v. Shute, 499 U.S. 585, 595 (1991) ("Any litigation to enforce this agreement shall be instituted in Los Angeles, California, and nowhere else."). For further discussion on the enforceability of forum selection clauses, see __.
116. 28 U.S.C. §§ 1391(a)(1)–(2), (b)(1)–(2).
117. 28 U.S.C. § 1391(a)(3).
118. 28 U.S.C. § 1391(b)(3).
119. Schwarzer, Tashima & Wagstaffe, Cal. Prac. Guide: Fed. Civ. Pro. Before Trial ¶ 4:202 (The Rutter Group 2007).
120. 28 U.S.C. § 1400(a).
121. *See* Milwaukee Concrete Studios, Ltd. v. Fjeld Mfg., 8 F.3d 441, 445–47 (7th Cir. 1993).

CHAPTER

11

Preliminary Remedies

"There is a place in our jurisprudence for Ex Parte Issuance, without notice, of temporary restraining orders of short duration...."
—Carroll v. President and Commissioners of Princes Anne[1]

a. Search and Seizure	166
b. Temporary Restraining Orders and Preliminary Injunctions	170
c. Knock 'n Talks	173
d. Cease and Desist Correspondence	174

In the criminal context, law enforcement officials are allowed to search for evidence without obtaining a search warrant if the circumstances would cause a "reasonable person" to believe that entry was necessary to prevent the destruction of relevant evidence.[2] The rationale for such a rule is obvious: If one is willing to commit a crime, he probably has no reservations about hiding evidence and, of course, cannot be trusted to honestly respond to a subpoena asking for the production of all relevant evidence. To prevent such an improper frustration of justice, courts carved out an "exigent circumstances" exception to the Fourth Amendment's safeguards against unreasonable searches and seizures.[3]

The general rule in civil litigation, however, provides that a defendant is served with a summons and complaint and afforded between twenty and

---

1. Carroll v. President and Commissioners of Princes Anne, 393 U.S. 175, 180 (1968).
2. United States v. McConney, 728 F. 2d 1195, 1199 (9th Cir. 1984) (en banc), *cert denied*, 469 U.S. 824 (1984).
3. *Id.* at 1199.

thirty days before being obligated to respond.[4] During this time period, a defendant typically selects an attorney, takes measures to ensure that all potentially relevant evidence is preserved,[5] and begins contemplating the litigation strategy. If the defendant is less honorable, however, it will endeavor to take advantage of this calm before the litigation storm by doing everything possible to revise history; documents will be shredded, electronic evidence will be scrubbed, and any other indicia of culpability will disappear.[6]

In addition to destroying evidence, there are other practices that can vex brand owners. For example, many defendants will treat the allegations in a complaint as simply *allegations*. Operating under the strategy that these allegations can be debunked through explanation or denial, these defendants will stay the course and make no modifications to their business model. Until a judge or jury orders otherwise, sales of potentially infringing products will continue during the next several months or years of litigation. Once a brand owner concludes that litigation is necessary, it must therefore examine whether it should avail itself to any of the preliminary remedies designed to preemptively prohibit unlawful activity. The following pages examine these remedies.

a. Search and Seizure

If destruction of incriminating evidence is a concern, it is necessary to consider whether a surprise search and seizure is warranted. In the digital age, it is not uncommon for the strongest evidence of culpability to also be the evidence most susceptible to destruction. With a few keystrokes or clicks of a mouse, the e-mail, instant message (IM), or text message that shows the defendant's intent to deceive a brand owner can be erased forever.[7]

---

4. *See e.g.*, Fed. R. Civ. P. 12(a)(1)(A) (unless statute provides otherwise, a defendant shall serve an answer within twenty days after being served with the summons and complaint); *see also* Cal. Civ. Proc. § 412.20(a)(3) (unless extended by stipulation or court order, defendant's answer is due within thirty days after service of the complaint).
5. *See e.g.*, Rambus, Inc. v. Inineon Tech. AG, 222 F.R.D. 280, 288 (E.D. Va. 2004) ("[O]nce a party reasonably anticipates litigation, it has a duty to suspend, as to documents that may be relevant to the anticipated litigation, any routine document purging system that might be in effect; failure to do so constitutes spoliation.").
6. *See e.g.*, Kurt Eichenwald, *Andersen Auditors Knew About Federal Inquiry, Records a Trial Show*, N.Y. Times, May 15, 2002, at C10 (describing Arthur Andersen's auditors shredding Enron documents while simultaneously working on and being aware of the S.E.C.'s inquiry of Enron).
7. *See e.g.*, Thomas J. Fitzgerald, *CIRCUITS: Basics; Deleted But Not Gone*, N.Y. Times, Jan. 3, 2005, at C9 ("When normal deletion methods like the Recycle Bin or the delete command are used, the computer's operating system, for the sake of speed, creates an illusion that data

Executing a surprise search and seizure provides brand owners with the best opportunity to discover these *smoking gun* documents.

The Federal Rules of Civil Procedure allow for the issuance of such preliminary orders without prior notice to the defendant if the plaintiff can "clearly show" that irreparable harm will occur if the defendant is afforded the opportunity to oppose the requested order.[8] The opportunity to erase computer disks, burn, shred, or hide documents, and coach potential witnesses is present in virtually every civil case. Therefore, a plaintiff must do more than assert that the defendant *could* destroy evidence if given the chance. Instead, a plaintiff must show that giving notice to the defendant would render further prosecution of the action fruitless[9] because the defendant *will* disregard a direct court order and dispose of evidence prior to any hearing.[10] To meet this burden, a plaintiff must show that its adversary has a history of disposing evidence or violating court orders or that persons similar to the defendant have such a history.[11]

In addition to the destruction of documentary and electronic evidence, a search and seizure may be necessary to recover the actual products that infringe a plaintiff's trademark or copyright. In the context of trademark infringement, 15 U.S.C. § 1116(d)(1)(A) provides a court with the authority to grant an order for "the seizure of goods and counterfeit marks involved in such violation and the means of making such marks, and records documenting the manufacture, sale, or receipt of things involved in such violation."

With respect to copyright infringement, 17 U.S.C. § 503(a) provides that, "[a]t any time while an action under this title is pending, the court may order the impounding, on such terms as it may deem reasonable, of all copies or phonorecords claimed to have been made or used in violation of the copyright owner's exclusive rights, and of all plates, molds, matrices, masters,

---

has been deleted. In fact, it merely earmarks that region of a disk or drive as being available for new data to overwrite the old data. Until that overwriting occurs, the old data can be retrieved with undelete programs and tools used by data recovery labs and law enforcement agencies. . . . To delete individual files there are programs, often called file shredders, which also use overwriting to render data unrecoverable. For example, Window Washer from Webroot Software ($29.95 at www.webroot.com) includes a feature called bleaching that offers several overwriting methods, including a National Security Agency standard of seven overwrites, and the Gutmann standard of 35 overwrites.").

8. Fed. R. Civ. P. 65(b) ("A temporary restraining order may be granted without written or oral notice to the adverse party or that party's attorney only if (1) it clearly appears from specific facts shown by affidavit or by the verified complaint that immediate and irreparable injury, loss, or damage will result to the applicant before the adverse party or that party's attorney can be heard in opposition, and (2) the applicant's attorney certifies to the court in writing the efforts, if any, which have been made to give the notice and the reasons supporting the claim that notice should not be required. . . .").
9. *In re* Vuitton et Fils S.A., 606 F.2d 1, 5 (2d Cir. 1979).
10. First Tech. Safety Sys., Inc. v. Depinet, 11 F.3d 641, 650 (6th Cir. 1993).
11. *Id.* at 651.

tapes, film negatives, or other articles by means of which such copies or phonorecords may be reproduced."

Similar to the Federal Rules of Civil Procedure discussed above, to obtain a Section 1116(d) order a plaintiff must provide specific facts showing, among others, that "the person against whom seizure would be ordered, or persons acting in concert with such person, would destroy, move, hide, or otherwise make such matter inaccessible to the court, if the applicant were to proceed on notice to such person."[12] The same proof is required in seizures under the Copyright Act.[13]

Of course, proving a history of disposing evidence before litigation has even begun can be a challenge. In the event the court is not satisfied with the plaintiff's proof on this issue, it will typically deny the request and order the plaintiff to serve the defendant with the complaint and provide the defendant an opportunity to oppose any requests for preliminary remedies. Although adhering to the court's order, the plaintiff should simultaneously have a strategy in place designed to expose any efforts to eliminate evidence. Rather than hire a process server to simply serve the lawsuit and wait to hear from the defendant or its counsel, a plaintiff would be well-advised to hire a reputable private investigator to have a team of individuals conduct surveillance of the defendant and all relevant locations where evidence of wrongdoing could be found. When the team is in place conducting surveillance from a public location, the defendant should be served with the complaint. From there, the defendant and all relevant locations must be observed and taped. Dumpster diving should also be considered. As discussed in Chapter 9, searching through another's trash is, in certain instances, perfectly legal.

The moment the defendant is seen doing anything to conceal or destroy evidence, the plaintiff should renew its request for a surprise search and seizure. Proof that the defendant is in the process of hiding or destroying evidence should be sufficient to have the court quickly reconsider its prior order and authorize a search and seizure before it is too late.

Because of the severity of the remedy, it is important to be mindful of the potential downsides of requesting a surprise search and seizure. Because of the immediate and dramatic disruption to the defendant's business, counterclaims for wrongful seizure are common. For example, in *Martin's Herend Imps., Inc. v. Diamond & Gem Trading USA, Co.*,[14] the Fifth Circuit Court examined a trial court's rulings awarding the plaintiff an injunction while denying the defendant's counterclaim for wrongful seizure. Curiously, the court affirmed the trial court's injunction but reversed the denial of the wrongful seizure claim.

---

12. 15 U.S.C. § 1116(d)(4)(B)(vii).
13. *See e.g.*, Time Warner Entm't Co. v. Does Nos. 1–2, 876 F. Supp. 407, 411 (E.D.N.Y. 1994).
14. Martin's Herend Imps., Inc. v. Diamond & Gem Trading USA, Co., 112 F.3d 1296 (5th Cir. 1997).

When the *Martin's* lawsuit was initiated, the plaintiff alleged that the defendants were selling fake porcelain products with a forged trademark. An affidavit from the plaintiff's president averred that the plaintiff had purchased several products from defendants that were not authentic.[15] Based on these claims, the trial court allowed the plaintiffs, through counsel and with the assistance of U.S. marshals, to raid the defendants' premises and seize various goods and records.[16]

As the case progressed, however, the plaintiff's theory evolved from a black market to a gray market case. Unable to establish that the defendants were selling fakes, the plaintiff argued that the defendants nonetheless infringed their trademark. The plaintiff, as the sole importer of foreign manufactured porcelain products, argued that defendant's gray market products, which were not authorized for importation, were materially different from the plaintiff's products.

Although the Court agreed with the plaintiff's gray market theory of liability,[17] it held that the trial court erred in granting summary judgment against the defendants on their wrongful seizure claim. The Court reasoned that the draconian nature of the *ex parte* remedy demanded that 15 U.S.C. § 1116(d) be construed narrowly. To wit, the statute does not expressly refer to gray market goods or goods with marks affixed by the manufacturer or some authorized holder of the marks. Therefore, the court held that "[g]ray market goods are not subject to this provision even if they are materially different from those selected for the domestic market."[18]

The court noted that the result would have been different if fake pieces were seized among other gray pieces. Given the plaintiff's failure to make this showing, however, the court concluded that the trial court erred in granting summary judgment in favor of the plaintiff and remanded the case accordingly.

The remedies for wrongful seizure are significant. Under 15 U.S.C. § 116(d)(11), "[a] person who suffers damage by reason of a wrongful seizure under this subsection has a cause of action against the applicant for the order under which such seizure was made, and shall be entitled to recover such relief as may be appropriate, including damages for lost profits, cost of materials, loss of good will, and punitive damages in instances where the seizure was sought in bad faith. . . ."

Once products find their way into the gray market, brand owners lose all control over their distribution and have no way of knowing, for example,

---

15. *Id.* at 1306.
16. *Id.* at 1299.
17. For further discussion on the substantive analysis of defendant's liability, see Chapter 17.
18. *Id.* at 1306.

whether its products are being commingled with black market products.[19] The use of brand protection purchases, *supra*, prior to a search and seizure is necessary to determine whether the gray marketer is doing anything more to justify a surprise search and seizure.

b. Temporary Restraining Orders and Preliminary Injunctions

Even in cases where the element of surprise is not necessary to seize evidence of wrongdoing, a preliminary remedy to maintain the status quo may be required to prevent the unlawful sale or distribution of gray market products. Such equitable relief can often be obtained at the beginning of a lawsuit by way of a temporary restraining order (TRO) and a preliminary injunction.

Federal Rule of Civil Procedure 65 addresses the general framework for obtaining a TRO or preliminary injunction. A TRO should be filed as soon as a plaintiff learns of the conduct rendering a TRO necessary.[20] A TRO is thus typically filed concurrently with the filing of a plaintiff's complaint. Depending on the circumstances, a TRO may be requested with or without giving notice to the defendant. Although the previous section described circumstances in which the plaintiff would not *want* to give notice to the defendant, there are instances when a moving party simply *cannot* provide notice.[21] Even in these latter instances, the moving party must show that immediate and irreparable injury will result without the issuance of a TRO.[22] In addition, the plaintiff's attorney must identify the efforts to provide the defendant notice of the requested TRO.[23] Perfunctory efforts to serve a defendant followed by a conclusory declaration that service could not be effectuated are insufficient, and can constitute grounds to deny an otherwise meritorious TRO request.[24]

After the TRO hearing, regardless of whether a TRO is issued, the court will typically schedule a subsequent hearing to determine whether a preliminary injunction should be entered. If a TRO was issued without notice,

---

19. *See e.g.*, U.S. v. Eighty-Three Rolex Watches, 992 F.2d 508, 510 (5th Cir. 1993) (plaintiff contended that gray market importers provide inferior inspection and testing of products and substitute non-genuine parts into products).
20. Miller v. California Pac. Med. Ctr., 991 F.2d 536, 544 (9th Cir. 1993) (delay before seeking injunction is relevant in determining whether relief is truly necessary).
21. Am. Can Co. v. Mansukhari, 742 F.2d 314, 322 (7th Cir. 1984) ("[A]n ex parte order is proper only when there is *no reasonable alternative*.").
22. Fed. R. Civ. P. 65(b).
23. *Id.*
24. *See e.g.*, Ziegman Productions Inc. v. City of Milwaukee, 496 F. Supp. 965, 967 (D.C. Wis. 1980) (inadequate efforts to serve defendants warranted denial of TRO request).

the preliminary injunction hearing must be "at the earliest possible time and takes precedence of all matters except older matters of the same character."[25]

To obtain a preliminary injunction a party must demonstrate: (1) that it will be irreparably harmed if an injunction is not granted; and (2) either (a) a likelihood of success on the merits, or (b) sufficiently serious questions going to the merits to make them a fair ground for litigation, and a balance of the hardships tipping in favor of the moving party.[26] When requesting a preliminary injunction in the context of trademark infringement, showing a likelihood of brand confusion constitutes the requisite showings of a likelihood of prevailing on the merits and irreparable harm.[27] Gray market plaintiffs, therefore, only need to show a likelihood of brand confusion to similarly obtain a preliminary injunction.

For example, in *Original Appalachian Artworks, Inc. v. Granada Elecs., Inc.*,[28] the Second Circuit Court examined a plaintiff's right to enjoin the importation of gray market goods. Specifically, the case involved the importation of Cabbage Patch Kids dolls, which were a wildly popular toy in the 1980s.[29] The plaintiff was the maker and licensor of the Cabbage Patch Kids dolls and initiated litigation against the defendant, who imported and distributed the dolls in the United States. The imported dolls at issue were manufactured by a company licensed by the plaintiff to sell only to certain foreign countries and only to those purchasers that similarly agreed not to use or resell the dolls outside those countries.[30]

The defendant argued that no trademark infringement had occurred because the imported dolls were authentic Cabbage Patch Kids dolls with a genuine trademark that accurately portrayed the plaintiff as the product's originator. Although the Second Circuit Court agreed that the dolls were genuine, it affirmed the trial court's injunction because the dolls were not intended to be sold in the United States and because the dolls were materially different from the dolls that were intended for sale in the United States.[31] The imported dolls, for example, came with Spanish-language boxes, birth certificates, adoption papers, and instructions. The court found that the

---

25. FED. R. CIV. P. 65(b).
26. Lusk v. Vill. Cold Spring, 475 F. 3d 480, 485 (2d Cir. 2007).
27. Hasbro, Inc. v. Lanard Toys, Ltd., 858 F.2d 70, 73 (2d Cir. 1988) ("In a Lanham Act case a showing of likelihood of confusion establishes both a likelihood of success on the merits and irreparable harm.").
28. Original Appalachian Artworks, Inc. v. Granada Elecs., Inc., 816 F.2d at 68.
29. See e.g., Fred Ferretti, *Cabbage Patch Kids: Born for "Adoption" at a Price*, N.Y. TIMES, Jan. 16, 1984, at B4 ("The craze reached its peak just before Christmas, according to Coleco, when the dolls were on sale, or sold out, at retail outlets across the country and news organizations carried stories of frustrated parents unable to find the dolls.").
30. *Id.* at 70.
31. For further discussion on what constitutes "material differences" for purposes of trademark infringement, see Chapter 17.

adoption process was an important element of the "mystique" of the Cabbage Patch Kids experience,[32] and that the sale of Spanish-language dolls caused sufficient public confusion to be actionable trademark infringement.[33]

A similar conclusion was reached in *Zino Davidoff SA v. CVS Corp.*[34] In *Davidoff,* the plaintiff obtained a TRO against the defendant, which prevented the defendant from selling any counterfeit goods and which also required the defendant to set aside certain products for the plaintiff's inspection.[35] During the inspection of the products, which were men's and women's fragrances manufactured abroad, it was found that 863 units were counterfeit and 16,600 units were gray market products.[36] When the plaintiff sought a preliminary injunction, the defendant did not oppose an injunction prohibiting the sale of counterfeit goods; however, the defendant did oppose any injunction against its right to sell gray market products.[37]

Although demonstrating a likelihood of brand confusion is usually sufficient to obtain a preliminary injunction, the court acknowledged the general rule that the sale of genuine goods typically does not violate trademark law because such a sale is unlikely to cause confusion.[38] One exception, however, pertained to goods that are subject to quality control standards imposed by the manufacturer. Gray markets goods that do not adhere to these quality control standards are not considered genuine, and their sale will constitute trademark infringement.[39]

Concluding that the plaintiff established and adhered to legitimate quality control standards and that the defendant's nonconforming sales would diminish the value of the plaintiff's mark, the court concluded that the plaintiff established the requirement of proving a likelihood of success on the merits of its trademark infringement claim.[40]

Although proving irreparable harm is also required to obtain a preliminary injunction, the court concluded in a sparse analysis that the plaintiff

---

32. See Ferretti, *supra* note 29, at B4 ("The Cabbage Patch Kids—those pudgy, homely, soft little dolls with no chins that seemed to be just about everywhere during the holidays—were so extraordinarily popular because they were designed to be substitute children, according to researchers and psychologists who helped with the development of the dolls.").
33. *Id.* at 71–72.
34. Zino Davidoff SA v. CVS Corp, 007 WL 1933932 (S.D.N.Y. 2007).
35. *Id.* at *1.
36. *Id.* at *2.
37. *Id.* at *3.
38. *Id.* at *3, *citing,* Polymer Tech. Corp. v. Mimran ("Polymer I"), 975 F.3d 74, 78 (2d Cir. 1994).
39. *Id., citing,* Polymer Tech. Corp. v. Mimran ("Polymer II"), 37 F.3d 74, 78 (2d Cir. 1994); *see also* Chapter 17 for further discussion on a gray marketer's failure to adhere to a manufacturer's quality control standards constituting trademark infringement.
40. *Id.* at *3–8.

made this requisite showing. The court first relied on the authority holding that the establishment of consumer confusion creates a legal presumption of irreparable injury.[41] Because the defendant had not come forward to rebut this legal presumption, the court concluded that the plaintiff had sufficiently established irreparable harm to warrant the issuance of a preliminary injunction.[42]

c. Knock 'n Talks

The foregoing has thus far required the filing of a formal complaint and additional pleadings requesting the court to issue preliminary remedies. In addition to the inherent uncertainty of litigation, search and seizures and preliminary injunctions require significant and costly attorney time. When the economics of such procedures are not feasible or warranted, a brand owner can consider some of the more cost-effective strategies aimed at either stopping illegal sales of its products or, if the illegal sales are going to continue, catching the dishonest entrepreneurs in the act.

One of the more low-cost strategies is to conduct an informal "knock 'n talk" wherein a brand owner's representative and counsel simply pay a visit to the establishment engaging in the illegal conduct. Such a visit can be prearranged or unannounced. During the actual knock 'n talk, the brand owner should outline their theory of liability and explain that the purpose of the meeting is to determine whether the matter can be resolved without initiating formal litigation. Before any knock 'n talk takes place, research should be done to determine whether the jurisdiction has any limitations with respect to such meetings.[43]

Such a visit may successfully convince the wrongdoer to stop the unlawful activity. Even if it is unlikely the infringing entity will be willing to immediately stop its infringing activity and make restitution, an unannounced knock 'n talk may still be appropriate. Simultaneous with the knock 'n talk, surveillance to observe the wrongdoer's actions after the conclusion of the meeting may reveal efforts to hide or destroy evidence of culpability.

---

41. *Id.* at *8 *citing*, Weight Watchers, Int'l, Inc. v. Luigino's Inc., 423 F.3d 137, 144 (2005).
42. *Id.* at *8.
43. *See e.g.*, CAL. RULES OF PROF. CONDUCT, Rule 2–100 ("While representing a client, a member shall not communicate directly or indirectly about the subject of the representation with a party the member knows to be represented by another lawyer in the matter, unless the member has the consent of the other lawyer.").

d. Cease and Desist Correspondence

Making a formal written demand that the gray marketer immediately stop its infringing activities is another option to be considered prior to initiating litigation. If, for example, the gray market activities infringe a brand owner's trademark, a letter putting the wrongdoer on formal notice of its illegal conduct can have two benefits. *First*, the conduct may stop. The gray marketer may understand, perhaps for the first time, that its conduct is illegal and decide to halt any continued wrongdoing. *Second*, in the event that the gray marketer ignores the cease and desist letter, receipt of the letter will prevent the gray marketer from arguing that it had no knowledge prior to the litigation that its conduct was improper.

CHAPTER 12

Civil Discovery

> *"[M]odern instruments of discovery serve a useful purpose. . . . They together with pretrial procedures make a trial less a game of blindman's bluff and more a fair contest with the basic issues and facts disclosed to the fullest extent."*
> —United States v. Procter & Gamble Co.[1]

a. E-Discovery: The Amended FRCP — 176

b. Forensic Preservation and Examination — 178

Both brand owners and alleged infringers have the right to discover "any matter, not privileged, that is relevant to the claim or defense of any party."[2] This rule, in practice, allows for relatively broad discovery. Information is typically discoverable if it "appears reasonably calculated to lead to the discovery of admissible evidence."[3] The skill, of course, is tailoring discovery requests so they are broad enough to obtain all needed information and yet also narrow enough that a court will order compliance if the responding party does not fully cooperate.

Like all modern commercial litigation, gray market cases require parties to understand the reality that the discovery process requires a great deal more than depositions, written interrogatories, and the exchange of paper documents. Although this conventional discovery was once sufficient, it is today a mere tip of the evidentiary iceberg. When the smoking gun document can be

---

1. United States v. Procter & Gamble Co., 356 U.S. 677, 682 (1958).
2. FED. R. CIV. PROC. 26(b)(1). Some states have broader discovery rules. For example, under California law, parties have the statutory right to discover any non-privileged matter that is "relevant to the *subject matter*." Cal. Civ. Proc. Code § 2017.010 (emphasis added).
3. FED. R. CIV. PROC. 26(b)(1).

found on an IM string, Blackberry, or key chain thumb drive, it is imperative that litigants understand how electronically stored information (ESI) works and the procedures necessary to ensure that it receives all ESI from its opponent.

This chapter discusses the practices and procedures gray market litigants should consider when engaged in the discovery phase of litigation.

a. E-Discovery: The Amended FRCP

When the most important information in a lawsuit is found in ESI, litigants are presented with several challenges. One of the more significant challenges is the sheer volume of ESI. Informal conversations that used to be in person or over the telephone are now memorialized in, unless privileged, discoverable e-mails.[4] In addition, such e-mail correspondence is often sent from one computer to another, replied to, forwarded, and replied to again thereby creating multiple records on multiple computers or servers. And, merely hitting the "delete" button does not really *delete* the e-mail. Deleting an e-mail simply changes the file's name and eliminates reference to it in the operating system's listing of *active* files.[5] But, make no mistake, unless more sophisticated efforts are taken, the file is still there.

Moreover, with more businesses having their most important documents and correspondence in electronic, as opposed to paper, form, efforts are being made to ensure that electronically stored information is periodically copied or replicated so that it can be restored should there ever be a disastrous loss of information. Although necessary and prudent, these backup media add to the volume of information that may be discoverable in litigation. Exacerbating the problem is that information on backup media may prove extremely difficult to search. Often the method in which such information is stored does not allow for easy retrieval of documents. In order to search for needed documents, the entire collection of stored electronic information must be restored—a costly and time-consuming endeavor. Finally, obsoletism can make the recovery and search efforts even more difficult; as hardware and software applications evolve, ESI on the backup media may no longer be compatible—and thereby accessible—with the business' current IT setup.[6]

---

4. *U.S. Workers Spared Junk Email*, BBC NEWS WORLD ED., Dec. 9, 2002, http://news.bbc.co.uk/2/hi/technology/2558113.stm (stating that 22 percent of U.S. employees receive more than 50 e-mails per day).
5. Kenneth J. Withers, *Electronically Stored Information: The December 2006 Amendments to the Federal Rules of Civil Procedure*, 4 NW. J. OF TECH. & INTELL. PROP. 2, 174 (Spring 2006), *available at* http://www.law.northwestern.edu/journals/njtip/v4/n2/3/J.%20Withers.pdf.
6. This information is referred to as "legacy data." *See e.g.*, The Sedona Conference, The Sedona Glossary: for E-Discovery and Digital Information Management, (2d ed. 2007), *available at*

Against this backdrop, a series of amendments to the Federal Rules of Civil Procedure (FRCP) governing electronic discovery (or e-discovery) were recently imposed. On December 1, 2006, the amended FRCP took effect in which a new category of information was created: "electronically stored information" or "ESI." The Advisory Committee Notes describe ESI as "[a]ny type of information that can be stored electronically."[7] Although the amendments to the FRCP essentially codify the already accepted assertion that electronic information is as susceptible to discovery rules as paper, the amended FRCP create express obligations on parties and their counsel to familiarize themselves early with location and recoverability of ESI.

For example, the amended FRCP requires attorneys to address ESI with each other before discovery even begins.[8] Some courts' local rules go even further and require attorneys to, prior to meeting with opposing counsel, have an intimate understanding of his or her client's digital systems as well as the identity of individuals with knowledge about his or her client's digital systems.[9] Once discovery begins, there is a distinction between "accessible" ESI and "inaccessible" ESI: "A party need not provide discovery of electronically stored information from sources that the party identifies as not reasonably accessible because of undue burden or cost. On motion to compel discovery or for a protective order, the party from whom discovery is sought must show that the information is not reasonably accessible because of undue burden or cost."[10]

---

http://www.thesedonaconference.org/content/miscFiles/TSCGlossary_12_07.pdf ("Legacy Data, Legacy Systems: Legacy Data is ESI in which an organization may have invested significant resources, but has been created or stored by the use of software and/or hardware that has become obsolete or replaced ('legacy systems'). Legacy data may be costly to restore or reconstruct when required for investigation or litigation analysis or discovery.").

7. Comm. on Rules of Practice and Procedure, Judicial Conference of the U.S., Report of the Civil Rules Advisory Comm. (2004), *available at* http:// www.uscourts.gov/rules/comment 2005/CVAug04.pdf.

8. FED. R. CIV. PROC. 26(f)(3) ("[T]he parties must, as soon as practicable and in any event at least 21 days before a scheduling conference is held or a scheduling order is due under Rule 16(b), confer to consider ... (3) any issues relating to disclosure or discovery of electronically stored information, including the form or forms in which it should be produced.").

9. *See e.g.*, Dist. of New Jersey, L. Civ. R. 26.1(d) ("[C]ounsel shall review with the client the client's information management systems including computer-based and other digital systems, in order to understand how information is stored and how it can be retrieved. To determine what must be disclosed pursuant to Fed. R. Civ. P. 26(a)(1), counsel shall further review with the client the client's information files, including currently maintained computer files as well as historical, archival, back-up, and legacy computer files, whether in current or historic media or formats, such as digital evidence which may be used to support claims or defenses. Counsel shall also identify a person or persons with knowledge about the client's information management systems, including computer-based and other digital systems, with the ability to facilitate, though counsel, reasonably anticipated discovery.").

10. FED. R. CIV. PROC. 26(b)(2)(B).

The best comparison of accessible ESI to inaccessible ESI was first articulated in *Zubulake v. UBS Warburg, LLC (Zubulake I)*.[11] In *Zubulake I*, Judge Shira A. Scheindlin divided ESI into two categories:

1. "[D]ata that is kept in an *accessible* format," broken into three subcategories, "listed in order from most accessible to least accessible:"
   a. "Active, online data," such as hard drives;
   b. "Near-line data," such as optical disks; and
   c. "Offline storage/archives . . . [which] lack 'the coordinated control of an intelligent disk subsystem,' . . . in the lingo, JBOD ('Just a Bunch of Disks')."
2. "Electronic data [that] is relatively *inaccessible*," broken into two subcategories, also ranked in order of accessibility:
   a. "Backup tapes;" and
   b. "Erased, fragmented or damaged data."[12]

There were other amendments to the FRCP.[13] Accordingly, brand owners and alleged infringers must familiarize themselves with the amended FRCP to understand their respective rights and obligations to ensure that the discoverability of ESI creates an opportunity and not a burden.

b. Forensic Preservation and Examination

Another characteristic of ESI is its vulnerability. Through either negligence[14] or design, digital files can be forever deleted and destroyed. It is thus important to consider early on in litigation whether to obtain a forensic preservation, recovery, and examination of all potential ESI sources.

The process begins with the creation of a forensic image or copy of the original digital media. After the forensic copy is verified as being identical to the original, all subsequent analysis is done on the copy; this process

---

11. Zubulake v. UBS Warburg, LLC, 217 F.R.D. 309 (S.D.N.Y. 2003).
12. *Id.* at 318.
13. *See* Fed. R. Civ. Proc. 16 (identify ESI issues in proposed discovery plan), 34 (redefining "document discovery" to include ESI), 37 (creates a "safe harbor" from discovery sanctions for the inadvertent loss of ESI based on the "routine, good faith operation" of an IT system).
14. B. Rothstein, R. Hedges, & E. Wiggins, Managing Discovery of Electronic Information: A Pocket Guide for Judges 3 (2007), *available at* http://www.fjc.gov/public/pdf.nsf/lookup/eldscpkt.pdf/$file/eldscpkt.pdf ("[C]omputer systems automatically recycle and reuse memory space, altering potentially relevant information without any specific direction or knowledge of the operator. Merely opening a digital file changes information about that file.").

preserves the evidentiary integrity of the original. In addition, the forensic copy preserves the entire contents of the original digital media, including any deleted files and file metadata that may be recoverable. Metadata provides information about an electronic file, such as the date it was created, its author, when and by whom it was edited, what edits were made, and, in the case of e-mail, the history of its transmission.

Notwithstanding the importance, complexity, and vulnerability of ESI, litigants often put their trust in opposing parties and counsel to make a competent production of evidence. When a single e-mail or text message can, and has in countless instances, mean the difference between winning and losing, litigants should not trust their opponents to have the competence or ethics to voluntarily produce all relevant information. A forensic examination is the only way to ensure a comprehensive production of ESI. The economic realities of litigation may cause a reluctance to add forensic computing consultants to an expensive legal team. Indeed, monitoring the costs of a lawsuit is good business. However, collecting relevant evidence from one's adversary is not the best place for a fiscal shortcut. In addition, computer forensic methodologies and tools can expedite the process of filtering and analyzing the vast quantities of data typically stored on today's computers. Thus, these processes can reduce the scope of reviewable material and costs attendant to its review.

Although the amended FRCP provides an opportunity to expressly ask one's opponent to agree to a forensic inspection, there is limited authority for the proposition that a party must immediately concede to a forensic inspection of their computers.[15] At a minimum, the party seeking a forensic inspection must show "that conventional discovery methods have failed to produce the information they need to litigate their case."[16]

When examining requests for the production or inspection of computers, courts typically consider (1) the needs of the case, (2) the amount in controversy, (3) the importance of the issues at stake, (4) the potential for finding relevant material, and (5) the importance of the proposed discovery in resolving the issues.[17] With respect to the "needs of the case," some courts have held that parties may not access its adversary's hard disk unless and until it makes a showing that the documents it seeks exist and have been unlawfully withheld.[18]

---

15. *See e.g.,* McCurdy Group LLC v. American Biomedical Group, Inc., 639 N.W. 2d 455, 465 (N.D. 2002) (Mere suspicion that an adversary has not produced all relevant documents will not warrant "such a drastic discovery measure.").
16. Lawyers Title Ins. Corp. v. United States Fid. & Guar. Co., 122 F.R.D. 567, 571 (1988).
17. *See e.g.,* E*TRADE Securities LLC v. Deutsche Bank AG, 2005 U.S. U.S. Dist. LEXIS 3038 (D.C. Minn. Jan. 31, 2005).
18. Bethea v. Comcast, 218 F.R.D. 328, 330 (D.D.C. 2003).

Notwithstanding the lack of authority or likely cooperation, it is good practice to request a forensic examination early in the litigation. Such an early request lays a proper foundation for a later request or motion. To show that this early request is reasonable, the party should make clear that the examination will be performed by a third-party forensic computing expert and that only relevant and responsive materials will be turned over to the requesting party. The request should also make clear that the forensic examination will (1) be pursuant to a mutually acceptable search protocol that would protect the other party's legitimate privacy and other interests, and (2) include an opportunity for the responding party to withhold documents for privilege (and that the forensic examiner's view of the documents does not constitute a waiver of any applicable privileges). Finally, the requesting party should propose that the parties split the cost of the forensic examination. The party can add that this last offer is more generous than the general rule, which provides that a party is required to bear its own costs for an adequate search and production of documents.[19]

If the requested party agrees with the above proposal, the requesting party can quickly move forward to negotiate the specific parameters of the inspection. More likely, however, the party will not agree. In this latter case, the requesting party will likely require a court to order the examination. To obtain a court order, the requesting party must show that its adversary failed to comply with its discovery obligations.

Towards this end, shortly after the responding party has produced documents, the requesting party should issue a deposition notice to obtain testimony from the party's *person most knowledgeable*[20] on issues related to the responding party's efforts to preserve documents once it learned that litigation was reasonably anticipated as well as the responding party's efforts to search for and produce all responsive documents.

With respect to the responding party's efforts to preserve documents, the law provides that once a dispute ripens to the point where litigation is "reasonably anticipated," there is a "duty to suspend any routine document purging system ... and to put in place a litigation hold to ensure the preservation of relevant documents."[21] The litigation hold notice should be sent to all persons who may possess and/or control relevant documents including, for example, key Human Resource and Information Technology personnel. Measures should also be taken to ensure adequate dissemination of the litigation hold notice. Using the e-mail system's return receipt confirmation feature

---

19. *See e.g.*, Oppenheimer Fund, Inc. v. Sanders, 437 U.S. 340, 358 (1978) ("the presumption is that the responding party must bear the expense of complying with discovery requests.").
20. *See* FED. R. CIV. PROC. 30(b)(6).
21. Rambus, Inc. v. Infineon Tech. AG, Inc., 222 F.R.D. 280, 288 (E.D. Va. 2004).

or having employees sign and acknowledge receipt of the notice are examples of ensuring adequate dissemination.

With respect to the efforts to actually produce documents, the propounding party should comprehensively examine the following issues during deposition:

- The identification of present and past system administrators and IT managers;
- The identification of all computer hardware including desktop computers, portable computers such as laptops and handheld devices, and home computers if used for work purposes;
- Information related to the creation, retention, deletion, back-up and retrieval of electronic information; and
- Information related to the production of documents in the pending and other litigation.

In many cases, a thorough scrutiny of the efforts to search for and produce responsive documents can catch a party flat-footed. Such depositions can often prove that the party's document production was woefully inadequate.

In the event the depositions prove that the responding party fell short of its duties to preserve or produce documents, the propounding party should immediately renew the initial request for a forensic examination. If the party still does not agree, the propounding party should seek relief from the court.

Of course, the substance of the motion will be dictated by the level of the responding party's failure to make an adequate production. Depending on the level of failure, the moving party has a variety of authorities to rely on to obtain the relief requested. When a party has refused to produce documents, Rule 37 of the Federal Rules of Civil Procedure provides the court with broad discretion to issue sanctions. Indeed, a District Court has wide discretion in imposing discovery sanctions, including "severe sanctions," and will only be reversed if its decision is an abuse of discretion.[22]

For example, in *GTFM, Inc. v. Wal-Mart Stores, Inc.*,[23] the plaintiffs brought a motion to compel an onsite inspection of the defendants' computer records detailing purchase and sale data. Prior to this motion, the plaintiffs had requested the production of all documents reflecting defendants' purchase and sale of products bearing plaintiffs' trademark since 1997. The defendants' counsel informed the plaintiffs that only information going back to 1998 could be produced. In a later deposition, however, an executive for

---

22. Daval Steel Products v. M/V Fakredine, 951 F. 2d 1357 (1991).
23. GTFM, Inc. v. Wal-Mart Stores, Inc., No. 98 Civ. 7724, 2000 U.S. Dist. LEXIS 3804 (S.D.N.Y. 2000).

the defendants admitted that the defendants did have the capacity to produce additional documents.

The court ordered the defendants to "make available to an expert designated by the plaintiffs' counsel all computer records and facilities within [the] defendants' possession, custody, or control, for the purpose of allowing [the] plaintiffs' expert to conduct an on-site inspection of [the] defendants' computer facilities to ascertain whether and how it is possible to extract information about the purchase of goods bearing [the] plaintiffs' trademarks . . ."[24] In addition, the court ordered the defendants to reimburse the plaintiffs for all legal and expert fees and expenses in connection with the onsite inspection.[25]

Forensic computing discovery is the *sine qua non* of comprehensive discovery in the twenty-first century. Being mindful of the foregoing authority increases the chances of efficiently and economically obtaining the needed discovery.

---

24. *Id.* * 6–7.
25. *Id.* * 6–7 ("[D]efendants' track record on compliance with discovery requests has been poor . . . Hopefully, these sanctions will serve as a deterrent against further discovery abuses by defendant in this case and in future cases.").

CHAPTER

13

Theories of Recovery

Breach of Contract

a. Introduction to Contract Law 184

b. Contract Law's Treatment of the Gray Market 186

c. Affirmative Defenses and the Gray Market 188

d. Remedies 189

Whenever a product is diverted from a brand owner's authorized supply chain, one of its partners has breached its obligations. Although the actual discovery of gray market products may be several transactions removed from the channel, one of the brand owner's top priorities must be to ascertain the identity of the originating diverter. Whether a manufacturing partner is overproducing products or a distributor is selling its inventory to gray market resellers, the brand owner must move quickly to plug the leak in its supply chain.

Once the culprit is identified, the brand owner must consider how to deal with its partner's deception. There are several issues to examine when making this consideration. Beyond the conventional analysis of liability and collectability, a brand owner should also analyze the prudence of making an example out of a partner that strayed from its obligations. In other words, a brand owner should consider the value of deterrence. Other partners similarly tempted to abandon their adherence to a supply chain's restrictions may be dissuaded upon learning that the brand owner aggressively pursues such infractions. Wishing to avoid a similar plight, the tempted partners immediately abdicate any contemplated infidelity.

This chapter examines a brand owner's ability to seek redress from its *authorized* partners that engage in gray market activity. Because these partners typically agree to refrain from certain transactions in their written agreement, brand owners have the ability to vindicate their rights by suing for breach of contract. In some ways, this cause of action can be simpler than the fact-intensive analysis of a copyright or trademark infringement claims.

As the cases below illustrate, however, a brand owner still must overcome some inevitable hurdles in order to prevail.

a. Introduction to Contract Law

A cause of action for breach of contract requires four elements: (1) the existence of a contract, (2) the plaintiff's performance or excuse for failure to perform, (3) the defendant's breach, and (4) damages suffered by the plaintiff.[1]

Proving the existence of a contract should rarely be a challenge for a brand owner. As discussed in Chapter 6, it is imperative that brand owners have written agreements with its authorized partner with unequivocal gray market prohibitions. Failing to have these requirements makes any contract litigation unnecessarily difficult. For example, in *Sebastian International v. Consumer Contacts (PTY) Ltd.*,[2] the plaintiff Sebastian International (Sebastian) manufactured and marketed beauty supplies and restricted retail sales only to professional salons. Sebastian had entered into an *oral contract* with the defendant Consumer Contacts d/b/a 3-D Marketing Services ("3-D") in which 3-D agreed to distribute the beauty products in South Africa and nowhere else.

After Sebastian shipped several hundred thousand dollars worth of product to 3-D in South Africa, 3-D reshipped them back to the United States. Once in the United States, codefendant Fabric, Ltd. (Fabric) was found to possess the products and Sebastian initiated litigation. Without a written contract with 3-D, any effort to allege that Fabric intentionally interfered with the contract would have been futile. Indeed, "[w]hen it became evident that Fabric had not known of the contractual limitations between Sebastian and 3-D, the district court lifted its initial restraining order."[3]

Assuming a written contract between the brand owner and its partner exists, the second element is usually unproblematic as well. Proving "the plaintiff's performance or excuse for failure to perform" essentially requires the brand owner to show that it fulfilled its end of the bargain. So long as the brand owner lived up to its obligations, the authorized partner is without legal excuse to perform any of its promises.[4] Because the gravamen of a brand owner's claim is that the partner engaged in prohibited activity as opposed

---

1. McKell v. Wash. Mutual, Inc., 142 Cal. App. 4th 1457, 1489 (2006); *accord* Anthony v. Yahoo!, Inc., 421 F. Supp. 2d 1257, 1260 (N.D. Cal. 2006); *see also* Roth v. Malson, 67 Cal. App. 4th 552, 557 (1998) (it is basic hornbook law that the existence of a contract is a necessary element to an action based on contract).
2. Sebastian International v. Consumer Contacts (PTY) Ltd., 847 F.2d 1093 (3d Cir. 1988).
3. *Id.* at 1095.
4. 17 Am. Jur. 2d *Contracts* § 699 (2007)

to non-performance, it will have limited ability to rely on any alleged "non-performance" to justify its illicit conduct. This does not mean, however, that a brand owner's conduct is never at issue. As explained below, a gray marketing partner may justify its conduct by the brand owner's chronic failure to ever complain or express disapproval of gray market activity.

Assuming the first two elements are satisfied, the brand owner will next need to establish the defendant's breach. A breach is simply the failure of the partner to perform one of its duties under the contract.[5] A breach can be material or immaterial to the contract; it is material when it relates to a matter of vital importance or goes to the essence of the contract.[6] Other courts have stated the standard of materiality as being when the non-breaching party receives something substantially less or different from that for which he bargained.[7] In the gray market context, the allegation is that the partner failed to perform its duty to maintain brand integrity by buying and/or selling products on the gray market. The standard of materiality for the purposes of deciding whether a contract was breached is necessarily imprecise and flexible. The determination depends on the nature and effect of the violation in light of how the particular contract was viewed, bargained for, entered into, and performed by the parties.[8]

Another common consideration is whether the breach was a total breach or a partial breach. Although every instance of noncompliance with the terms of a contract is deemed to be a breach, not every instance is sufficient to treat the contract as having been terminated.[9] This is rarely an issue in the brand owner/partner context because most contracts afford the brand owner full discretion to terminate the agreement with or without cause. Upon a breach, therefore, whether the brand owner considers the contract terminated is typically within their discretion.

Assuming the brand owner can establish breach, establishing damages is the next issue of contention. The language of the contract will dictate the ease or difficulty with which a brand owner can recover damages. Although a gray marketing partner may assert that the brand owner cannot prove by a preponderance of the evidence that the prohibited sales should inure to the brand owner's benefit, brand owners can preemptively debunk this argument by framing the damages calculation in the agreement itself.[10]

---

5. RESTATEMENT (SECOND) OF CONTRACTS § 235(2) (1981).
6. Thomas v. HUD, 124 F.3d 1439, 1442 (Fed. Cir. 1997).
7. Bernard v. Las Americas Commc'ns, Inc., 84 F.3d 103, 109 (2d Cir. 1995).
8. Stone Forest Indus., Inc. v. United States, 973 F.2d 1548, 1550–51 (Fed. Cir. 1992).
9. Superior Motels v. Rinn Motor Hotels, 195 Cal. App. 3d 1032, 1051 (1987).
10. For further discussion on the recommended clauses to strengthen a damages claim, see Chapter 6.

b. Contract Law's Treatment of the Gray Market

One of the early cases looking at a brand owner's ability to enforce gray market restrictions in a contract is the case of *Elizabeth Lincoln Mercury, Inc. v. Jones*.[11] In *Elizabeth Lincoln*, a car dealer sold a 1949 Lincoln automobile to the defendant. The purchase agreement provided that the defendant would not sell the vehicle for at least 12 months without first offering it to the dealer for the purchase price minus a handling charge of ten percent. The purchase agreement contained a liquidated damages clause, which provided a breaching party would pay the other party twenty-five percent of the invoice price.[12]

In violation of the parties' agreement, the defendant sold the Lincoln automobile to a third party one day after purchasing it from the dealer. After litigation ensued, the defendant argued that the restriction was unenforceable and void because it was contrary to public policy. The court disagreed and, in fact, concluded that the rationale for restricting the alienability of the automobile was a worthy practice to protect consumers:

> Contracts of this character are permitted and sanctioned in order to protect the interests of the public and to foster fair dealing. The public, as well as purchasers of commodities, have a right to be protected against the sale thereof at inflationary prices, in this case the sale of automobiles then scarce and in great demand, which fact created what is denominated a "gray market."[13]

Courts analyzing similar issues came to the same conclusion. The businesses looking to enforce such agreements similarly asserted that enforceability of the resale restriction was necessary to protect consumers: "[I]f the purchasers of [the plaintiff's] new cars immediately put them on the 'gray market' where new cars were at the time selling far above list price, it would cause the buying public in the trade area . . . to feel, and possibly believe, that [the plaintiff] was selling the new cars it received on the 'gray market,' and thus damaging its business reputation in that community."[14]

As mentioned above, a brand owner's ability to prove breach will be made easier or more difficult depending on the clarity of the parties' contract. *Computech International, Inc. v. Compaq Computer Corporation*,[15] illustrates this issue. The plaintiff Computech International, Inc. (CTI) was a reseller of computer equipment and software with particular experience in the video

---

11. Elizabeth Lincoln Mercury, Inc. v. Jones, 313 Ky. 321 (1950).
12. *Id.* at 322–23.
13. *Id.* at 324.
14. Stanford Motor Co. v. Westman, 151 Neb. 850, 852–53 (1949).
15. Computech International, Inc. v. Compaq Computer Corporation, 2002 WL 31398933 (S.D.N.Y. 2002).

editing market. In 2002, CTI was allegedly "induced" to help Compaq Computer Corporation (Compaq) enter the video editing market. As part of this alleged inducement, Compaq "represented to CTI that it would prepare an agreement with CTI which would memorialize its intention to offer special, discounted pricing to CTI across the board on sales of all Compaq product."[16] This representation was unusual because Compaq typically only offered such special pricing for products sold to resellers that were selling directly to end users. CTI, on the other hand, sold its products to other unauthorized resellers.[17]

In apparent reliance on Compaq's assurances, CTI invested "substantial time" to help Compaq develop a "'turnkey' product for an end user in the video production marketplace."[18] After development of the product, CTI alleged that Compaq discontinued its discounts given that CTI was a gray marketer. Specifically, Compaq stopped offering the discounts "due to Compaq's belief that CTI was competing with Compaq in the sale of Compaq product."[19] Making matters worse for CTI, Compaq allegedly "sent a 'blast' e-mail to authorized resellers of Compaq product whereby it labeled CTI as a 'broker' of 'gray market' Compaq product and barred authorized resellers from purchasing Compaq product from CTI."[20]

Compaq was able to dismiss CTI's claims given the lack of any clear contractual obligations between the parties: "The doctrine of definiteness or certainty is well established on contract law. In short, it means that a court cannot enforce a contract unless it is able to determine what in fact the parties have agreed to. . . . If an agreement is not reasonably certain in its material terms, there can be no legally enforceable contract."[21] On the other hand, the vagaries of the parties' agreement prevented Compaq from having the ability to assert any claims against CTI for its gray market transactions. Moreover, Compaq's failure to contractually restrict CTI's sales in any way makes the brand vulnerable to commingling of counterfeit products as well as estoppel defenses were it to assert gray market prohibitions against other parties.

Even when the contract is written, problems can arise of the terms are unclear. For example, in *KNK Tamex Corporation v. Medical-Dental Specialties, Ltd.*,[22] the case involved the allegedly impermissible selling of x-ray film into the gray market. KNK Medical-Dental Specialties, Ltd. (KNK) was in the business of buying and selling supplies to the medical and dental professions. It submitted a purchase order to Tamex Corporation ("Tamex") for the

---

16. *Id.* at *1.
17. *Id.*
18. *Id.*
19. *Id.*
20. *Id.* at *2.
21. *Id. citing* 166 Mamoroneck Ave. Corp. v. 151 East Post Road Corp., 78 N.Y.2d 88, 91 (1991).
22. KNK Tamex Corporation v. Medical-Dental Specialties, Ltd., 2000 WL 1470665 (E.D. Pa. 2000).

purchase of over $1 million worth of dental x-ray film. Although KNK paid for all of the film, it did not receive all of the film it ordered. Meanwhile, Tamex alleged that KNK "mix[ed] the dental x-ray film purchased from Tamex with 'gray market' dental X-ray film imported from China and reselling the product outside of the United States, allegedly in violation of the parties' agreement."[23]

KNK moved for summary judgment on Tamex's breach of contract cause of action arguing that the contract did not prohibit it from reselling the dental x-ray outside of the United States or from mixing the film with gray market film. The court was unable to grant summary judgment because "the parties dispute what activities were impermissible under their contract."[24] Although the opinion does not include the specific language of the parties' contract, it is reasonable to deduce that any gray market prohibition was equivocal. The fact that the parties' disputed interpretation of its meaning was sufficient to preclude summary judgment evidences that the plain meaning of the contract could not be ascertained from its language alone.

Contract litigation does not always flow from the brand owner to a rogue partner. Brand owners can also be vulnerable to litigation for failing to take sufficient steps to prevent the gray market. For example, in *Alleghany Pharmacal Corp. v. Parbel of Florida, Inc.*,[25] a brand owner was held liable when it "refused to participate in efforts to stop the gray market import into the United States" of its products. The defendant had licensed to the plaintiff its trademark for use in the United States. The plaintiff faced unwanted competition, however, when an independent British manufacturer produced products that found their way to the United States via the gray market. Given the court's conclusion that the defendant had not done enough to prevent the gray market, it awarded the plaintiff over $1 million as proven lost future profits attributable to the breach of contract.[26]

The foregoing case law underscores the importance of having clear contracts and adhering to their obligations. The above cases may have had very different results had the contracts been clearly drafted prior to any gray market activity.

c. Affirmative Defenses and the Gray Market

In the gray market context, the cases most often turn on the clarity of the diversion prohibition. However, there are a variety of affirmative defenses

---

23. *Id.* at *8.
24. *Id.*
25. Alleghany Pharmacal Corp. v. Parbel of Florida, Inc., 226 A.D.2d 104 (N.Y. 1996).
26. *Id.* at 105.

available in a breach of contract cause of action. Possible defenses include mistake, fraud, duress, and undue influence. "A mistake need not be mutual. Unilateral mistake is ground for relief where the mistake is due to the fault of the other party or the other party knows or has reason to know of the mistake.... To rely on a unilateral mistake of fact, [the party] must demonstrate his mistake was not caused by his 'neglect of a legal duty.'"[27] Fraud is, as its name suggests, an available affirmative defense where the other party made a misrepresentation that the contracting party reasonably relied on to its detriment.[28] Similarly, duress requires the defendant to prove it was compelled by force or coercion to execute the contract at issue.[29] Although available as a matter of law, their applicability is typically limited.

One potential affirmative defense that may be especially relevant is waiver or estoppel. The requirements to prove waiver or estoppel are the following: (1) the party to be estopped must know the facts; (2) he must intend that his conduct shall be acted on or must so act that the party asserting the estoppel has a right to believe it is so intended; (3) the latter must be ignorant of the true facts; and (4) he must rely on the former's conduct to his injury.[30] This defense may be availing when the facts establish that the brand owner has a history of *not* enforcing its reseller agreements. By showing a pattern of nonenforcement, a breaching reseller can argue that it believed the brand owner had no intention of enforcing any gray market prohibitions.[31]

d. Remedies

Beyond enjoining the gray market activity, the remedies that a brand owner will wish to recover when a partner engages in gray market activity are money damages. The parties' contract will typically dictate the amount and method of calculating this figure. For example, the contract may have a liquidated damages provision[32] that can make the calculation of damages very simple. To the extent that such a provision is not present, the type of damages

---

27. *See e.g.*, Architects & Contractors Estimating Serv., Inc. v. Smith, 164 Cal. App. 3d 1001, 1007–1008 (1985).
28. 17 CALIFORNIA FORMS OF PLEADING AND PRACTICE, *Duress, Menace, Fraud, Undue Influence, and Mistake*, §§ 215.50–215.57, 215.141 (Matthew Bender 2007).
29. Totem Marine Tub & Barge, Inc. v. Alyeska Pipeline Serv. Co., 584 P.2d 15, 21 (Alaska 1978).
30. *See e.g,* Hampton v. Paramount Pictures Corp., 279 F.2d 100 (9th Cir. 1960).
31. *But see,* Microsoft v. Compusource Distributors, Inc., 115 F. Supp. 2d 800 (E.D. Mich. 2000) (Microsoft's issuance of cease and desist correspondence was sufficient to prevent defendant from relying on estoppel defense).
32. For discussion on liquidated damages, see Chapter 6.

available is varied. A brand owner will have the right to seek consequential damages. These damages represent the losses that were caused by the breach that were foreseeable. Foreseeable damages means that each side reasonably knew that, at the time of the contract, there would be certain potential losses.[33]

Attorney fees may also be recoverable. As articulated in Chapter 6, the general rule in this country, known as the American Rule, states that attorney's fees incurred by the successful party in an action are not recoverable in the absence of a statute or an enforceable contract.[34] Thus, the recovery of attorney fees will turn on whether there is an enforceable fees provision in the agreement. Some states like California will interpret a *unilateral* fee provision as *mutual* fee provision.[35] Thus, even if the agreement provides that only the brand owner would be entitled to fees if it was the prevailing party, some states will interpret the contract to mean that the prevailing party—whether it is the brand owner or the partner—shall be entitled to recover attorney fees and costs.

---

33. *See e.g.,* GORDON D. SCHABER & CLAUDE D. ROHWER, CONTRACTS IN A NUTSHELL § 174, at 331–32 (2d ed. 1984).
34. Fleischmann Distilling Corp. v. Maier Brewing Co., 386 U.S. 714, 717 (1967); *see also* Alyeska Pipeline Serv. Co. v. Wilderness Soc'y, 421 U.S. 240, 247–62 (1975) (discussing the history and development of the American Rule).
35. CAL. CIV. CODE § 1717(a) (2008) ("In any action on a contract, where the contract specifically provides that attorney's fees and costs, which are incurred to enforce that contract, shall be awarded either to one of the parties or to the prevailing party, then the party who is determined to be the party prevailing on the contract, whether he or she is the party specified in the contract or not, shall be entitled to reasonable attorney's fees in addition to other costs.").

CHAPTER
14

Theories of Liability

Intentional Interference with Contract (IIWC)

a.	Introduction to IIWC	191
b.	IIWC's Treatment of the Gray Market	194
c.	Affirmative Defenses	197
d.	Remedies	197

a. Introduction to IIWC

As this book has endeavored to establish, brand owners are behooved to ensure that their distribution partners are, once appropriately vetted, bound by written agreements that clearly identify the parties' respective rights and obligations. Specifically, distributor agreements must identify with particularity the obligation to *only* sell the brand owners' products to authorized resellers. Moving down the distribution chain, reseller agreements should identify the obligation to only sell products to end users and perhaps only end users in a particular geographic region. Armed with these contracts, brand owners can have the confidence that their rights will be vindicated if they discover a channel partner supplementing its business by participating in the gray market.

But, what about the other gray market participants? Suppose, for example, that ABC Brand Owner (ABC) had a contract with its foreign distributor that expressly prohibited the distributor from selling ABC's widgets to anyone other than ABC's foreign authorized resellers. For years, ABC honored the agreement until it was approached by GRAY Gray Marketer (GRAY). Seeing an arbitrage opportunity, GRAY offered to purchase a vast amount of the distributor's inventory for purposes of importing and selling the widgets in the United States. The distributor explained to GRAY that it had a contract with ABC and, because GRAY was not an authorized reseller of ABC, it could not sell GRAY any widgets. GRAY explained to the distributor that there was "nothing wrong" with its proposed transaction: ABC would be the benefactor of additional revenue from the distributor's sales, the distributor would be the benefactor of additional revenue and profit from GRAY's purchase, and American consumers would benefit because they would enjoy more opportunities to purchase ABC's widgets. Tempted by GRAY's offering and satisfied with GRAY's rationale, the distributor makes the sale.

When ABC discovers the distributor's breach and the facts underlying the transaction, it takes appropriate action against the distributor. ABC would also like to take action against GRAY. However, it does not have any contractual relationship with GRAY. In addition to exploring potential copyright or trademark causes of action against GRAY, *infra*, ABC would like to know whether it has any claims for GRAY's activity that essentially induced the distributor to breach its settlement agreement.

One theory of potential recovery for ABC against GRAY is the tort of intentional inference with contract (IIWC). Although it is closely related to a breach of contract cause of action, IIWC is a fundamentally different cause of action. As an initial matter, IIWC is a tort. A tort is the name given to a body of law that creates civil wrongs that do *not* arise out of contractual duties.[1]

The significance of this legal distinction is important to brand owners for two reasons: *First*, and most obvious, a defendant in a breach of contract cause of action must indeed be a party to the contract at issue. IIWC is not so limited. Any third party that unlawfully *interferes* with a contract between two parties can be held liable. *Second*, the scope of damages available in a cause of action for IIWC is much broader than typically awardable in a breach of contract cause of action. A breach of contract cause of action is typically limited to direct economic damages that flow from the failure of one party to perform the obligations identified in the contract. The damages in an IIWC case are not so limited. A plaintiff is entitled to recover damages that flow from the breach; additionally, a plaintiff may also be entitled to more extensive compensatory damages and, if the defendant's conduct was malicious, punitive damages.

To establish a claim for IIWC a plaintiff must show "(1) the existence of a valid contract . . . ; (2) the defendant's knowledge of that contract; (3) the defendant's intentional procuring of the breach of that contract . . . , and (4) damages" resulting from the breach.[2] Where the breaching party acted in accordance with the contributing third party, the IIWC claim may also be seen as aiding and abetting breach.[3]

---

1. "Tort" is the Norman word for "wrong." As traditionally used, this kind of wrong is distinct from a contractual or criminal wrong. G. EDWARD WHITE, TORT LAW IN AMERICA xxiii (Oxford Publishing 2003).
2. Israel v. Wood Dolson Co., 134 N.E.2d 97 (N.Y. 1956).
3. Steelvest, Inc. v. Scansteel Serv. Ctr., Inc., 807 S.W.2d 476 (Ky. 1991).

The initial existence of a valid contract is important for IIWC. If a plaintiff is trying to sue for interference in a situation where a contract *has not* yet been formed, he must sue under intentional interference with prospective economic advantage (IIEA) instead, *infra*.[4]

Aside from requiring an underlying contract, a claim for IIWC must show that the defendant was aware of the contract's existence.[5] In *Lanius v. Najman*,[6] the former tenant-operators of a parking lot sued the owner of an adjacent parking lot for zoning violations and IIWC with regard to their parking lot business.[7] When the plaintiffs failed to show that the defendants *knew* of the plaintiffs' existing business relations and contracts, the court dismissed the plaintiffs' case.[8]

An IIWC plaintiff must also show that the defendant interfered *intentionally*, and not just out of normal business practice or even negligence. For example, in *Alvord and Swift v. Stewart M. Muller Constr. Co., Inc.*,[9] a subcontractor had contractually scheduled building improvement services for a general contractor as part of the general contractor's agreement with the building's owner.[10] In general, the project suffered various setbacks, which created unexpected expenses to the subcontractor in performing its subcontract duties. The subcontractor sued for IIWC, alleging that the general contractor, in its failure to prevent the schedule setbacks, was liable for interference with the plaintiff's performance of the subcontract.[11] Ruling against the subcontractor, the court held that it lacked the necessary evidence to show that the general contractor "intentionally and unjustifiably interfered with the work to be done by the subcontractor."[12] Rather, it appeared that the delays occurred in the normal course of business and were not caused purposefully by the general contractor—thus, the subcontractor was not entitled to compensation.[13]

The purposeful action element of IIWC also generally requires that the defendant has acted with "improper means." At least one jurisdiction equates "improper means" with "actual malice."[14] Regardless of the title, most jurisdictions consider the following factors in evaluating improper means (or actual malice) in this context: "(a) The nature of the actor's conduct, (b) the actor's

---

4. Buckaloo v. Johnson, 537 P.2d 865, 872 (Cal. 1975).
5. Lanius v. Najman, 472 N.E.2d 170 (Ill. App. Ct. 1984).
6. *Id.*
7. *Id.* at 171, 174.
8. *Id.* at 174.
9. Alvord and Swift v. Stewart M. Muller Constr. Co., Inc., 385 N.E.2d 1238 (N.Y. 1978).
10. *Id.* at 1239–40.
11. *Id.* at 1240.
12. *Id.* at 1241.
13. *Id.*
14. *See* Shea v. Emmanuel Coll., 682 N.E.2d 1348, 1351 (Mass. 1997).

motive, (c) the interests of the other with which the actor's conduct interferes, (d) the interests sought to be advanced by the actor, (e) the proximity or remoteness of the actor's conduct to the interference and (f) the relations between the parties."[15]

Though the damage element of IIWC is important, a defendant's conduct need not cause a complete breach of contract—the plaintiff can still sustain an IIWC action by using damages resulting from burdened performance. For example, in *Pac. Gas & Elec. Co. v. Bear Stearns & Co.*,[16] a power company entered into a long-term contract to purchase power from a hydroelectric dam. When energy prices rose, the defendant Bear Stearns offered to handle the procedures of withdrawing the dam owner from the contract, so that the dam owner could seek a more profitable buyer.[17]

Fearing the loss of its contract, the power company brought an IIWC claim against the financial company for preparing to induce the dam company's breach. Bear Sterns argued that IIWC could not be used because no breach occurred yet. The court rejected this argument recognizing "that interference with the plaintiff's performance may give rise to a claim for interference with contractual relations if plaintiff's performance is made more costly or more burdensome" even if there was no actual breach.[18]

b. IIWC's Treatment of the Gray Market

IIWC represents a convenient way of reaching gray market defendants who may not have direct contractual ties with a brand owner. IIWC may even be used as an investigatory tool of sorts for brand owners investigating leaks in its distribution chain. In *Quiksilver Inc. v. Shoe Fantasy*,[19] a clothing and accessory manufacturer sought to discover such distribution chain leaks when it asserted IIWC against a store selling the manufacturer's goods without authorization.[20] Not only did the court allow the manufacturer to proceed with suing the store for IIWC, but it also condoned the manufacturer's other intent of obtaining the identity of the store's supplier: a distributor who was directly breaching contract with the manufacturer.[21]

---

15. Adler, Barish, Daniels, Levin & Crecksoff v. Epstein, 393 A.2d 1175, 1184 (Pa. 1978) (quoting RESTATEMENT (SECOND) OF TORTS § 767 (1979)).
16. Pac. Gas & Elec. Co. v. Bear Stearns & Co., 791 P.2d 587, 592 (Cal. 1990).
17. *Id.* at 588.
18. *Id.* In this particular case, however, the financial company's actions were not linked to the power company's burdens, so the court ruled against the plaintiff. *Id.* at 598.
19. Quiksilver Inc. v. Shoe Fantasy, 2005 WL 1274412 (Cal. Ct. App. 2005).
20. *Id.* at *1.
21. *Id.* at *3.

In another instances, efforts taken by gray market IIWC defendants "to circumvent direct importation" was enough to support the requisite *knowledge* element of IIWC.[22] To illustrate, in *Schmid, Inc. v. Zucker's Gifts, Inc.*,[23] the plaintiff Schmid was the American distributor of figurines and porcelain products manufactured by Goebel, which was located in Germany. Although Schmid was the exclusive distributor in the United States, the contract between Schmid and Goebel provided that Goebel would "use its best efforts, consistent with applicable laws to prevent unauthorized importation of [the porcelain figurines] into the United States and Puerto Rico."[24] The lawsuit was initiated when Schmid discovered that various retail dealers were selling the figurines throughout the United States. Specifically, the defendant Zucker's Gifts, Inc. (ZGI) was alleged to be "one of the principal gray marketers of [the porcelain figurines] in this country."[25] Schmid alleged that ZGI was able to import the figurines in the United States by setting up a shell corporation in Panama where it would divert figurines from Central America to New York City where their sales would compete with Schmid's authorized sales.

ZGI conceded that Schmid might be suffering additional competition by virtue of the imported figurines. However, ZGI argued that Schmid could not state a viable legal theory against it. Specifically, ZGI argued that Schmid had failed to allege that ZGI *knew* about the exclusive distributorship agreement between Schmid and Gloebel. Schmid successfully argued that the conduct of ZGI—to wit, setting up a shell company to prevent Gloebel from knowing that the figurines were going to the United States—was sufficient to support the "inference" that ZGI knew of the exclusive contract between Schmid and Gloebel.[26]

In order to avail themselves of the remedies in an IIWC cause of action, brand owners must ensure that their contracts are substantively consistent and consistently applied. Failing to adhere to either of these practices can render cases vulnerable to "waiver" defenses by gray marketers. Such failures can also provide a gray marketer with the opportunity to argue that it did not have "knowledge" of the contract to which it allegedly interfered. For example, in *Matrix Essentials, Inc. v. Cosmetic Gallery, Inc.*,[27] a hair product manufacturer maintained distribution clauses in *some* contracts requiring sales only to salons; however, not all distribution contracts contained such restrictions. The defendants received the manufacturer's products from several sources, and only some of these sources were found to have a contractual

---

22. *See e.g.*, Schmid, Inc. v. Zucker's Gifts, Inc., 766 F. Supp. 118 (S.D.N.Y. 1991).
23. *Id.*
24. *Id.* at 120.
25. *Id.*
26. *Id.* at 121.
27. Matrix Essentials, Inc. v. Cosmetic Gallery, Inc., 870 F. Supp. 1237 (D.N.J. 1994).

obligation to the manufacturer regarding distribution.[28] Given this inconsistency, the court concluded that there was no evidence that the defendants were aware of the anti-diversion clauses in *some* of the distribution contracts.[29]

The next challenge for brand owners is showing that the gray marketer *intentionally caused* a breach. Some courts, for example, have held that even if a defendant is found to have knowledge of a distribution contract and reasonable certainty that he would be causing breach of that contract, the requisite intent might *not* be satisfied if the defendant was only acting for personal gain and not expressly to cause breach or burden.[30] This challenge is compounded if there is evidence that the authorized reseller or distributor was already predisposed to *not* adhere to its contractual obligations.

For example, in *John Paul Mitchell Systems v. Quality King Distributors, Inc.*,[31] there was a dispute over whether the defendant Quality King did indeed have knowledge of the contract between the brand owner Paul Mitchell and its foreign distributor. What was more problematic for Paul Mitchell, however, was the fact that it could not prove that it was Quality King that *induced* the foreign distributor to breach its contract. From the evidence, the court concluded that the foreign distributor "never intended to abide by the terms of its contracts with [Paul Mitchell]."[32] In fact, there was evidence that the foreign distributor had already sought to sell products in the United States before Quality King came along: "Quality King was certainly a willing buyer, but there is no substantial evidence that *induced* [the foreign distributor] to breach its contract."[33] Given these problems for Paul Mitchell, the court denied its request for a preliminary injunction.[34]

Finally, brand owners must be prepared to substantiate the damages it has suffered by the unwanted gray market activity. In *Railway Exp. Agency Inc. v. Super Scale Models, Ltd.*,[35] Railway Express Agency, Inc. (REA) entered into a contract with E.P Lehmann (EPL) wherein it would purchase a certain volume of model train equipment. In return, EPL granted REA the exclusive right to purchase, import, and sell EPL's model railroad equipment in the United States. Problems began when REA discovered that Super Scale Models, Ltd. (Super Scale) was selling EPL railroad products in the United States. Although Super Scale was not purchasing the equipment directly from EPL, it was obtaining the equipment from various European model dealers

---

28. *Id.* at 1247.
29. *Id.*
30. W. Microtechnology, Inc. v. Goold Elec. Corp., 1993 WL 424244, slip op. at *2 (N.D.Ill. 1993) (citing R. E. Davis Chem. Corp. v. Diasonics, 826 F.2d 678, 685 (7th Cir. 1987).
31. John Paul Mitchell Systems v. Quality King Distributors, Inc., 106 F. Supp. 2d 462 (S.D.N.Y. 2000).
32. *Id.* at 477.
33. *Id.* (emphasis added).
34. *Id.* at 478.
35. Railway Exp. Agency Inc. v. Super Scale Models, Ltd., 934 F.2d 135 (7th Cir. 1991).

(who had purchased the equipment from EPL) and was then importing and selling the merchandise in competition with REA.[36]

REA's cause of action for IIWC ultimately failed, however, because the Court was never satisfied that it had established any harm. Specifically, the court noted that "[t]he facts . . . do not demonstrate that Super Scale was the cause of injury to REA."[37] In pedantic dicta, the Court explained that REA could have established damages in several ways. REA could have presented evidence that Super Scale had sold an inferior product or that Super Scale made sales to REA's existing clientele. Because no such showings were made, REA's claim failed.[38]

c. Affirmative Defenses

In addition to challenging every requisite element in an IIWC cause of action, gray marketers can also make the "justification defense." With this defense, the defendant attempts to essentially excuse his interfering acts. The viability of this defense is evaluated given the "importance, social and private, of the objective advanced by the interference against the importance of the interest interfered with, considering all circumstances including the nature of the actor's conduct and the relationship between the parties."[39] In the gray market context, the gray marketer would argue that societal interests were advanced by providing the manufacturer's products at cheaper prices through arbitrage. However, there are no cases that endorse this theory.

d. Remedies

Because IIWC is a tort, the scope of damages is broader than a mere breach of contract cause of action. Compensatory and punitive damages are both recoverable. The most widely and discussed damages award in an intentional interference with contract claim is the 1986 suit by the Pennzoil Corporation against Texaco resulting in $7.53 billion in compensatory damages and $3 billion in punitive damages.[40] Brand owners should similarly follow the

---

36. *Id.* at 136–37.
37. *Id.* at 140.
38. *Id.*
39. Herron v. State Farm Mut. Ins. Co., 363 P.2d 310, 312 (Cal. 1961). *See also* Restatement of Torts § 767(a)–(e).
40. *See* Stephen Landsman, *The Civil Jury in America: Scenes from an Unappreciated History*, 44 HASTINGS L.J. 579, 616–17 (1993).

advice offered in *Railway Exp. Agency Inc. v. Super Scale Models, Ltd.*,[41] *supra*, and provide several illustrations with respect to how the unwanted interference has cause harm.

In addition, when the IIWC claim is coupled with a trademark or copyright claim, brand owners may also request injunctive relief.[42] Especially if the gray market activity in question is ongoing and likely to further damage a brand owner by the continuation of interfering activity, injunctive relief would be an appropriate remedy.

---

41. Railway Exp. Agency, 934 F.2d at 135.
42. *See e.g.*, Graham Webb, 916 F. Supp. at 917 (but here, all claims, including one for IIWC were defeated on motion for summary judgment).

CHAPTER

15

Theories of Liability

Intentional Interference with Prospective Economic Advantage (IIEA)

a. Introduction to IIEA	199
b. IIEA's Treatment of the Gray Market	202
c. Affirmative Defenses and the Gray Market	204
d. Remedies	205

a. Introduction to IIEA

Intentional interference with prospective economic advantage ("IIEA") is an interference tort closely related to IIWC. Both theories of recovery were listed together in the original Restatement of Torts[1] because they essentially deal the same type of harm: the lost benefits arising from a business relationship.[2] Although IIWC compensates a plaintiff for conduct that interferes with the performance of an already-formed contract, IIEA does the same for conduct that interferes with the *formation of a contract before* the contract is formed.[3]

To establish a claim for IIEA a plaintiff must show "(1) an economic relationship between [the plaintiff] and [a third party] containing the probability of future economic benefit to the [the plaintiff], (2) knowledge by the defendant of the existence of the relationship, (3) intentional acts on the part of the defendant designed to disrupt the relationship, (4) actual disruption of the relationship, [and] (5) damages to the plaintiff proximately caused by the acts

---

1. RESTATEMENT OF TORTS § 766(a)–(b) (1939) ("one who . . . induces or otherwise purposely causes a third person not to (a) perform a contract . . . or (b) enter into or continue a business relation . . . is liable").
2. Builders Corp. of Am. v. United States, 148 F. Supp 482, 484 n. 1 (N.D.Cal. 1957).
3. *Id.*

of the defendant."[4] Most jurisdictions also recognize an additional element that, although not always expressly enumerated, requires that the interference be conducted with "improper means or methods" before liability can be found.[5]

The most notable distinction between IIEA and IIWC is that a disrupted business relationship can fulfill the requirements of IIEA even if the legal requirements for a contractual relationship are not fulfilled. On some occasions, the elements of IIEA can be met even if a contractual relationship may never develop.[6] In *Buckaloo v. Johnson*, the plaintiff real estate broker found prospective buyers for a particular parcel of land owned by the defendant.[7] The prospective buyers later completed the purchase without the plaintiff's participation but the defendant refused to pay a required commission for the plaintiff's "procuring cause" of the sale.[8] Here, the California Supreme Court held that, even though the plaintiff had no enforceable contract with the buyer or with the seller regarding a commission, his claim for IIEA could not be dismissed as a matter of law.[9] The court reasoned that plaintiff's procuring actions alone, in light of local real estate customs, constituted a sufficient relationship to support a claim for IIEA.[10]

Of course, not all potential business prospects qualify as relationships actionable under IIEA. In *Binns v. Flaster Greenberg, P.C.*,[11] for example, the case dealt with an IIEA claim in the context of the attorney-client relationship. The defendants were two partners in a New Jersey law firm. The partners had represented an individual for years in various legal matters. When the Securities and Exchange Commission served the client with a subpoena that foreshadowed possible criminal implications, the defendants recommended that the client also consult with the plaintiff, who was a Pennsylvania lawyer with extensive experience in complex commercial litigation as well as a particular expertise in white collar defense and securities litigation.

The client agreed and the plaintiff essentially joined the client's "defense team" and worked on all matters relating to the client. Although a member of this defense team, the plaintiff was not a member of the defendant's law firm: the plaintiff's work was billed separately, he was referred to as "of counsel," and would refer to his own firm when making appearances in court on behalf of the client. Moreover, the client entrusted the defendants to properly staff

---

4. Buckaloo v. Johnson, 537 P.2d 865, 872 (Cal. 1975).
5. Maximus, Inc. v. Lockheed Info. Mgmt. Sys. Co., 493 S.E.2d 375, 378 (Va. 1997). *See also* Della Penna v. Toyota Motor Sales, U.S.A., Inc., 902 P.2d 740 (Cal. 1995).
6. Buckaloo, 537 P.2d 865, 873 n. 7.
7. *Id.* at 867.
8. *Id.*
9. *Id.* at 873–74.
10. *Id.* at 873.
11. Binns v. Flaster Greenberg, P.C., 480 F. Supp. 2d 773 (E.D.Pa. 2007).

the defense team and the plaintiff and client never executed their own engagement letter.

Problems arose when the defendant's insurance carrier advised the plaintiff and defendants that it was capping any further litigation costs at $150,000.00. Given the depleting funds available to defend the client, the defendants terminated the plaintiff. After the termination, there were various disputes revolving around the client's representation and the plaintiff's compensation. When the plaintiff did not receive what he believed to be sufficient compensation his work in the case, he initiated litigation.[12]

The plaintiff alleged that the defendants interfered with his contractual relations with the client (IIWC) as well as his prospective contract with the client (IIEA). By way of summary judgment, the court dismissed both causes of action. Missing from IIWC was the essential contract element. Although the plaintiff was on the "defense team," he did not have any oral or written agreement with the client articulating the client's engagement of the plaintiff.

Because an actual contract was not essential to the plaintiff's IIEA claim, the court focused on whether the plaintiff had sufficiently shown a "prospective contractual relationship." Describing this element as "something less than a contractual right [but] something more than a mere hope,"[13] the court explained that a plaintiff was required to show "a reasonable probability that a contract will come into existence."[14] Given this standard, the court ultimately concluded that the plaintiff had not made a sufficient showing to withstand summary judgment. Germane to the court's analysis was the fact that the plaintiff was unable to identify any facts that manifested a prospective contractual relationship. Merely serving on the client's "defense team" was not sufficient to create any realistic expectation that a separate contract would be obtained with the client.[15]

The intent element of IIEA must be satisfied by a targeted "design or purpose to inflict injury. . . ."[16] As mentioned, courts often use this element to additionally require the plaintiff to show that the defendant exercised "improper means" to carry out the alleged interference. The importance of this element is to distinguish an IIEA claim from cases of interferences that are incidental to conduct that is motivated by business decisions.[17] The distinction between wanting to injure a competitor for improper or proper means is rarely clear. For example, in *Top Serv. Body Shop, Inc. v. Allstate Ins. Co.*, the defendant insurance company referred its clients (in need of auto repairs)

---

12. *Id.* at 776–77.
13. *Id.* at 778 *citing* Santana Prods., Inc. v. Bobrick Washroom Equip., 401 F.3d 123, 140 (3d Cir. 2005).
14. *Id. citing* Kachmar v. SunGard Data Sys., Inc., 109 F.3d 173, 184 (3d Cir. 1997).
15. *Id.*
16. Top Serv. Body Shop, Inc. v. Allstate Ins. Co., 582 P.2d 1365, 1372 (Or. 1978).
17. *Id.* at 1371.

to repair services that were in competition with the plaintiff's repair service. Plaintiff brought a claim for IIEA and was awarded compensatory and punitive damages by the jury. After the trial, the court rejected the jury's verdict reasoning that "'there was no evidence that defendant's conduct was the result of a specific intent directed at the plaintiff or that its purpose was to interfere with the plaintiff, as such.'"[18] The Oregon Supreme Court affirmed, holding that the insurance company's actions in discouraging use of plaintiff's services was consistent with its own business interests and not motivated by an intent to harm the plaintiff.

b. IIEA's Treatment of the Gray Market

IIEA fits modestly in gray market litigation. Participants of an authorized distribution chain are easily involved in business relationships that are, if not full-blown contractual relationships, typical of IIEA causes of action. In addition, distribution relationships are of such character that any future economic advantage is "more than mere hope."[19] Meanwhile, unauthorized distributors or resellers are clearly outsiders to these relationships and are typically aware of the restrictions imposed on the participating business. Distinguishing "improper means" from benign business motivations can be shown by any other conduct injurious to the brand owner. For example, it can be illustrative to reveal that the unauthorized business is also palming off or using the brand owner's trademark without authorization.[20] Causation and damages resulting from gray market activity can also be satisfied provided that any successful undercutting resale amounts to lost profits and a lost customer for the authorized participants.

In an IIEA cause of action, a brand owner must also show that the purpose of its authorized distribution chain and corresponding restrictions are legitimate. For example, where a distribution chain is created for no other reason than to perpetuate "mystique" and inflate prices, an IIEA action will not survive unless the gray market activity actually reduces revenue.

To illustrate, in *Graham Webb International Partnership v. Emporium Drug Mart, Inc.*,[21] the case involved a manufacturer of hair products that only permitted its products to be sold in salons where customers could receive consultation to select the best suited product. The lawsuit was initiated when

---

18. *Id.*
19. *See* Thompson Coal Co. v. Pike Coal Co., 412 A.2d 466, 471 (PA S.C. 1979).
20. *See e.g.*, Dell, Inc. v. This Old Store, Inc., 2007 WL 2903845, slip op. at 1 (S.D.Tex. 2007).
21. Graham Webb Int'l Partnership v. Emporium Drug Mart, Inc., 916 F. Supp. 909, 916 (E.D. Ark 1995).

an exclusive distributor of the hair products discovered that a drug store was also selling the exclusive brand at low prices.[22] It was not clear how the drug store obtained the products, but the distributor was concerned that the product would lose its prestige when offered at a mere drug store without any pre-sale consultation. The court rejected the distributor's claims. As an initial matter, the court was not impressed with the argument that the authorized distribution furthered a legitimate quality control of the product given that there were many sales at salons unaccompanied by any pre-sale consultation.[23]

Moreover, the distributor could not establish any loss in revenue from having this product available outside of the intended salons, despite the lowered prices at the consumer level.[24] The court granted a judgment as a matter of law in favor of the drug store, holding that loss of revenue (and not damage to the product's public image per se) was needed to satisfy the damage element of IIEA.[25]

There have also been instances of gray market resellers using IIEA *against* authorized distribution chain participants. In *Della Penna v. Toyota Motor Sales, U.S.A., Inc.*,[26] Toyota developed concerns that its then-new Lexus division and cars (manufactured in Japan but sold in the U.S.) would be resold in the Japanese gray market.[27] To prevent this, Toyota "inserted into its dealership agreements a 'no export' clause. . . ."[28] Dealers who sold outside of the United States or sold to parties for later export and resale were subject to funding cuts or even a loss of franchise. The plaintiff in this case was one such exporter/reseller, who eventually could find no Lexus dealers willing to sell to him, because of Toyota's measures. The reseller sued Toyota for IIEA, as Toyota's anti-gray-market measures had interfered with the reseller's business.[29]

At trial, the jury rendered a verdict in favor of Toyota.[30] On appeal, the issue was whether the jury was properly instructed to require the plaintiff to prove what was essentially an "improper means" element of its IIEA claim.[31] The Supreme Court of California agreed that "improper means" was a required element of IIEA and that the specific instruction was proper.[32] *Della Penna* underscores the importance of brand owners having contractually

---

22. *Id.*
23. *Id.* at 916–917.
24. *Id.* at 918.
25. *Id.*
26. Della Penna v. Toyota Motor Sales, U.S.A., Inc., 902 P.2d 740 (Cal. 1995).
27. *Id.* at 742.
28. *Id.*
29. *Id.*
30. *Id.* at 743.
31. *Id.*
32. *Id.* at 751.

established distribution chains and also provides brand owners with the confidence that gray marketers will not be able to undermine their enforceability with IIEA causes of action.[33]

c. Affirmative Defenses and the Gray Market

As business prospects can easily be damaged by negative information, a substantial amount of IIEA cases involve some form of speech as the interfering activity. Thus, IIEA allows some speech-related defenses that do not apply to the gray market field. For instance, speech given during official proceedings is privileged and does not invoke liability even if it causes interference with prospective economic advantage.[34] The First Amendment may also be claimed as a defense in IIEA: "[[I]it does not matter whether the defendant's speech was motivated by economic self interest because motives are irrelevant when it comes to public debate."[35]

Similar to IIWC, *supra*, the gray marketer can argue that liability should not attached given the "importance, social and private, of the objective advanced by the interference against the importance of the interest interfered with, considering all circumstances including the nature of the actor's conduct and the relationship between the parties."[36] Related to the justification defense is the claim that the conduct was part of normal business competition. This is also related to the "improper means" element of the action, and may be applied as a defense where that element is not outright required for a *prima facie* case. All competitive business involves a high probability of incidentally interfering with the possible prospects of a competitor. For instance, suppose Buyer and Seller are about to close their hundred-widget deal when Competitor appears. Competitor promotes the superior quality of his widgets to Buyer and wins the contract instead, to the detriment of Seller. Since normal product promotion is not an "improper means," there is no liability for Competitor here.[37]

---

33. *See also*, Intercont'l Parts, Inc. v. Caterpillar, Inc., 631 N.E.2d 1258, 1269 (Ill. App. Ct. 1994) (denying an IIEA claim to a gray market reseller because the reseller had no reasonable expectancy of dealing with an authorized distributor).
34. *See e.g.,* CAL. CIV. CODE § 47(b) (2007).
35. Hoffman Co. v. E. I. Du Pont Nemours & Co., 202 Cal. App. 3d 390, 395 (Cal. Ct. App. 1988) (citing Hustler Magazine v. Falwell, 485 U.S. 46, 52).
36. Herron v. State Farm Mut. Ins. Co., 363 P.2d 310, 312 (Cal. 1961); *see also* RESTATEMENT OF TORTS § 767(a)–(e).
37. *Id. See also* WILLIAM L. PROSSER, PROSSER ON TORTS 954 (4th ed. 1971) ("it is considered to be in the interest of the public that any competitor should be free to divert [a potential customer] by all fair and reasonable means").

If the gray market conduct in question can be shown to be acceptable business practice (i.e., it breaks no contracts formed by the manufacturer, breaks no laws, and otherwise lacks obvious moral reprehensibility), it can escape IIEA liability. Companies worried about the damages of gray market activity should address the threat in their distributor contracts, so that subsequent breaches can eliminate the use of this strategy.[38]

d. Remedies

As for the damages element of IIEA, any actual damages to business relations qualify as recoverable damages.[39] In *Adventure Outdoors, Inc. v. Bloomberg*, a district court found that the plaintiff's IIEA claim was properly pled, including the damages element, even though they only amounted to "damages . . . to 'business relations,' [with] no economic loss. . . ."[40] In contrast, the court cited a case where IIEA claims were dismissed "because plaintiff could not 'identify a single client that he has lost or failed to acquire'" as a result of the tort.[41]

The remedies sought in IIEA cases are also sought along with other related causes of action. For example, for cases in which trademark claims are also involved, injunctive relief is typically sought as well.[42] Injunctive relief is also appropriate if the gray market activity in question is threatened to continue and the brand owner needs a court order for it to stop. In most instances, however, the normal IIEA compensation of business damages should apply to the harm incurred. Finally, because IIEA is a tort, punitive damages are also an option if the defendant acted in malice or reprehensibility, as seen in *Top Body*,[43] *supra*.

---

38. Use of contracts to avoid the gray market has been successful in *Della Penna* and *Dell v. This Old Store* cases, *supra*.
39. Adventure Outdoors, Inc. v. Bloomberg, 519 F. Supp. 2d 1258, 1276 (N.D.Ga. 2007).
40. *Id.* at 1274, 1276.
41. *Id.* at 1276 (quoting Lively v. McDaniel, 522 S.E.2d 711, 714 (Ga.App. 1999)).
42. Graham Webb, 916 F. Supp. at 917.
43. Top Body, 582 P.2d 1365 (reversed, but not because of the punitive damages).

CHAPTER 16

Theories of Liability

Copyright

a. Introduction to Copyright Law 208
   i. Copyright Infringement 209
   ii. Copyright Registration 211
   iii. International Protection 212

b. Copyright Law's Treatment of the Gray Market 213
   i. Performance Rights 214
   ii. Importation Rights 216
      (a) Importation Rights: Authorization to Import Goods 217
      (b) Importation Rights and the First Sale Doctrine 218
      (c) Importation Rights and the First Sale Doctrine: Goods Manufactured and Sold Abroad 219
      (d) Importation Rights and the First Sale Doctrine: Goods Manufactured and Sold Domestically 222
      (e) Importation Rights and the First Sale Doctrine: The United States Supreme Court 224
   iii. Software Licenses and the First Sale Doctrine: An End Run Around the First Sale Doctrine? 227
   iv. Software Licenses and the First Sale Doctrine: An End Run Around the First Sale Doctrine *Beyond* Software? 232

c. Affirmative Defenses 233
   i. Fair Use 233
   ii. Waiver or Abandonment of Copyright 235
   iii. Estoppel 236
   iv. Innocent Intent 237

d. Remedies		237
	i. Injunctive Relief	238
	ii. Impoundment and Destruction	239
	iii. Damages and Profits	239
	iv. Attorney Fees	240
	v. Criminal Penalties	240

a. Introduction to Copyright Law

At its core, copyright law—as its name suggests—gives the creator of an original work the exclusive right to *copy* the work. This exclusive right is designed to ensure that the creator is fairly compensated for the time, effort, and costs to prepare the work. Writing a book, movie, song, or software program requires a substantial investment of time, money, and risk. Once the work is completed, however, copies can be made at virtually no cost. To reward creators and provide a sufficient incentive to invest in innovation, copyright laws seek to prohibit the production and sale of unauthorized copies that divert revenues from the creator.

Copyright law was borne from Johannes Gutenberg's invention of the printing press. After its development, printing companies in England claimed exclusive rights over written works of authors. It was not until the enactment of the Statute of Anne in 1710 that authors gained control over the reproduction of their work.[1]

The importance of protecting such intellectual property was of such paramount importance to America's Founding Fathers that it was specifically included among the neophyte Congress' authority. Specifically, the Patent and Copyright Clause—Article I, Section 8, Clause 8—of the U.S. Constitution provides that Congress has the authority "[t]o promote the Progress of Science and useful Arts, by securing for limited Times to Authors and Inventors the exclusive Right to their respective Writings and Discoveries." Congress passed its first copyright statute in 1790[2] along with revisions in 1831, 1870, 1909, and 1976.[3]

---

1. The Statute of Anne, passed by the English Parliament in 1710, is the first copyright statute and was intended by Parliament to be an "Act for the Encouragement of Learning, by Vesting the Copies of Printed Books in the Authors or Purchasers of Such Copies, during the Times therein mentioned." Act for the Encouragement of Learning, 1709, 8 Ann., c. 19 (Eng.).
2. The 1790 statute designated only "maps, charts, and books;" other forms of expression, such as music, drama, and works of art, achieved statutory recognition only in later amendments. *See* Deborah F. Buckman, J.D., Annotation, *Copyright Protection of Computer Programs*, 180 A.L.R. Fed. 1 (2002).
3. *See* 17 U.S.C. §§ 101–1332 (2008). The Copyright Act of 1976 was Congress' response to developments made in technology and science. H.R. Rep. No. 94–1476, at 47 (1976), *reprinted in* 1976 U.S.C.C.A.N. 5659, 5660; *see also* Buckman, *supra*, at 1.

Today, the term copyright means a great deal more than merely the right to *copy*. The 1976 Copyright Act (the Copyright Act) is the primary piece of legislation that articulates the rights of copyright holders. The Copyright Act provides that owners have the following exclusive rights (1) to reproduce, distribute, and, in the case of certain works, publicly perform or display the work; (2) to prepare derivative works; (3) in the case of sound recordings, to perform the work publicly by means of a digital audio transmission; or (4) to license others to engage in the same acts under specific terms and conditions.[4] Moreover, as the mediums on which copies can be made have evolved from vellum to bytes, copyright law has evolved as well. Copyright protections are now available for a wide range of original works of authorship, including literary, dramatic, musical, architectural, cartographic, choreographic, pantomimic, pictorial, graphic, sculptural, and audiovisual creations.[5]

For something to be copyrightable it must be *original*. As used in the context of copyright law, however, proving originality is not too high of a burden. As articulated by the United States Supreme Court, "[o]riginal ... means only that that the work was independently created by the author (as opposed to copied from other works), and that it possesses at least some minimal degree of creativity."[6] Unlike, for example a patent, there is no novelty requirement in proving originality. Thus, a work may be similar to an earlier work and still be copyrightable. A compilation of noncopyrightable facts may also constitute copyrightable subject matter. Although the facts themselves are not copyrightable, the "particular selection or arrangement" may deserve protection.[7] Copyright protections do not, however, extend to "any idea, procedure, process, system, method of operation, concept, principle, or discovery, regardless of the form in which it is described, explained, illustrated, or embodied in such work."[8]

i. Copyright Infringement

To establish infringement under the Copyright Act, a plaintiff is generally required to prove (1) ownership of a valid copyright, and (2) violation of any of the copyright owner's exclusive rights.[9] With respect to the first prong, the Copyright Act provides that a certificate of registration creates a rebuttable

---

4. 17 U.S.C. § 106(1)–(6) (2008).
5. *Id.*
6. Feist Publ'n, Inc. v. Rural Tel. Serv. Co., 499 U.S. 340, 345 (1991).
7. *Id.* at 348.
8. 17 U.S.C. § 102(b) (2008).
9. 17 U.S.C. § 501(a); *see also* Feist, 499 U.S. 340, 361 (1991) ("To establish infringement, two elements must be proven: (1) ownership of a valid copyright, and (2) copying of constituent elements of the work that are original.").

presumption of validity and ownership.[10] Ownership is a required element because only the *owner* of a copyright or one of its exclusive rights has standing to initiate an action for infringement.[11] The law provides that ownership initially vests in the author or authors of the work.[12] In the event there are two or more authors, the authors of a joint work are co-owners of copyright.[13]

An exception to this rule is present where the author or authors created a "work made for hire." In these instances, the employer or other person for whom the work was prepared is considered the author and thus the *owner* of the copyright.[14] The work-made-for-hire doctrine is present in two situations. *First*, the work is prepared pursuant to an employer-employee relationship. *Second*, the work is prepared pursuant to a contract wherein one party is commissioned to prepare a specific piece of work.[15] To determine whether a work is indeed for hire, courts typically look at the rules of agency to see if the work was prepared by an employee or an independent contractor.[16] Although a work prepared by an employee will typically qualify as a work-made-for-hire under agency principles, a work prepared by independent contractor will not. A work prepared by an independent contractor may, however, qualify as a work for hire under agency principles if it was a *commissioned* work. To determine whether a "commissioned work" constitutes a work for hire, it must fall within the specific statutory enumerated works.[17] In addition, an agreement must specify the work as a work-made-for-hire.[18]

Ownership of a copyright can also be transferred by written assignment. To establish a valid written assignment, the Copyright Act requires a signed written instrument to transfer copyright ownership.[19]

---

10. 17 U.S.C. § 410(c) (2008); *see also* Johnson Controls, Inc. v. Phoenix Control Sys., Inc. , 886 F.2d 1173, 1175 (9th Cir. 1989) ("[Plaintiff's] copyright registration is prima facie evidence of ownership.").
11. 17 U.S.C. § 501(b) (2008); *see also* Parfums Givenchy, Inc. v. Drug Emporium, Inc., 38 F.3d 477, 479–80 (9th Cir. 1994) (The plaintiff had the right to initiate an action for copyright infringement because it "owned the United States copyright . . . *when the infringement occurred*.") (Emphasis added).
12. 17 U.S.C. § 201(a).
13. *Id.*; *see also* Cmty. for Creative Non-Violence v. Reid, 490 U.S. 730, 737 (1989) ("As a general rule, the author is the party who actually creates the work, that is, the person translates an idea into a fixed, tangible expression entitled to copyright protection.").
14. 17 U.S.C. § 201(b) (2008).
15. 17 U.S.C. § 101(1), (2) (2008).
16. Cmty. for Creative Non-Violence, 490 U.S. at 730.
17. *See* 17 U.S.C. § 101 (Defining each of the nine categories of "specially ordered or commissioned" works).
18. *See* 490 U.S. 730, 738 (1989).
19. 17 U.S.C. § 204(a) (2008); *see also* Twin Peaks Prods., Inc. v. Publ'n Int'l, Ltd., 996 F.2d 1366, 1372 (2d Cir. 1993) (Oral assignment followed by a written agreement ratifying the transfer is also sufficient).

Once ownership is established, a plaintiff is then required to prove infringement. In other words, the plaintiff must prove that the defendant violated one or more of the copyright owner's exclusive rights. Similar to a crime being proven by direct or circumstantial evidence, copyright infringement can be shown in one of two ways. Like a bystander witnessing a crime, infringement can be proven with direct evidence of copying.[20] Or, like a corrupt bank security guard found with bags of cash, infringement can be shown with evidence that (1) the accused infringer had *access* to the copyrighted work, and (2) the accused work and the copyrighted work are substantially similar.[21]

ii. Copyright Registration

Although a copyright comes into existence once a work is created or when it is fixed in a copy for the first time, there are benefits only obtainable by registering the copyright. As an initial matter, a registration within five years of the work's first publication is accompanied by a presumption that the copyright is valid.[22] In addition, a copyright owner cannot commence a lawsuit for infringement unless the copyright is registered with the U.S. Copyright Office.[23] Similarly, a defendant cannot bring a counterclaim for copyright infringement unless it has likewise registered its copyright.[24]

One exception to the preregistration rule applies when the work in question consists of sounds, images, or both and the first fixation of it is made simultaneously with its transmission.[25] An example of such a work is a television news program where the first fixation of the work is made simultaneously with its transmission.[26] In these instances, the copyright owner does not need to preregister the mark prior to litigation so long as the owner (1) serves notice upon the infringer the intent to secure copyright protections of the work, and (2) registers the work within three months after the transmission.[27]

In addition to the right to litigate an action for infringement, registering as early as possible is also necessary to give an owner the best opportunity to recover statutory damages and attorney fees. Section 412 of the Copyright

---

20. *See e.g.*, Rogers v. Koons, 960 F.2d 301, 307 (2d Cir. 1992).
21. *See e.g.*, Wildlife Express Corp. v. Carol Wright Sales, Inc., 18 F.3d 502, 508 (7th Cir. 1994).
22. 17 U.S.C. § 410(c) (2008).
23. 17 U.S.C. § 411(a) (2008).
24. *See e.g.*, Xoom, Inc. v. Imageline, Inc., 323 F.3d 279, 283 (4th Cir. 2003).
25. 17 U.S.C. § 411(b) (2008).
26. *See e.g.*, NBC Subsidiary (KCNC-TV), Inc. v. Broad. Info. Serv., Inc., 717 F. Supp. 1449 (D.Co. 1988).
27. 17 U.S.C. § 411(b)(1–2) (2008).

Act provides that, with limited exceptions, such remedies are not awardable if *commencement of the infringement* occurred prior to registration.[28] Commencement of the infringement means the time when the first act of infringement occurs.[29] Even if there is a series of ongoing infringements, commencement of the infringement occurs on the *first* infringement.[30] If the commencement of the infringement occurred prior to registration, then statutory damages and attorney fees are barred even regarding those infringements that continue after registration,.[31] Because statutory damages can often be more than actual damages, there is a compelling incentive for owners to register their copyrights upon the earliest opportunity.

Finally, registering a copyright provides added protection from the U.S. Customs Service. When registering copyrights with the U.S. Copyright Office, an additional certificate must be filed with the U.S. Customs Service.[32] Upon recordation, the U.S. Customs Service will endeavor to bar the importation of any piratical copies of the registered work.[33]

iii. International Protection

Efforts to stop black or gray market activity cannot be accomplished exclusively through litigation. Such a strategy is destined to fail because, in many instances, unlawful acts that occur outside of the United States are not actionable in the United States. In the context of copyright infringement, this limitation is equally applicable. Although the Copyright Act endeavors to bar importation of infringing material and holds liable those who play part of an "act" of infringement that occurs in the United States but is completed in a foreign jurisdiction,[34] infringing activity taking place beyond our borders is essentially beyond the reach of the Copyright Act.

A large majority of developed countries extend copyright protection to works prepared by American authors by virtue of a treaty or other agreement. Most notably, the United States became a party to the Berne Convention on March 1, 1989.[35] Under the Berne Convention, its members recognize the copyright of works of authors from other member countries in the same way they recognize the copyrights of its own nationals.[36] In other words, if the

---

28. 17 U.S.C. § 412 (2008).
29. *See* Johnson v. Jones, 149 F.3d 494, 505 (6th Cir. 1998).
30. *Id.*
31. Fournier v. Erickson, 202 F. Supp. 2d 290, 297–98 (S.D.N.Y. 2002).
32. 19 C.F.R. § 133.33(a) (2008).
33. 19 C.F.R. § 133.33(a)(1) (2008).
34. *See* Subafilms, Ltd. v. MGM-Pathe Commc'n Co., 24 F.3d 1088, 1094 (9th Cir. 1994).
35. Berne Convention Implementation Act of 1988, Pub. L. No. 100–568, 102 Stat. 2853.
36. World Intellectual Property Organization (WIPO), *Summary of the Berne Convention for the Protection of Literary and Artistic Works (1886)*, http://www.wipo.int/treaties/en/ip/berne/

work's country of origin is a member of the Berne Convention, the work is entitled to protection in all member nations. Copyright under the Berne Convention is automatic; it requires no formalities in order to offer protection outside the country of origin.[37]

In addition to the Berne Convention, a number of countries have exchanged notes or otherwise indicated to the United States that they will extend copyright protections to American nationals.[38] Although Sweden and Italy will protect works by American nationals even if the works are first published in the United States, many countries will only extend protections if the work is first published in such foreign country.[39] France, meanwhile, will protect the work of all foreign authors even without an exchange of notes or other agreement unless there is a total lack of reciprocity.[40]

Unfortunately, notwithstanding the above, many countries lack the legal infrastructure to provide foreigners with the needed tools to enforce their intellectual property rights effectively. Some countries simply do not have the legislation sufficient to address the problem. Other countries may have the appropriate laws; however, a corrupt or fledgling legal system may strip the laws of all potency. It is in this latter group of countries where many brand owners elect to manufacture their products. This leaves many brand owners vulnerable as they end up sharing their intellectual property with countries least equipped to protect it. Accordingly, to prevent black and gray market economies, brand owners must use litigation to supplement its overall efforts to control their distribution channels.

b. Copyright Law's Treatment of the Gray Market

Because trademark law has not provided brand owners with the desired breadth of authority to prevent gray market activity, many have turned to copyright law for their desired relief. Because the vast majority of gray market products incorporate a label, design, instruction manual, or other material that can be subject to copyright protection, brand owners have sought to

---

summary_berne.html; *Summary of the Berne Convention for the Protection of Literary and Artistic Works (Paris Act of July 24, 1971)*, www.wipo.int/treaties/en/ip/berne/trtdocs_wo001.html (last visited Oct. 14, 2008). WIPO is one of 16 specialized agencies of the United Nations system or organization, and it administers 23 international treaties regarding intellectual property, including the Berne Convention.

37. Heather Nehila, *International Copyright Law: Is It Music to American Ears?*, 16 TEMP. INT'L & COMP. L.J. 199, 200, fn. 19 (2002).
38. 4–17 NIMMER ON COPYRIGHT § 17.04(E) (2008).
39. *Id.*
40. *Id.*

characterize gray market activity as unlawful copyright infringement. As explained below, determining whether gray market activity constitutes copyright infringement is not a simple task. The analysis involves a complex examination of the interplay among various provisions of the Copyright Act, which requires reconciling the seemingly competing interests between a copyright owner's "importation right" and a gray marketer's "first sale" defense.

i. Performance Rights

As articulated above, the Copyright Act provides that the right to *publicly perform* a copyrighted work is among an owner's exclusive rights. This issue was addressed in the context of the gray market in *Red Baron-Franklin Park, Inc. v. Taito Corporation*.[41] The case was part of a more extensive antitrust litigation between the parties and dealt specifically with the once popular video game "Double Dragon." Taito, the owner of Double Dragon's copyright, argued that Red Baron had committed copyright infringement by operating gray market Double Dragon video games in its arcade.[42]

The actual video game resided on a circuit board, which interfaced with a video game console. Double Dragon players would insert coins into the video game console in order to activate various audiovisual images—some of which are controlled by the players. Rather than purchase circuit boards or a license to operate the circuit boards from Taito, Red Baron acquired circuit boards on the gray market and imported them without Taito's consent. Although Taito had originally sold these gray market circuit boards in Japan without retaining any control over their resale, the game exhibited the following restrictive notice upon the game's activation: "This game is for use in Japan only. Sales, exports, or operation outside this territory may violate international copyright and trademark law and the violator [will be] subject to severe penalties."[43]

Taito argued that Red Baron was infringing its exclusive right of "public performance" when it installed the circuit boards in units in its video arcades and made them available to the public for play. At the trial court level, the district court held that Taito's claims were barred by the "first sale doctrine." According to the district court, Taito's right under the copyright laws, including the right of public performance, extinguished once it initially sold the Double Dragon circuit boards in Japan.

Taito conceded that Red Baron had the right to purchase, import, and even sell Double Dragon circuit boards. Taito's argument on appeal, however, was

---

41. Red Baron-Franklin Park, Inc. v. Taito Corporation, 883 F.2d 275 (4th Cir. 1989).
42. *Id.* at 277.
43. *Id.*

that it had a separate and distinct right to "perform" Double Dragon. Because it had not conferred this right, Red Baron was infringing its copyright by making the circuit boards available for a "public performance" upon a fee.

In determining whether Red Baron's use of the Double Dragon circuit boards constituted a "public performance" within the meaning of the Copyright Act, the Fourth Circuit Court first acknowledged that video games such as Double Dragon are indeed "audiovisual works" entitled to copyright protection.[44] The court then examined the Copyright Act to understand with precision what it means to "perform" the work and to perform it "publicly."

"Perform" means "to recite, render, play, dance, or act [a work], either directly or by means of any device or process or, in the case of a motion picture or other audiovisual work, to show its images in any sequence or to make the sounds accompanying it audible."[45] To perform a work "publicly" means "to perform . . . it at a place open to the public or at any place where a substantial number of persons outside of a normal circle of a family and its social acquaintances is gathered. . . ."[46]

Applying these definitions to the facts of the case, the court concluded that Red Baron's operation of the Double Dragon circuit boards at its arcades constituted a public performance. *First*, it was a *performance* because the television monitor displayed a sequence of images with accompanying sounds. Although the exact order of images will vary somewhat each time the game is played, it would always be a *sequence* of images rather than its mere *display*.[47] *Second*, it was a *public* performance because the Red Baron arcade was open to the public and aimed to attract as many people as possible. Although the game was typically viewed by Double Dragon's player, any other interested patron could similarly view the performance.[48]

Turning to the first sale doctrine, the court concluded that it did not apply to Red Baron's public performances of Double Dragon. By the Copyright Act's own terms the first sale doctrine does not apply to the performance right of a copyright. Section 109(a), which is the codification of the first sale doctrine, only prohibits the copyright owner from restricting further sales or dispositions of the copied work. Section 109(a) had no application to the

---

44. 17 U.S.C. § 101 of the Copyright Act provides that "audiovisual works" are works which "consist of a series of related images which are intrinsically intended to be shown by the use of machines or devices . . . together with accompanying sounds, if any, regardless of the nature of the material objects . . . in which the works are embodied." It is well settled that video games are copyrightable as audiovisual works. *See e.g.*, M. Kramer Mfg. Co. v. Andrews, 783 F.2d 421, 435–36 (4th Cir. 1986); *accord* United States v. Goss, 803 F.2d 638, 641 (11th Cir. 1986).
45. 17 U.S.C. § 101 (2008).
46. 17 U.S.C. § 101(1) (2008).
47. A "display" is defined as a non-sequential showing of individual images. 17 U.S.C. § 101.
48. Red Baron, 883 F.2d 179.

other rights of a copyright owner, including the right to perform the work publicly.[49] Because the first sale doctrine did not apply, the court held that Red Baron was indeed liable for copyright infringement.

ii. Importation Rights

In addition to the exclusive rights identified above, Section 602(a) of the Copyright Act affords owners the right to prevent *importation* of copies that have been acquired outside of the United States.[50] This importation right is designed to prohibit wholesale distribution. Thus, Section 602(a) expressly excludes three activities that do not constitute such prohibited importation:

(1) importation of copies or phonorecords under the authority or for the use of the Government of the United States or of any State or political subdivision of a State, but not including copies or phonorecords for use in schools, or copies of any audiovisual work imported for purposes other than archival use;
(2) importation, for the private use of the importer and not for distribution, by any person with respect to no more than one copy or phonorecord of any one work at any one time, or by any person arriving from outside the United States with respect to copies or phonorecords forming part of such person's personal baggage; or
(3) importation by or for an organization operated for scholarly, educational, or religious purposes and not for private gain, with respect to no more than one copy of an audiovisual work solely for its archival purposes, and no more than five copies or phonorecords of any other work for its library lending or archival purposes, unless the importation of such copies or phonorecords is part of an activity consisting of systematic reproduction or distribution, engaged in by such organization in violation of the provisions of section 108(g)(2).[51]

A cursory examination of Section 602(a) thus appears to be the much needed weapon for brand owners to prevent the importation of gray market products. Indeed, one of the early cases concluded without dispute or analysis that the importation of gray market goods constituted copyright infringement.

---

49. *Id.* at 280.
50. 17 U.S.C. § 602(a) ("Importation into the United States, without the authority of the owner of copyright under this title, of copies or phonorecords of a work that have been acquired outside the United States is an infringement of the exclusive right to distribute copies or phonorecords under section 106, actionable under section 501.").
51. 17 U.S.C. § 602(a).

In *Original Appalachian Artworks, Inc. v. J.F. Reichert, Inc.*,[52] *supra*, the case considered the importation of the once popular Cabbage Patch Kids dolls. The plaintiff, Original Appalachian, granted an exclusive license to Coleco to manufacture, market, and sell full-sized copies of the dolls in the United States. Original Appalachian also granted similar licenses to companies outside of the United States for distribution outside of the United States.[53]

The defendant Reichert meanwhile sought to take advantage of the dolls' popularity in the United States. Operating a "limited export/import business," he became aware that retailers were having difficulty meeting the domestic demand for the Cabbage Patch Kids dolls. Reichert contacted various U.S. Customs Offices and even contacted Coleco to determine whether there was any objection to him importing foreign-manufactured dolls for domestic distribution. After not receiving any affirmative objection, he proceeded to purchase and import various European Cabbage Patch Kids dolls.[54]

Original Appalachian brought a lawsuit seeking various injunctive and monetary relief. The court concluded without objection that Reichert committed copyright infringement. Without any mention of the "first sale doctrine" or the relevance of where the dolls were first manufactured and sold, the court summarily concluded that the defendant had infringed the plaintiff's copyrights by violating Sections 501(a) and 602(a) of the Copyright Act. Since *Original Appalachian*, however, the breadth of Section 602(a) has come under much more scrutiny.

(a) Importation Rights: Authorization to Import Goods

In *Disenos Artisticos E Industriales, S.A. v. Costco Wholesale Corporation*,[55] the Ninth Circuit Court examined the ability of a brand owner to rely on Section 602(a) to prohibit gray market sales. Litigation was initiated when the plaintiff discovered that Costco, a well-known chain of retail stores throughout the United States, was found selling plaintiff's decorative figurines without purchasing them from plaintiff or plaintiff's authorization. Relevant to the Court's analysis was whether the requisite "authority" of Section 602(a) had to be "express" or "implied." The court concluded that "implied" authority was sufficient because "[w]hen Congress resolved the gray market battle between retailers and copyright owners under section 602(a), it did not do it with the words 'express consent' or 'written consent.' Instead it said 'authority,' which ordinarily includes implied authority."[56]

---

52. Original Appalachian Artworks, Inc. v. J.F. Reichert, Inc., 658 F. Supp. at 458.
53. *Id.* at 461.
54. *Id.* at 462.
55. Disenos Artisticos E Industriales, S.A. v. Costco Wholesale Corporation, 97 F.3d 377 (9th Cir. 1996).
56. *Id.* at 381.

Turning to whether Costco was liable for violating Section 602(a), the Court focused on whether the *owner* of the copyright had authorized importation of the figurines into the United States. The parent corporation of the plaintiff had a contract with an American subsidiary promising that it would not sell figurines to anyone else or knowingly cause anyone else to sell them in the United States. However, neither the parent corporation nor the American subsidiary owned the copyright. Instead, another intermediary owned the copyright and it had different contractual agreements with its license manufacturers: The licensed manufacturers had the contractual freedom to sell the figurines "to all countries of the world, without the existence of any limitations or exclusions of territory."[57] The court therefore concluded that the authority provided by the copyright *owner* flowed downstream to all subsequent purchasers. Thus, Costco could not be liable for importing copyrighted goods without the owner's authority in violation of Section 602(a).

The *Disenos* case illustrates the importance of contracts between brand owners and their channel partners. Although some of the corporate entities properly delineated the boundaries in which the figurines could be sold, the most relevant contract between the copyright *owner* and the licensed manufacturers contained no such restriction. As explained in Part II, the most effective way to combat gray market activity is through prophylactic as opposed to reactive measures. The litigation could have had a very different conclusion had the copyright owner had a different contractual arrangement.

The case is also noteworthy given the legal theories that were *not* pursued by the plaintiff. The plaintiff made no argument that the defendants were liable for trademark infringement or otherwise selling tampered goods. The parties stipulated that the products were "genuine goods."[58] However, the opinion reveals that "[m]ost of the boxes in the Costco stores had a portion of the boxes sliced off."[59] It is unclear how or why portions of the boxes were cut. As explained in Chapter 17, such tampering can often be for purposes of concealing the person or company responsible for the product leak. Because such tampering can impair a brand owner from being able to do a product recall, it can constitute trademark infringement.

(b) Importation Rights and the First Sale Doctrine

The plain language of Section 602 provides that "[i]mportation ... without the authority of the owner of the copyright ... is an infringement of the exclusive right to distribute copies or phonorecords under section 106, actionable under section 501." Because the brand owner has not authorized such gray

---

57. *Id.* at 378.
58. *Id.* at 379.
59. *Id.*

market imports, Section 602(a) appears to make clear that such conduct is an actionable infringement. The phrase "under section 106," however, has proven to be a controversial portion of the statute wherein parties and courts can rarely agree on its meaning.

Section 106 of the Copyright Act lists the exclusive rights granted to a copyright owner.[60] Section 106 also states that the exclusive rights are limited by Sections 107 through 120. One of these limiting sections, Section 109, is the statutory codification of common law's first sale doctrine. Specifically, Section 109 states the following: "Notwithstanding the provisions of section 106(3), the owner of a particular copy or phonorecord lawfully made under this title, or any person authorized by such owner, is entitled, without the authority of the copyright owner, to sell or otherwise dispose of the possession of that copy or phonorecord."[61] In other words, the first sale doctrine allows the owner of a legally manufactured copyrighted product to dispose of the item without the permission of the copyright owner.[62] The challenge presented by these statutes therefore is determining how the first sale doctrine of Section 109(a) impacts a copyright owner's Section 602(a) importation right.

(c) Importation Rights and the First Sale Doctrine: Goods Manufactured and Sold Abroad

The first case to address the tension between Section 602(a)'s importation right and Section 109(a)'s first sale doctrine was *Columbia Broadcasting Systems, Inc. v. Scorpio*.[63] The plaintiff CBS owned United States copyrights to various sound recordings. In 1981, CBS consented to a contract wherein

---

60. 17 U.S.C. § 106 ("Subject to sections 107 through 122, the owner of copyright under this title has the exclusive rights to do and to authorize any of the following: (1) to reproduce the copyrighted work in copies or phonorecords; (2) to prepare derivative works based upon the copyrighted work; (3) to distribute copies or phonorecords of the copyrighted work to the public by sale or other transfer of ownership, or by rental, lease, or lending; (4) in the case of literary, musical, dramatic, and choreographic works, pantomimes, and motion pictures and other audiovisual works, to perform the copyrighted work publicly; (5) in the case of literary, musical, dramatic, and choreographic works, pantomimes, and pictorial, graphic, or sculptural works, including the individual images of a motion picture or other audiovisual work, to display the copyrighted work publicly; and (6) in the case of sound recordings, to perform the copyrighted work publicly by means of a digital audio transmission.").
61. 17 U.S.C. § 109(a) (2008).
62. Indeed, Section 109(a) applies only if the copies are "lawfully made under this title." Therefore, any resale of pirated copies would be an infringement even if the reseller acquiring ownership had no notice that the product was an infringing copy. Circumstantial evidence indicating that the copies or phonorecords in issued had been unlawfully made may render irrelevant the first sale issue. *See e.g.,* Dowling v. United States, 473 U.S. 207 (1985) (e.g., low prices, false names and addresses etc.).
63. Columbia Broadcasting Systems, Inc. v. Scorpio, 569 F. Supp. 47 (E.D. Pa. 1983).

Vicor Music, a Philippine corporation, was granted the exclusive right to manufacture and sell such recordings in the Philippines. Vicor's contract was later terminated and it was given sixty days to liquidate its stock. Vicor thus sold its inventory to Rainbow Music; Rainbow Music re-sold the inventory to International Traders; and International Traders imported the copyrighted recordings and re-sold them to the defendant Scorpio Music Distributors (Scorpio).[64]

CBS sued Scorpio for copyright infringement, alleging that the recordings were unlawfully imported without CBS's required consent pursuant to Section 602(a). In response, Scorpio contended that Vicor's sale to Rainbow Music constituted a "first sale" and therefore Section 109(a) barred CBS from controlling any subsequent sales of the copyrighted works.[65]

The court rejected the application of the Section 109(a). It held that Section 109(a)'s term "lawfully made under this title" meant that its protections applied to copies legally *made and sold* within the United States but not to *foreign-manufactured* products.[66] The court explained that American statutes do not typically have extraterritorial effect. Thus, absent any congressional intent to the contrary the court would not assume it existed in the statutes at bar. The court further reasoned that applying the first sale doctrine to the facts presented would essentially eviscerate Section 602(a)'s importation prohibition. Anyone could simply purchase copyrighted goods indirectly, import them, and then hide behind the immunity provided by first sale doctrine. In addition to rendering Section 602(a) impotent against such imports, such a holding would frustrate the statute's purpose of enabling United States copyright owners to control imported copies that would compete with their copies intended for domestic distribution. Thus, the court held that Scorpio was liable for copyright infringement and that the first sale doctrine only applied to copies legally made and sold in the United States.[67]

The next case to examine the first sale doctrine's application to the importation right was *Hearst Corp. v. Stark*.[68] The plaintiff Hearst Corporation (Hearst) entered into various agreements with authors wherein Hearst was the exclusive U.S. copyright owner of their works. The same authors granted publication and distribution rights to various United Kingdom publishers. A wholesaler in the United Kingdom purchased books from United Kingdom publishers and sold them to Stark, a California corporation. Stark imported the books into the United States and was sued by Hearst. Hearst alleged

---

64. *Id.* at 47–48.
65. *Id.* at 49.
66. *Id.*
67. *Id.*
68. Hearst Corp. v. Stark, 639 F. Supp. 970, 977 (N.D. Cal. 1986).

that Stark violated Section 602(a)'s importation right whereas Stark raised Section 109(a) first sale defense.[69]

Similar to *Scorpio*, the court held that the first sale defense did not apply. However, the *Hearst* court came to the same conclusion through an alternate analysis. The court focused its attention on the distinction between Section 109(a)'s reference to a "particular copy or phonorecord," whereas Section 602(a) referred to "*wholesale* importations into the United States of copyrighted materials manufactured outside of this country."[70] Because Stark was importing a large quantity of books and not a "particular copy" as identified by Section 109, the first sale defense did not apply. This rationale has been criticized. Section 109 must apply to multiple distributions because, holding otherwise, there would be no right to operate a large second-hand bookstore.[71] Moreover, *Hearst* could have relied on the same rationale as *Scorpio*: The first sale defense was not available when the goods are manufactured and sold abroad.

Years later, in *Parfums Givenchy, Inc. v. Drug Emporium, Inc.*,[72] this issue was revisited in a case involving the importation and sale of Amarige, a perfume that was manufactured in France by Parfums Givenchy, S.A. (Givenchy France). Givenchy France imported Amarige to the United States and later sold its copyright interests to Parfums Givenchy, Inc. (Givenchy USA), a wholly owned subsidiary. Givenchy USA then registered the copyright in the United States and began a multimillion dollar campaign to advertise and market the product.[73] At the same time, third parties lawfully purchased bottles of Amarige oversees and then imported the perfume into the United States without the authorization of Givenchy France or Givenchy USA. When Givenchy USA agents discovered the perfume for sale on the shelves of Drug Emporium, it brought a lawsuit for copyright infringement.

Drug Emporium defended its sales by relying on the first sale doctrine of Section 109(a). Specifically, Drug Emporium argued that Section 109 precluded liability because, after "lawfully made sales" were made abroad, neither Givenchy France nor Givenchy USA had any authority to control or limit subsequent sales. The Ninth Circuit Court rejected Drug Emporium's reasoning. The court held instead that the first sale doctrine did not apply until and unless there has been a "first sale" in the United States. To reach this conclusion, the court relied on Section 602(a) and concluded it was designed to prevent the unauthorized importation of copies sold abroad as a means of circumventing a copyright owner's distribution right in the United States.[74]

---

69. *Id.* at 974.
70. *Id.* at 976.
71. 4–8 NIMMER ON COPYRIGHT § 8.12[B][6][a] (2008).
72. Parfums Givenchy, Inc. v. Drug Emporium, Inc., 38 F.3d 477 (1994).
73. *Id.* at 479.
74. *Id.* at 481.

(d) Importation Rights and the First Sale Doctrine: Goods Manufactured and Sold Domestically

A different holding from the above cases was reached in *Cosmair v. Dynamite Enterprises*.[75] Well-known clothing designer Ralph Lauren copyrighted a package label for his fragrance and cosmetic products through his company and plaintiff Cosmair. Litigation was initiated when Cosmair sought to prevent entry of goods consigned by the defendant Dynamite Enterprises (Dynamite). Cosmair alleged that Dynamite's conduct violated Section 602(a) because it did not have Cosmair's consent to import the copyrighted goods. Unlike the goods in *Scorpio*, however, the goods at issue in *Cosmair* were manufactured in the United States. The court refused to issue a preliminary injunction. The court reasoned that the first sale doctrine in Section 109(a) limited the application of Section 602(a) when the products are made and sold in the United States.[76] Thus, a judicial distinction was created between goods manufactured and sold in the United States compared to goods manufactured and sold abroad. The first sale defense applied in the former category of goods whereas it did not in the latter.

A similar—albeit more hostile—conclusion was reached in *Sebastian International v. Consumer Contacts (PTY) Ltd.*,[77] *supra*. In *Sebastian*, the strategy of using copyright law to prevent the importation of gray market products was, for the first time, met with hostility by the court. The court foreshadowed its holding in its opening condemnation of the plaintiff's legal theory: "This case comes to us in the guise of an alleged copyright infringement but, in reality, is an attempt by a domestic manufacturer to prevent the importation of its own product by the 'gray market.'"

The plaintiff Sebastian manufactured and marketed beauty supplies and restricted retail sales only to professional salons. It also registered copyrights for the text and artistic content of the supplies' labels. Sebastian had entered into an oral contract with the defendant Consumer Contacts d/b/a 3-D Marketing Services in which 3-D agreed to distribute the beauty products in South Africa and nowhere else. After Sebastian shipped several hundred thousand dollars worth of product to 3-D in South Africa, 3-D reshipped them back to the United States. Once in the United States, codefendant Fabric, Ltd. was found to possess the products and Sebastian initiated litigation.

According to Fabric, it was not aware of the contractual limitations that prohibited 3-D sales outside of South Africa. Nonetheless, Sebastian alleged that, as copyright owner, it had the right to control *importation* of the copies under Section 602(a) of the Copyright Act. The court acknowledged the confusion of reconciling Sections 602(a) and 109(a) but concluded the facts

---

75. Cosmair v. Dynamite Enterprises, 1985 WL 2209 (S.D. Fla.) (unpublished).
76. *Id.* at *4.
77. 847 F.2d 1093 (3d Cir. 1988).

did not demand a resolution of the uncertainty. The case did not "involve a license agreement or copies produced in a foreign country under that agreement by someone other than the owner; instead this case centers on actual copies of labels printed *in this country by the copyright owner*. Sebastian produced and sold the same copies which it now seeks to control."[78] Once the owner made these sales the first doctrine prohibited Sebastian from controlling subsequent distribution. The fact that the sales were abroad did not change the court's analysis. It explained that nothing in the language of Section 109 "intimate[s] that a copyright owner who elects to sell copies abroad should receive 'a more adequate reward' than those who sell domestically."[79]

Finally, although the analysis centered on copyright law, the court remarked in its opinion that copyright law was not the appropriate method to resolve gray market disputes: "This twist has created the anomalous situation in which the dispute at hand superficially targets a product's label, but in reality rages over the product itself. We think that the controversy over 'gray market' goods, or 'parallel importing,' should be resolved directly on its merits by Congress, not by judicial extension of the Copyright Act's limited monopoly."[80] Notwithstanding the court's judicial editorial, its holding was essentially consistent with the rationale of *Scorpio* and *Hearst* in that the first sale applied to products that were initially manufactured and sold in the United States.

Neutrogena Corporation v. United States[81] is a similar case. The plaintiff brought a lawsuit against the United States to refrain the entry of certain personal care products. The plaintiff Neutrogena sold various products to one of its distributors in Hong Kong. The Hong Kong distributor sold it to a third party who in turn sold it to Federal Airport Services Transport (FAST). FAST shipped the product back to the United States wherein U.S. Customs officials notified Neutrogena of the shipment. Neutrogena confirmed that the products were genuine products. However, given that Neutrogena did not want gray market products competing with its domestic products, it initiated litigation against both the United States and FAST.

At issue for the District Court was whether Neutrogena was entitled to a preliminary restraining order due to FAST's alleged violation of the copyright laws.[82] Although there were a variety of factors for a court to consider, it focused on the first factor: Whether the plaintiff would be able to prevail on the merits of its copyright claim. This analysis required the court to examine the interplay between Sections 602(a) and 109(a). Without reaching an express

---

78. *Id.* at 1098 (emphasis added).
79. *Id.* at 1099.
80. *Id.*
81. Neutrogena Corporation v. United States, 1988 WL 166236 (D.S.C.).
82. Without further explanation, the court explains that another court issued a Temporary Restraining Order enjoining the United States from releasing the identified shipment of goods. *Id.* at *1.

conclusion, the court acknowledged the holdings of *Scorpio* and *Hearst*, *supra*, which concluded that the first sale doctrine did not apply to goods that were manufactured and sold overseas.

Because the products in *Neutrogena* were originally manufactured domestically, the court concluded that the "the first sale defense *may* be applicable." Accordingly, the court could not conclude that the plaintiff would likely prevail on its copyright infringement claim and the request for a preliminary injunction was denied.

In a similar case, *Summit Technology, Inc. v. High-Line Medical Instruments*,[83] *infra*, California's Central District Court took a close look at the controversy surrounding the efforts to reconcile Sections 602(a) 109(a). The plaintiff Summit Technology manufactured and sold laser systems to ophthalmologists for use abroad and in the United States. It sued the defendant High-Line Medical (High-Line) for a number of causes of action related to its importation, promotion, and sales of used or serviced laser systems in the United States. High-Line had legally acquired laser systems that had been sold in foreign countries and then reimported them into the United States for distribution in the United States. Because copyrighted software resided on the laser systems, Summit Technologies alleged that High-Line infringed its copyrights by importing the laser systems and selling them domestically.

In determining whether Summit Technology had a viable legal theory, the court focused its attention on whether the copyright *owner*—Summit Technology—had extinguished its right to control importation of those goods. Following the holding of *Sebastian*, *supra*, the court remarked that because Summit Technology had manufactured and sold the goods itself, it had received its "reward" for its work and thus the first sale rule of Section 109(a) applied. Regardless of where the sale took place, the first sale by the copyright owner extinguished any right to later control importation of those goods. This factual scenario was different, the court explained, from instances where the United States copyright owner, typically as a licensor, has never actually owned the goods that were "first sold." In these latter factual scenarios, sales by the manufacturer-licensee did not transfer "ownership" to the United States copyright owner and there was thus no applicable "first sale."

(e) Importation Rights and the First Sale Doctrine: The United States Supreme Court

Seeking to resolve the tension among the lower courts in their efforts to reconcile Section 602(a)'s importation right with Section 109(a)'s first sale doctrine, the United States Supreme Court examined in the issue in

---

83. Summit Technology, Inc. v. High-Line Medical Instruments, 922 F. Supp. 299 (C.D. Cal. 1996).

Quality King Distributors, Inc. v. L'anza Research Intern., Inc.[84] The plaintiff L'anza Research Intern., Inc. (L'anza) manufactured and sold hair products throughout the United States to distributors who had agreed to resell them within limited geographic areas and only to authorized resellers. L'anza also sold its products in foreign markets and, in typical gray market fashion, products intended for distribution in the United Kingdom found their way back into the United States by the defendant Quality King Distributors, Inc. (Quality King) for domestic sales. L'anza sued Quality King for copyright infringement.

Quality King argued that the first sale doctrine shielded itself from liability. Although several facts were not clearly established, it was undisputed that the goods at issue were originally manufactured by L'anza in California and sold to a foreign purchaser. Thus, Quality King argued that L'anza had no legal authority to control any subsequent transactions.[85]

In its analysis, the Court examined the rationale that was applied the first time it endorsed the first sale doctrine.[86] Specifically, in *Bobbs-Merrill Co. v. Strauss*,[87] the 1908 United States Supreme Court had stated the following: "It is not denied that one who has sold a copyrighted article, without restriction, has parted with all right to control the sale of it. The purchaser of a book, once sold by authority of the owner of the copyright, may sell it again, although he could not publish a new edition of it."[88] Congress later codified the United States Supreme Court's holding that the right to control sales was limited to the *first* sale of the work.[89]

L'anza relied on Section 602(a) to argue that the unauthorized importation of L'anza's products into the United States infringed L'anza's exclusive right of distribution. As noted above, Section 602(a) provides that importation of copies into the United States without the copyright owner's authority infringes the copyright owner's exclusive right of distribution *under Section 106*.[90] Similar to the limited right to distribute articulated in *Bobbs-Merrill, supra*, Section 106 states that the rights granted by that section are limited by the provisions of Sections 107 through 120.[91] Among the limitations identified in Sections 107 through 120 is Section 109, which is a codification of the

---

84. Quality King Distributors, Inc. v. L'anza Research Intern., Inc., 523 U.S. 135 (1998).
85. *Id.* at 139.
86. Bobbs-Merrill Co. v. Straus, 210 U.S. 339 (1908).
87. *Id.*
88. *Id.* at 350.
89. 17 U.S.C. § 109(a) provides the right "the owner of a particular copy or phonorecord lawfully made under this title, or any person authorized by such owner, is entitled, without the authority of the copyright owner, to sell or otherwise dispose of the possession of that copy or phonorecord...."
90. *See* 17 U.S.C. § 602(a) (emphasis added).
91. 17 U.S.C. § 106.

"first sale" doctrine. Section 109 expressly permits the owner of a lawfully made copy to sell that copy "[n]otwithstanding the provisions of Section 106(3)."[92]

Writing for a unanimous Court, Justice Stevens considered the foregoing statutes and concluded following:

(1) After the first sale of a copyrighted item, any subsequent purchaser, *domestic or otherwise*, is an "owner" of that item;
(2) Section 109(a) provides that such an "owner" has an unfettered right to sell that item;
(3) While Section 602(a) prohibits the unauthorized importation of copies, the scope of the prohibition is limited by Section 106; and
(4) Because Section 106 is limited by Section 109's first sale doctrine, Section 602(a) is inapplicable to domestic and foreign "owners" of L'anza's products who decide to import and sell them into the United States.[93]

The Court concludes its opinion with some parting comments on the parties' use of the terms "gray market" and "parallel importation." Although the Court acknowledged the use of the terms in *K Mart Corp. v. Cartier, Inc.*,[94] wherein the defendant imported foreign manufactured goods with a valid U.S. trademark without the trademark holder's consent, it is uncomfortable using such terms in the present case:

> We are not at all sure that those terms appropriately describe the consequences of an American manufacturer's decision to limit its promotion efforts to the domestic market and to sell its products abroad at discounted prices that are so low that its foreign distributors can compete in the domestic market. But even if they do, whether or not we think it would be wise policy to provide statutory protection for such price discrimination is not a matter that is relevant to our duty to interpret the text of the Copyright Act.[95]

Seemingly unsympathetic of L'anza's plight, the Court adds in a footnote that L'anza could have avoided the consequences of such competition by providing advertising support abroad, charging higher prices abroad, or selling its products abroad under a different name.[96]

---

92. 17 U.S.C. §109(a).
93. Quality King, 523 U.S. at 145.
94. K Mart Corp. v. Cartier, Inc., 486 U.S. 281 (1988).
95. *Id.* at 153.
96. *Id.* at 153, fn. 29.

Finally, noting that the products at issue involved a "round trip" journey wherein they were first manufactured in the United States, Justice Ginsburg offered a brief concurring opinion articulating that the Court's opinion does not "resolve cases in which the allegedly infringing products were manufactured abroad. . . . The rights granted by the Copyright Act extend no farther than the nation's borders."[97]

The Court described this category of goods as not being affected by its ruling: "[Section] 602(a) applies to a category of copies that are neither piratical nor 'lawfully made under this title.' That category encompasses copies that were 'lawfully made' not under the United States Copyright Act, but instead, under the law of some other country."[98] Indeed, *Quality King* did not overrule the aforementioned cases in which Courts refused to apply the first sale doctrine when the products were manufactured and sold overseas. According to at least the Ninth Circuit Court, such cases are still binding authority.

In 2008, *Omega S.A. v. Costco Wholesale Corp.*[99] dealt with such gray market goods. The plaintiff Omega S.A. (Omega) manufactured watches in Switzerland and sold them globally through a network of authorized distributors and retailers.[100] The defendant Costco Wholesale Corp. (Costco) obtained Omega watches from the gray market for resale in its stores. "Omega first sold the watches to authorized distributors overseas . . . [and a]lthough Omega authorized the initial foreign sale of the watches, *it did not authorize their importation into the United States or the sales made by Costco.*"[101] Although the trial court found nothing improper with Costco acquisition and sale of these gray market goods, the Ninth Circuit Court of Appeals concluded that the first sale doctrine is *not* applicable in cases that involve foreign-made, non-piratical copies of a U.S. copyrighted work unless those same copies have already been sold in the United States with the copyright owner's authority.[102]

iii. Software Licenses and the First Sale Doctrine: An End Run Around the First Sale Doctrine?

Another way in which manufacturers have sought to avoid the reach of the first sale doctrine is through software license agreements. Because of the

---

97. Quality King, 523 U.S. at 154 (concurring opinion).
98. *Id.* at 147.
99. Omega S.A. v. Costco Wholesale Corp., 541 F.3d 982 (9th Cir. Sept. 3, 2008).
100. *Id.* at 983–84.
101. *Id.* (emphasis added).
102. For further discussion of *Omega S.A. v. Costco Wholesale Corp.*, see Chapter 19.

unique nature of software, it has received some special treatment from the Copyright Act. To illustrate, the owner of a particular copy of a copyrighted work has the right to sell or otherwise dispose of the possession of that copy.[103] However, the owner does not have the right to *copy* the copyrighted work. That right to copy is retained by the copyright owner.[104] In order to effectively use software, however, making a copy is necessary. Using software requires the computer to make a copy of that software and transfer the copy from the computer's permanent storage to the active memory location.[105] This transfer constitutes making a *copy* because the original copy remains on the computer's permanent storage while the user actively operates the copy residing on the active memory.[106]

To ensure that purchasers of software can use it without infringing any copying rights, Congress enacted Section 117 of the Copyright Act.[107] Section 117 provides that " . . . it is not a[] [copyright] infringement for the owner of a copy of a computer program to make or authorize the making of another copy or adaptation of that computer program provided: (1) that such a new copy or adaptation is created as an essential step in the utilization of the computer program in conjunction with a machine and that it is used in no other manner, or (2) that such new copy or adaptation is for archival purposes only and that all archival copies are destroyed in the event that continued possession of the computer program should cease to be rightful."[108] In other words, creating another "copy" of software by virtue of using a software program is not an infringement because it is an "essential step in the utilization" of the program.

Summit Technology, Inc. v. High-Line Medical Instruments,[109] *supra*, examined Section 117 as it related to the gray market and the first sale doctrine. On a related theory of liability, Summit Technology sued two end user ophthalmologists who had purchased and used gray market laser systems. Summit Technology's theory was that every time the laser systems were turned on, the copyrighted software was *copied* onto their Random Access Memory (RAM) chips. Because the ophthalmologists were not authorized to *copy* the software, they were liable for copyright infringement.

---

103. 17 U.S.C. § 109(a).
104. 17 U.S.C. § 106; *see also* Picker Int'l Corp. v. Imaging Equip. Srvs., Inc., 931 F. Supp. 18, 38 (D. Mass. 1995) (Where the plaintiff's parts department accidentally sold one copy of plaintiff's service handbook, the buyer could use and distribute that one copy under the first sale doctrine, but not could make any copies of it.).
105. A computer's active memory location is also known as Random Access Memory (RAM).
106. *See* MAI Sys. Corp. v. Peak Computer, Inc., 991 F.2d 511, 517–19 (9th Cir. 1993) ("[T]he loading of software into the RAM creates a copy under the Copyright Act.").
107. 17 U.S.C. § 117(a).
108. *Id.*
109. Summit Technology, 922 F. Supp. at 299.

The court rejected this theory pursuant to Section 117. As a matter of law, it was not an infringement for the owner of a copy of a computer program to make another copy provided that the new copy was "an essential step in the utilization of the computer program in conjunction with a machine."[110] Summit did not challenge the fact that rightful owners were allowed to make these essential copies. Instead, its theory was that the end users were not rightful end users pursuant to its overall theory of copyright infringement and, since that theory failed (pursuant to the first sale doctrine), the court rejected this theory as well.

In practice, however, the first sale doctrine and Section 117 have limited application. The rights afforded by first sale doctrine and Section 117 only apply to "owners" of software.[111] Software, however, is rarely sold. Instead of selling programs, software developers *license* their products. Because a licensee cannot transfer away any more rights than what was originally received, software developers can effectively prevent the secondary marketing of its programs through agreements. A typical license agreement will thus permit the customers to use a program for *their own use*; however, the license will expressly prohibit any subsequent transfers of the licensed rights.

This practice of preventing customers from transferring their copies of software allows developers to sell its programs to different users at different prices.[112] For example, educational and nonprofit entities are often entitled to preferred pricing schemes than those typically offered to for-profit concerns. Another justification for the enforcement of licenses is intended to preserve the rights of owners and creators.[113]

This right to control the alienability of software programs has sparked a debate over whether software agreements should be interpreted as "sales" agreements rather than "license" agreements. If the agreements are interpreted as "sales" agreements, the first sale doctrine would apply and purchasers

---

110. 17 U.S.C. § 117.
111. 17 U.S.C. § 109(a) provides that the first sale doctrine only extends to an "owner of a particular copy." Similarly, 17 U.S.C. § 117(a) has the same restriction. A prior version of Section 117 proposed that it would not be a copyright infringement for a "rightful possessor" of a copy of software to make copies in the course of using it. *See* DSC Commc'n Corp. v. Pulse Commc'n, Inc., 170 F.3d 1354, 1360 (Fed. Cir. 1999) *citing* Final Report of the National Commission on New Technological Uses of Copyrighted Works 30, U.S. Dept. of Commerce, PB-282141 (July 31, 1978). Congress replaced the words "rightful possessor" with "owner." Thus Congress intended Section 117 not to licenses, leases, loans or other transfers beyond sales.
112. *See e.g.*, ProCD, Inc. v. Zeinberg, 86 F.3d 1447, 1450 (7th Cir. 1996) ("To make price discrimination work . . . the seller must be able to control arbitrage.").
113. *See* Gardner v. Nike, Inc., 279 F.3d 774, 780–81 (9th Cir. 2002) ("On the one hand, the 1976 [Copyright] Act reflects Congress' growing awareness for free alienability and divisibility. Yet, both Congress and this Circuit have always been aware of the necessity to preserve the rights and control of the owners and creators.").

could freely sell or distribute their acquired copy and enjoy the protections of the first sale doctrine. Although there appears to be a growing consensus that software agreements should be interpreted as licenses, there are a few cases that have interpreted such agreements as sales.

For example, in *SoftMan Products v. Adobe Systems*,[114] Adobe distributed bundles of software at a price lower than the aggregate retail price of the individual software programs in the bundle. Adobe distributed these bundles under an agreement that permitted redistribution as a bundle, but not as individual programs. Defendant SoftMan obtained Adobe Software bundles from Adobe distributors, split the programs apart, and redistributed them individually at higher prices. SoftMan argued that it had no contractual privity with Adobe and that under the first sale doctrine was immunized from any redistribution limitations. Adobe contended that the first sale doctrine did not apply because the software was merely *licensed* to its distributors. Thus, SoftMan was limited by the scope of the distributors' licenses, which precluded unbundled redistribution. The court held that "the circumstances surrounding the transaction strongly suggest that the transaction is in fact a sale rather than a license."[115] The court downplayed the express terms of the Adobe license agreement, endorsing the view that "[o]wnership of a copy should be determined based on the actual character, rather than the label, of the transaction by which the user obtained possession. Merely labeling a transaction as a lease or license does not control."[116]

SoftMan is, however, sandwiched between two other Adobe cases that reached opposite conclusions. The latter opinion, *Adobe Systems v. Stargate Software*,[117] expressly refused to endorse the *SoftMan* analysis, in part, because it saw no reason to disturb Adobe's distributor agreements: "[T]his Court finds that no colorable reason exists in this case as to why Adobe and its distributors should be barred from characterizing the transaction that has been forged between them as a license. In light of the restrictions on title that have been incorporated into the OCRA, as well as the Parties' free and willing consent to enter into and execute its terms, the Parties should be free to negotiate and/or set a price for the product being exchanged, as well as set the terms by which the product is exchanged."[118]

The debate has seen continued controversy in 2008. Two district courts in the Ninth Circuit Court have examined the "license" versus "sale" issue and

---

114. SoftMan Products v. Adobe Systems, 171 F. Supp. 2d 1075 (C.D. Cal. 2001).
115. *Id.* at 1085.
116. *Id.* at 1086.
117. Adobe Systems v. Stargate Software, 216 F. Supp. 2d 1051 (N.D. Cal. 2002). The first of the *Adobe* Trilogy was Adobe Systems Inc. v. One Stop Micro, Inc., 84 F. Supp. 2d 1086 (N.D. Cal. 2000).
118. *Id.* at 1059.

arrived at different conclusions. Both courts acknowledged and summarized the legal uncertainty and apparent conflict among various courts.

In *Vernor v. Autodesk, Inc.*,[119] Mr. Vernor wished to sell used copies of Autodesk's copyrighted AutoCAD software on eBay. Mr. Vernor brought a declaratory relief action seeking a declaration that his resale of the AutoCAD was lawful. Autodesk claimed that the sales were unlawful because the AutoCAD software was originally sold with its Licensing Agreement, which imposed various restrictions on its users. The court first acknowledged that if there were no license, there would be no dispute that Mr. Vernor's resale of the software packages would be legal pursuant to the first sale doctrine.

However, given the license agreement, the court explained that the case turned on the issue of whether, because of the license agreement, the transfer of the AutoCAD packages was or was not a sale. Relying on *United States v. Wise*,[120] the court concluded that the critical factor was whether the transferee kept the copy acquired from the copyright holder. Given this permanent transfer of possession, the court concluded that the transaction was a "sale," and the onerous restrictions on transfer of the copies merely modified this "sale" as a "sale with restrictions on use." The important byproduct of this nuance is that any subsequent purchasers of the software are not in contractual privity with the copyright owner and can thus avoid liability.

A more recent case, *MDY Industries, LLC v. Blizzard Entertainment, Inc.*,[121] acknowledged but declined to follow *Vernor*. *MDY* involved a multiplayer online role-playing game known as "World of Warcraft" (WoW). WoW's creator and plaintiff Blizzard Entertainment owned the WoW copyright and required its users to agree to WoW's license agreement before playing the game. The defendant MDY Industries, LLC (MDY) meanwhile created a software program called WowGlider (Glider). Glider was a program known as a "bot" and automatically played WoW for players while they were away from their computers. Glider thus enabled its owners to advance more quickly than players who would otherwise need to take time out from playing while away from their computers.[122]

Blizzard argued that MDY was liable for contributory copyright infringement because Glider essentially induced WoW users to infringe WoW's copyright.[123] WoW's license agreement permitted users to copy the game software to their computer's RAM in order to play the game. However, the

---

119. Vernor v. Autodesk, Inc., 555 F. Supp. 2d 1164 (W.D. Wa. 2008).
120. United States v. Wise, 550 F.2d 1180, 1187 (9th Cir. 1977).
121. MDY Industries, LLC v. Blizzard Entertainment, Inc., 2008 WL 2757357 (D. Ariz. July 14, 2008).
122. *Id.* at *7.
123. A person commits contributory copyright infringement "by intentionally inducing or encouraging direct infringement." MGM Studios Inc. v. Grokster, Ltd., 545 U.S. 913, 930 (2005).

WoW license agreement expressly prohibited the use of bots. Therefore, Blizzard argued that when users launch WoW using Glider, they exceed their license agreements and create infringing copies of the WoW software.

MDY argued that the bot prohibition was a mere contract term. Pursuant to this argument, Blizzard may assert a breach of contract claim against its users for playing Glider but not any claims for copyright infringement.[124] Using Section 117 to bolster its argument, MDY contended that WoW's users were expressly permitted to make a copy of WoW to RAM because it was an "essential step" in using the game. Thus, the act of copying the game was not an infringement—whether it was or was not done with Glider.[125]

The court rejected this argument because it did not agree that *users* of WoW were *owners* of WoW. Although acknowledging the controversy in the license versus sale debate, the district court ultimately rejected the reasoning of *Vernor* and endorsed other Ninth Circuit Court opinions that simplify the license/sale analysis into a two-part test: (1) whether the copyright owner makes clear that it is granting a license to the copy of the software; and (2) whether the copyright holder imposes significant restrictions on the use or transfer of the copy.

iv. Software Licenses and the First Sale Doctrine: An End Run Around the First Sale Doctrine *Beyond* Software?

The majority of courts endorse the argument that software license agreements are enforceable to prevent unwanted copies and transfers. From cars to calculators, software programs are ubiquitous in consumer products today. Although the first sale doctrine prevents any restrictions on subsequent sales of the *physical goods*, can restrictive software licenses give manufacturers of any products containing the ability to effectively prevent the secondary or gray market of any products?

At least some manufacturers are relying on software license agreements to restrict the alienability of its products. Cisco is a well-known example. Cisco manufactures and sells various networking technologies. With respect to the sales of these products, such as routers and switches, Cisco takes the position that it is only selling the hardware. With respect to the software embedded in these products, Cisco asserts that purchasers are only acquiring a license. Therefore, when the original purchaser sells the product, Cisco has the ability to rely on the above case law and argue that the subsequent purchaser has

---

124. Breach of contract damages are typically limited to actual loss caused by the breach. *See e.g.*, 24 RICHARD A. LORD, WILLISTON ON CONTRACTS § 65:1 (4th ed. 2007).
125. 2008 WL 2757357 at *8.

committed a copyright infringement.¹²⁶ Cisco employs this strategy and argues that end users should not buy its products from eBay or the gray market because it will not be the rightful *owner* of the software embedded in the hardware. The ability of using these restrictive licenses to essentially preclude subsequent sales of hardware has not yet been tested by the courts. Accordingly, the ability to use restrictive licenses in these circumstances remains an open issue.

c. Affirmative Defenses

Assuming that a brand owner is able to present the judge or jury with facts sufficient to show copyright infringement, a defendant may still escape liability establishing an affirmative defense against the plaintiff's allegations. Below is a discussion of some of these affirmative defenses.

i. Fair Use

Certain acts of copying are defensible as fair use. This affirmative defense allows courts to avoid rigid application of the copyright statutes when it would stifle the very creativity the law is designed to foster.[127] Courts are required to consider several factors when deciding whether a defendant's use of copyrighted work is worthy of this defense.[128] Courts balance these factors to determine whether the public interest in the free flow of information outweighs the copyright holder's interest in exclusive control over the work.[129]

The first factor is the purpose and character of the use of the copyrighted work, including whether such use is of a commercial nature or is for non-profit educational purposes.[130] When the purpose is for commercial use, most courts tend to presume that the infringement is an unfair exploitation and therefore not a fair use.[131] Thus, although commercial motivation and fair use can theoretically exist side by side, a court is permitted to consider whether the alleged infringing use was primarily for the public benefit or for private commercial gain.[132] Because gray marketers are always in business for

---

126. *See e.g.*, Craig Zimmerman, *Fear, Uncertainty, Doubt, And Cisco*, POWERSOURCE ONLINE, Aug. 2008, at 6.
127. Iowa State Univ. Research Found., Inc. v. Am. Broad. Cos., 621 F.2d 57 (2nd Cir. 1980).
128. 17 U.S.C. § 107 (2008).
129. DC Comics, Inc. v. Reel Fantasy, Inc., 696 F.2d 24, 27 (2nd Cir. 1982).
130. 17 U.S.C. § 107(1) (2008).
131. Sony Corp. of Am. v. Universal City Studios, Inc., 464 U.S. 417, 455 (1984).
132. MCA, Inc. v. Wilson, 677 F.2d 180 (2nd Cir. 1981).

commercial purposes, this factor would almost invariably tip in favor of the copyright owner.

The second factor requires an examination of the nature of the copyrighted work.[133] Under this factor, the more creative a work, the more protection is afforded. Conversely, the more informational the work, the fair use defense is applied more broadly.[134] In the context of the gray market, the copyrighted works are typically labels, designs, instruction manuals, or other materials uniquely and creatively identify the brand owner. Thus, this factor typically tips in favor of the brand owner.

The third factor is the amount and substantiality of the portion used in relation to the copyrighted work as a whole.[135] This factor is designed to ensure that there is both a quantitative and qualitative analysis to determine whether the use is unfair. Thus, the general standard for determining whether alleged copyright infringement is "fair use" is that defendant must copy no more than is reasonably necessary to enable him to pursue an aim that the law recognizes as proper.[136] This factor is rarely germane in the gray market context because the product at issue does not contain a *portion* of the brand owner's copyrighted work. In many circumstances, the gray marketer will sell genuine and unadulterated products. On other occasions, the gray marketer will insert copies of domestic materials like instruction manuals or labels with a product procured overseas to ensure the product can be sold seamlessly in the United States. Under either scenario, the gray marketer cannot argue that it only used a portion of the brand owner's copyrighted work.

Finally, the fourth factor requires an examination of how the defendant's infringement affects the value or potential value of the copyrighted work.[137] The purpose of this factor is to strike a balance between the benefit the public will derive if the use is permitted compared to the personal gain by the copyright owner if the use is denied.[138] In the gray market context, this factor invites a debate between two competing policies. On the one hand, the gray marketer will argue that the public benefits by the importation of genuine goods as consumers will have an opportunity to purchase genuine products at cheaper prices. By allowing such imports, the gray marketer will argue, it will prevent brand owners from engaging in unfair price discrimination between the goods being sold in the United States and other emerging markets. Brand owners, on the other hand, would likely dispute the argument that there is any public benefit from the gray market and would also argue

---

133. 17 U.S.C. 107(2) (2008).
134. Harper & Row, Publishers, Inc. v. Nation Enter., 471 U.S. 539, 563 (1985) ("The law generally recognizes a greater need to disseminate factual works than works of fiction or fantasy.").
135. 17 U.S.C. § 107(3) (2008).
136. Chicago Bd. of Educ. v. Substance, Inc., 354 F.3d 624 (7th Cir. 2003).
137. 17 U.S.C. § 107(4) (2008).
138. MCA, Inc. v. Wilson, 677 F.2d 180, 183 (2d Cir. 1981).

that its potential market value suffers significantly from the infringement. The latter point is easiest to prove as the brand owner will be able to show that it must lower its prices to adequately compete against gray market imports. The brand owner would also assert that the public is potentially deceived when it purchases a product outside of its controlled channels of distribution. Although the price may be cheaper, the brand owner would argue that the customers unknowingly are buying a product that is potentially inferior as a result of incompetent packaging, storing, or shipping.

These factors are nonexclusive[139] and the Copyright Act does not indicate how much weight should be ascribed to each. To date, there are no cases in which a gray marketer has successfully proven that its conduct amounted to a fair use of a brand owner's copyright.

ii. Waiver or Abandonment of Copyright

Waiver is the intentional relinquishment of a known right with knowledge of its existence and the intent to relinquish it.[140] In the context of copyright law, waiver or abandonment occurs if there is an intent by the copyright proprietor to surrender rights in his work.[141] Most courts require an overt act by the copyright owner that manifests an intent to abandon the copyright. Passive allowance of an environment that implicitly encourages infringement is not sufficient. For example, in *A&M Records v. Napster*,[142] the defendant Napster was a downloadable software program that facilitated the transmission of MP3[143] files between and among its users. The plaintiff A&M Records, Inc. (A&M) claimed that Napster users were engaged in the wholesale reproduction and distribution of copyrighted works. On defense, Napster argued that the A&M had abandoned its copyrights by knowingly providing consumers with technology designed to copy and distribute MP3 files over the Internet. Thus, Napster argued, A&M waived any legal authority to exercise exclusive control over the creation and distribution of MP3 files. The Ninth Circuit Court rejected this argument and endorsed the district court's holding that

---

139. *See* Fisher v. Dees, 794 F.2d 432, 435 (9th Cir. 1986).
140. United States v. King Features Entm't, Inc., 843 F.2d 394, 399 (9th Cir. 1988).
141. A&M Records, Inc. v. Napster, Inc., 239 F.3d 1004, 1026 (9th Cir. 2001).
142. *Id.*
143. In 1987, the Moving Picture Experts Group set a standard file format for the storage of audio recordings in a digital format called MPEG-3, abbreviated as "MP3." Digital MP3 files are created through a process colloquially called "ripping." Ripping software allows a computer owner to copy an audio compact disk ("audio CD") directly onto a computer's hard drive by compressing the audio information on the CD into the MP3 format. The MP3's compressed format allows for rapid transmission of digital audio files from one computer to another by electronic mail or any other file transfer protocol. *Id.* 1011.

A&M did no more than seek partners for their commercial downloading ventures and develop music players or files they planned to sell over the Internet.[144]

The gray market has similarly been justified as existing solely from the creation of price discrimination by manufacturers. Even if such reasoning accurately explains the creation of the gray marketer's opportunity for price arbitrage, such conduct by the manufacturers does not constitute copyright abandonment.

iii. Estoppel

Estoppel is closely related to the doctrine of waiver and abandonment. It is a doctrine that is applicable elsewhere in the law and, reduced to its essence, prevents a party from adopting a position in a legal proceeding that contradicts his past statements or actions. In the context of copyright infringement, a defendant must show the following: (1) the plaintiff knew the facts of defendant's infringing conduct; (2) the plaintiff intended that its conduct would be acted on or the defendant reasonably believed that the plaintiff intended that its conduct would be acted on; (3) the defendant was ignorant of the true facts; and (4) the defendant relied on the plaintiff's conduct to its injury.[145] The defense is especially applicable in situations where the plaintiff has aided the defendant in the acts of the alleged infringement or has induced or caused the defendant to perform such acts.[146]

Of the available affirmative defenses, brand owners are most vulnerable to the defense of estoppel. To the extent a gray marketer can show that the brand owner somehow communicated its acquiescence to any infringing activity, the gray marketer will have an opportunity to argue against any findings of liability. For example, a gray market importer may sell infringing products to a brand owner's authorized reseller. To the extent the representations of the authorized reseller can be attributed to the brand owner, the gray marketer could argue that it believed its transactions were entirely lawful. To avoid this risk, brand owners should communicate clearly and regularly its position on gray market transactions.

For example, in *Microsoft v. Compusource Distributors, Inc.*,[147] Microsoft sued a distributor for selling counterfeit software and hardware. After Microsoft discovered this unlawful activity, it issued a cease and desist letter to Compusource demanding that it immediately stop selling counterfeit

---

144. *Id.* at 1026.
145. Hampton v. Paramount Pictures Corp., 279 F.2d 100, 104 (9th Cir. 1960).
146. 4–13 NIMMER ON COPYRIGHT § 13.07 (2008).
147. Microsoft, 115 F. Supp. 2d at 800.

products. Rather than heed Microsoft's warning, Compusource continued to acquire Microsoft products from suspicious sources. During discovery, however, Compusource's president testified that he telephoned his Microsoft suppliers to discuss the matter with them. According to the president, the suppliers assured him that the products were legitimate and that the products were simply cheaper because they were bought on the gray market.[148] Microsoft was able to rebut any argument that it has somehow acquiesced or implicitly approved Compusource's conduct by its cease and desist correspondence. Specifically, the court concluded that notwithstanding the assurances Compusource had received about the products' legitimacy, Compusource had in fact turned a "blind eye to the clear indications" that it was acquiring counterfeit and infringing software.[149] Similarly, brand owners wanting to prevent the viability of an estoppel defense should (1) ensure that they do not communicate any approvals to gray market activity, and (2) ensure that their position with respect to gray market activity is enforced with regularity.

iv. Innocent Intent

There are several instances in which an infringer may not realize that his conduct violates the owner's copyrights. For example, an infringer may copy the owner's work but, in good faith, forget the source upon which he is drawing. A defendant may also intentionally copy the owner's work and believe, again in good faith, that his conduct does not constitute an infringement.[150] However, lack of intent is neither an element of a plaintiff's case nor a defense to infringement. Although intent or knowledge is relevant when considering damages, it is not relevant in determining liability.

d. Remedies

Because copyright infringement is often an ongoing activity, especially in the gray market, mere monetary remedies are usually insufficient. Even after receiving a damages award, a copyright holder can continue to be injured unless the defendant stops all unlawful activity. Fortunately for brand owners, the Copyright Act provides for a variety of remedies designed to adequately compensate victims of unlawful infringement.

---

148. *Id.* at 804.
149. *Id.* at 808.
150. 4–13 NIMMER ON COPYRIGHT § 13.07 (2008).

i. Injunctive Relief

Accordingly, the Copyright Act provides a court with the authority to issue orders prohibiting any further infringing activity.[151] Of course, the court's power is limited to the United States—activities occurring purely abroad by a foreign defendant may be beyond the reach of any court-ordered injunction.[152]

A court's injunctive power in copyright cases includes injunctions and permanent injunctions.[153] A preliminary injunction temporarily stops infringing activity before a case is decided.[154] In the gray market copyright infringement context, the normal rules for preliminary injunctions apply: the plaintiff must show the following: (1) he will likely succeed on the merits of the case; (2) he will suffer irreparable harm if the injunction is not granted; (3) the harm to the defendant imposed by the injunction does not outweigh the irreparable harm to the plaintiff; (4) that granting the injunction is not contrary to public interest.[155]

The likelihood-of-success element is important. No court wants to prevent a defendant from engaging in certain activities only to later learn that nothing improper was taking place. However, so long as the plaintiff provides sufficient evidence to satisfy the likelihood-of-success element in a copyright infringement case, the second element of proving irreparable harm is *presumed* to exist. For example, in *Ty v. Publications International*,[156] the maker of Beanie Babies sued an unauthorized publisher of Beanie Babies books for copyright and trademark infringement. Once the court concluded that the plaintiff was likely to succeed on the merits of its copyright infringement claim, it granted the injunction even though the harm to the *defendant* in granting an injunction slightly outweighed the harm to the plaintiff in denying it.

Courts are also given the discretion to tailor an injunction to best fit the facts presented in the case. For example, in *Montblanc-Simplo GmbH v. Staples, Inc.*,[157] a pen manufacturer with very limited U.S. distribution brought copyright and trademark claims against a retailer who removed manufacturer serial numbers and sold the pens without authorization.[158] The manufacturer argued that all sales of the pens should be barred, whereas the retailer argued that they should be allowed to continue sale on the condition

---

151. 17 U.S.C. § 502(a). *E.g.*, Bayer Corp. v. Custom School Frames, LLC, 259 F. Supp. 2d (E.D. La. 2003) (injunction granted for a gray market plaintiff).
152. 17 U.S.C. § 502(b).
153. *Id.*
154. For more discussion on preliminary remedies and injunctions, see Chapter 11.
155. Montblanc-Simplo GmbH v. Staples, Inc., 172 F. Supp. 2d 231 (D. Mass. 2001).
156. Ty v. Publications International, 81 F. Supp. 2d 899 (N.D. Ill. 2000).
157. Montblanc-Simplo GmbH, 172 F. Supp. 2d at 231.
158. *Id.* at 233.

that they notified customers of the pens' origins.[159] There, the court issued a compromise ruling, barring sales only of pens which lacked the manufacturer's marks while requiring informative signage for pens whose marks were intact.[160]

ii. Impoundment and Destruction

Similar to, but separate from, a normal preliminary injunction, a court presiding over a copyright action has the discretion to impound inventories of infringing materials as well as the means to make more infringing materials, such as manufacturing plans and equipment.[161] For a plaintiff seeking to stop gray market activities, this can be a powerful early remedy that does not require the same test of a preliminary injunction. So long as the judge finds it reasonable, the gray market activities can be effectively halted in this manner at any time during the action.

At the conclusion of a case, a court can also order the destruction of infringing inventories and the means to make them.[162] This measure is effective in the same ways as impounding and can be a permanent solution.

iii. Damages and Profits

Copyright holders can choose between two different bases for monetary damages: actual damages and incidental profits or statutory damages.[163] Plaintiffs who elect to recover actual damages are entitled to recover the damages suffered by the copyright owner as a result of the infringement as well as any profits from the infringement not already taken into account.[164] In establishing the infringer's profits, the copyright owner is required to present proof only of the infringer's gross revenue; the infringer is then required to prove any deductible expenses or show that any elements of profit are attributable to factors other than the copyrighted work.[165] The Copyright Act does not specify which expenses will be regarded as deductible costs. Resolution of this issue generally turns on the definition of costs under generally accepted

---

159. *Id.* at 249.
160. *Id.*
161. 17 U.S.C. § 503(a).
162. 17 U.S.C. § 503(b).
163. 17 U.S.C. § 504(a).
164. 17 U.S.C. § 504(b).
165. *Id.*

accounting practices (GAAP).[166] Prejudgment interest is also awarded.[167] If the plaintiff can show large monetary harm resulting from the infringement or large sums of profit by the defendant, the actual damages route is more favorable.

Many gray market plaintiffs opt for statutory damages, however, when actual damages are difficult to determine or are estimated to be low.[168] This amount is decided by the judge, ranging from $750 to $30,000 per work infringed.[169] Where the plaintiff can prove that the infringement was willful, the maximum increases to $150,000. If the plaintiff tries to increase this maximum but the defendant manages to prove that the infringement was not willful, the minimum drops to $200.[170] The amount is further reduced if the defendant can show that he reasonably believed he was operating under nonprofit, educational, fair use.[171]

iv. Attorney Fees

At the court's discretion, the prevailing party in a copyright action may be awarded full costs and reasonable attorney fees.[172] This is a relatively common remedy seen in gray market copyright cases.[173]

v. Criminal Penalties

In the event that a gray market defendant is prosecuted by the government (perhaps at the request of a manufacturer or distributor) rather than sued by a private plaintiff, criminal penalties may apply. Following conviction, the court may order forfeiture and destruction of infringing material and the means for producing it. Defendants can also be fined up to $2,500 for knowingly using a false copyright notice or removing a valid existing one from the product or its packaging. Criminal penalties typically occur in the gray market case when the products are also co-mingled with counterfeit products.

---

166. 4–14 NIMMER ON COPYRIGHT § 14.03(C) (2008).
167. R. J. Reynolds Tobacco Co. v. Premium Tobacco Stores, Inc., 2005 WL 293512, slip op. at *1 (N.D. Ill. 2005).
168. *E.g.*, Microsoft Corp. v. Compusource Distrib., Inc., 115 F. Supp. 2d 800 (E.D. Mich. 2000); Original Appalachian Artworks, Inc. v. J. F. Reichert, Inc., 658 F. Supp. 458 (E.D. Pa. 1987).
169. 17 U.S.C. § 504(c)(2).
170. *Id.*
171. *Id.*
172. 17 U.S.C. § 505.
173. *E.g.*, Microsoft, 115 F. Supp. 2d at 811; Original Appalachian, 658 F. Supp. at 467.

CHAPTER 17

Theories of Liability
Trademark

a. Introduction to Trademark Law — 242
    i. Importance of Trademarks — 242
    ii. Trademark Causes of Action — 244
b. Trademark Law's Treatment of the Gray Market — 246
    i. The Early Cases and the Gray Market — 246
    ii. Tariff Act and the Gray Market — 249
    iii. The Lanham Act and the Gray Market — 254
        (a) Prong One: Is the Plaintiff Entitled to Trademark Protection? — 256
        (b) Prong Two: Are the Goods "Materially Different"? — 260
            (i) Materially Different Goods When the Goods are Artistic — 260
            (ii) Materially Different Goods When the Post-Sale Services are Different — 263
            (iii) Materially Different Goods When the Quality Controls are Different — 265
            (iv) Materially Different Goods When the Ingredients are Different — 272
            (v) Materially Different Goods When the Warranty Protections are Different — 273
            (vi) Materially Different Goods When there are Differences in the Aggregate — 276
        (c) The Lanham Act Applied: The "Salon" Cases — 277
        (d) Factors Beyond the "Material Difference" Factor? — 281
c. Affirmative Defenses — 282
    i. The First Sale Doctrine — 282
    ii. Not "Gray Market" Goods? — 285
d. Remedies — 286

a. Introduction to Trademark Law

> *"If this business were to split up, I would give you the land and bricks and mortar, and I would take the brands and trade marks, and I would fare better than you."*
>
> —John Stuart, chairman of Quaker (1900).

Thirty-five hundred years ago, a potter's "mark" was used to identify the source of clay pots.[1] Through this mark, which was nothing more than scratchy signature, a potter could be identified and thus associated with the quality and craftsmanship found in these pots.[2] Today, the purpose of trademarks remains essentially the same. A trademark is designed to associate a product with a particular source. Trademarks are afforded legal protection to protect the reputation and goodwill of the product's source.[3]

i. Importance of Trademarks

The importance of protecting a brand owner's trademark cannot be overstated. The brand is the most valuable and sustainable asset of any organization.[4] In 2001, the world's two most powerful brands (Coca-Cola and Microsoft) were worth $134 billion.[5] To put this figure into perspective, the gross domestic product of Thailand that same year was $115 billion.[6] Trademarks are important because they allow customers to quickly associate a product with the brand owner sponsoring the product. Rather than read a long list of components or ingredients present in particular products, customers are able to make faster purchasing decisions when they are familiar with the products at issue. In other words, most customers will not do a side-by-side comparison of the components inside a Porsche and a Prius. From first-hand experience, word of mouth, or marketing efforts, the vast majority of consumers understand that a Porsche will have a powerful engine built for speed whereas the Prius is a hybrid engine built for fuel efficiency.

---

1. Gerard Ruston, *On the Origin of Trademarks*, 45 TRADEMARK REP. 127 (1955).
2. *Id.*
3. Smith v. Dental Products Co., 140 F.2d 140, 144 (7th Cir. 1944).
4. CLIFTON, *supra* note 13, at 2.
5. *Id.*
6. *Id.*

Consumer trust or *mistrust* of brands and trademarks provides consumers with the confidence to make informed purchasing decisions. This reality puts immense pressure on brand owners to maintain the quality and relevance of their brands. Trends come and go and styles change; today, one of the world's most popular brands is Apple Computer. Dedicated consumers line up outside the doors of their fashionable stores to purchase Apple's latest gadgets.[7] This was not always the case. In 1997, Apple was a beleaguered company believed by many to be on the brink of bankruptcy. *Wired* Magazine published an article called "101 Ways to Save Apple" wherein the number one reason for the company's ostensible failures was the following:

> 1. **Admit it**. You're out of the hardware game. Outsource your hardware production, or scrap it entirely, to compete more directly with Microsoft without the liability of manufacturing boxes.[8]

Years later, Apple was back on top, touting a variety of popular hardware products that it *manufactured*. Acknowledging its comeback, *Wired* Magazine credited Apple's branding efforts: "'It's a really powerful brand,' said Robin Rusch, editor or Brandchannel.com, which awarded Apple 'Brand of the Year' in 2001. 'The overwhelming presence of Apple comes through in everything they do.'"[9]

The Apple trademark has won back the confidence of consumers. Consumers have a renewed faith that a product from Apple is a product of quality. Apple's revival reveals the vulnerability and value of trademarks. As one commentator has explained, a trademark is essentially a contract between the brand owner and consumer:

> The real power of successful brands is that they meet the expectations of those that buy them or, to put it another way, they represent a promise kept. As such they are a contract between a seller and a buyer: if the seller keeps to its side of the bargain, the buyer will be satisfied; if not, the buyer will in the future look elsewhere.[10]

---

7. John Markoff, *In Line for an iPhone, and Then Prevented From Turning It On*, N.Y. TIMES, July 12, 2008, at C1 ("Apple's stores opened at 8 a.m. At the store in downtown San Francisco at 11:30 a.m., there was still a line of more than 300 customers stretching down one block and around the corner waiting for iPhones. Some customers said they had hired placeholders to stand overnight in line.").
8. James Daly, *101 Ways to Save Apple*, WIRED, June 1997, *available at* http://www.wired.com/wired/archive/5.06/apple_pr.html.
9. Leander Kahney, *Apple: It's All About the Brand*, WIRED, Dec. 4, 2002, *available at* http://www.wired.com/gadgets/mac/commentary/cultofmac/2002/12/56677.
10. CLIFTON, *supra* note 13, at 18 (2003).

Because the marketplace is sufficient to jeopardize the value of a trademark, the last thing brand owners need is other individuals or companies selling inferior products under the same trademark. Fortunately for American brand owners, there is a body of law designed to prevent and punish those that look to unfairly capitalize on the brand value of another.

ii. Trademark Causes of Action

Congress enacted the first federal trademark statute in 1870.[11] However, the United States Supreme Court ruled it unconstitutional on the ground that it was beyond the constitutional scope of Congress' authority to enact legislation.[12] The Trademark Protection Act of 1881 included the appropriate revisions and remained in effect until it was replaced by the 1905 Act.[13] The 1905 Act and a supplemental Act passed in 1920 were supplanted in 1946 by the Lanham Act, which took effect July 5, 1947.[14] The United States Supreme Court has likewise recognized the importance of protecting trademarks to foster competition and protect the goodwill and reputation of brand owners.[15]

The Lanham Act establishes a system of trademark protection.[16] Section 45 of the Lanham Act defines a trademark as any word, name, symbol, or device adopted and used by merchants or manufacturers to identify and distinguish their goods from other merchants.[17] Section 32(1) of the Lanham Act[18] governs claims for infringement of a registered trademark, prohibiting the use in commerce of "any reproduction, counterfeit, copy, or colorable imitation of a registered mark in connection with the sale, offering for sale, distribution, or advertising of any goods or services on or in connection with which such use is likely to cause confusion, or to cause mistake, or to deceive."[19]

The Lanham Act also provides claims for *dilution*. Dilution of a famous trademark takes two forms: "tarnishment," which is when a mark is linked to substandard goods or services such that the goodwill and positive associations

---

11. 16 Stat. 210 (1870).
12. United States v. Steffens, 100 U.S. 82 (1879).
13. 33 Stat. 724 (1905).
14. 15 U.S.C. § 1051 (2008).
15. San Francisco Arts & Ath. v. United States Olympic Comm., 483 U.S. 522, 531 (1987).
16. *Id.*
17. *Id.*
18. 15 U.S.C. § 1114(1).
19. *Id.*

to the mark are diminished; and "blurring," which is the gradual diminution of a mark's value through unauthorized uses of the mark.[20]

To be successful on a claim of dilution, one must prove the famousness of the mark, the defendant's commercial use of the mark, and actual dilution on the quality of the mark.[21] The federal dilution statute provides eight factors courts may use, along with other relevant factors, in determining whether a mark is distinctive and famous.[22] The eight factors are the following: (1) the degree of inherent or acquired distinctiveness of the mark; (2) the duration and extent of use of the mark in connection with the goods or services with which the mark is used; (3) the duration and extent of advertising and publicity of the mark; (4) the geographical extent of the trading area in which the mark is used; (5) the channels of trade for the goods or services with which the mark is used; (6) the degree of recognition of the mark in the trading areas and channels of trade used by the marks' owner and the person against whom the injunction is sought; (7) the nature and extent of use of the same or similar marks by third parties; and (8) whether the mark was federally registered.[23]

When the defendant substitutes its products for the plaintiff's without notice to the purchaser, the defendant is normally found liable for palming off or passing off, if not counterfeiting.[24] Although palming off as such is not an essential ingredient of a trademark infringement action, as long as likelihood of confusion can be shown, palming off itself constitutes trademark infringement and unfair competition.[25] Palming off has generated a related offshoot known as "reverse palming off."[26] It occurs when a wholesaler or retailer removes the original trademark or name from the product without the originator's consent, and then resells the product as his own.[27] An essential element to proving a passing off claim is a showing of a likelihood of confusion.[28] If the defendant modifies the product to the extent that it is converted into a different product, then there is no liability for reverse passing off.[29]

---

20. Deborah Heart & Lung Found.v.Children of the World Found., 99 F. Supp. 2d 481, 493 (D.N.J. 2000).
21. 15 U.S.C. § 1125(c) (2008).
22. Playboy Enter. v. Netscape Comm'n, 354 F.3d 1020, 1031 (9th Cir. 2004).
23. Id. at 1031–32.
24. 5-5 GILSON ON TRADEMARKS § 5.09(6) (2008).
25. Id.
26. Id.
27. Playboy Enters. v. Frena, 839 F. Supp. 1552, 1562 (M.D. Fla. 1993).
28. Lipscher v. LRP Publs., Inc., 266 F.3d 1305, 1313 (11th Cir. 2001).
29. Id.

b. Trademark Law's Treatment of the Gray Market

i. The Early Cases and the Gray Market

One of the early gray market cases was in New York's Circuit Court in 1886. In *Apollinaris Co. v. Scherer*,[30] the court examined a trademark holder's ability to block the importation of genuine products intended for foreign distribution. The plaintiff Apollinaris Company (Apollinaris) purchased from Andreas Saxlehner the sole right to export certain mineral water from Hungary to Great Britain and America and use the Andreas Saxlehner trademark to sell the water in these countries.[31] In an effort to ensure the protection of their rights, labels affixed to the bottles identified their respective authorizations. The labels on bottles sold by Saxlehner stated the following: "CAUTION. This bottle is not intended for export, and if exported for sale in Great Britain, her colonies, America, or other transmarine places, the public is cautioned against purchasing it. ANDREAS SAXLEHNER."[32] The bottle used by Apollinaris stated the following: "Sole exporters. The Apollinaris Company, Limited, London."[33]

Aware of the parties' contract, the defendant Scherer purchased mineral water from parties who had purchased it from Saxlehner. Scherer then imported and sold the water in the United States for prices lower than those offered by Apollinaris. Apollinaris contended that it could not maintain its own prices and brought its lawsuit to enjoin continued gray market imports and sales. In its ruling, the court acknowledged the various ways in which Apollinaris was harmed by the unauthorized imports. The court agreed that Apollinaris could no longer enjoy the full benefits of the contract rights it purchased from Saxlehner. Indeed, Apollinaris could no longer protect itself against "a spurious articled being palmed off upon the public as its own."[34] However, the court ultimately concluded that the plaintiff was without a viable legal theory for recovery.

With respect to trademark infringement, the court reasoned that there could be no infringement because the water offered by the defendant was the "genuine" water associated with the trademark. Unless the defendant was using the trademark to falsely claim that some other product was Saxlehner water, the law of trademark could not be invoked.

---

30. Apollinaris Co. v. Scherer, 27 F. 18 (C.C.N.Y. 1886).
31. *Id.* at 19. According to the complaint, the mineral water was from a certain mineral spring of Hungary owned by Andreas Saxlehner.
32. *Id.* at 19.
33. *Id.*
34. *Id.* at 20.

The court then analyzed whether Scherer was unlawfully interfering with any exclusive right owned by Apollinaris. The court acknowledged that if Saxlehner was the party trying to compete domestically with Apollinaris there would indeed be a valid claim. Likewise, a valid claim would exist if Saxlehner had colluded with Scherer to compete with Apollinaris. It was not possible, the court concluded, for Apollinaris and Sexlehner to create a "territorial right to the products."[35] The court explained that "any purchaser of the water, wherever he purchases it, acquires a valid title to treat it as his own property."[36] Accordingly, Scherer was "legally justified in buying where he can and selling where he chooses, it [was] not material whether he [was] actuated by a desire to annoy the complainant or to promote his own pecuniary interests."[37]

In 1921, the Second Circuit Court followed *Appollinaris* in its *A. Bourjois & Co. v. Katzel*[38] opinion. The controversy stemmed from the plaintiff's 1913 purchase of goodwill and trademarks in the United States from A. Bourjois & Co., E. Wertheimer & Cie., Successeurs (Bourjois). Bourjois manufactured and sold face powder and the plaintiff, with its purchase of Bourjois' American trademark rights, imported and sold the face powder throughout the United States. The defendant operated a pharmacy in New York City and was found selling the same Bourjois face powder acquired from the gray market.

At issue was whether the plaintiff had the right to enjoin the defendant pharmacy from selling the face powder under the trademarks owned by the plaintiff. Although the Second Circuit Court noted a couple of *de minimus* differences in the defendant's products from the products sold by the plaintiff, it considered the products to be the same: "The article sold by the plaintiff and covered by its registered trade-marks is the face powder actually manufactured by the French firm, imported in bulk and packed here by the plaintiff, which is the precise article imported by the defendant in the French firm's original boxes and sold here."[39]

Rather than consider whether the differences between the products were *material* and could cause any consumer confusion, the court instead considered whether the defendant had the right to sell the face powder under the trademarks that *truthfully* indicate its origin. Under this analysis, the court concluded that the defendant had not infringed any of the plaintiff's rights. The court interpreted the Trademark Act to prohibit the entry of imported merchandise that *copied or simulated* a trademark. Because the goods imported by the defendant were *genuine*, there was no law that prohibited a

---

35. *Id.* at 21.
36. *Id.*
37. *Id.* at 22.
38. A. Bourjois & Co. v. Katzel, 275 F. 539 (2d Cir. 1921).
39. *Id.* at 540.

party from buying genuine goods in a foreign country, importing them into the United States, and selling them in the United States.[40]

The United States Supreme Court reversed the Second Circuit Court's ruling.[41] In a two-page opinion, the Court concluded that the defendant's sales infringed the plaintiff's trademark rights. Justice Holmes authored the opinion and reasoned that ownership of goods "does not necessarily carry the right to sell them at all in a given place."[42] Axiomatically, the French manufacturers who sold its U.S. trademarks to the plaintiff could not have come to the United States and sold its face powder in competition with the plaintiff. Similarly, the French manufacturer could not have conspired with the defendant to engage in such sales. Although no such conspiracy was evident in the case, the defendants could not have sold the face powder without the "opening of a door" by the French manufacturer. The plaintiff owned the U.S. trademark, it purchased goodwill of the French manufacturer, and the public understood that the goods came from the plaintiff (although not made by it). Accordingly, the face powder could only be sold by the plaintiff in the United States.[43]

Although Justice Holmes seemed willing to grant certain prohibitive rights to trademark owners in *Katzel*, he established one year later that the rights were not without limitation. In *Prestonettes v. Coty*,[44] the United States Supreme Court examined a case wherein a defendant bought, dramatically altered, and then sold goods bearing the plaintiff's trademarks "Coty" and "L'Origan." The plaintiff's goods were toilet powders and perfumes. Specifically, the defendant would repackage the powders and perfumes and sell them in different metal cases and bottles, respectively. The district court permitted the sales to continue so long as the containers contained a clear and obvious disclaimer articulating that the goods were repackaged by the defendant.[45] The Circuit Court of Appeals extended the district court's holding and issued a preliminary injunction, which prohibited the use of the trademarks except for original packages marked and sold by the plaintiff.[46]

The United States Supreme Court disagreed with the Court of Appeal's ruling finding that it went too far. Drawing the distinction between copyrights

---

40. *Id.* at 544.
41. *See* A. Bourjois & Co., Inc. v. Katzel, 260 U.S. 689 (1923).
42. *See id.* at 692.
43. *Id.*
44. Prestonettes v. Coty, 264 U.S. 359 (1924).
45. *Id.* at 367 (The district court's decree stated that the defendant could continue to sell the rebottled perfume with the following language on the container: "Prestonettes, Inc., not connected with Coty, states that the contents are Coty's independently bottled in New York." The disclaimer for the powder required similar language: "Prestonettes, Inc., not connected with Coty, states that the compact of face powder herein was independently compounded by it from Coty's loose powder and its own binder. Loose powder-per cent., Binder-per cent.")
46. *Id.*

and trademarks, the Court explained that a trademark holder does not have the right to prohibit the use of words. A trademark, explained the Court, only gives the right to prohibit the use of it so far as to protect the owner's goodwill against the sale of another's product as his. Thus, the plaintiff could not prevent or complain about the defendant stating the source from which its repackaged goods derived if it did not use the trademark in doing so. The Court distinguished the case from *Katzel* on the grounds that there was no potential for confusion with respect to the goods' source. So long as the public was not deceived about who did the repackaging and rebottling—and thus no potential for deception—the Court was unwilling to prevent the use of the trademarked word to simply tell the truth.[47]

ii. Tariff Act and the Gray Market

In addition to the United States Supreme Court reversing the Second Circuit Court's *A. Bourjois & Co. v. Katzel*[48] opinion, *supra*, Congress also felt compelled to take action in response to the apparent unfairness that was afforded to Bourjois & Co. Congress thus enacted Section 526 of the Tariff Act of 1922, later reenacted as Section 526(a) of the Tariff Act of 1930.[49] The United States Supreme Court later characterized Section 526 as a "hastily drafted provision" that was "introduced as a 'midnight amendmen[t]' on the floor of the Senate."[50] With respect to its substance, the statute sought to prohibit the importation into the United States of any merchandise:

> [1] of foreign manufacture . . . [2] bearing a trademark owned by a citizen of, or by a corporation or association created or organized within . . . the United States, [3] and registered in the Patent and Trademark Office by a person domiciled in the United States . . . [4] unless written consent of the owner of such trademark is produced at the time of making entry.[51]

After Section 526's enactment, the U.S. Customs Service enacted implementing regulations. These regulations provided that merchandise with the above characteristics were subject to seizure and forfeiture as prohibited importations.[52] However, the regulations provided two exceptions to the importation ban. First, the "common-control" exception applied when either

---

47. *Id.* at 368.
48. A. Bourjois & Co. v. Katzel, 275 F. 539 (2d Cir. 1921).
49. 19 U.S.C. § 526.
50. K Mart v. Cartier, 486 U.S. 281, 303 (1988).
51. 19 U.S.C. § 526.
52. 19 C.F.R. § 133.21(b).

(1) the foreign and the U.S. trademark or trade name were owned by the same person or business entity; or (2) the foreign and the U.S. trademark or trade name owners were parent and subsidiary companies or were otherwise subject to common ownership or control.[53] Second, the "authorized-use" exception applied when the foreign manufactured merchandise bears a trademark or trade name applied under authorization of the U.S. owner.[54]

These regulations were challenged in *K Mart Corp. v. Cartier, Inc.*[55] The plaintiffs were an association of trademark owners, which the Court collectively referred to as COPIAT. COPIAT commenced litigation in the District Court of Columbia to challenge the U.S. Customs Service Regulations. COPIAT sought a judicial declaration that the U.S. Customs Service Regulations were invalid because the "common control" and "authorized use" exceptions were inconsistent with Section 526 of the 1930 Tariff Act and Section 42 of the Lanham Act. K Mart and 47th Street Photo, Inc. intervened as defendants in the case. To adequately frame the issues, the Court began its opinion identifying the typical contexts in which the gray market case arose.[56]

The first context was described as the "prototypical gray-market victim." In this context, a domestic company buys from a foreign company the right to (1) use its trademark, and (2) sell its foreign-manufactured products domestically. Especially when the foreign company has already registered its trademark or earned a reputation for quality, purchasing the trademark rights can be very valuable. The domestic company becomes the victim of the gray market, however, if the foreign company imports and distributes its products domestically. The same result occurs when the foreign company sells its products to a third party abroad who similarly imports them for domestic distribution. As a result of these imports, the domestic company is left to compete with the very trademark it purchased.

The second context occurs when a foreign company wishes to control the distribution of its products domestically. Towards this end, the foreign company will incorporate a subsidiary in the United States. The subsidiary then registers a United States trademark that is identical to its foreign parent company's trademark. The parallel importation, or gray market, occurs when a third party purchases goods abroad from a foreign company (or the foreign trademark holder itself), imports the goods, and distributes the goods domestically.

A variation of the second context occurs when a domestic company establishes abroad a manufacturing subsidiary or its own manufacturing division

---

53. 19 C.F.R. § 133.21(c)(1), (2).
54. 19 C.F.R. § 13321(c).
55. K Mart Corp. v. Cartier, Inc., 485 U.S. 176 (1988).
56. *See id.* at 286–87 (The Supreme Court describes these general contexts as case 1, case 2, and case 3).

to produce its United States trademarked goods for importation and domestic distribution. A gray market is created if the products are sold abroad by the manufacturing company to a separate third party who imports them for domestic competition.

Finally, the third context occurs when a domestic trademark holder authorizes an independent foreign manufacturer to use it. Typically, the domestic trademark holder sells to the foreign manufacturer an exclusive right to use the trademark, but the use is conditioned on the foreign manufacturer promising not to import its trademarked goods into the United States. A gray market is created if the foreign manufacturer or a third party imports the goods into the United States to compete against the domestic trademark holder's goods.

Turning to the legality of the U.S. Customs Service Regulations, the United States Supreme Court upheld the "common-control" exceptions. Applying the traditional analysis to determine whether a regulation was a permissible construction of the relevant statute, the Court reasoned that Section 526 was sufficiently ambiguous such that the regulation did not create an irreconcilable conflict with the statute.

The United States Supreme Court did, however, conclude that the "authorized-use" exception was inconsistent with Section 526. The Court concluded that allowing the "authorized-use" regulation to stand would prevent a trademark owner from prohibiting the importation of goods made by an independent foreign manufacturer authorized to use the trademark. Because the regulations were severable, the Court ordered Section 133.21(c)(3) to be invalidated for its conflict with Section 526.

Although concurring in part and dissenting in part, Justice Brennan offered an alternative justification for affirming the common control exception. Examining the language and design of the statute along with the legislative history, Justice Brennan concluded that Section 526 was intended to only protect domestic interests. In addition to the "characteristic of the times," the language of Section 526 reflected a "protectionist, almost jingoist, flavor." Specifically, Section 526 required "consent of the trademark owner to import a United States trademarked product if (1) the product was "of foreign manufacture"; (2) the trademark it bore was 'owned by' either a United States citizen or 'a corporation . . . created or organized . . . [in] the United States'; and (3) 'a person domiciled in the United States' registered the trademark."[57]

These protections for domestic interests would be undermined, however, if a foreign company could simply incorporate a shell domestic subsidiary with the United States trademark as its only asset. Allowing a foreign manufacturer to so easily insulate itself from the competition of gray markets, Justice Brennan reasoned, was entirely at odds with the protectionist sentiment

---

57. *Id.* at 297–298.

that inspired Section 526. To avoid such a result, Justice Brennan concluded that the U.S. Customs Service's regulations properly interpreted Section 526 to have a common control exception.

The result of the Court's holding in *K Mart* appeared to deny the owners of U.S. trademarks the protections of Section 526 when they are affiliated with foreign manufacturers. Although the United States Supreme Court was contemplating its decision in *K Mart*, the Ninth Circuit Court considered a similar set of gray market circumstances and arrived at such a conclusion. In *NEC Electronics v. Cal Circuit Abco*,[58] a Japanese manufacturer of computer chips (NEC-Japan) assigned its United States trademark rights to its California subsidiary (NEC-USA). NEC-USA was vexed to discover the defendant (Abco) buying NEC-Japan's chips in foreign companies for purposes of importing and selling them domestically.[59] NEC-USA thus sued Abco for trademark infringement under Sections 32 and 43 of the Lanham Act.[60]

Notwithstanding Section 526 and its enacting regulations discussed above, NEC-USA argued that its case was guided by *A. Bourjois & Co. v. Katzel*.[61] Examining *Katzel*, the Ninth Circuit Court discerned two rationales—neither of which was present in the case at bar—underlying the *Katzel* opinion. Unlike NEC-USA, the American company paid a large sum of money for the trademarks and goodwill associated with them in an arm's-length transaction. Second, as a result of the transaction, the foreign manufacturer had surrendered all rights to its trademark in the United States.

Accordingly, the American owner in *Katzel* had full control over the quality and control of the goods sold under the mark. Unlike the parent-subsidiary relationship present in *NEC Electronics*, the *Katzel* opinion was justified on the American owner's "real independence from the foreign manufacturer."[62] The Ninth Circuit Court reinforced its opinion by citing the U.S. Customs Service's regulations outlined above, which created an exception to Section 526's importation bar when the American trademark owner is in such a parent/subsidiary relationship.[63] Although the United States Supreme Court had not yet issued its *K Mart* opinion, the Ninth Circuit Court foreshadowed their consistent holdings: "If in [*K Mart*], the Supreme Court upholds the challenged regulations, then our holding today will be consistent: foreign producers will not be able to accomplish under trademark law what they cannot do under the Tariff Act."[64] Given the relationship

---

58. NEC Electronics v. Cal Circuit Abco, 810 F.2d 1506 (9th Cir. 1987).
59. *Id.* at 1507.
60. 15 U.S.C. §§ 1114, 1125.
61. A. Bourjois & Co. v. Katzel, 260 U.S. 689 (1923).
62. NEC Electronics, 810 F.2d at 1509.
63. *Id.* at 1510, n. 4.
64. *Id.*

between NEC-Japan and NEC-USA, the court concluded that no trademark infringement could exist.

Even after the United States Supreme Court issued its opinion, the reach of *K Mart* was challenged shortly after its holding in *Weil Ceramics & Glass, Inc. v. Dash*.[65] The plaintiff Weil Ceramics & Glass, Inc. (Weil) was the wholly owned subsidiary of a Spanish corporation (Lladro),[66] which manufactured fine porcelain. In 1966, Weil became the exclusive distributor in the United States of Lladro porcelain. Weil obtained a valid U.S. registration for the "LLADRO" trademark and continued as the exclusive distributor of the porcelain for years.[67]

In 1982, the defendant Jalyn Corporation and its president Bernard Dash (collectively, "Jalyn") began importing and selling Lladro porcelain, which it had obtained in Spain from Lladro distributors, in the United States. Weil filed a complaint in the District Court of New Jersey seeking declaratory and injunctive relief against any further imports.[68] Among other causes of action, Weil argued that Jalyn's imports violated Section 526 of the Tariff Act.

In the court's analysis of whether Weil had a viable theory of recovery, it summarized the recently articulated opinion of *K Mart*.[69] Turning to *Weil*, the Third Circuit Court had previously concluded that the case was most similar to the situation described in *K Mart* wherein a foreign company incorporates a subsidiary in the United States. After the subsidiary registers a U.S. trademark that is identical to its foreign parent company's trademark, a gray market is created when a third party purchases goods abroad from another third party (or the foreign company itself), imports the goods, and distributes the goods domestically. *K Mart* concluded that Section 133.21's "common control" exception applied to preclude the applicability of Section 526's importation ban.

In an effort to distinguish the case from *K Mart*, Weil argued that *K Mart* only endorsed the application of Section 133.21 to instances of *sham* incorporation; situations where a foreign corporation incorporates a shell domestic corporation so that it can control the distribution of product without American competition. According to Weil, the applicability of Section 133.21 was not—or at least should not be—absolute. Weil argued that Section 133.21 merely created a *presumption* that Section 526 is not applicable. Because Weil had established that it was an independent subsidiary that truly owned the

---

65. Weil Ceramics & Glass, Inc. v. Dash, 878 F.2d 659 (3d Cir. 1989).
66. Specifically, Lladro Exportadora, S.A. was a sister corporation of Lladro, S.A. In 1977, Lladro Exportadora obtained Ladro, S.A.'s shares of Weil stock, as well as the remaining fifty percent of Weil stock thus becoming the sole owner of Weil. *Id.*
67. *Id.* at 662.
68. *Id.*
69. *See id.* at 664–66.

LLADRO trademark, it should have the ability to preclude unwanted imports.[70]

The court was not persuaded. Whether or not Weil's incorporation was a sham or a legitimate business endeavor, the court concluded that the foreign manufacturer's ownership provided it the opportunity to control the United States market. In addition, the court did not interpret *K Mart* to create anything less than an *absolute* exception from Section 526 under the facts presented by *Weil*.

With Section 526 unavailable, Weil's next argument was that Jalyn's conduct was deemed unlawful by *A. Bourjois & Co. v. Katzel*.[71] Specifically, Weil relied on the theory that there are separate trademark rights in each territory they have been registered.[72] The court rejected Weil's argument and concluded that the case was not sufficiently analogous to *Bourjois*. The most significant difference was the fact that Bourjois, unlike Weil, was "completely independent from the foreign manufacturer."[73] Detailing the differences, the court explained that "[Bourjois had] entered into an arms-length exchange to acquire the rights to the trademark with the clear intent that the foreign manufacturer would not market the trademarked good in the United States."[74]

Rejecting Weil's attempt to align its plight with that suffered by Bourjois, the Third Circuit Court concluded that its conclusion was consistent with *K Mart* and *Katzel*. In fact, it concluded that its opinion "illustrate[d] the synthesis between those Supreme Court decisions."[75] Section 526 was designed to provide trademark act protection to domestic trademark holders that are "truly independent of the foreign manufacturer." Neither *Katzel* nor *K Mart* should be read to extend beyond that circumstance. Thus, because Weil was not *truly independent* from its foreign parent, its claims failed.

This does not mean, however, that trademark law denies these owners all recourse. As explained below, the Lanham Act can be a successful—albeit complex—road to recovery.

iii. The Lanham Act and the Gray Market

Section 32(1) of the Lanham Act[76] governs claims for infringement of a registered trademark, prohibiting the use in commerce of "any reproduction, counterfeit, copy, or colorable imitation of a registered mark in connection

---

70. *See id.* at 666.
71. A. Bourjois & Co. v. Katzel, 275 F. 539 (2d Cir. 1921).
72. Weil Ceramics & Glass, Inc. v. Dash, 878 F.2d at 667.
73. *Id.*
74. *Id. citing* Katzel, 260 U.S. at 691.
75. *Id.* at 669.
76. 15 U.S.C. § 1114(1).

with the sale, offering for sale, distribution, or advertising of any goods or services on or in connection with which such use is likely to cause confusion, or to cause mistake, or to deceive."[77]

Section 42 of the Act[78] bars merchandise that "cop[ies] or simulate[s] the name of . . . any domestic manufacture, or manufacturer . . . or which shall copy or simulate a trademark registered . . . or shall bear a name or mark calculated to induce the public to believe that the article is manufactured in the United States, or that it is manufactured in any foreign country or locality other than the country or locality in which it is in fact manufactured[.]"[79] This section "undeniably bespeak[s] an intention to protect domestic trademark holders from foreign competitors who seek a free ride on the goodwill of domestic trademarks."[80] However, "the importation of a . . . good *identical* to a good authorized for sale in the domestic market does not violate section 42," so long as the identical good is sold under the identical mark.[81]

Section 43(a) of the Act[82] governs claims for infringement of an unregistered trademark and also acts a "a broad federal unfair competition provision."[83] Specifically, Section 43(a) prohibits the use in commerce of "any word, term, name, symbol, or device, or any combination thereof, or any false designation of origin, false or misleading description of fact, or false or misleading representation of fact, which . . . is likely to cause confusion, or to cause mistake, or to deceive as to the affiliation, connection, or association of such person with another person, or as to the origin, sponsorship, or approval of his or her goods, services, or commercial activities by another person."[84]

Whether a claim for trademark infringement is brought under Section 32(1), 42 or 43(a) of the Lanham Act, it is analyzed under a two-prong test. The test first looks to whether the plaintiff's mark is entitled to protection. The second test looks to whether the defendant's use of the mark is likely to cause consumers confusion as to the origin or sponsorship of the defendant's goods.[85] A certificate of registration of the plaintiff's registration on the principal register is prima facie evidence that the plaintiff's mark satisfies the first prong of the test.[86] When analyzing whether a defendant's use of a mark is likely to

---

77. Id.
78. 15 U.S.C. § 1124.
79. Id.
80. Lever Bros. Co. v. United States, 877 F.2d 101, 105 (D.C. Cir. 1989).
81. Société Des Produits Nestlé, S.A. v. Casa Helvetia, Inc., 982 F.2d 633, 639 (1st Cir. 1992).
82. See 15 U.S.C. § 1125(a)(1)(A).
83. Chambers v. Time Warner, Inc., 282 F.3d 147, 155 (2d Cir. 2002).
84. 15 U.S.C. § 1125(a)(1)(A).
85. See e.g., Virgin Enters. Ltd. v. Nawab, 335 F.3d 141, 146 (2d Cir. 2003).
86. See 15 U.S.C. § 1057(b) ("A certificate of registration of a mark upon the principal register provided by this chapter shall be prima facie evidence of the validity of the registered mark and of the registration of the mark, of the registrant's ownership of the mark, and of the registrant's exclusive right to use the registered mark in commerce. . . .").

cause consumer confusion, courts typically weigh the eight *Polaroid* factors[87] articulated by Judge Henry Friendly in 1961.

In gray market cases, however, courts have generally simplified the second test and, instead of weighing the eight *Polaroid* factors, examine the following: (1) whether "material differences" exist between the goods sold by the trademark holder and its authorized or licensed dealers and those sold by the unauthorized dealer(s); and (2) whether the unauthorized dealer(s) sell the materially different goods in a manner that would be likely to cause confusion and/or dilute the strength of the trademark owner's mark.[88] Although this abridged second test is simpler, it has spawned a body of case law where courts throughout the country are looking at detailed fact patters in an effort to ascertain whether various difference are "material" and whether such "material" differences may confuse the consumer or harm the trademark holder. Courts have not applied these standards in predictable uniformity. However, there are enough cases to give trademark owners strong guidance on what fact patterns will or will not succeed.

(a) Prong One: Is the Plaintiff Entitled to Trademark Protection?

An important lesson when negotiating distribution rights is found in *DEP Corp. v. Interstate Cigar Company, Inc.*[89] The plaintiff learned the necessity of being the trademark *owner* to bring a trademark infringement action. The case involved soap products that were manufactured by a company called A&P Pears Ltd. (Pears). Pears was the owner of the "Pears" mark, which was registered in the United States. Meanwhile, Pears granted Unilever Export Ltd. (Unilever) the exclusive right to distribute Pears soap worldwide. Unilever then entered into an agreement with the plaintiff DEP Corporation (DEP) wherein DEP was appointed as the exclusive distributor of Pears soap in the United States.[90]

Shortly after DEP entered into its contract with Unilever, it discovered that the defendants Interstate Cigar Company, Inc. and others (collectively, "Interstate") were selling Pears soap in the United States that had been purchased from "European middlemen" who were able to sell the soap at

---

87. *See* Polaroid Corp. v. Polorad Elecs. Corp., 287 F.2d 492, 495 (2d Cir. 1961) (The eight factors are: (1) the strength of the plaintiff's mark; (2) the similarity of the plaintiff's and defendant's marks; (3) the proximity of the products; (4) the likelihood that the prior owner will bridge the gap; (5) actual confusion; (6) the defendant's good faith in adopting its own mark; (7) the quality of defendant's product; and (8) the sophistication of the buyers.).
88. *See e.g.*, Original Appalachian Artworks, Inc. v. Granada Elecs., Inc., 816 F.2d 68 (2d Cir. 1987).
89. DEP Corp. v. Interstate Cigar Company, Inc., 622 F.2d 621 (2d Cir. 1980).
90. *Id.* at 621.

lower prices.[91] DEP sued Interstate for trademark infringement and unfair competition. The trial court dismissed the case and the Second Circuit Court affirmed.

The dismissal of the trial court was based on the fact that DEP did not own the Pears' trademarks. The court examined the contract between DEP and Unilever and noted that not only was there no conveyance of trademark rights, but the contract expressly articulated the fact that DEP was not acquiring any trademark rights:

> You (DEP) shall not during the continuance of this arrangement or thereafter have or claim any right whatsoever whether of user or otherwise to or in any such trade marks, trade names or brands used in connection with Products. . . . In the event of any infringement of any such trade marks, trade names or brands coming to your notice, you shall promptly notify us and shall take at our expense such steps as we may reasonably require for their protection.[92]

The Lanham Act provides that only the "registrant" may bring an action for trademark infringement.[93] "Registrant" is defined to include legal representatives, predecessors, successors and assigns of the registrant.[94] Thus, because the DEP contract provided that it had no rights in the Pears trademarks, trade names or brands, it could not reasonably establish that it was the "registrant" for purposes of pursuing a trademark infringement cause of action.

The *DEP* case illustrates the importance of acquiring trademark rights when acquiring the right to distribute products in restricted territories. Not only must the distributor acquire an assignment of the trademark, the Lanham Act does not recognize the assignment unless it is in writing[95] and unless it also assigns the goodwill of the business in which the mark is used.[96] Even though the court recognized the reality that DEP was losing business to its gray market competitors, its lack of trademark ownership rendered its trademark cause of action fatally defective.[97]

Although DEP was missing the essential element of a written agreement transferring ownership of the trademark, a parties' agreement is not always

---

91. *Id.* at 622.
92. *Id.*
93. 15 U.S.C. § 1114(1).
94. 15 U.S.C. § 1127.
95. 15 U.S.C. § 1060(a)(3).
96. 15 U.S.C. § 1060(a)(1) ("A registered mark or a mark for which an application to register has been filed shall be assignable with the good will of the business in which the mark is used, or with that part of the good will of the business connected with the use of and symbolized by the mark.")
97. DEP, 622 F.2d at 624.

dispositive in settling the question of ownership. The ownership of the product's goodwill must also be determined. These issues were closely examined in *Premier Dental Products Company v. Darby Dental Supply, Inc.*[98] The case involved the unauthorized importation of various dental products. The plaintiff Premier Dental Products Company (Premier) was a wholesale distributor of dental products. Among the products it sold was a denture impression material that was manufactured by ESPE Fabrik Pharmazeutischer Praparate, GmbH (ESPE), a West German company. In 1974, ESPE granted Premier the exclusive right to market and sell IMPREGUM. IMPREGUM was a registered trademark owned by ESPE and used in a variety of dental procedures.[99]

For years, the defendant Darby Dental Supply Company (Darby) purchased its IMPREGUM from Premier to sell to dentists and dental supply companies. Beginning in 1982, however, Darby began purchasing the European-marketed version of IMPREGUM, and was able to sell in the United States at lower prices than those offered by Premier.[100] As of 1982 Premier had the exclusive right to market and sell IMPREGUM; however, it did not have any ownership rights over its U.S. trademark. Prior to litigation, therefore, ESPE and Premier entered into a contract wherein "ESPE assigned to Premier all its 'rights, title, and interest' in the United States trademark 'IMPREGUM.'"[101] Premier then sent cease and desist correspondence to Darby demanding that it immediately refrain from importing and selling the European-marketed IMPREGUM. When Darby refused to acquiesce, Premier sued Darby and moved for a preliminary injunction.

After the district court granted Premier's request for a preliminary injunction, the Third Circuit Court examined the court's ruling and focused its attention on the issue of whether Premier was indeed the valid owner of the IMPREGUM trademarks. Although it was not disputed that Premier and ESPE had contractually agreed that Premier should own the U.S. trademark in IMPREGUM, the contract was not conclusive: "While the parties' agreement is *important* in settling the question of ownership, it is not dispositive. The ownership of the product's goodwill must also be determined."[102] On this latter issue, the parties' intent is "circumstantial proof" that a particular firm or legal entity is standing behind the mark. Absent evidence to the contrary, this circumstantial proof will be sufficient, as a matter of law, to establish that what the parties intended to be the public perception was in fact the actual perception.[103]

---

98. Premier Dental Products Company v. Darby Dental Supply, Inc., 794 F.2d 850 (3d Cir. 1986).
99. *Id.* at 851.
100. *Id.*
101. *Id.*
102. *Id.* at 854.
103. *Id.*

In addition, an exclusive distributor does not have to manufacture the products at issue in order to prove that it possesses the goodwill associated with the products. Showing evidence of goodwill ownership can be established, for example, "[i]f the public believes that the exclusive distributor is responsible for the product, so that the trademark has come, 'by public understanding, to indicate that the goods bearing the trademark come from plaintiff although not made by it.'"[104] Similarly, the distributor can also show that it "has obtained 'a valuable reputation for himself and his wares by his care in selection of his precautions as to transit and storage, or because his local character is such that the article acquires a value by his testimony to its genuineness.'"[105]

To prove ownership of goodwill under these standards, Premier highlighted several facts. Premier noted the fact that it has been the exclusive American distributor of IMPREGUM since 1974. Since then, Premier spent a great deal of time and money promoting the product in the United States and creating its domestic goodwill. Although IMPREGUM was not made by Premier, Premier guaranteed its customer satisfaction, had provided seminars and instructions to those wishing to learn about the product, and provided a toll-free telephone number for the use of those with questions or problems with the product. Given its establishment of domestic goodwill, Premier argued that ESPE effectively transferred to it the IMPEGRUM trademark and its attendant goodwill.[106]

Darby contested Premier's claimed goodwill ownership on two grounds. Darby first argued that the parties' contract was invalid. Given that ESPE retained substantial control over the use of the mark including the right to require that it be reassigned, Darby argued that the parties' assignment was a sham. The court rejected this argument. Although the assignment contained limitations over Premier's right to the trademark, "[i]t is a well-established principle both of contract law and trademark law that limitations in an otherwise valid assignment do not invalidate it."[107]

Darby's next challenge was that Premier failed to establish that consumers of the product (i.e., dentists and dental technicians) associated IMPEGRUM with Premier. The court ruled that consumers need not know the trademark owner by name so long as they perceive the product coming from a single source: "[I]t is of little significance to the establishment of trademark rights whether the public can identify correctly by name the owner of the mark.... What is relevant is whether the trademark has become sufficiently associated with Premier to justify the inference that buyers under that name are its customers. It is

---

104. *Id. citing* A. Bourjois & Co. v. Katzel Co., 260 U.S. 689, 692 (1923).
105. *Id. citing* E. Leitz, Inc. v. Watson, 152 F. Supp. 631, 635–36 (D.D.C. 1957).
106. *Id.* at 855.
107. *Id.* at 855–56.

enough 'if the article be known as coming from a single, though anonymous source.'"[108] Although consumers did not necessarily recognize Premier as the source for IMPREGUM products, consumers did recognize that they all emanated from a single domestic source. This anonymity did not impair Premier's status as the trademark owner, and the court affirmed the trial court's ruling.[109]

(b) Prong Two: Are the Goods "Materially Different"?

As articulated, determining whether gray market goods infringe a brand owner's mark requires an examination of whether the differences between the gray goods and the authorized goods are sufficient to create a likelihood of confusion, mistake, or deception.[110] In other words, are the goods "materially different"? In this analysis, a plaintiff is not required to provide proof of *actual* confusion.[111] Federal courts routinely grant injunctions in gray market goods cases without any evidence of actual confusion.[112] Instead, once a plaintiff establishes the existence of material differences, consumer confusion is presumed as a matter of law. The alleged infringer may attempt to rebut this presumption.[113] In order to shift this burden, the defendant must prove by preponderance of the evidence that the differences are not the kind that consumers, on average, would likely consider in purchasing the product.[114]

(i) Materially Different Goods When the Goods are Artistic

In *Martin's Herend Imps., Inc. v. Diamond & Gem Trading USA, Co.*,[115] Martin's Herend Imports, Inc. (Martin) was an American corporation that had an exclusive distributorship agreement with Herendi Pocelangyar (Herendi). Herendi was a Hungarian corporation that manufactured high-end porcelain tableware, figurines, and other pieces. Pursuant to the parties' distributorship agreement, Martin was authorized as the sole importer of Herendi's products. Martin and Herendi would collectively select the Herendi

---

108. *Id.* at 856 *citing* Weil Ceramics & Glass, Inc. v. Dash, 618 F. Supp. 700, 712 (D.N.J. 1985); Coty, Inc. v. LeBlume Import Co., Inc., 292 F. 264, 267 (S.D.N.Y. 1923).
109. *Id.* at 856–57.
110. Société Des Produits Nestlé, S.A. v. Casa Helvetia, Inc., 982 F.2d 638 (1st Cir. 1992).
111. *See id.* at 640; *see also* Coach Leatherware Co. v. AnnTaylor, Inc., 933 F.2d 162, 171 (2d Cir. 1991).
112. *See id. citing* Ferrero U.S.A., Inc. v. Ozark Trading, Inc., 753 F. Supp. 1240, 1247 (D.N.J.) *aff'd* 935 F.2d 1281 (3d Cir. 1991).
113. Coach Leatherware Co. v. AnnTaylor, Inc., 933 F.2d 162, 170 (2d Cir. 1991).
114. Nestlé, 982 F.2d at 641.
115. Martin's Herend Imps., Inc. v. Diamond & Gem Trading USA, Co., 112 F. 3d 1296 (5th Cir. 1997).

pieces to be sold in the United States, and Martin would then sell the pieces to upscale retailers.[116]

Martin and Herendi sued Judit and Frank Juhasz along with their business, Diamond & Gem Trading, USA, Co. (collectively, "Juhasz") for selling counterfeit goods bearing Herendi's trademarks. Simultaneous with the filing of the lawsuit, which alleged trademark infringement and false designation of origin, the plaintiffs sought and obtained an *ex parte* search and seizure order. The plaintiffs, through counsel and with the assistance of U.S. Marshals, raided Juhasz's premises and seized various goods and records.[117] After the plaintiffs prevailed at trial, Juhasz appealed.

On appeal, the Fifth Circuit Court first examined whether the trial court properly awarded judgment for trademark infringement. The plaintiffs initially sought judgment on the theory that Juhasz was selling fake Herendi products. Juhasz denied that it ever sold fake Herendi products; instead, Juhasz averred that it sold "genuine" Herendi products that it acquired from (1) Herendi company stores in Hungary, and (2) other American and foreign sources. Juhasz did admit, however, that the Herendi products it sold were not offered by Martin.[118] When seeking judgment, the plaintiff argued that the pieces sold by Juhasz, even if genuine, were materially different from those imported by Martin. The material difference, according to the plaintiffs, was between the Herendi products Martin imported and those lines it did not import.

The Fifth Circuit Court affirmed judgment in plaintiffs' favor under this trademark infringement theory. Relying on *Sociétée Des Produits Nestlé, S.A. v. Casa Helvetia, Inc.*,[119] and *Original Appalachian Artworks, Inc. v. Granada Electronics, Inc.*,[120] *supra*, the court stated that, at least when the goods are highly artistic, luxury goods, infringement may be found if the goods sold by the authorized domestic distributor are materially different from the foreign goods sold by the defendant.[121] The court reasoned that the importance of marketing such goods and imparting on the domestic consumer the belief that the goods are "rare, collectable, elegant, chic or otherwise desirable pieces to own" is one of the valuable attributes of a trademark. Maintaining this valuable attribute may depend on the stores where the goods are sold, advertising, the selection pieces will be offered domestically, and other factors.[122]

---

116. *Id.* at 1299.
117. *Id.*
118. *Id.* at 1299 n.1.
119. *Nestlé*, 982 F. 2d at 633.
120. Original Appalachian Artworks, Inc. v. Granada Elecs., Inc., 816 F. 2d at 68.
121. Martin's Herend Imps., Inc. v. Diamond & Gem Trading USA, Co., 112 F. 3d 1301–02 (5th Cir. 1997).
122. *Id.* at 1302.

Although Juhasz agreed that the pieces were different, it argued that no infringement occurred given that the pieces were of the same grade and quality, as they were authentic Herendi products. Relying on *Nestlé, infra*, the court rejected that argument as irrelevant: "[T]he plaintiff need not prove that the defendant's imports are of inferior quality to establish trademark infringement, only that they are materially different."[123]

Juhasz also argued that his sales of Herendi products were allowed under the "first sale" rule, *infra*. The court rejected this argument because the rule only applied to *identical* genuine goods. The rule does not apply when genuine, but unauthorized, imports differ materially from authentic goods authorized for sale in the domestic market. The court was again relying on *Nestlé*, which recognized the legal distinctions it was placing on imported products: "[A]n unauthorized importation may well turn an otherwise 'genuine' product into a 'counterfeit' one."[124] Holding otherwise would result in the gray market importer always escaping liability since unauthorized resellers are never the first seller.[125]

Even though the trial court's theory of liability was affirmed, the court narrowed the scope of the injunction that was entered. The trial court enjoined Juhasz from selling any Herendi products that were different from the Herendi products that were "at that time being sold in the United States by plaintiffs."[126] The court reasoned that Juhasz should not be barred from selling any Herendi products that, at *some* time, were approved for importation in the United States. Because no material difference existed if the products sold by Juhasz were once approved for importation, the trademark owner's right to control its goodwill through an exclusive distributorship arrangement is outweighed by policies of limiting restraints on trade and alienation.[127]

Similarly, in *Davidoff & CIE, S.A. v. PLD International Corporation*,[128] the plaintiff Davidoff & Cie, S.A. (Davidoff) manufactured and owned the U.S. trademark to various fragrance products. Davidoff exclusively licensed its American sales and distribution to a third-party company. However, the defendant PLD International Corporation (PLD) acquired Davidoff fragrances that were intended for overseas sales or duty-free sales and sold them to discount retail stores in the United States.[129] When PLD acquired the products, codes on the boxes were covered with white stickers and batch

---

123. *Id.* at 1303, *citing* Nestlé, 982 F. 2d at 640.
124. *Id.*, *citing* 982 F. 2d at 640.
125. *Id.* at 1303.
126. *Id.* at 1304.
127. *Id.* at 1304.
128. 263 F.3d 1297 (11th Cir. 2001).
129. *Id.* at 1299.

codes on the bottles themselves were removed with an etching tool.[130] PLD explained that the batch codes were removed to prevent Davidoff from discovering who sold the fragrances to PLD because Davidoff would stop selling to those vendors.[131]

Davidoff sued PLD for trademark infringement, alleging that PLD's sale of fragrances with the batch codes removed rendered the products materially different from genuine Davidoff fragrances. PLD argued that no infringement could exist because "[w]ith or without a manufacturer or batch code on its packaging, the product is absolutely the same."[132]

In its analysis, the court noted that in order to succeed in its trademark claim, Davidoff would have to show that PLD sold products that were "materially different" than those sold by the trademark owner. To meet this burden, Davidoff would have to show that the difference between the products is one that consumers consider relevant to a decision about whether to purchase a product.[133] Put another way, Davidoff would have to show that two products creates the existence of a "likelihood of confusion" among consumers. As a matter of law, the court explained that the resale of a trademarked product that has been altered, resulting in physical differences in the product, can create a likelihood of consumer confusion.[134]

Turning to the facts of the case, the court adopted Davidoff's contention that a consumer examining a fragrance bottle with a missing batch code could very likely believe that the bottle had been tampered with.[135] The court further reasoned that in marketing a fragrance, a vendor is not only selling the product inside the bottle, it is also selling the "commercial magnetism" of the trademark that is affixed to the bottle.[136]

(ii) Materially Different Goods When the Post-Sale Services are Different

In *SKF USA Inc. v. International Trade Commission*,[137] the Federal Circuit Court examined whether material differences between gray market and authorized goods need to be physical in order to establish trademark infringement.

---

130. *Id.*
131. *Id.*
132. *Id.* at 1300.
133. *Id.* at 1302 citing Martin's Herend Imports v. Diamond & Gem Trading USA, Co., 112 F.3d 1296, 1302 (5th Cir. 1997).
134. *Id.* citing Société Des Produits Nestlé, S.A. v. Casa Helvetia, Inc., 982 F.2d 633, 643-33 (1st Cir. 1992); Original Appalachian Artworks, Inc. v. Granada Electronics, Inc., 816 F.2d 68, 73.
135. *Id.* at 1303.
136. *Id.* at 1303 citing Mishawaka Rubber & Woolen Mfg. Co. v. S.S. Keresge Co., 316 U.S. 203, 205 (1942).
137. 423 F.3d 1307 (Fed. Cir. 2005).

The plaintiff SKF USA, Inc. (SKF USA) sold ball bearings that it manufactured in the United States as well as ball bearings that it imported from SKF Manufacturing Units (SKF Manufacturing). SKF USA and SKF Manufacturing were both owned by the same parent company, AB SKF, a Swedish corporation.

SKF USA filed a complaint with the International Trade Commission (ITC) against various companies alleging that they had infringed SKF USA's trademarks by importing and selling various SKF ball bearings. There were no physical differences between the bearings that SKF USA sold compared to the bearings sold by the defendants. However, SKF USA employed a number of engineers to provide technical support and assistance to its customers in the form of troubleshooting, installation supervision, and end user training. Thus, SKF argued that the existence of these technical and engineering services offered with authorized bearings compared to the gray market bearings constituted material differences for purposes of trademark liability.

At the ITC level, the Commission implicitly agreed with SKF USA that material differences in a gray market case can be based solely on nonphysical differences. However, the Commission refused to rule in SKF USA's favor because the material differences were not present in "all or substantially all of" SKF USA's ball bearing sales. Specifically, the Commission found that over 12 percent of SKF USA's sales were to "nonauthorized" distributors, with which the post-sale services did not accompany the sale. Because SKF USA had elected to distribute through authorized and nonauthorized channels in order to "maximize its bearing sales," it had "undermined its own quality control and failed to provide the same level of service to bearings sold through alternate channels."[138]

On appeal, the Federal Circuit Court agreed that the distinction between domestic and gray market goods does not need to be physical in nature to satisfy the "material difference" test for purposes of trademark infringement.[139] The court first reiterated the established rule that courts have "applied a low threshold of materiality, requiring no more than showing that consumers would be likely to consider the differences between the foreign and domestic products to be significant when purchasing the product, for such differences would suffice to erode the goodwill of the domestic source."[140] Given this standard, the court reasoned that nonphysical differences may be material for purposes of trademark infringement. Specifically, there may be nonphysical characteristics, including services, which customers associate with trademarked goods. When customers purchase unauthorized goods lacking these characteristics, they may mistakenly believe that the goods

---

138. *Id.* at 1311–12.
139. *Id.* at 1312.
140. *Id.* at 1313.

originated from the trademark owner and their misled dissatisfaction can damage the trademark owner's goodwill.[141]

Although the court embraced SKF USA's argument that the differences need not be physical to be material, the court affirmed the Commission's holding on the basis that SKF USA was unable to establish that all or substantially all of its sales were accompanied by its post-sale services. As a matter of law, the court agreed with the Commission that a plaintiff in a gray market case is required to establish that "all or substantially all of its sales" were materially different from gray market goods. There could be no material differences if the trademark owner is putting into the stream of commerce a substantial quantity of goods that lack these post-sale services. To permit recovery in such circumstances would allow the owner to contribute to the customer confusion that it accuses gray market imports of creating.[142] Because almost 13 percent of SKF USA's sales were not accompanied by the post-sale services, the court affirmed the Commission's ruling that SKF USA failed to establish that "all or substantially all of its sales" were materially different from the gray market imports.

(iii) Materially Different Goods When the Quality Controls are Different

Another way of proving material differences is to show that the trademark owner adheres to certain quality control procedures in the distribution of its products. If a brand owner can show that a gray marketer sells its goods without adhering to such standards, it can show that the physically identical goods are, in fact, materially different. An early example of this rule is found in *Adolph Coors Co. v. A. Genderson & Sons, Inc.*[143] To ensure the quality of its beer, the plaintiff Adolph Coors Company (Coors) required that its distributors follow various procedures. Distributors were required to transport and deliver the beer in refrigerated or insulated carriers as well as limit the time in which the beer could be sold.[144] Taking advantage of beer shortages in various parts of the country, the defendant Genderson purchased large quantities of Coors from licensed retailers in Colorado and other states for purposes of reselling the beer in Maryland and other nearby states.

Ruling against Genderson, the court reasoned that Genderson's use of the Coors' trademark constituted a representation that the beer it sold had been subject to the same quality standards typically enforced by Coors. When Genderson sold the beer that had instead been unrefrigerated for long

---

141. *Id.*
142. *Id.* at 1315.
143. Adolph Coors Co. v. A. Genderson & Sons, Inc., 386 F. Supp. 131 (D. Col. 1980).
144. *Id.* at 133.

periods of time and was thus of an inferior quality, the goodwill of Coors suffered. Even though Genderson had not taken any affirmative steps to adulterate the beer, the court concluded that his conduct "pose[d] a threat to the quality assurance function of trademarks."[145] To prevent any continued threats and injury to Coors' goodwill, the district court enjoined any continued unauthorized distribution of Coors beer and ordered that all existing beer in Genderson's inventory be destroyed.

El Greco Leather Products Company, Inc. v. Shoe World, Inc.[146] arrived at the same conclusion with a clearer analysis than *Coors*. El Greco was a shoe designer and had contracted with Solemio, a Brazilian shoe factory, to manufacture 25,000 pairs of shoes that bore El Greco's trademark, "CANDIE'S." The shoes were to be made and sent in several shipments. Prior to each shipment, El Greco's agent in Brazil was to inspect the shoes to confirm that they met El Greco's specifications and quality standards.[147] During the parties' contract, El Greco became unsatisfied with Solemio[148] and cancelled its last two orders. Notwithstanding the cancellation, Solemio manufactured the final orders and sold the shoes, through an intermediary, to the defendant Shoe World, Inc. (Shoe World).[149]

El Greco sued Shoe World upon its discovery that it was selling CANDIE'S shoes in its retail stores that had been manufactured and sold by Solemio without El Greco's authorization. El Greco's theory to hold Shoe World liable was that the shoes were not "genuine" CANDIE'S shoes because they were manufactured and sold without El Greco's inspection to confirm the shoes' quality.

Reversing the district court's prior rulings, the Second Circuit Court concluded that Shoe World had indeed violated El Greco's trademarks. The court explained that "[o]ne of the most valuable and important protections afforded by the Lanham Act is the right to control the quality of the goods manufactured and sold under the holder's trademark."[150] Under this right, "the actual quality of the goods is irrelevant; it is the control of the quality that a trademark holder is entitled to maintain."[151] Applying these principles to the present case, the court concluded that El Greco's inspection policy was an integral part of the procedure to determine whether to accept shoes and sell them

---

145. *Id.* at 135.
146. 806 F.2d 392 (2d Cir. 1986), *cert. denied*, 484 U.S. 817 (1987).
147. *Id.* at 393.
148. It was unclear whether the dissatisfaction was because of Solemio's inferior quality or production delays. *See id.* at 393–94.
149. *Id.* at 394.
150. *Id.* at 395, *citing* Menendez v. Faber, 345 F. Supp. 527 (S.D.N.Y. 1972), *Aff'd in relevant part and modified*, 485 F.2d 1355 (2d Cir. 1973), *modification rev'd sub nom.*
151. *Id. citing* Professional Golfers Association of America v. Bankers Life & Casualty Co., 514 F.2d 665, 670–71 (5th Cir. 1975).

under its trademark. Even though El Greco had previously ordered and authorized Solemio to manufacture its shoes under its trademark, the manufactured goods—without the quality control inspection—could not be considered "genuine" El Greco products and were thus infringing goods.[152]

A factually similar albeit distinguishable case from *El Greco* is *Monte Carlo Shirt, Inc. v. Daewoo International, Corp.*[153] The plaintiff Monte Carlo had contracted with Daewoo to purchase twenty-four hundred dozen men's dress shirts in accordance with Monte Carlo's specifications and bearing its label. Monte Carlo wanted the shipment for Christmas sales so, when the shirts arrived in the United States too late, Monte Carlo rejected the shipment. Daewoo's American subsidiary therefore purchased the shirts and sold them to various discount stores without Monte Carlo's permission.[154]

To justify its various legal theories, Monte Carlo argued that the imported shirts were not genuine Monte Carlo shirts because it was unable to determine the quality of the shirts manufactured by Daewoo without inspecting them upon delivery and supervising their distribution. Unlike *El Greco*, the Ninth Circuit Court rejected this argument. The case should not be read to be legally distinguishable from *El Greco*, however, because the court's rejection of this theory was on the basis that it was not supported by the facts of the case.

To illustrate, the efforts to control the quality of the shirts were completed prior to the shipment; Monte Carlo's president had visited Korea and thoroughly investigated Daewoo's production capabilities. Because Monte Carlo was able to ascertain the quality of the shirts before receipt of the goods, the court was unwilling to accept that its inability to inspect the goods after receipt rendered them "not genuine." Monte Carlo's argument was further undermined by its admitted willingness to accept the shirts for their spring delivery.[155]

El Greco's reasoning was endorsed in *Shell Oil Co. v. Commercial Petroleum, Inc.*[156] The plaintiff Shell Oil (Shell) produced motor oils for heavy-duty trucks under the trademarks "Rotella" and "Shell Rotella T." The oils were sold through various distributors that were contractually bound to adhere to stringent quality control standards. Shell mandated that its distributors follow Shell's procedures for the transportation, delivery, and storage of oil. Such measures were necessary to ensure that the oil did not become contaminated during the distribution process.[157] The defendant Commercial Petroleum (Commercial) resold Shell oil and employed its own standards that "guaranteed"

---

152. *Id.* at 396.
153. 707 F.2d 1054 (9th Cir. 1983).
154. *Id.* at 1055.
155. *Id.* at 1058, n. 5.
156. 928 F.2d 104 (4th Cir. 1991).
157. *Id.* at 106.

the quality of the oil. Shell sued Commercial on the theory that Commercial was infringing its marks by selling oil that was not "genuine."

Echoing the holding of *El Greco*, the court explained that "a product is not truly 'genuine' unless it is manufactured and distributed under quality controls established by the manufacturer."[158] The fact that Commercial employed its own quality control standards was irrelevant because "in order to maintain the genuineness of the bulk oil, the quality standards must be controlled by Shell."[159]

Commercial next argued that, even if the oil was not "genuine," it should still avoid liability because there was no "likelihood of confusion" because its customers knew it was not an authorized distributor of Shell. The court was not persuaded. As an initial matter, proof of *actual* confusion was unnecessary. Moreover, the court remarked that "the use of the Shell marks implies that the product has been delivered according to all quality control guidelines enforced by the manufacturer."[160] Because Commercial did not adhere to these standards, "the use of Shell's marks was deceptive and likely to confuse consumers who rely on the trademarks as symbols of Shell quality."[161]

In *Matrix Essentials, Inc. v. Emporium Drug Mart, Inc.*,[162] the Fifth Circuit Court examined the quality control issue in connection with the sale of hair products. Like many manufacturers of hair products,[163] the plaintiff Matrix manufactured and sold specialty hair-care products only in hair-cutting salons. The products bore the plaintiff's trademark and a label stating that the products were intended to only be sold in hair salons. Matrix's distributors, who sold the products to the hair salon retailers, were contractually restricted to only sell Matrix products to licensed cosmetologists. Matrix further intended that its products be sold in these hair salons along with a consultation so that the consumer would be directed to the most appropriate product for his or her hair and scalp condition.[164]

The defendant Drug Emporium owned and operated two large drug stores and sold various Matrix products. Matrix sued Drug Emporium for trademark infringement on the theory that Drug Emporium was selling its products without the requisite consultation to assist the consumer in selecting the most appropriate product. Without this essential step in the transaction,

---

158. *Id.* at 107 *citing* El Greco, 806 F.2d at 395.
159. *Id.*
160. *Id.* at 108.
161. *Id.*
162. Matrix Essentials, Inc. v. Emporium Drug Mart, Inc., 988 F.2d 587 (5th Cir. 1993).
163. A further discussion applying trademark law in the context of gray market hair salon products is found in __.
164. Matrix, 988 F.2d at 589.

Matrix argued that consumers were not purchasing the "full, complete, and *genuine* Matrix product."[165]

The court was unwilling to consider Matrix's argument as analogous to the successful quality control arguments of *Shell Oil, El Greco,* or *Coors, supra.* What was missing in the *Matrix* case compared to those cases, the court explained, was the element of consumer confusion. Matrix's argument was that products sold by Drug Emporium without a salon consultation could result in consumers purchasing an ill-suited product that could damage their hair and, correspondingly, Matrix's goodwill. The court was unwilling to endorse this as a viable theory because there was no evidence that a consumer was confused or deceived as to whether such a consultation was provided.

In the above cited cases, each case involved some defect (or potential defect) in the *product itself* that the customer could not readily detect: "The oil, shoes, and beer from *Shell, El Greco,* and *Coors* all contained or could potentially contained a latent product defect due to the unauthorized distributor's failure to observe the manufacturer and mark owner's rigorous quality control standards."[166]

Without any defect or potential defect, the court concluded that the case was more analogous to *Hayden Co. of N.Y., Inc. v. Siemens Medical Systems, Inc.*[167] In *Siemens,* the defendant sold dental equipment that was ordinarily sold by authorized distributors who would deliver and install the equipment. When the defendant imported and sold gray market equipment without any installation services, the plaintiff argued that the products were not "genuine" for purposes of trademark infringement. The Second Circuit Court rejected the argument on the grounds that the customers were not deceived. The customers understood at the time of purchase that the product did not include installation.[168] Applying the same rationale, the *Matrix* court concluded that no infringement could exist when there was no evidence that consumers were confused as to whether they received any consultation.[169]

Although the foregoing cases acknowledged the right of trademark holders to use the existence of quality control measures to establish a material difference from "genuine" goods, *Warner-Lambert Co. v. Northside Development Corp.*[170] established a more clearly defined rule to test the

---

165. *Id.* at 590 (emphasis added).
166. *Id.* at 591.
167. Hayden Co. of N.Y., Inc. v. Siemens Medical Systems, Inc., 879 F.2d 1005 (2d Cir. 1989).
168. *Id.* at 1022–24.
169. Matrix, 988 F.2d at 592. The court also added that Matrix's argument was further undermined by the fact that Matrix did not require, monitor, or attempt to ensure that consumers in salons were assisted by cosmetologists. "We cannot ignore the fact that if a pre-sale consultation is a necessary part, in Matrix's opinion, of a "genuine" Matrix product, then many of the sales that occur in salons are not sales of 'genuine' Matrix products either."
170. Warner-Lambert Co. v. Northside Development Corp., 86 F.3d 3 (2d Cir. 1996).

viability of this theory. The plaintiff Warner-Lambert Company (Warner-Lambert) was the maker and trademark owner of HALLS cough drops. According to Warner-Lambert, the cough drops could remain in acceptable condition for up to thirty months. To ensure that consumers purchased adequate cough drops, Warner-Lambert established a shelf life for the product of 24 months. To ensure adherence to this shelf-life policy, Warner-Lambert enforced various quality control procedures.[171] Warner-Lambert initiated litigation when it learned that the defendants Quality King Distributors and Northside Associates (collectively, "Quality King") had sold large qualities of the cough drop more than 24 months old.

Warner-Lambert argued that the cough drops sold by Quality King were infringing goods because the cough drops were not subject to Warner-Lambert's quality control standards. Although Quality King conceded that its cough drops were more than 24 months old, it argued that Warner-Lambert did not have the right to preclude such sales because Warner-Lambert's quality standards were not foolproof. Since Warner-Lambert's own standards allowed at least some stale cough drops to be sold to consumers, Quality King should not be prevented from distributing *its* stale cough drops to customers as well.

The court rejected Quality King's argument. The court agreed that Warner-Lambert could have employed more stringent measures to ensure freshness. However, the law does not require the trademark holder to employ the *most stringent* quality control measures to be entitled to relief. After all, the court reasoned, a trademark holder must be afforded the ability to exercise its business judgment to select the most appropriate measures. Accordingly, the court held that the trademark holder must only demonstrate the following: (1) That it has established legitimate, substantial, and nonpretextual quality control procedures, (2) that it abides by these procedures, and (3) that the nonconforming sales will diminish the value of the mark.[172] Applying this test, the court ordered the district court to enjoin Quality King from selling any cough drops that were more than 24 months old.[173]

---

171. *Id.* at 5 (The quality control measures were the following: (i) shipping HALLS within 18 months from the date of manufacture; (ii) marking the shipping cases ("shippers") and display trays contained in the shippers with the shelf life of the product; (iii) informing its wholesale and retail customers about the product shelf life; (iv) sending sales representatives to stores that sell HALLS cough drops to monitor the product's freshness and issuing credits for new HALLS to replace outdated supply; (v) segregating lots manufactured at different times; and (vi) supervising the destruction of outdated product. In addition, a Warner-Lambert representative testified that the company initiates legal action against, or discontinues selling to, customers that refuse to comply with its freshness policy.").
172. *Id.* at 7.
173. *Id.* at 8.

Of course, the ability of a manufacturer to control the quality of its products through distribution channels is not limited. In *Summit Technology, Inc. v. High-Line Medical Instruments*,[174] *supra*, the plaintiff Summit Technology manufactured and sold laser systems to ophthalmologists for use abroad and in the United States. It sued the defendant High-Line Medical for a number of causes of action related to its importation, promotion, and sale of used or serviced laser systems in the United States. High-Line had legally acquired laser systems that had been sold in foreign countries and then reimported them into the United States for distribution in the United States. Among several legal theories, Summit Technology alleged that High-Line had violated various provisions of the Lanham Act because the reimported products were not subject to the same quality control standards as the domestic systems.[175]

Because Summit manufactured and already sold the laser systems at issue to end users, the court distinguished the case from *Shell Oil Co. v. Commercial Petroleum*,[176] *supra*, on the ground that *Shell* involved a plaintiff suing distributors or licensees who purported to sell "new" goods but failed to maintain them in accordance with the trademark holder's quality standards. The holding of *Summit* is probably correct albeit with imprecise reasoning. For example, *Shell Oil* made no mention that the defendant distributor represented the oil as "new" oil. To the contrary, the defendant purchased bulk Shell oil from Shell's authorized distributors and then resold it. In its sales to customers, the defendant included a disclaimer indicating that it had no affiliation with Shell.

Rather than relying on the "new" versus "used" distinction, the *Summit* court could have more properly distinguished its holding by noting the limitations in which a trademark holder can retain control of the use of its trademark in the sale of its product. Specifically, and as articulated in *Shell Oil*, the right to control these quality standards is retained to the *end user*.

Axiomatically, trademark owners cannot mandate that end user customers meet their quality control standards prior to any re-sales. In *Summit*, the defendants were various end users and a corporation that was "engaged in the business of buying and selling used medical equipment."[177] In other words, the defendants purchased the goods from prior end users. The limitation of controlling quality standards beyond the end user—instead of the "new" versus "used" distinction—provides a more practical way for courts to distinguish whether a trademark holder may avail itself to the right of controlling the quality of its products' distribution.

---

174. Summit Technology, Inc. v. High-Line Medical Instruments 922 F. Supp. 299 (C.D. Cal. 1996).
175. Summit, 922 F. Supp. at 308.
176. Shell Oil Co. v. Commercial Petroleum, 928 F.2d 104 (4th Cir. 1991).
177. Summit, 922 F. Supp. at 302.

(iv) Materially Different Goods When the Ingredients are Different

An example in which different ingredients have successfully constituted a material difference can be found in *R.J. Reynolds Tobacco Co. v. Cigarettes Cheaper!*[178] The plaintiff R.J. Reynolds sold cigarettes domestically and internationally. The defendant Cigarettes Cheaper! operated a chain of retail outlets and sold, among others, R.J. Reynolds cigarettes that it reimported[179] for domestic sale. Reynolds initiated litigation by alleging that Cigarettes Cheaper! violated the Lanham Act by its sale of gray market Reynolds cigarettes.[180]

With respect to Reynolds' Lanham Act claim, Cigarettes Cheaper! argued to the district court that, as a matter of law, the use in the United States of trademarks affixed by their proprietor is always permissible. The district court rejected Cigarettes Cheaper!'s legal argument and ruled that reimported products could be unlawful if the products designed for domestic and foreign markets were materially different. To prove material differences, Reynolds argued that additives and taste in its Winston cigarettes were different.[181] Reynolds sold its Winston cigarettes in the United States with the representation that they were simply tobacco and water. Because Winstons intended for foreign distribution contained additional additives, the cigarettes were materially different.[182] The district court, its jury, and the Seventh Circuit Court all endorsed this theory and concluded the goods were indeed materially different.[183]

Ferrero U.S.A. Inc. v. Ozark Trading, Inc.[184] is another example of ingredients constituting a material difference for purposes of trademark

---

178. R.J. Reynolds Tobacco Co. v. Cigarettes Cheaper!, 462 F.3d 690 (7th Cir. 2006).
179. Although the court used the term "reimportation," it acknowledged that some of the cigarettes in question were manufactured outside the United States by firms licensed to use the trademarks in their own countries.
180. In addition to defending Reynolds' allegations, Cigarettes Cheaper! responded to the lawsuit by bringing its own claims for antitrust violations. *Id.* at 693.
181. Reynolds initially argued that the additives and taste were different with respect to all of its cigarettes. When pressed to disclose what specific ingredients are in its foreign and domestic cigarettes, Reynolds withdrew this contention with respect to all brands except Winston. See *id.* at 700.
182. In addition to the material differences with respect to taste, Reynolds also argued that its domestic cigarettes were materially different with respect to its loyalty programs. For example, domestic packages of Camels cigarettes included coupons called "C-Notes" that could be collected and redeemed for merchandise. Finally, Reynolds argued that domestic cigarettes were inspected and removed from sale at the end of their shelf life. Reimported gray market cigarettes, on the other hand, were not. See *id.*
183. *Id.* at 701.
184. Ferrero U.S.A. Inc. v. Ozark Trading, Inc., 952 F.2d 44 (3d Cir. 1991) (At issue in the opinion was the award of attorney fees. However, the opinion recites and endorses its previous "memorandum opinion" affirming the plaintiff's trademark infringement claim.).

infringement. The plaintiff Ferrero U.S.A. (Ferrero) was the exclusive U.S. distributor of Tic Tac mints. Ferrero successfully argued that the defendant Ozark's importation of Tic Tac mints constituted a trademark infringement because they differed in size and calorie content from those it imported, sold, and advertised.[185]

Specifically, Ozark imported and sold Tic Tacs that were manufactured for distribution throughout the United Kingdom. The Tic Tacs intended for domestic distribution had 1.5 calories per mint, contained sugar, and were sold in packages labeled with nutritional information that conformed to FDA requirements. The Tic Tacs intended for the United Kingdom, meanwhile, had 2 calories per mint, a fructose sweetener, and were packaged with labeling under European standards. Although both versions were authentic Tic Tacs, there were sufficient differences to create a likelihood of confusion among consumers.[186]

(v) Materially Different Goods When the Warranty Protections are Different

In *Dan-Foam v. Brand Name Beds, LLC*,[187] *supra*, the District Court of New York examined a gray marketer's motion for summary judgment, which argued that its sales of various foam-based bed products could not, as a matter of law, infringe the brand owner's trademarks. The plaintiff Tempur-Pedic manufactured and distributed mattresses, pillows, and other foam-based bed products. Although it sold its products through authorized resellers, the defendant Brand Name Beds sold Tempur-Pedic products on the Internet.

Tempur-Pedic objected to BNB's sales and alleged that such sales infringed and diluted its registered TEMPUR-PEDIC trademark. Because BNB was a gray marketer that had obtained its products from authorized resellers,[188] Tempur-Pedic was unable to rely on any physical differences to support its trademark infringement claims. Instead, Tempur-Pedic asserted several non-physical differences between its authorized products and the unauthorized gray market products.

---

185. *Id.* at 45–46.
186. *Id.* at 46.
187. 500 F. Supp. 2d 296 (S.D.N.Y. 2007).
188. Only some of Tempur-Pedic's authorized resellers had signed agreements with Tempur-Pedic. Beginning in 2006, Tempur-Pedic implemented a program requiring all authorized resellers to execute new written agreements prohibiting sales to anyone other than end users of the products. BNB asserted that it purchased its products from authorized resellers that had not yet signed any agreements with Tempur-Pedic. Thus, BNB argued, the resellers who sold BNB branded goods were not in breach of any contract with Tempur-Pedic. *Id.* at 301–303.

For example, Tempur-Pedic provided a twenty-year warranty that was only valid so long as the product was sold directly by Tempur-Pedic or an authorized reseller.[189] The warranty was also voided if the products were "physically abused, damaged, burned, cut or torn."[190] Tempur-Pedic's authorized resellers were thus trained in the proper delivery and handling of the TEMPUR-PEDIC products. Specifically, the products were sensitive to the heat and cold and, if not handled properly, their performance could be compromised. BNB, on the other hand, did not adhere to the same quality standards imposed on Tempur-Pedic's authorized resellers. BNB shipped its products in shipping crates or cardboard boxes that were smaller than the boxes used by Tempur-Pedic. In addition, BNB essentially dropped the products off at customers' front doors whereas Tempur-Pedic's authorized resellers were trained to properly unpack and unfold the products in a method designed to prevent damage.

For purposes of summary judgment, the court concluded that Tempur-Pedic had produced sufficient evidence to deny BNB's motion. The court concluded that there were questions that needed to be resolved by a jury regarding the validity of Tempur-Pedic's warranty. Specifically, the court explained that a reasonable juror could conclude that the invalidity of Tempur-Pedic's warranty for BNB-sold products could constitute a material difference that presented a likelihood of consumer confusion for purposes of trademark infringement.[191]

Rather than argue that a Tempur-Pedic product without a Tempur-Pedic warranty was not materially different, BNB argued that Tempur-Pedic's warranty still applied to any products sold by BNB. The court rejected this argument for two reasons. *First*, the court concluded that BNB's repackaging and shipping procedures may void Tempur-Pedic's warranty. Because the warranty was void if the product was abused, the court reasoned that BNB's relatively crude shipping and delivery methods may impair the integrity of the product and constitute "abuse" for purposes of voiding the warranty. *Second*, the plain language of the warranty indicated that it was void unless the products were sold by Tempur-Pedic or an authorized reseller. BNB argued for an alternative interpretation. However, since the court was evaluating BNB's motion for summary judgment, all inferences were construed in a light most favorable to Tempur-Pedic. Thus, the court denied BNB's motion.

A similar holding is found in *Swatch S.A. v. New City, Inc.*[192] The plaintiff Swatch was the manufacturer and seller of watches, watch parts, jewelry, and other electronics under a number of registered trademarks. The plaintiff TSG

---

189. *Id.* at 300–301.
190. *Id.* at 300.
191. *Id.* at 320.
192. Swatch S.A. v. New City, Inc., 454 F. Supp. 2d 1245 (S.D. Fla. 2006).

was the exclusive Swatch distributor in the United States. The defendant New City, Inc. (New City) was a watch distributor that sold Swatch branded goods without Swatches consent. After Swatch and TSG (collectively, "Swatch") sued New City for trademark infringement, it sought summary judgment to affirmatively adjudicate its rights.[193]

There was no contention that the Swatch products sold by New City were counterfeit. To the contrary, Swatch conceded that the products at issue were genuine Swatch products. To argue that the products sold by New City were materially different from authorized Swatch products, Swatch argued that New City was selling Swatch products with void warranties.[194] Swatch's warranty advised its customers of the following:

> Your swatch is warranted by Swatch Ltd. for a period of twenty-four months from the date of purchase under the terms and conditions of the warranty ... **The warranty only comes into force if the warranty certificate is dated, fully and correctly completed and stamped by an official Swatch dealer.**[195]

Because New City was not an "official Swatch dealer," it could not provide the warranty's requisite stamp. Thus, the theory went, any Swatch products sold by New City lacked warranty protection and this missing element rendered the products materially different from authorized Swatch products. In response, New City argued that Swatch had essentially waived the ability to deny warranty coverage to consumers of unauthorized Swatches because Swatch had honored its warranties on similarly unendorsed warranties in the past.[196]

The court rejected New City's "waiver" argument. The fact that Swatch had exercised its business discretion to honor otherwise void warranties could not shield New City from liability for trademark infringement. Such voluntary warranty coverage would not constitute a waiver to demand validly endorsed warranties in the future.[197] Given this rejection of New City's waiver argument, the district court held that the Swatches it sold were different from

---

193. *Id.* at 1248.
194. Swatch also argued that New City (or some other third party in the unauthorized chain of distribution) made physical alterations to the packaging thereby rendering the products no longer "genuine" for purposes of trademark infringement. The physical alterations included the stripping of product reference numbers, SKU, bar codes, and batch codes.
195. *Swatch*, 454 F. Supp. 2d at 1250–51 (emphasis added).
196. *Id.* at 1251.
197. *Id.*; *see also* Osawa & Co. v. B&H Photo, 589 F. Supp. 1163 (S.D.N.Y. 1984) (finding that a camera manufacturer that provided warranty coverage to consumers of camera's that lacked valid warranties did so not out of stupidity or neglect, but because its management perceived that dissatisfied purchasers of the company's cameras would damage the reputation of the company's trademark).

authorized Swatches. However, the court denied Swatch's motion for summary judgment so that the jury could decide whether this intangible difference between authorized and unauthorized Swatches was material to a consumer's decision to purchase the watch.[198]

(vi) Materially Different Goods When there are Differences in the Aggregate

In certain cases, the totality of the circumstances reveals that the goods at issue are materially different. An example of this is found in Société *Des Produits Nestlé, S.A. v. Casa Helvetia, Inc.*[199] The case involved PERUGINA chocolates that were made in Italy and sold throughout the world. *Société Des Produits Nestlé, S.A.* (Nestlé) owned the PERUGINA trademark. For years, Nestlé authorized defendant Casa Helvetia to be its authorized distributor of PERUGINA chocolates in Puerto Rico. In 1988, however, Nestlé canceled Casa Helvetia's distributorship and awarded an affiliate to be its authorized Puerto Rico distributor.[200]

Meanwhile, Nestlé had authorized an independent company to manufacture and sell chocolates bearing the PERUGINA mark throughout Venezuela. Beginning in 1990, Casa Helvetia began purchasing these Venezuelan-made PERUGINA chocolates through middlemen in order to import and sell them in Puerto Rico. Asserting that Casa Helvetia's sales of these chocolates infringed its trademark, Nestlé commenced litigation in the district court of Puerto Rico wherein the court denied Nestlé's request for a preliminary injunction and dismissed the case.[201]

On appeal, the First Circuit Court explained that trademark rights have a territorial component.[202] Specifically, a trademark's reputation and goodwill often differ from nation to nation.[203] As a result, the importation of goods properly trademarked abroad but not intended for sale locally may confuse consumers and threaten the local mark owner's goodwill.[204] Of course, the court explained, this danger of customer confusion does not exist if the products are identical: The analysis "boils down to whether material differences exist between the Italian-made product and the Venezuelan-made

---

198. *Id.*
199. Société Des Produits Nestlé, S.A. v. Casa Helvetia, Inc., 982 F.2d 633 (1st Cir. 1992).
200. *Id.* at 635.
201. *Id.* at 635–36.
202. *Id.* at 636.
203. *Id. citing* Osawa & Co. v. B&H Photo, 589 F. Supp. 1163, 1173 (S.D.N.Y. 1984).
204. *Id.*

product sufficient to create a likelihood of consumer confusion, mistake, or deception."[205]

The court went on to explain how the burden of showing material differences is very low. Especially when dealing with the importation of gray goods, subtle differences are important considerations. "[T]he threshold of materiality must be kept low enough to take account of potentially confusing differences—differences that are not blatant enough to make it obvious to the average consumer that the origin of the product differs from his or her expectations."[206] Any higher requirement, the court warned, would endanger a manufacturer's goodwill and unduly subject consumers to potential confusion.

Applying these standards to the chocolates at issue, the court concluded that there were enough differences to warrant a conclusion that the dissimilarities were "material in the aggregate."[207] Among the differences identified by the court were differences in quality control, composition, configuration, packaging, and price. These dissimilarities, the court concluded, were each relevant in the court's analysis.

(c) The Lanham Act Applied: The "Salon" Cases

Because the resale of genuine trademarked goods generally does not constitute trademark infringement,[208] trademark owners have petitioned the courts with several theories to advocate that gray market products are materially different and therefore infringing products. One industry that has aggressively combated the gray market is the hair products market. To maintain their prestige, several manufacturers limit the sale of their products to authorized hair salons. When these manufacturers discover their products being sold in grocery stores, drug stores, or other discount retail outlets, they have often turned to the courts for relief. In these cases, the factual scenarios are all very similar; however, the results are not. Although a casual examination of

---

205. *Id.* at 638.
206. *Id. See also* Lever Bros., 877 F.2d at 103, 108 (finding minor differences in ingredients and packaging between versions of deodorant soap to be material); Ferrero U.S.A. Inc. v. Ozark Trading, Inc., 753 F. Supp. at 1241–49, 1247 (finding a one-half calorie difference in chemical composition of breath mints, coupled with slight differences in packaging and labeling, to be material); PepsiCo Inc. v. Nostalgia, 18 U.S.P.Q.2d at 1405 (finding "differences in labeling, packaging and marketing methods" to be material); PepsiCo v. Giraud, 7 U.S.P.Q.2d at 1373 (finding differences not readily apparent to the consumer-container volume, packaging, quality control, and advertising participation to be material); Dial Corp. v. Encina Corp., 643 F. Supp. 951, 952 (S.D. Fla. 1986) (finding differences in formulation and packaging of soap products to be material).
207. *Id.* at 644.
208. *See e.g.*, Matrix Essentials, Inc. v. Emporium Drug Mart, Inc., 988 F.2d 587, 590 (5th Cir. 1993); NEC Electronics v. CAL Circuit Abco, 810 F.2d 1506, 1509 (9th Cir. 1987).

278   Chapter 17   *Theories of Liability: Trademark*

these cases suggests a murky and inconsistent body of case law, a closer examination illuminates what facts are consistently held to be important *vel non*.

One strategy has been to identify any physical alterations to the products sold by gray marketers. For example, serial numbers or batch codes are often affixed to products. These numbers can be useful to track manufacturing, sales, and if necessary, product recalls. To prevent trademark owners from being able to identify the distributor or reseller that engaged in gray market transactions, these serial numbers or batch codes are often covered up or erased.

In *Graham Webb International Limited Partnership v. Emporium Drug Mart, Inc.*,[209] the district court was unwilling to conclude that bottles with batch codes removed were materially different precuts for purposes of trademark infringement. The plaintiff Graham Webb International (Graham Webb) sued Emporium Drug Mart, Inc. (Drug Emporium) when it learned that it was selling its hair, bath, cosmetic, and related products with obliterated batch codes. As owner of the "Graham Webb" trademark, Graham Webb sold its products through authorized distributors. The authorized distributors were restricted to reselling the Graham Webb products only to certain salons. To ensure that customers received proper instructions with respect to the use of the products, as well as to create a certain "mystique" about the products' prestige, Graham Webb did not permit its products to be sold anywhere else.[210]

Prior to litigation, Graham Webb sent Drug Emporium correspondence demanding that all Graham Webb products be removed from Drug Emporium's shelves. Instead of complying to Graham Webb's demands, Drug Emporium did two things: *First*, it informed its customers that it was not affiliated in any way with the manufacturer of the products. *Second*, it posted a disclaimer that stated the following:

> Graham Webb International cannot guarantee the authenticity of any product sold by an unauthorized retailer such as Drug Emporium. Graham Webb International states that its products are guaranteed only when sold through professional salons. If the UPC codes or other tracing codes are missing from any product container of a Graham Webb International product purchased by you, please retain your purchase receipt to assist in the tracing of that product in the unlikely event it is defective.[211]

---

209. Graham Webb International Limited Partnership v. Emporium Drug Mart, Inc., 916 F. Supp. 909 (E.D. Ark. 1995).
210. *Id.* at 912.
211. *Id.* at 913.

Because Drug Emporium's sales continued, Graham Webb commenced litigation alleging, among other theories, that Drug Emporium sales of products with obliterated batch codes constituted trademark infringement. In its motion for summary judgment, Drug Emporium argued that no trademark infringement could exist given that the products at issue were genuine Graham Webb hair products.

The district court agreed. The court first focused its attention on the fact that the products were not inferior, defective, nor counterfeit.[212] Because the "quality" of the products sold by Drug Emporium were "essentially identical" to those sold at salons, the court was unwilling to concede that a likelihood of confusion could exist: "The mere removal of batch codes from product containers, as occurred in this case, does not give rise to the element of likelihood of consumer confusion necessary for a Lanham Act claim."[213]

The court also rejected the argument that consumer confusion could exist when the Graham Webb products were sold without the salons' professional consultation. As a matter of law, the court expressed its own skepticism that such consultation was even needed. Moreover, the court relied on evidence that many salons were selling the Graham Webb products without any analysis or advice. Finally, the court rejected the argument that Drug Emporium's disclaimer was ineffective. The court concluded that such a disclaimer communicating no affiliation with Graham Webb was an effective means to prevent consumer confusion.

A similar result is found in *John Paul Mitchell Systems v. Randalls Food Markets, Inc. (Paul Mitchell II)*.[214] John Paul Mitchell Systems (Paul Mitchell) sued an unauthorized distributor (Jade) and an unauthorized retailer (Randalls) in connection with the sale of its hair products outside of Paul Mitchell's intended distribution chain. Similar to the plaintiff in *Graham Webb*, Paul Mitchell only authorized the sale of its hair products to take place in authorized salons. Sales in grocery stores or other retail outlets were prohibited. These restrictions were justified on the theories that such restricted sales allowed Paul Mitchell to monitor the quality of its products, provide professional advice as to the products' proper use, and enhance the reputation and desirability of its products.[215]

Batch codes were affixed to all products so that John Paul Mitchell could monitor products as well as trace leaks in its supply chains. When Paul Mitchell discovered that Randalls was selling Paul Mitchell products with defaced batch codes that had come from Jade, it sued both companies. Although the jury awarded Paul Mitchell more than $15 million including

---

212. *Id.* at 916.
213. *Id.*
214. 17 S.W.3d 721 (Court of Appeals Texas 2000).
215. *Id.* at 726–27.

injunctive relief, the trial court issued a post-trial order disregarding the jury verdict and awarding Paul Mitchell nothing. Surprising no one, Paul Mitchell appealed.[216]

On appeal, the Texas Court of Appeals affirmed the trial court's ruling, including its reversal of the trademark infringement cause of action. The court began its analysis by reiterating the general rule that the unauthorized sale of *genuine* goods does not give rise to a trademark infringement claim.[217] Thus, for Paul Mitchell to prevail it had the burden of proving that material differences existed between the products found at defendants' retail locations versus Paul Mitchell's authorized salons.

Paul Mitchell relied on the fact that the products contained defaced batch codes. The court rejected this argument on the ground that "there was no evidence that removal of batch codes defaced the bottles or compromised the quality of the products."[218] The court seemed to conclude that unless there was evidence that the products were tainted or mishandled, there could be no material difference.[219] The court further reasoned that "[t]here [was] no evidence in the record that customers who purchased these hair products from Randalls were confused or deceived by thinking that they would receive professional consultation with their purchase."[220] Without evidence of customer confusion or tainted products, the court concluded that Paul Mitchell could not prevail: "The lack of material difference or defect leading to confusion of customers is fatal to Paul Mitchell's claim of unfair competition, as well as its trademark protection claims."[221]

The ruling is somewhat curious because, six years earlier, John Paul successfully persuaded the Western District Court of New York to deny a defendant's motion for summary judgment that made similar arguments. Before ruling on the batch code obliteration issue, the court in *John Paul Mitchell Systems v. Pete-N-Larry's Inc. (Paul Mitchell I)*[222] first examined the seemingly different approaches that courts have taken to determine whether a product is "genuine" or "materially different" for purposes of trademark infringement. Given the semantic differences among the courts, the *Paul Mitchell II* court created more questions than answers. For example, the *Graham Webb* court based its ruling in part on the fact that there was no defect or potential defect in the "product itself." *Paul Mitchell II* articulated the difficulty in determining the parameters of what is "the product itself— for instance, whether such should include the bottle that contains a treating

---

216. *Id.* at 727–28.
217. *Id.* at 735.
218. *Id.* at 736.
219. *See id.*
220. *Id.*
221. *Id.*
222. John Paul Mitchell Systems v. Pete-N-Larry's Inc., 862 F. Supp. 1020 (W.D.N.Y. 1994).

material, the information printed on such bottle, the box that in turn contains the bottle, the instructions placed in and printed on the box, or the carton that contains several boxes."[223]

Given that the *Paul Mitchell I* court was merely ruling on a defendants' motion for summary judgment, however, it did not feel obligated to synthesize or even choose the soundest approach to these cases. Instead, the court considered several factual assertions submitted by Paul Mitchell and concluded that they, in the aggregate, were sufficient to form a basis for a viable Lanham Act claim. Specifically, the court relied on Paul Mitchell's contention that the defendants' effort to obliterate batch codes were done so crudely that trademarks, instructions, ingredient lists, and other writings were similarly compromised. On at least one occasion, the obliteration was so indelicate that the bottle itself was punctured.[224] Along with other factors such as the right to control the quality and ensure professional consultation, the court was unwilling to dismiss Paul Mitchell's trademark claim.

(d) Factors Beyond the "Material Difference" Factor?

As the preceding pages have made clear, courts have repeatedly turned their analysis of gray market cases on whether material differences between genuine and gray goods exist that are sufficient to cause confusion among consumers. In *Dan-Foam v. Brand Named Beds, LLC*,[225] *supra*, the Southern District of New York opined that this analysis was insufficient. In *Dan-Foam*, the court acknowledged that courts have generally used the material differences standard "as a proxy for the likelihood of confusion test traditionally used in trademark infringement cases, permitting gray market goods to be sold unless the goods are 'materially different' from those sold through authorized distribution channels."[226] The court also noted, however, that courts in the Second Circuit Court were required to consider the factors known as the *Polaroid* factors as articulated in *Polaroid Corp. v. Polarad Electronics Corp.*[227]

Polaroid was not a gray market case. The case involved a defendant marketing and selling Polaroid television equipment, which Polaroid argued, infringed Polaroid's trademark. The case is particularly noteworthy because it established a *non-exhaustive* list of eight factors that are now commonly used to analyze trademark infringement: (1) the strength of the mark; (2) the degree of similarity between the two marks; (3) the proximity of the products,

---

223. *Id.* at 1025–26.
224. *Id.* at 1026.
225. Dan-Foam v. Brand Named Beds, LLC, 500 F. Supp. 2d 296 (S.D.N.Y. 2007).
226. *Id.* at 311.
227. Polaroid Corp. v. Polarad Electronics Corp., 287 F.2d 492 (2d Cir. 1961).

(4) the likelihood that the prior owner will bridge the gap; (5) actual confusion; (6) the defendant's good faith in adopting its own mark; (7) the quality of defendant's product; and (8) the sophistication of the buyers.[228]

As *Dan-Foam* acknowledged, the first two *Polaroid* factors are never at issue in a gray market case because the marks are the same.[229] The third factor, the proximity of the products, is relevant to the issue of customer confusion resulting from material differences in gray market cases. The fourth factor, the likelihood that the plaintiff will "bridge the gap" is not relevant in a gray market case because the plaintiff and defendant are selling the same products to the same market.[230] According to the *Dan-Foam* court, factors five through eight are "highly relevant" in the consumer confusion analysis. The seventh factor—the quality of defendant's product—should be given particular attention because the crux of the consumer confusion often turns on whether consumers are likely to be confused by differences between products that they assume are identical.[231]

The holding of *Dan-Foam* would have been the same under the simpler material differences test versus the *Polaroid* factors test. Although its holding is relatively recent, it is not binding authority given that it came from a federal district courthouse. Thus, it remains to be seen whether other courts are persuaded to similarly put their gray market cases through the more rigorous *Polaroid* factors test.

c. Affirmative Defenses

i. The First Sale Doctrine

The affirmative defense most commonly raised in gray market cases is the "first sale" doctrine defense. It should be noted at the outset, however, that there often lies a distinction of mere semantics when determining whether the defense is applicable or whether the gray market goods are simply non-infringing goods. Put another way, when gray market goods are not materially different from a trademark owner's authorized goods, no infringement has occurred. Notwithstanding this reality, some courts have felt compelled to find no infringement pursuant to the affirmative defense of the "first sale" doctrine. This has resulted in some confusion and inconsistency in the defense's applicability.

---

228. *Id.* at 495.
229. Dan-Foam v. Brand Name Beds, LLC, 500 F. Supp. 2d 312.
230. *Id.*
231. *Id.*

Sebastian Intern., Inc. v. Longs Drug Stores Corp.[232] is a good example. The plaintiff Sebastian manufactured various hair products with its trademark, a large stylized "S," to the front of each container. Like so many of the salon cases articulated above, Sebastian wanted its products to only be sold in professional salons that were members of an organization created and controlled by Sebastian called the "Sebastian Collective Membership Program." Members of the Collective agreed to only sell Sebastian's products to other members of the Collective or to salon clientele (i.e., end users).[233]

Sebastian brought the lawsuit when it discovered that Longs Drugs was buying and reselling Sebastian products in its stores. Sebastian alleged that Longs Drugs had violated its trademark rights when it sold products bearing the mark "Sebastian Collective Salon Member" when it was not a member of the Collective.

The district court preliminarily enjoined Longs Drugs from continuing to sell Sebastian products and the Ninth Circuit Court reversed. The Ninth Circuit Court based its decision on the first sale doctrine defense. Citing *Prestonettes v. Coty*,[234] *supra*, the court explained that courts have "consistently" held that the right of a producer to control distribution of its trademarked products does "not extend beyond the first sale of the product."[235] Resale by the first purchaser of the original article, according to the *Sebastian* court, is neither trademark infringement nor unfair competition.

Turning to the specific facts of the case, the court noted that Longs Drugs had not done anything more than merely stock and resell genuine Sebastian products.[236] It is an overstatement to suggest that the first sale doctrine would shield the resale of Sebastian products by Longs Drugs under any circumstances. As the preceding pages have revealed, the removal of batch codes or other defacement to the products may have created a material difference sufficient for a finding of infringement. Sebastian may have also established quality controls over its products to the end user to justify an injunction. These circumstances may have rendered the Sebastian products "not genuine" for purposes of trademark infringement. Moreover, the first sale doctrine would not have given Long Drugs any immunity to sell these infringing goods.

However, because Longs Drug did nothing more than stock and resell genuine Sebastian products, it was not selling any infringing goods—it was selling *genuine goods*. The Ninth Circuit Court did not have to expressly rely on the first sale doctrine to reverse the district court's preliminary injunction.

---

232. Sebastian Intern., Inc. v. Longs Drug Stores Corp., 53 F.3d 1073 (9th Cir. 1995).
233. *Id.* at 1074.
234. Prestonettes v. Coty, 264 U.S. 359 (1924). .
235. Sebastian, 53 F.3d at 1074.
236. *Id.* at 1076.

It could have instead relied on the well-settled principle that trademark law does not reach the sale of goods bearing a true mark even though such sale is without the trademark owner's consent.[237]

In *Summit Technology, Inc. v. High-Line Medical Instruments*,[238] *supra*, the plaintiff Summit Technology manufactured and sold laser systems to ophthalmologists for use abroad and in the United States. The defendant High-Line had acquired laser systems that had been sold in foreign countries and had then reimported them into the United States for distribution in the United States. Summit averred that the reimported products were not genuine products because they used systems that were not approved by the FDA and because they were not subject to the same quality control standards as the domestic systems.[239] However, the district court dismissed Summit's cause of action concluding that it was barred by the first sale doctrine. Even though the products sold for foreign use were materially different, it did not change the fact that the reimported laser systems were genuine Summit products, manufactured and sold by Summit itself.

The district court endorsed the Ninth Circuit Court's reasoning in *Sebastian Int'l, Inc. v. Longs Drug Stores Corp.*,[240] *supra*, stating that "Summit simply cannot use trademark law to control downstream distribution of products that Summit *itself* manufactured and sold. The mere fact that Summit sold its goods abroad rather than domestically [did] not create an exception to the 'first sale doctrine.'"[241] The district court was equally unmoved by the fact that Summit sold *different* goods in different markets for different prices. Again, relying on the reasoning of *Sebastian*, the court explained that if Summit chose to price or manufacture its goods differently for different countries, it did so at its own peril. Instead of looking for relief from the courts, the district court opined that Summit should look to exclusive licensing or other restrictive agreements instead of trademark law for support.[242] Rather than focusing on the fact that the goods were manufactured and sold by Summit, the court could have relied on the fact that Summit's sales were to end users. Once the end users possessed the products, Summit lost its ability—pursuant to the first sale doctrine—to control further dissemination of the products.

---

237. *See e.g.*, NEC Electronics v. CAL Circuit Abco, 810 F.2d 1506, 1509 (9th Cir. 1987) ("Trademark law generally does not reach the sale of genuine goods bearing a true mark even though such sale is without the mark owner's consent.").
238. Summit, 922 F. Supp. 299 (C.D. Cal. 1996).
239. *Id.* at 308.
240. Sebastian, 53 F.3d 1073 (9th Cir. 1995).
241. Summit, 922 F. Supp. at 309.
242. *Id.* at 309.

ii. Not "Gray Market" Goods?

The district court in *Summit Technology, supra,* incorrectly concluded that any "gray market" cases were inapplicable to its analysis because "'gray-market goods' [only] refer to foreign manufactured goods, for which a valid United States trademark has been registered, that are legally purchased abroad and imported into the United States without the consent of the American trademark holder."[243] Although the products may have had material differences, the court concluded that they were not gray market goods because they were all manufactured by Summit.[244]

The district court was incorrect to conclude that goods manufactured domestically cannot be considered gray market goods. This same argument was rejected by the Federal Circuit Court in 2006. Specifically, in *Bourdeau Bros., Inc. v. International Trade Com'n.*[245] Deere & Co. (Deere) sold a 5000 and 6000 series of forage harvesters in the United States and Europe through a network of authorized dealers and distributors. The 5000 series was manufactured exclusively in the United States, regardless of the market for which it was destined. The 6000 series was manufactured exclusively in Germany. Both series of forage harvesters fell into two general categories: the North American version forage harvesters, which were manufactured for sale in North America, and the European version forage harvester, which were manufactured for sale in Europe. Although the products were sold under the same name, they had certain differences, including different labeling and safety features.

Bourdeau Bros., Inc. (Bourdeau) was involved in the importation and distribution of the European version of the forage harvesters in the United States. Deere filed a complaint with the ITC alleging violations of 19 U.S.C. § 1337 (Section 1337) by claiming Bourdeau's importation and distribution of the European forage harvesters infringed Deere's trademarks. Deere alleged that its forage harvesters, which were manufactured solely for sale in Europe, were materially different from its forage harvesters manufactured and authorized for domestic distribution.

Bourdeau argued that because the 5000 series forage harvesters were manufactured in the United States, they could not be "gray market goods" and therefore could not violate Section 1337. Relying on *K Mart*,[246] *supra,* Bourdeau argued that a gray market good must be a "foreign-manufactured good, bearing a valid United States trademark, that is imported without the

---

243. *Id.* at 309 *citing* Weil Ceramics & Glass, Inc. v. Dash, 878 F.2d 659, 662, n. 1 (3d Cir.), *cert. denied*, 493 U.S. 853 (1989).
244. Summit, 922 F. Supp. at 310.
245. Bourdeau Bros., Inc. v. International Trade Com'n, 444 F.3d 1317 (Fed. Cir. 2006).
246. K Mart v. Cartier, 486 U.S. 281 (1987).

consent of the United States trademark holder."[247] Because the 5000 series are not foreign-manufactured and the scenarios discussed in K Mart only identified foreign-manufactured products, they could not be unlawful gray market goods.

The court rejected Bourdeau's argument that the 5000 series forage harvesters could not be gray market goods. With respect to Bourdeau's reliance on K Mart, the court pointed out that the Lanham Act was not addressed in that case. Instead, the United States Supreme Court was examining whether certain customs regulations were consistent with Section 526 of the Tariff Act of 1930.[248] Because both the statute and the regulations at issue in K Mart referred to "[f]oreign-made articles" or "merchandise of foreign manufacture" it was not surprising that the Court's description of gray market theory focused on goods of foreign manufacture. Nonetheless, K Mart should not be read to limit gray market theory to goods of foreign manufacture.[249]

d. Remedies

The Lanham Act provides injunctive relief for many situations that give rise to trademark infringement.[250] The court is granted leeway in how it chooses to use the power to grant injunctions.[251] This power is used according to the principles of equity and upon such terms as the court may deem reasonable, to prevent the violation of any right of the registrant of a mark registered in the Patent and Trademark Office.[252] One court has held that even the threat of infringement is sufficient to issue an injunction and that the plaintiff would not have to wait until actual infringement had occurred in order to bring the action.[253] The injunction can be as simple as enjoining the defendant from further infringing use of the mark or it can be as specific as enjoining the defendant in destroying all items on which the infringing mark was impressed.[254]

---

247. Bourdeau, 444 F.3d at 1321 *citing K Mart*, 486 U.S. at 285.
248. 19 U.S.C. § 1526
249. Several other district courts have held that the importation or sale of products manufactured domestically exclusively for export may constitute trademark infringement. *See e.g.*, R.J. Reynolds Tobacco Co. v. Premium Tobacco Stores, Inc., 2004 WL 1613563 (N.D. Ill. 2004); Am. HomeProds v. Reliance Trading Co., 2000 WL 1263465 (C.D. Cal. 2000); Philip Morris Inc. v. Cigarettes for Less, 69 F. Supp. 2d 1181 (N.D. Cal. 1999), *aff'd* 215 3d 1333 (9th Cir. 2000).
250. 15 U.S.C. § 1114(2) (2008).
251. 15 U.S.C. § 1116(a) (2008).
252. *Id.*
253. Chemical Corp. of Am. v. Anheuser-Busch, Inc., 306 F.2d 433, 439 (5th Cir. 1962).
254. Gatson's White River Resort v. Rush, 701 F. Supp. 1431, 1441 (W.D. Ark. 1988).

When a violation of a registered plaintiff is proven, the plaintiff shall be entitled to recover (1) defendant's profits, (2) any damages sustained by the plaintiff, and (3) the costs of the action.[255] Section 1117 of the Lanham Act gives the district court broad discretion over the amount of damages, limited only by principles of equity and restricted from making any award that is punitive instead of merely compensatory.[256] In assessing profits, the plaintiff shall be required to prove defendant's sales only; defendant must prove all elements of cost or deduction claimed.[257] In assessing damages the court may enter judgment, according to the circumstances of the case, for any sum above the amount found as actual damages, not exceeding three times such amount.[258] If the court shall find that the amount of the recovery based on profits is either inadequate or excessive, the court may in its discretion enter judgment for such sum as the court shall find to be just, according to the circumstances of the case.[259]

Although the court is afforded substantial leeway, damages may not be awarded on the basis of speculation or conjecture.[260] Although to set a damage figure "arbitrarily" or through "pure guesswork" is impermissible,[261] once the existence of damages has been shown, all that an award of damages requires is substantial evidence in the record to permit a fact finder to draw reasonable inferences and make a fair and reasonable assessment of the amount of damages.[262]

---

255. 15 U.S.C. § 1117(a) (2008).
256. Dial One of the Mid-South, Inc. v. BellSouth Telcomms., Inc., 269 F.3d 523, 526 (5th Cir. 2001).
257. Martin's Herend Imports v. Diamond & Gem Trading USA, 112 F.3d 1296, 1304 (5th Cir. 1997).
258. Id.
259. Id.
260. Porous Media Corp. v. Pall Corp., 173 F.3d 1109, 1122 (8th Cir. 1999).
261. Agricultural Servs. Assoc. v. Ferry-Morse Seed, 551 F.2d 1057, 1072 (6th Cir. 1977).
262. Broan Mfg. Co. v. Associated Distribs., Inc., 923 F.2d 1232, 1236 (6th Cir. 1991).

CHAPTER

18

Theories of Liability

State Law

a.	Gray Market Statutes in California	289
b.	Gray Market Statutes in Connecticut	293
c.	Gray Market Statutes in New York	294
d.	Gray Market Statutes in Washington D.C. and Michigan: Gray Market Cigarette Statutes	295

The vast majority of gray market litigation turns on claims related to copyright, trademark, or contract. A few states, however, have enacted their own gray market legislation. Specifically, California, Connecticut, and New York (the District of Columbia and Michigan have statutes pertaining to gray market cigarettes) have enacted gray market statutes designed to prevent consumers from unwittingly purchasing gray market products.

As observed in Chapter 4, several manufacturers have policies of not providing warranty support or other services for products procured from the gray market. To prevent consumers from unknowingly purchasing a product devoid of warranty support, these states have imposed specific obligations on gray marketers to either provide their own warranty support or clearly advise their customers that their purchase will not be covered by the brand owner's express warranties. Although these statutes were crafted with consumers in mind, brand owners can likely rely on such violations to bolster unfair competition claims against gray markets. Although these statutes are not new, they have remained surprisingly dormant since their enactment. Notwithstanding their underutilization, they do provide consumers and brand owners with some additional litigation fodder.

a. Gray Market Statutes in California

California has two gray market statutes. The first is a disclosure statute designed to protect consumers from unknown or undisclosed risks that may accompany gray market purchases. Specifically, California's Civil Code Section 1797.81 requires retailers of gray market goods to provide their own warranty support for the product[1] or otherwise conspicuously label the product as being "not covered by a manufacturer's express written warranty valid in the United States...."[2]

When Section 1797.81 applies, retailers must also disclose through labeling or signage on the product any "incompatibility or nonconformity with relevant domestic standards known to the seller" including compatibility with U.S. electric power systems, the availability of replacement parts from domestic distributors, compatibility with accessories available domestically, English instructions, and rebate eligibility.[3] These disclosures must also appear on all advertising for gray market products.[4]

Retailers who fail to comply with these provisions are liable to buyers who return the gray market goods[5] and the contract of sale can be rescinded.[6] Violating retailers are also liable for unfair competition under Sections 17200 and 1770.[7] Despite its 1986 vintage, Section 1797.81 has gone practically unseen in court opinions so far. It is only mentioned in one case, and only for the purposes of arguing legislative intent for a largely unrelated issue of misrepresentation.[8] Still, the statute does appear to be a viable weapon for brand owners wishing to keep the gray market out of some stores. Although the initial provisions are aimed only at consumer protection,[9] the latter portion declares violations to be statutory unfair competition. So long as a brand

---

1. § 1797.81(b). A retailer's warranty in lieu of disclosure must provide equal or greater protections than the normal manufacturer's warranty. § 1797.81(b)(1). The product must also be labeled to inform consumers that copies of the warranty are available on request. § 1797.81(b)(3). Lastly, the warranty and retailer practices must comply with the Song-Beverly Consumer Warranty Act and the Magnuson-Moss Warranty-Federal Trade Commission Improvement Act. § 1797.81(b)(2), (4); see CAL. CIV. CODE § 1790 et seq., 15 U.S.C. § 2302(b)(1)(A), 16 C.F.R. § 702.1 et seq.
2. CAL. CIV. CODE § 1797.81(a)(1). Despite the lack of express warranty, implied warranties still exist. Id.
3. § 1797.81(a)(2)–(8).
4. § 1797.82.
5. § 1797.85.
6. § 1797.86. See § 1689.
7. § 1797.86. See CAL. BUS. & PROF. CODE § 17200, CAL. CIV. CODE § 1770.
8. See Chamberlain v. Ford Motor Co., 2003 WL 25751413 slip op. at *5 (N.D.Cal. 2003). The statute also appears as support for a Lanham Act claim in one gray market case that was recently before a federal district court in Illinois. See Hyundai Constr. Equip. U.S.A., Inc. v. Chris Johnson Equip., Inc., 2008 WL 4210785, slip op. (N.D. Illinois 2008); Plaintiff Hyundai Constr. Equip. U.S.A., Inc.'s Memorandum in Support of its Motion for Summary Judgment, 2008 WL 2325353. On summary judgment, the plaintiff prevailed on the Lanham Act claim, though the court's opinion doesn't mention the influence that this statute had on this decision. Hyundai, 2008 WL 4210785, slip op. at *4.
9. See CAL. CIV. CODE § 1797.85.

owner's foreign-distributed products have appreciable differences from its domestically-distributed products (especially regarding the warranty), the brand owner can use this statute in conjunction with Section 17200 against any retailer selling the gray market good without the proper disclosures.[10]

California's second gray market statute is a criminal statute that protects supply-chain integrity by outlawing interference with manufacturer identification marks.[11] Specifically, Section 537e states that it is a public offense to buy, sell, receive, dispose of, conceal, or possess "any personal property from which the manufacturer's serial number, identification number, electronic serial number, or any other distinguishing number or identification mark has been removed, defaced, covered, altered, or destroyed. . . ."[12]

As discussed in Chapter 17, removing product or serial numbers is a common strategy among gray marketers to obfuscate their suppliers as well as the location of the actual leak in a brand owner's distribution channel. Fortunately for brand owners, Section 537e renders this practice illegal. Violations of Section 537e are punishable by up to six months imprisonment in county jail;[13] up to one year if the property's value is over $400;[14] up to three years in state prison if the property is a computer chip or circuit board with a value over $400.[15]

Section 537e's application has been expressly endorsed in the gray market context by the California Court of Appeal. In *People v. Superior Court (Shayan)*,[16] a retailer/wholesaler possessed over one thousand car stereo parts that were missing the manufacturer's serial numbers.[17] When law enforcement suspected that the goods were stolen, the retailer/wholesaler insisted that they were lawful gray market imports. With respect to the Section 537e, the retailer argued that his gray market activities were not illegal and the statute was thus not applicable. In addition, the retailer argued that the marks were not removed with any fraudulent intent.[18]

The court rejected all of the retailer's arguments, holding that intent to defraud need not be proven.[19] With respect to the ostensible right to remove the marks, the court held that only the *original* manufacturer of a product could authorize removal of an identifying mark.[20] Finally, regardless of the

---

10. § 1797.86; *see* CAL. BUS. & PROF. CODE § 17200 et. seq.
11. *See* CAL. PENAL CODE § 537e.
12. § 537e(a). If the item is a firearm, Section 12090 of the Penal Code may also apply. If the item is a motor vehicle, Section 10751 of the Vehicle Code may apply.
13. § 537e(a)(1).
14. § 537e(a)(2).
15. § 537e(a)(3).
16. People v. Superior Court (Shayan), 21 Cal. App. 4th 621 (Cal. Ct. App. 1993).
17. *Id.* at 623.
18. Shayan, 21 Cal. App. 4th at 626.
19. *Id.*
20. *Id.* at 629.

alleged legitimacy of the defendant's business, a violation of Section 537e had occurred nonetheless. The court reasoned that manufacturer marks needed to stay intact for the purposes of product recalls, defenses against product liability suits, and for the tracking of products after they have left the factory.[21]

In *Sebastian Int'l, Inc. v. Russolillo*, a federal district court in California reached a similar conclusion.[22] In *Sebastian*, a hair care product brand owner desired to sell its wares exclusively through salons and beauty schools.[23] Accordingly, it created a tight distribution network and bound each participating salon to contractual provisions that prohibited distribution outside of the manufacturer's intended venues.[24] Many of the products were holographically labeled for tracking and identification purposes.[25] Despite the brand owner's efforts to maintain exclusivity for their products, however, it discovered that several unauthorized retailers and distributors had induced salons to divert distribution of some products, contrary to the brand owner's partner contracts.[26] In some cases, this also involved the removal of the holographic labels.[27]

Among many other claims, the brand owner brought suit alleging Section 17200 Unfair Competition[28] via violations of Section 537e.[29] The defendants filed a motion to dismiss on the grounds that the statute was only intended to deter theft. Since there were no such allegations, the defendants argued that there could not be any liability. The court disagreed with the defendants' overly narrow interpretation of the statute. Instead, the court observed that Section 537e was intended to facilitate the tracking and identification of products by the brand owner.[30] Because the brand owner used holographic labels for those very purposes, Section 537e was fully applicable here. Accordingly, the court refused to dismiss the claim for unfair competition.[31]

Although Section 537e is a criminal statute, brand owners can use their violations in civil actions by characterizing its violations as "unfair competition" the plaintiff did in *Sebastian*. Using this strategy, Section 537e will essentially become another gateway for an unfair competition claim.

---

21. *Id.* at 627.
22. Sebastian Int'l, Inc. v. Russolillo, 186 F. Supp. 2d 1055 (C.D.Cal. 2000).
23. *Id.* at 1061.
24. *Id.*
25. *Id.*
26. *Id.* at 1062.
27. *Id.*
28. *See* CAL. BUS. & PROF. CODE § 17200.
29. *Id.* at 1072.
30. *Id.* at 1073.
31. *Id.*

b. Gray Market Statutes in Connecticut

Like California, Connecticut has a civil statute requiring the disclosure of information for gray market products.[32] Section 42-210 of the Connecticut General Statutes defines gray market goods in almost the same way that California's Civil Code does: "[A]ny brand-name consumer product normally accompanied by a warranty valid in the United States which is imported into the United States through channels other than the manufacturer's authorized United States distributor . . . and which . . . may not be accompanied by a manufacturer's express written warranty. . . ."[33]

Similar to California's disclosure statute, Section 42-210 requires retailers to conspicuously label gray market products to inform consumers that the products lack a valid U.S. warranty, lack English instructions, and/or are ineligible for manufacturer rebate, if any are the case.[34] Unlike the California statute, however, which also requires retailers to disclose *all* "incompatibility or nonconformity with relevant domestic standards[,]"[35] the requirements of Section 42-210 are only limited to the three enumerated items.[36] Also unlike the California statute, Section 42-210 only requires such disclosures in product advertisements for retailers which engage in mail-order sales.[37]

Connecticut retailers have the option of providing their own express written warranties for gray market products, so long as "equal or greater protection than the manufacturer's warranty" is provided.[38] Also like the California statute, Section 42-210 creates liability for violating retailers to sellers who wish to return the gray market product.[39] However, this liability under Section 42-210 is limited to "twenty days from the date of purchase,"[40] and does not carry the indefinite time window offered in California.[41] Lastly, similar to California's treatment, violations of Section 42-210 constitute "unfair or deceptive trade practice" under Connecticut's version of unfair competition law.[42]

---

32. *Compare* CONN. GEN. STAT. § 42–210 *to* CAL. CIV. CODE. §§ 1797.8–1797.86.
33. CONN. GEN. STAT. § 42-210(a).
34. § 42-210(b).
35. CAL. CIV. CODE § 1797.81(a)(8).
36. CONN. GEN. STAT. § 42-210(b).
37. § 42-210(c).
38. § 42-210(f). Section 42-210 expressly labels this as an affirmative defense, as opposed to California's Section 1797.81(b), which treats the retailer-warranty as more of a qualifier of the elements of the claim. *See* CAL. CIV. CODE § 1797.81(b).
39. *Compare* § 42-210(d) *to* CAL. CIV. CODE § 1897.85. Both assume that the consumer has not used the product in a manner contrary to written instructions.
40. CONN. GEN. STAT. § 42-210(d).
41. CAL. CIV. CODE § 1797.85.
42. CONN. GEN. STAT. § 42-210(e). *See* § 42.110b et. seq.

Section 42-210 has not yet appeared in any Connecticut state or federal court opinions.[43] Despite being relatively narrower than its counterpart in California, Section 42-210 still generally provides the same gray market enforcement opportunities that are available in California.[44] Most importantly, it acts as a gateway to an unfair competition claim[45] wherever a gray market retailer lacks the diligence to properly label the product.

c. Gray Market Statutes in New York

New York carries a gray market disclosure statute[46] akin to the ones found in California and Connecticut. The New York legislature has defined gray market goods using almost the exact same wording used by Connecticut's legislature:[47] "[A]ny brand-name consumer product normally accompanied by a warranty valid in the United States of America which is imported into the United States through channels other than the manufacturer's authorized United States distributor . . . and which . . . may not be accompanied by a manufacturer's express written warranty. . . ."[48]

Also identical to Connecticut's statute, New York's Section 218-aa requires retailers to disclose, if applicable, that a gray market product lacks a valid U.S. warranty, lacks English instructions, and/or is ineligible for manufacturer rebate.[49] The requirement for disclosure in advertising is limited to mail-order businesses[50] and the liability to returning buyers is available for twenty days from the time of sale.[51] Lastly, as seen in all the disclosure statutes, Section 218-aa allows retailers to provide their own express warranty in lieu of disclosing the lack of a manufacturer's warranty.[52]

---

43. The statute *appears* to have been cited in just one case, but further investigation reveals that the case instead cited a probate statute that once occupied the citation number in which Section 42-210 now resides. *See* Guaranty Bank & Trust Co. v. Kaminsky, 356 A.2d 909 (Conn. Super. 1976).
44. *See* CAL. CIV. CODE § 1797.86.
45. CONN. GEN. STAT. § 42-210(e).
46. N.Y. GEN. BUS. LAW § 218-aa.
47. Actually, it is more likely that Connecticut followed New York with this language as New York's Section 218-aa precedes Connecticut's Section 42-210 by one year.
48. N.Y. GEN. BUS. LAW § 218-aa(1).
49. § 218-aa(3).
50. § 218-aa(4).
51. § 218-aa(5).
52. § 218-aa(7). Like in Section 42-210, Section 218-aa calls this an affirmative defense for retailers. *See* CONN. GEN. STAT. § 42-210(f). As with all the disclosure statutes, the retailer's warranty must provide equal or greater protection than a manufacturer's warranty normally would have. Gen. Bus. Law. § 218-aa.

As for remedies beyond the issue of consumer returns, New York's Section 218-aa contains a major departure from the gray market disclosure statutes of California and Connecticut. Since New York does not have an equivalent unfair competition statute to California's Section 17200 or Connecticut's Section 42.110b,[53] it cannot declare violations of the gray market disclosure provisions to be unfair competition in the way that Connecticut and California have. Instead, Section 218-aa directly allows for injunctions of the retailer's unlawful conduct without need for proof of injury,[54] additional costs of up to $2,000 from each defendant to each plaintiff,[55] direct restitution,[56] and civil penalties of up to $500 for each violation.[57]

Section 218-aa has not appeared in any New York state or federal court opinions.[58] Although Section 218-aa does not make unfair competition claims available against violating retailers, it has a substantial amount of its own remedies available to manufacturers wishing to sue.

d. Gray Market Statutes in Washington D.C. and Michigan: Gray Market Cigarette Statutes

Both the District of Columbia and the state of Michigan have statutes which prohibit the possession and sale of gray market cigarettes.[59] Both define "gray market cigarette" as the following:

> [A]ny cigarettes the package of which bears any statement, label, stamp, sticker, or notice indicating that the manufacturer did not intend the

---

53. *See* CAL. BUS. & PROF. CODE § 17200; CONN. GEN. STAT. § 42.110b. Rather, New York seems to prefer a the strict common-law definition of unfair competition, which is limited to the passing off of one's goods as another's or the passing off of another's goods as one's own. *See* Chapter 19 of this book.
54. N.Y. GEN. BUS. LAW § 218-aa(6).
55. N.Y. C.P.L.R. § 8303(a)(6); *see* N.Y. GEN. BUS. LAW § 218-aa(6) ("allowances to the attorney general provided in paragraph six of subdivision (a) of section eighty-three hundred three of the civil practice law and rules").
56. Gen. Bus. Law § 218-aa(6).
57. *Id.* Civil penalties under Section 218-aa are similar to, but much lesser than, the civil penalties available under California's and Connecticut's unfair competition statutes ($2,500 and $25,000, respectively). CAL. BUS. & PROF. CODE § 17206(a); Ct. St. § 42-1100(a).
58. Section 218-aa does appear alongside California's Section 1797.81 as support for the Lanham Act claim in the *Hyundai* case. *Hyundai*, 2008 WL 4210785; Plaintiff Hyundai Constr. Equip. U.S.A., Inc.'s Memorandum in Support of its Motion for Summary Judgment, 2008 WL 2325353. Recall that, on summary judgment, the plaintiff prevailed on the Lanham Act claim but the court's opinion doesn't mention the influence that either statute had on this decision. Hyundai, 2008 WL 4210785, slip op. at *4.
59. D.C. CODE § 47-2419; MICH. COMP. LAWS § 205.428.

cigarettes to be sold, distributed, or used in the United States, including, but not limited to, a label stating "For Export Only," "U.S. Tax Exempt," "For Use Outside U.S.," or similar wording.[60]

In the District of Columbia, where it is also illegal to alter any such labeling, gray market cigarettes in the jurisdiction are "subject to seizure, forfeiture, and destruction by the Mayor under § 47-2409."[61] In Michigan, unlicensed possessors of gray market cigarettes are personally liable for state taxes on those cigarettes and must pay "a penalty of 500% of the amount of tax. . . ."[62] This is a misdemeanor offense, "punishable by a fine of not more than $1,000.00 or 5 times the retail value of the tobacco products involved, whichever is greater, or imprisonment for not more than 1 year, or both."[63] If 3,000 or more gray market cigarettes are involved (or cigarettes together worth $250 or more), the possessor "is guilty of a felony, punishable by a fine of not more than $50,000.00 or imprisonment for not more than 5 years, or both."[64]

Copyright, trademark, and contract causes of action are the most common and effective tools brand owners typically have to wield against gray marketers. However, brand owners should be sure to examine the relevant state statutes to determine whether additional theories may be viable.

---

60. D.C. CODE § 47-2419(1)(A)(i); MICH. COMP. LAWS § 205.422(h).
61. D.C. CODE § 47-2423. See § 47-2409(a).
62. MICH. COMP. LAWS § 205.428(1). See MICH. COMP. LAWS Ch. 205 et seq. for cigarette taxation details.
63. MICH. COMP. LAWS § 205.428(5).
64. § 205.428(3).

CHAPTER

19

Approaches to Gray Market around the Globe

a.	Canada	300
b.	Mexico	301
c.	Europe	302
d.	Russia	304
e.	China	306
f.	India	308

Given that gray market activity is often borne from a brand owner's efforts to manufacture and sell its products around the world, a familiarity with the protections offered by other countries is necessary. Because not every gray market issue can be litigated in the United States, brand owners should preemptively acquaint themselves with the rules and customs in nations where gray or black market issues may arise. Specifically, brand owners should look very carefully into the particular IP laws of their target country to see (1) if business is viable there, and (2) if so, what procedures should be followed to be included under the protections of the country's laws. Multinational corporations typically consider the following factors for determining the stability and safety of IP in a given country:

(1) [The] presence of a stable and facilitating political and economic base and a transparent and non-discretionary legal and regulatory framework; (2) an attractive market characterized by a strong and sustained rate of growth, an equitable distribution of domestic income, expansion and integration of the regional market; and (3) the existence of adequate human capital and technical capabilities.[1]

---

1. Horacio Teran, *Intellectual Property Protection and Offshore Software Development: An Analysis of the US Software Industry*, 2 MINN. INTELL.PROP. REV. 1 (2001).

Although an exegesis of every country's treatment of the gray market is beyond the scope of this book, the following pages provide a brief overview of some of the more noteworthy rules and countries commonly examined in an international gray market analysis.

As an initial matter, countries are essentially left on their own to create and enforce their laws. Although international law exists, it is more akin to a contract than a statute. To illustrate, once state or federal statutes are ratified in the United States, the rules therein are imposed on its citizens. Rights found in a contract, however, are only imposed on parties that voluntarily submit to their application. Similarly, international law—especially with respect to intellectual property—is essentially derived from treaties and multilateral agreements among various countries and states that voluntarily submit to their application.

In an effort to ensure fair treatment and enforcement of multilateral agreements pertaining to intellectual property, most are now adjudicated by The World Intellectual Property Organization (WIPO), an organization of the United Nations. WIPO is comprised of 175 countries[2] and, according to its Web site, "is dedicated to developing a balanced and accessible international intellectual property (IP) system, which rewards creativity, stimulates innovation and contributes to economic development while safeguarding the public interest."[3] Today, WIPO administers 24 treaties.[4] In these efforts, WIPO seeks to "harmonize national intellectual property legislation and procedures" and "facilitate the resolution of private intellectual property disputes."[5]

For example, WIPO administers the Berne Convention for the Protection of Literary and Artistic Works (Berne Convention), which seeks to provide international copyright protection to various forms of intellectual property. The Berne Convention respects the copyright works of authors from other member parties as though the authors were its own citizens.[6] Accordingly, a copyright author is not required to register its copyright in every conceivable nation where a threat of infringement exists.[7] With respect to trademarks,[8]

---

2. WIPO, Member States, http://www.wipo.int/members/en/ (last visited Oct. 25, 2008).
3. WIPO, What is WIPO?, http://www.wipo.int/about-wipo/en/what/ (last visited Oct. 25, 2008).
4. Id.
5. WIPO, WIPO Treaties—General Information, http://www.wipo.int/treaties/en/general/ (last visited Oct. 25, 2008).
6. See 17 U.S.C. §§ 410, 411; see also In re Peregrine Entm't, Ltd., 116 Bankr. 194, 200 n.7 (C.D. Cal. 1990).
7. The registration of copyrights is still highly recommended in any target country. Beyond merely facilitating the evidentiary issue of who-created-first, the registration of copyrights provides concrete certification of IP ownership and can speed the response of a foreign government to infringement. Registered copyrights are also more effective in nations where enforcement of copyright is generally softer. See Frank X. Curci, Protecting Your Intellectual Property Rights Overseas, Symposium: Transnational Business Law in the Twenty-First Century, 15 TRANSNAT'L LAW. 15, fn. 45 (2002).
8. Trademarks, which must always be registered anyway, should be registered prior to any commencement of business activity in a foreign nation—otherwise, a competitor may swoop in

WIPO administers an international registry of trademarks under the Madrid Agreement Concerning the International Registration of Marks and the Madrid Protocol.[9] The Madrid System allows simultaneous trademark registration in 83 countries and protection attaches automatically for all countries that do not refuse the registration within a certain timeframe.[10]

Although countries are essentially left on their own with respect to their treatment of the gray market, efforts are underway to harmonize the laws. For example, the International Trademark Association has publicly disapproved gray market activity and states that eradicating the gray market is "in the best interests of the brand owners and their customers (the consumers) and of orderly markets."[11]

Notwithstanding the efforts of organizations and nations to reach a level of uniformity in the protection of intellectual property, brand owners must acknowledge the reality that most countries retain a great deal of autonomy to set and enforce their own rules. More troublingly for brand owners, most countries fall dramatically short of the United States' efforts to protect intellectual property. There are several reasons for the disparity in legal treatment. The simplest explanation is practicality: many countries simply cannot afford to pursue infringers.[12] Others are financially capable of enforcement, but see no monetary benefit as a consequence.[13] In other countries, intellectual property might only be protected in its physical manifestations, ruling out protection for things such as software.[14] Former and current enemies of the United States may even see intellectual property as an American or Western idea unworthy of protection.[15]

Given this spectrum of enforceability, a brand owner's familiarity with the rules of the countries in which its distribution channels traverse is therefore a worthy endeavor.

---

to register first. This is especially important in countries which follow a first-to-file rule, in which ownership of a mark is given to the first entity to register it, even if another entity had been actively using the mark in the country for several years. *See id.*

9. WIPO, Madrid System for the International Registration of Marks, http://www.wipo.int/madrid/en/ (last visited Oct. 25, 2008).
10. *See id.*
11. International Trademark Association ("INTA"), *Position Paper on Parallel Imports* (July 2007), http://www.inta.org/images/stories/downloads/PDA/parallelimportspositionpaper.pdf (last visited Oct. 25, 2008).
12. Mary Kopczynski, *Robin Hood Versus the Bullies: Software Piracy and Developing Countries*, 33 RUTGERS COMPUTER. & TECH. L. J. 299 (2007) (citing Jishnu Guha, *Time for India's Intellectual Property Regime to Grow Up*, 13 CARDOZO J. INT'L & COMP. L. 225, 239 (2005).
13. Frank X. Curci, Protecting Your Intellectual Property Rights Overseas, Symposium: Transnational Business Law in the Twenty-First Century, 15 TRANSNAT'L LAW. 15, fn. 45 (2002).
14. Bradley S. Butterfield et al., *Human Resources and Intellectual Property in a Global Outsourcing Environment: Focus on China, India and Eastern Europe*, 15 INT'L HUMAN RESOURCES J., 2, 1 (2006).
15. Kopczynski, *supra* note 12.

a. Canada

As detailed in Chapter 2, Canada has a keen familiarity with the gray market. With divergent tax schemes on cigarettes in its provinces, the country faced a robust diversion epidemic that commentators compared to the smuggling of liquor during the Prohibition Era. Notwithstanding its proximity to and shared experiences with the United States, its treatment of the gray market is not entirely consistent.

For example, in May 2007 Canada's Supreme Court examined a case with facts very similar to the United States Supreme Court case of *Quality King Distributors, Inc. v. L'anza Research Intern., Inc.*[16] The plaintiff Kraft Canada Inc. (Kraft) sued Euro-Excellence Inc. (Euro Excellence) for violating Canada's Copyright Act.[17] From 1997 through 2000, Euro Excellence was the exclusive distributor of Cote D'Or chocolates, which were manufactured by Kraft's parent company, Kraft Foods Belgium S.A. (KFB). When Euro Excellence's distribution agreement expired, KFB registered an artistic copyright in Canada for the Cote D'Or logo—an elephant. Meanwhile, Kraft Foods Schweiz AG (KFS) registered an artistic copyright for its Toblerone chocolate bars and both KFS and KFB registered license agreements that gave Kraft the exclusive rights to use the copyrights and sell the chocolate bars in Canada.

The controversy arose because Euro Excellence continued to sell its Cote d'Or chocolate bars as well as Toblerone bars. Kraft therefore sued Euro Excellence for copyright infringement with respect to its unauthorized sales of the copyrighted works. The trial court endorsed this theory of copyright infringement as did the court of appeal. The Supreme Court of Canada, however, reversed explaining that "[f]or [Kraft] to succeed, it must show that Euro imported works that would have infringed copyright if they had been made in Canada by the persons who made them."[18] Because the products were gray market chocolate bars originally manufactured by KFB and KFS, the Supreme Court of Canada held that no infringement could have occurred.

The *Kraft* opinion is an illustrative example in which Canada and the United States reached departing conclusions in similar fact patterns. In *Quality King*, the court implied that when the copyrighted goods were first manufactured and sold overseas, such a transaction does not constitute a first sale to deprive the copyright holder from enforcing its rights.[19] *Quality King's* implication was expressly endorsed in *Omega v. Costco*, in which Omega was

---

16. 523 U.S. 135 (1998).
17. S. 27(2)(e) of the Copyright Act, R.S.C. 1985, c. C-42.
18. Euro-Excellence Inc. v. Kraft Canada Inc., 2007 SCC 37 (Can.).
19. *See* 523 U.S. 135 (1998).

able to successfully move forward with its claims notwithstanding the fact that the goods were manufactured and sold overseas by the plaintiff's parent company.[20] Accordingly, brand owners must be mindful that proving that a gray market's imports violate their copyrights will be more difficult if they must litigate the issue in Canada.

b. Mexico

Like Canada, Mexico has experienced its fair share of black and gray market activity. Unlike the United States and Canada, Mexico is a country where gray market goods typically leave rather than arrive. Given Mexico's poverty levels, brand owners must offer their goods at lower prices. As a result, gray market importers will aggressively court Mexican distributors to purchase goods for resale in the United States. Especially if there is unrealistic pressure on authorized partners in Mexico to sell a large volume of goods, the ability to sell to gray market importers is often too tempting to resist.

In addition to gray market offenses, Mexico is equally notorious for being a source of black market goods. To combat these problems, Mexico created the Mexican Institute of Industrial Property (IMPI) to address counterfeiting and comply with NAFTA regulations.[21] IMPI is broad in application, providing protections for trademarks and copyrights. However, Mexico is still considered a chronic abuser of intellectual property rights. The U.S. Embassy recently summarized the dismal reality and outlook with respect to Mexico's efforts to protection of intellectual property:

> Losses to Mexican and international companies due to trademark counterfeiting, copyright piracy, and patent infringements lie in the hundreds of millions of dollars annually and are growing. Solutions to this problem, which significantly affects the film, music, software, pharmaceutical, and textile industries, are hampered by limited political will, a lack of capacity and coordination among law enforcement entities, competing crime-fighting priorities, weak application of IPR laws, and insufficient planning and coordination among industry sectors. The protection of IPR is complicated by Mexico's extensive poverty and corruption.[22]

---

20. *See* 2008 WL 4058640.
21. DAVID M. HOPKINS, Counterfeiting Exposed 10 (2003) at 288.
22. U.S. Embassy, Overview of Mexico's IPR Environment, http://www.usembassy-mexico.gov/IPRtoolkit_overview.html (last visited Oct. 25, 2008).

c. Europe

The European Union (EU) is comprised of 27 member states,[23] which are among the wealthiest countries in the world. Their high prices for consumer and health care good make them a chronic target for gray market activity. There have been efforts in Europe for the intellectual property laws to be harmonized. For example, the United Kingdom's Trade Marks Act of 1994 reflects the European Trade Mark Harmonization Directive (Directive) and states that a trademark is "any sign which is both (a) capable of being represented graphically; and (b) capable of distinguishing goods or services undertaking from those of other undertakings."[24] The Directive is a model for many other countries to consider when they are adopting new legislation governing trademarks.

Similar to the first sale doctrine, several countries as well as the EU adhere a doctrine known as the exhaustion of rights theory. The scope of the exhaustion theory typically turns on whether the country follows a national exhaustion of rights theory or an international exhaustion of rights theory.

National (or regional) exhaustion of rights is closer to the American rule, and it holds that once a brand owner has sold its goods in relation to which the trademark is used in a particular country, it has only "exhausted" its trademark rights in relation those goods in that particular country.[25] If the same goods are sold in another country, the brand owner can rely on its trademark rights in that country to prevent the further sale of the goods.[26] The EU, for example, applies this concept regionally. Therefore, a brand owner consenting to sell its trademarked goods in a country within a certain region has exhausted its trademark rights with respect to all of the countries in that region.

International exhaustion of rights, however, holds that once a brand owner has sold its trademarked goods in one country, it has exhausted its trademark rights in relation to those goods all over the world. Similar to the holding in *Omega v. Costco*,[27] INTA advocates a national or regional exhaustion theory so that brand owners can prevent the unwanted and unwelcomed importation of its goods without first sale doctrine or exhaustion theories impeding such efforts.

---

23. European Comm'n, *The EU at a Glance: European Countries*, http:// europa.eu/abc/European_countries/index_en.htm (last visited Oct. 25, 2008).
24. RITA CLIFTON, Brands and Branding 2(2d ed. 2004) (2003) at 158.
25. International Trademark Association ("INTA"), *Position Paper on Parallel Imports* (July 2007), http://www.inta.org/images/stories/downloads/PDA/parallelimportspositionpaper.pdf (last visited Oct. 25, 2008).
26. *Id.*
27. For further discussion of *Omega v. Costco*, see Chapter 2.

There is currently no treaty or consensus dictating a standard of the first sale doctrine, national exhaustion, or international exhaustion.[28] For example, the Trade Related Aspects of Intellectual Property (TRIPS) Agreement, which was negotiated in an effort to standardize intellectual property protection throughout the world, is expressly neutral in its treatment of the exhaustion of rights theory:

> For the purposes of dispute settlement under this agreement . . . nothing in this Agreement may be used to address the issue of the exhaustion of intellectual property rights.[29]

Although Europe and the United States face similar gray and black market challenges, they will commonly reach differing conclusions in cases with similar facts presented. For example, Chapter 3 explained how U.S. courts have been generally unwilling to hold eBay liable for the infringing conduct of its users. In *Hendrickson v. eBay Inc.*,[30] eBay was sued when pirated copies of the movie "Manson" were found being offered for sale. The movie's owner alleged that eBay was liable for copyright infringement because it participated in and facilitated the unlawful sale and distribution of unauthorized copies of the film. Although the court acknowledged that eBay manifests the characteristics of an online swap meet where organizers can be held liable, it refused to find liability pursuant to the "safe harbor" provision of the Digital Millennium Copyright Act,[31] which protects Internet service providers from liability for direct, vicarious, and contributory infringement.

In July 2008, a French court came to a different conclusion and ordered eBay to pay Louis Vuitton and other luxury brand owners €40 million ($63.2 million) for allowing fake and unauthorized goods to be sold online. The brand owners LVMH Möet Hennessy Louis Vuitton (Louis Vuitton) and Christian Dior SA (Christian Dior) alleged that eBay had not done enough to ensure that goods sold on the site were not counterfeit.[32] eBay was also found liable for unauthorized gray market sales. The court ruled that although legitimate perfumes were found on the site, Louis Vuitton strictly limited its perfume sales to authorized dealers such as perfume chains and department stores.

---

28. International Trademark Association ("INTA"), *Position Paper on Parallel Imports* (July 2007), http://www.inta.org/images/stories/downloads/PDA/parallelimportspositionpaper.pdf (last visited Oct. 25, 2008).
29. Trade Related Aspects of Intellectual Property ("TRIPS") Agreement, a*vailable at* http://www.wto.int/english/docs_e/legal_e/27-trips.pdf (last visited Oct. 25, 2008).
30. 165 F. Supp. 2d 1082 (C.D. Cal. 2001).
31. 17 U.S.C. § 512 (2008).
32. Christina Passariello, *eBay Fined Over Selling Counterfeits*, WALL ST. J., July 1, 2008, at B1.

Although the *Louis Vuitton* opinion was criticized by some as favoritism for a French company,[33] it reflects the potential for fundamentally diverging rulings in cases that are virtually identical. Although the gray market challenges are the same, the law is not.

d. Russia

In April 2008, The United States named Russia among the worst offenders for failing to protect American intellectual property rights.[34] Although some progress had been made in recent years, the United States Trade Representative's office observed that "weak enforcement against piracy and counterfeiting in Russia remains a serious problem."[35] Notwithstanding Russia's chronic failure to protect and respect foreign intellectual property, brand owners continue to invest in Russia to manufacture, distribute, and sell their branded goods. As one commentator noted, the appeal of Russia is obvious:

> The country has the oil reserves of Saudi Arabia, the mineral reserves of South Africa, the timber reserves of the Amazon, the fertile farmland of the American Midwest, the inexpensive labor of Mexico or Malaysia, a population the size of Japan, a land mass almost the size of the U.S. and Canada combined, engineers and scientists that compare to any western country, but with a GDP roughly the size of Indonesia's. Each of these reasons makes doing business in Russia attractive to a variety of companies.[36]

Given the panoply of resources beneficial to business, Russia has seen investment from various companies such as British Petroleum and Exxon Mobil to Motorola and Caterpillar.[37] Meanwhile, crime, corruption, and stifling bureaucracy continue to present significant challenges to its entire economy as well as to brand owners looking to capitalize on the advantages available in the country's landscape.

---

33. *Did French Retailers Win 'Hometown' Verdict Against eBay*, http://blogs.wsj.com/law/2008/06/30/did-french-retailers-win-hometown-verdict-against-ebay/ (June 30, 2008, 14:05 EST).
34. *See* U.S. Trade Rep., 2008 Special 301 Report 34 (2008), *available at* http://www.ustr.gov/assets/Document_Library/Reports_Publications/2008/2008_Special_301_Report/asset_upload_file553_14869.pdf.
35. *Id.*
36. A. Carter Balkcom et al., *Russia: Western Investment in Heavy Manufacturing*, Global Initiatives Mgmt., Winter 2001, http://www.arcci.org/publications/Kellogg Papers/ManufacturinginRussia.htm (last visited Oct. 25, 2008).
37. *Id.*

The gray market presents a specific challenge for brand owners. After the fall of communism, for example, Ford Motor Company (Ford) decided that its Focus would be a popular car in Russia.[38] The Focus was already popular in Europe; with a few modifications to better suit the vehicle for Russia's winters, the Focus would be made available to Russian consumers. Ford's initial strategy was to import the vehicle from its manufacturing plant in Germany. However, Russia's steep import duties would have made the car too expensive for most Russians. Therefore, Ford invested $100 million in a manufacturing plant in Vsevolozhsk to build Russian Focuses in Russia.

By the turn of the century, Ford faced many challenges in its Focus strategy. Among the top challenges was "the huge gray market for new and used automobiles."[39] Because of lax duty enforcement, gray marketers were able to illegally import new or used vehicles from Europe without paying any duty. As a result, these lower priced gray market cars were able to beat the prices Ford offered for its Russian-made Focuses.[40] Fortunately, the demand for cars has steadily increased; in August 2008, "Russia's car market overtook Germany . . . as the biggest in Europe."[41] And, "Ford [was] its leading brand."[42] By 2007, Ford was increasing its annual production of Focuses from 72,000 to 100,000.[43]

Efforts to combat the gray market in Russia remain vital to a brand owner's viability. Similar to Ford, GM saw an opportunity in Russia and established sales outlets in Russia in an effort to counter the gray market importation of its vehicles:

> GM had changed some of its business practices in the U.S. regarding Hummer in an effort to curb the Hummer gray market trade, such as offering incentives on leasing instead of purchases to make it more difficult for the Hummer to leave the country. GM also told its U.S. Hummer dealers to be on guard for certain warning signs that would indicate customers were likely buying Hummers for gray market export. Paying cash is the biggest red flag.[44]

---

38. *Id.*
39. *Id.*
40. *Id.*
41. Maria Antonova, *A Generation Later, Russians Still Waiting For Their Cars*, MOSCOW TIMES, Aug. 4, 2008, *available at* http://www.iht.com/articles/2008/08/04/ business/auto.php.
42. Dietwald Claus, *Ford Adds Modeo to its Product Range in Russia*, Dec. 7, 2007, *available at* http://www.mnweekly.ru/business/20070712/55261715.html.
43. *Id.*
44. Michelle Krebs, *One of Russia's Richest Men Talks to GM about Buying Hummer, Report Says*, EDMONDS AUTOOBSERVER, Aug. 14, 2008, *available at* http://www.autoobserver.com/2008/08/one-of-russias-richest-men-talks-to-gm-about-buying-hummer-report-says.html.

In addition to brand owners, Russian authorities are beginning to show signs of combating the gray market importation of unauthorized goods. In December 2007, the *Moscow News* reported that Russian authorities decided to combat the illegal importation of electronic goods by passing a resolution that temporarily suspended all import duties on digital cameras and cellular-phone components.[45] The measure was designed to prevent the advantages gray marketers receive when they illegally import goods and avoid these duties. By putting authorized and unauthorized importers on equal footing, gray marketers were not able to undercut the prices of its authorized competitors.

Although progress is being made, brand owners must be diligently cognizant of the potential hazards of manufacturing and selling in Russia. Although the country has bountiful qualities inviting to business, brand owners electing to participate in Russian commerce must take vigilant efforts to protect their brands.

e. China

A Chinese trader who has lived in Japan for three years says trademark violation is nothing more than a legal concept in a capitalist society. "Forged cigarettes don't kill people. Chinese who manufacture them never feel a sense of guilt," the trader said.[46]

China is constantly being featured in the news as a chronic and notorious abuser of intellectual property. From food[47] to car tires,[48] China is under a chronic indictment for its failure to acknowledge and combat intellectual property abuses. Making the harm even more problematic is the lack of a reliable legal system where rights can be adequately adjudicated and enforced.[49] Indeed, some see China's IP enforcement efforts as window dressing devoid of real substance:

> The Chinese government and some Chinese companies appear to have an interesting philosophy about piracy. They point to their robust laws

---

45. Igor Korolyov, *Crackdown on 'Gray Market' Goods*, Moscow Times, Dec. 7, 2007, *available at* http://www.mnweekly.ru/business/20070712/55261663.html.
46. *Chinese villages produce fake cigarettes for Japan*, Asian Economic News, Aug. 7, 2000, *available at* http://findarticles.com/p/articles/mi_m0WDP/is_2000_August_7 /ai_63946759.
47. Nicholas Zamiska, *Who's Monitoring Chinese Food Exports?*, Wall St. J., Apr. 9, 2007.
48. David Barboza and Andrew Martin, *Chinese Tire Maker Denies Defective Work, and Sees an Effort to Undercut its Exports*, N.Y. Times, June 27, 2007, at C3 (the safety feature was designed to prevent tire separation).
49. Richard S. Post & Penelope N. Post, Global Brand Integrity Management 58 (2008).

on intellectual property, show attempts at enforcement with a televised raid of a market stall, and describe their involvement in the issue by lending you education materials for high schools on the importance of respecting intellectual property. Piracy, they claim, is not to be tolerated. Yet the reality is that not only is piracy tolerated, but also the government typically turns a blind eye to allow the benefits of piracy to accrue to Chinese consumers. These cheaper products, it is argued, provide the Chinese population with the luxury items they desire but may not be able to afford.[50]

Although the present state of intellectual property protection is grim, there is reason for cautious optimism. After all, in 1886 the United States refused to sign the Berne Convention because it felt that, as a developing country, it was entitled to benefit from the creations in the more developed world.[51] As the United States evolved to become the most prodigious innovator, it established a legal system to protect and encourage innovation: "No country respects and protects intellectual property better than America."[52]

As China undergoes a similar evolution, its government will have no choice but to create an environment that protects innovation.[53] There are already signs of progress. On December 11, 2001, China joined the World Trade Organization. With its membership, Beijing agreed to follow the same global rules governing imports, exports, and foreign investments that most countries follow. China's Quality Brands Protection Committee (QBPC), an international brand-holder coalition, has observed increases in criminal enforcement against counterfeiters "mainly due to an increased willingness by local and national police to accept their cases and devote the required manpower."[54]

In addition, the consulting firm Interbrand predicts that several Chinese firms will be among the top global brands within the next five years.[55] Some Chinese brands are already emerging as big players in the world marketplace. Chinese appliance-maker Haier Group (Haier) is now the fourth-largest maker of major appliances in the world.[56] With $1.4 billion in sales, Haier has

---

50. Howard L. Berman, *Intellectual Property Theft in China and Russia*, Hearing before the Subcommittee on Courts, the Internet, and Intellectual Property of the Committee on the Judiciary House of Representatives, 109th Congress, First Session, May 17, 2005, 109–34, *available at* http://commdocs.house.gov/committees/judiciary/hju21217.000/ hju21217_0.htm.
51. HOPKINS, *supra* note 11, at 135.
52. FRIEDMAN, *supra* note 2, at 333.
53. Butterfield et al., *supra* note 14 (citing TODD FURNISS, CHINA, THE NEXT BIG WAVE IN OFFSHORE OUTSOURCING (Outsourcing Center 2003)).
54. *See* DAVID M. HOPKINS ET AL., COUNTERFEITING EXPOSED 234 (2003).
55. Anthony Lin, *A Haier Power*, IP LAW AND BUS., Apr. 2008, *available at* http://www.iplawandbusiness.law.com/display.php/file=/texts/0408/haier
56. *Id.*

ambitions to be as recognizable as Samsung and General Electric.[57] For such a brand to succeed, protection is imperative. When discussing brand protection, Haier's in-house attorney's strategy is no different than the recommended strategy for American brand owners:

> Su [Xiaoxi] says Haier combats counterfeiters by training both its own staff and sales agents to spot and report fakes. The company keeps a close eye on its distribution channels, says Su, ensuring that its products are only available in China through its network of authorized retailers.... Haier also says the government, specifically the State Administration on Industry and Commerce, has taken strong action on Haier's behalf.

Other commentators agree that China's innovation is the real impetus behind its increased efforts to protect intellectual property: "The emergence of Chinese intellectual property and the globalization of Chinese business are responsible for a greater willingness to protection intellectual property rights, at least for the Chinese, and are proving to be far more effective than any U.S. pressure to control IP theft."[58]

Although many remain dubious of China's ability to turn itself around with respect to the protection of intellectual property, it is worth considering the speed at which China has established itself as a world economic power: "[T]wenty-five years ago [China] was still emerging from the chaos of the Cultural Revolution and decades of turmoil under Mao Tse-tung. Within a single generation, China has become one of the most important trading powers in the world."[59]

f. India

Like China, India has established itself as a country with strong and recent ambitions to participate in the global marketplace. With a large population of educated and inexpensive employees, India has been the benefactor of countless multinational companies outsourcing everything from troubleshooting hotlines to software design work. With several political and governmental reforms aimed at freeing its citizenry taking place, India has grown at similar rates as China in recent years.[60]

---

57. Id.
58. POST, supra note 49, at 19.
59. JEFFREY D. SACHS, THE END OF POVERTY 17 (Penguin Books 2006) (2005).
60. FRIEDMAN, supra note 2, at 181.

Again, like China, because India is a developing economy, it is a neophyte with respect to intellectual property protection. Some brand owners have delayed or refused to sell their products in India. Similar to Russia, India has high import taxes. As a result, many imported goods are out of reach to most Indians.[61] Apple is a recent example: "Indians have a taste for all things Apple. But it's a taste very few can satisfy since all imported computer goods are so heavily taxed they are out of reach to all but the most affluent Indians."[62] As a result of the goods becoming too expensive, a burgeoning gray market has been created, causing Apple to have some reluctance to selling in India:

> Even though demand for iPods is as great in India as anywhere else in the world, Apple seems to have cold feet about expanding its presence in the country. In May, Apple closed down its only call center in Bangalore and halted plans to hire 3,000 new employees by 2007. Though Apple said only that it had "re-evaluated" its plans in India, it appears that high taxes, a strong gray market and a thriving environment for Windows systems have given the company pause.[63]

Today, enforcing intellectual property rights in India is a hopeless endeavor[64] India's "IT Act" is a set of statutes that covers theft of information, but only when an Indian citizen or company was the direct victim![65] Outsiders operating within India or contracting among parties in India do not enjoy the same protections.[66] However, realizing the necessity to protect intellectual property to adequately participate in the global marketplace, India became a signatory to the TRIPS agreement, signifying a willingness to standardize intellectual property protections with the rest of the world. As India evolves to an innovating nation, a transformation to genuinely protect intellectual property is inevitable.

---

61. Scott Carney, *iPod Gray Market Booms in India*, WIRED, Aug. 23, 2006, *available at* http://www.wired.com/gadgets/mac/news/2006/08/71639.
62. *Id.*
63. *Id.*
64. POST, *supra* note 49, at 58.
65. Michael Fitzgerald, *At Risk Offshore*, CIO MAGAZINE, November 15, 2003, fn. 1 (quoting Elliot Turrini, an attorney working for McElroy, Deutsch & Mulvaney).
66. *Id.*

Table of Cases

3 Lab, Inc. v. Kim, 2007 WL 2177513 (D.N.J. 2007) 100
151 East Post Road Corp., Mamoroneck Ave. Corp. v., 78 N.Y.2d 88 (1991) 187

A. Bourjois & Co. v. Katzel, 260 U.S. 689 (1923) 252, 254, 259
A. Bourjois & Co. v. Katzel, 275 F. 539 (2d Cir. 1921) 247–249
A. Genderson & Sons, Inc., Adolph Coors Co. v., 386 F. Supp. 131
   (D. Col. 1980) 265, 266, 269
Aapata Off-Shore Co., M/S Bremen v., 407 U.S. 1 (1972) 92
Abercrombie & Fitch v. Fashion Shops of Kentucky, Inc, 363 F. Supp. 2d 952
   (S.D. Ohio 2005) 16
Adams Golf, Inc., In re, No. 199CV00371 (D. Del. 2008) 69
Adams Golf, Inc. Securities Litigation, 381 F.3d 267 (3d Cir. 2004) 68
Adobe Systems, SoftMan Products v., 171 F. Supp. 2d 1075 (C.D. Cal. 2001) 230
Adobe Systems Inc. v. One Stop Micro, Inc., 84 F. Supp. 2d 1086
   (N.D. Cal. 2000) 230
Adobe Systems v. Stargate Software, 216 F. Supp. 2d 1051 (N.D. Cal. 2002) 230
Adolph Coors Co. v. A. Genderson & Sons, Inc., 386 F. Supp. 131
   (D. Col. 1980) 265, 266, 269
Adventure Outdoors, Inc. v. Bloomberg, 519 F. Supp. 2d 1258
   (N.D.Ga. 2007) 205
Agricultural Servs. Assoc. v. Ferry-Morse Seed, 551 F.2d 1057 (6th Cir. 1977) 287
Alan's of Atlanta, Inc. v. Minolta Corp, 903 F.2d 1414 (11th Cir. 1990) 41, 42
Alleghany Pharmacal Corp. v. Parbel of Florida, Inc., 226 A.D.2d 104
   (N.Y. 1996) 97, 188
Allied Van Lines, Knowlton v., 900 F.2d 1196 (8th Cir. 1990) 160
Allstate Ins. Co., Jazzabi v., 278 F.3d 979 (9th Cir. 2002) 158
Allstate Ins. Co., Top Serv. Body Shop, Inc. v., 582 P.2d 1365
   (Or. 1978) 201, 202, 205
Alvord and Swift v. Stewart M. Muller Constr. Co., Inc., 385 N.E.2d 1238
   (N.Y. 1978) 193
Alyeska Pipeline Serv. Co., Totem Marine Tub & Barge, Inc. v., 584 P.2d 15
   (Alaska 1978) 189
Alyeska Pipeline Serv. Co. v. Wilderness Soc'y, 421 U.S. 240 (1975) 95, 190
Am. Broad. Cos., Iowa State Univ. Research Found., Inc. v., 621 F.2d 57
   (2nd Cir. 1980) 233
Am. Can Co. v. Mansukhari, 742 F.2d 314 (7th Cir. 1984) 170

Am. HomeProds v. Reliance Trading Co., 2000 WL 1263465
(C.D. Cal. 2000) 286
American Biomedical Group, Inc., McCurdy Group LLC v.,
639 N.W. 2d 455 (N.D. 2002)...179
Amoco Egypt Oil Co. v. Leonis Navigation Co., Inc., 1 F.3d 848
(9th Cir. 1993)..161
A&M Records, Inc. v. Napster, Inc., 239 F.3d 1004 (9th Cir. 2001)......... 235, 236
Andrews, M. Kramer Mfg. Co. v., 783 F.2d 421 (4th Cir. 1986).................215
Andros Compania Maritima, S.A. (March Rich & Co.), Matter of,
579 F.2d 691 (2d Cir. 1978).. 149, 149
Anheuser-Busch, Inc., Chemical Corp. of Am. v., 306 F.2d 433
(5th Cir. 1962)..286
AnnTaylor, Inc., Coach Leatherware Co. v., 933 F.2d 162 (2d Cir.1991) 260
Anthony v. Yahoo!, Inc., 421 F. Supp. 2d 1257 (N.D. Cal. 2006) 184
Apollinaris Co. v. Scherer, 27 F. 18 (C.C.N.Y. 1886) 21, 246, 247
Apple Corp. v. Int'l Collectors Soc'y, 15 F. Supp. 2d 456 (D.N.J. 1998)...... 136, 138
Architects & Contractors Estimating Serv., Inc. v. Smith, 164 Cal.
App. 3d 1001 (1985)...189
Arctic Sales, Inc., Midwest Motor Sports v., 347 F.3d 693 (8th Cir. 2003) ... 137, 138
Associated Distribs., Inc., Broan Mfg. Co. v., 923 F.2d 1232 (6th Cir. 1991) 287
Autodesk, Inc., Vernor v., 555 F. Supp. 2d 1164 (W.D. Wa. 2008) 231, 232

Bankers Life & Casualty Co., Professional Golfers Association of
America v., 514 F.2d 665 (5th Cir. 1975) 266
BASIS Int'l, Ltd., EDIAS Software Int'l, L.L.C. v., 947 F. Supp. 413
(D. Az. 1996)...162
Bathalter, National Acceptance Co. v., 705 F.2d 924 (7th Cir. 1983)..............155
Bayer Corp. v. Custom School Frames, LLC, 259 F. Supp. 2d (E.D.La. 2003) 238
BDO Seidman v. Hirshberg, 93 N.Y.2d 382, 712 N.E.2d 1220 (N.Y. 1999).........93
Bear Stearns & Co., Pac. Gas & Elec. Co. v., 791 P.2d 587 (Cal. 1990)............194
Bell ExpressVu Ltd. P'ship v. Rex, [2002] 2 S.C.R. 559 (Can.) 22, 22
BellSouth Telcomms., Inc., Dial One of the Mid-South, Inc. v., 269 F.3d 523
(5th Cir. 2001)..287
Benguet Consol. Mining Co., Perkins v., 342 U.S. 437 (1952) 161
Bernard v. Las Americas Commc'ns, Inc., 84 F.3d 103 (2d Cir. 1995)............185
Bethea v. Comcast, 218 F.R.D. 328 (D.D.C. 2003) 179
Bhd. of R.R. Trainmen, Denver & Rio Grande W. R.R. Co. v.,
387 U.S. 556 (1967) 163
B&H Photo, Osawa & Co. v., 589 F. Supp. 1163 (S.D.N.Y. 1984)..... 21, 50, 275, 276
Binns v. Flaster Greenberg, P.C., 480 F. Supp. 2d 773 (E.D.Pa. 2007)....... 200, 201
Bloomberg, Adventure Outdoors, Inc. v., 519 F. Supp. 2d 1258
(N.D.Ga. 2007)...205
Blue Bell, Inc. v. Western Glove Works Ltd., 816 F. Supp. 236
(S.D.N.Y. 1993).. 149, 150
Bobbs-Merrill Co. v. Straus, 210 U.S. 339 (1908) 225
Bobrick Washroom Equip., Santana Prods., Inc. v., 401 F.3d 123
(3d Cir. 2005) 201

Bourdeau Bros., Inc. v. International Trade Com'n,
　444 F.3d 1317 (Fed. Cir. 2006) 4, 147, 148, 285, 286
Brand Name Beds, LLC, Dan-Foam v., 500 F. Supp. 2d 296
　(S.D.N.Y. 2007)....................... 65, 80, 81, 85, 86, 91, 273, 274, 281, 282
Braunstein, United States v., 281 F.3d 982 (9th Cir. 2002) 40, 42, 43, 62, 87–89
Broad. Info. Serv., Inc., NBC Subsidiary (KCNC-TV), Inc. v., 717 F.
　Supp. 1449 (D.Co. 1988) 211
Broan Mfg. Co. v. Associated Distribs., Inc., 923 F.2d 1232
　(6th Cir. 1991)..287
Buckaloo v. Johnson, 537 P.2d 865 (Cal. 1975) 193, 200
Builders Corp. of Am. v. United States, 148 F. Supp 482
　(N.D.Cal. 1957)..199
Burger King Corp. v. Rudzewicz, 471 U.S. 462 (1985)........................161
Burnham v. Sup. Ct., 495 U.S. 604 (1990) 160

C3, Inc. v. United States, 4 Cl.Ct 790 (1984) 156
CAL Circuit Abco, NEC Electronics v., 810 F.2d 1506
　(9th Cir. 1987) 115, 252, 253, 277, 284
California Pac. Med. Ctr., Miller v., 991 F.2d 536 (9th Cir. 1993) 170
California v. Greenwood, 486 U.S. 35 (1988)........................... 140, 141
Campaniello Imports, Ltd., Gidatex v., 82 F. Supp. 2d 119
　(S.D.N.Y. 1999)... 135, 137, 138
Canon USA, Inc., P & S Business Machines, Inc. v., 331 F.3d 804
　(11th Cir. 2003)...92
Capital City Micro, Inc, Hewlett-Packard Co. v., 2006 WL 149034
　(M.D.Tenn. 2006).. 127, 128
Carnival Cruise Lines, Inc. v. Shute, 499 U.S. 585 (1991) 92, 163
Carol Wright Sales, Inc., Wildlife Express Corp. v., 18 F.3d 502
　(7th Cir. 1994)...211
Carroll v. President and Commissioners of Princes Anne, 393 U.S. 175
　(1968)..165
Cartier, Inc., K Mart Corp. v., 485 U.S. 176 (1988).................. 250, 252, 254
Cartier, Inc., K Mart Corp. v., 486 U.S. 281 (1988)............... 226, 249, 285, 286
Casa Helvetia, Inc., Société Des Produits Nestlé, S.A. v.,
　982 F.2d 633 (1st Cir. 1992) 18, 255, 260–263, 276, 277
Caterpillar, Inc., Intercont'l Parts, Inc. v., 631 N.E.2d 1258
　(Ill. App. Ct. 1994) 204
Chamberlain v. Ford Motor Co., 2003 WL 25751413 slip op. at
　*5 (N.D.Cal. 2003) 290
Chambers v. Time Warner, Inc., 282 F.3d 147 (2d Cir. 2002) 255
Chemical Corp. of Am. v. Anheuser-Busch, Inc., 306 F.2d 433
　(5th Cir. 1962)...286
Cherry Auction, Inc., Fonovisa, Inc. v., 76 F.3d 259 (9th Cir. 1996) 33
Chicago Bd. of Educ. v. Substance, Inc., 354 F.3d 624 (7th Cir. 2003)............234
Chris Johnson Equip., Inc., Hyundai Constr. Equip. U.S.A., Inc. v.,
　2008 WL 4210785, slip op. (N.D. Illinois 2008)....................... 290, 295
Cigarettes Cheaper!, R.J. Reynolds Tobacco Co. v., 462 F.3d 690
　(7th Cir. 2006)... 14, 272

Cigarettes for Less, Philip Morris Inc. v., 69 F. Supp. 2d 1181
  (N.D. Cal. 1999) 286
Cisneros, United States v., 203 F.3d 333 (5th Cir. 2000) 154
City of Milwaukee, Ziegman Productions Inc. v., 496 F. Supp. 965
  (D.C. Wis. 1980)..170
Cmty. for Creative Non-Violence v. Reid, 490 U.S. 730 (1989) 210
Coach Leatherware Co. v. AnnTaylor, Inc., 933 F.2d 162 (2d Cir.1991)..........260
Columbia Broadcasting Systems, Inc. v. Scorpio, 569 F. Supp. 47
  (E.D. Pa. 1983) 219, 224
Comcast, Bethea v., 218 F.R.D. 328 (D.D.C. 2003)..........................179
Compaq Computer Corporation, Computech International, Inc. v.,
  2002 WL 31398933 (S.D.N.Y. 2002) 186, 187
Compusource Distributors, Inc., Microsoft v., 115 F. Supp. 2d 800
  (E.D. Mich. 2000).. 21, 189, 236, 237, 240
Computech International, Inc. v. Compaq Computer Corporation,
  2002 WL 31398933 (S.D.N.Y. 2002) 186, 187
Consumer Contacts Ltd., International, Inc. v., 847 F.2d 1093
  (3d Cir. 1988) 83
Consumer Contacts (PTY) Ltd., Sebastian International v.,
  847 F.2d 1093 (3d Cir. 1988) 184, 222–224
Cosmair v. Dynamite Enterprises, 1985 WL 2209 (S.D. Fla.) 222
Cosmetic Gallery, Inc., Matrix Essentials, Inc. v., 870 F. Supp. 1237
  (D.N.J. 1994) 194, 195
Costco Wholesale Corporation, Disenos Artisticos E Industriales,
  S.A. v., 97 F.3d 377 (9th Cir. 1996) 217, 218
Coty, Inc. v. LeBlume Import Co., Inc., 292 F. 264 (S.D.N.Y. 1923) 260
Coty, Prestonettes, Inc. v., 264 U.S. 359 (1924) 154, 248, 283
Custom School Frames, LLC, Bayer Corp. v., 259 F. Supp. 2d
  (E.D.La. 2003) 238
CVS Corp., Zino Davidoff SA v., 2007 WL 1933932 (S.D.N.Y. 2007) 91, 172

Dal International Trading Co., Johnson Products, Inc. v., 798 F.2d 100
  (3d Cir. 1986) 84, 104, 105
Dan-Foam v. Brand Name Beds, LLC, 500 F. Supp. 2d 296
  (S.D.N.Y. 2007) 65, 80, 81, 85, 86, 91, 273, 274, 281, 282
Darby Dental Supply, Inc., Premier Dental Products Company v.,
  794 F.2d 850 (3d Cir. 1986) 258, 260
Dash, Weil Ceramics & Glass, Inc. v., 618 F. Supp. 700 (D.N.J. 1985) 260
Dash, Weil Ceramics & Glass, Inc. v., 878 F.2d 659 (3d Cir. 1989) 253, 254, 285
Daval Steel Products v. M/V Fakredine, 951 F. 2d 1357 (1991) 181
Davidoff & CIE, S.A. v. PLD International Corporation 262, 262, 263, 263
DC Comics, Inc. v. Reel Fantasy, Inc., 696 F.2d 24 (2nd Cir. 1982) 233
Deborah Heart & Lung Found.v.Children of the World Found.,
  99 F. Supp. 2d 481 (D.N.J.2000) 245, 245
Deerfield Specialty, Golden Quality Ice Cream Co., Inc. v.,
  87 F.R.D. 53 (D.C.Pa. 1980) 157
Dees, Fisher v., 794 F.2d 432 (9th Cir. 1986) 235

Dell, Inc. v. This Old Store, Inc., 2007 WL 2903845, slip op. at 1
  (S.D.Tex. 2007) 202, 205
Della Penna v. Toyota Motor Sales, U.S.A., Inc., 902 P.2d 740
  (Cal. 1995) 200, 203, 205
Denckla, Hanson v., 357 U.S. 235 (1958) 161
Dental Products Co., Smith v., 140 F.2d 140 (7th Cir. 1944) 242
Denver & Rio Grande W. R.R. Co. v. Bhd. of R.R. Trainmen,
  387 U.S. 556 (1967) 163
DEP Corp. v. Interstate Cigar Company, Inc., 622 F.2d 621
  (2d Cir. 1980) 256, 257
Depinet, First Tech. Safety Sys., Inc. v., 11 F.3d 641 (6th Cir. 1993) 167
Deutz Ag, Gen. Elec. Co. v., 270 F.3d 144 (3d Cir. 2001) 93
Dial Corp. v. Encina Corp., 643 F. Supp. 951 (S.D. Fla. 1986) 277
Dial One of the Mid-South, Inc. v. BellSouth Telcomms., Inc.,
  269 F.3d 523 (5th Cir. 2001) 287
Diamond & Gem Trading USA, Martin's Herend Imports v.,
  112 F.3d 1296 (5th Cir.1997) 168, 260–263, 287
Diasonics, R. E. Davis Chem. Corp. v., 826 F.2d 678 (7th Cir. 1987) 195
Disenos Artisticos E Industriales, S.A. v. Costco Wholesale
  Corporation, 97 F.3d 377 (9th Cir. 1996) 217, 218
District of Columbia, Horn v., 210 F.R.D. 13 (2002) 157
Does Nos. 1–2, Time Warner Entm't Co. v., 876 F. Supp. 407
  (E.D.N.Y. 1994) 168
Dowling v. United States, 473 U.S. 207 (1985) 219
Dresser, SEC v., 628 F.2d 1368 (D.C. Cir. 1980) 156
Drug Emporium, Inc., Parfums Givenchy, Inc. v., 38 F.3d 477
  (9th Cir. 1994) 16, 210, 221
DSC Commc'n Corp. v. Pulse Commc'n, Inc., 170 F.3d 1354
  (Fed. Cir. 1999) 229
Dynamite Enterprises, Cosmair v., 1985 WL 2209 (S.D. Fla.) 222

E. I. Du Pont Nemours & Co., Hoffman Co. v., 202 Cal. App. 3d 390
  (Cal. Ct. App. 1988) 204
E. Leitz, Inc. v. Watson, 152 F. Supp. 631 (D.D.C. 1957) 259
EBay Inc., Hendrickson v., 165 F. Supp. 2d 1082 (C.D. Cal. 2001) 33, 303
Edberg v. Neoge Corp., 17 F. Supp. 2d 104 (D.C. 1998) 162
EDIAS Software Int'l, L.L.C. v. BASIS Int'l, Ltd., 947 F. Supp. 413
  (D. Az. 1996) 162
Effron v. Sun Line Cruises, Inc., 67 F.3d 7 (2nd Cir. 1995) 92
Eighty-Three Rolex Watches, United States v., 992 F.2d 508 (5th Cir. 1993) 170
El Greco Leather Products Company, Inc. v. Shoe World, Inc. 266, 266, 268,
                                                                       268, 269, 269
Elizabeth Lincoln Mercury, Inc. v. Jones, 313 Ky. 321 (1950) 186
Emich Motors v. General Motors, 340 U.S. 558 (1951) 156
Emmanuel Coll., Shea v., 682 N.E.2d 1348 (Mass. 1997) 193
Emporium Drug Mart, Inc., Graham Webb International Limited
  Partnership v., 916 F. Supp. 909 (E.D. Ark. 1995) 202, 203, 205, 278, 279

Emporium Drug Mart, Inc., Matrix Essentials, Inc. v., 988 F.2d 587
   (5th Cir. 1993) 268, 269, 277
Encina Corp., Dial Corp. v., 643 F. Supp. 951 (S.D. Fla. 1986) 277
EPA, Indep. Equip. Dealers Ass'n v., 372 F.3d 420 (2004) 75
Erickson, Fournier v., 202 F. Supp. 2d 290 (S.D.N.Y. 2002) 212
Estes-El v. Long Island Jewish Med. Ctr., 916 F. Supp. 268 (S.D.N.Y. 1995) 156
E*TRADE Securities LLC v. Deutsche Bank AG, 2005 U.S. U.S. Dist.
   LEXIS 3038 (D.C. Minn. Jan. 31, 2005) 179
Euro-Excellence Inc. v. Kraft Canada Inc., 2007 SCC 37 (Can.) 300

Faber, Menendez v., 345 F. Supp. 527 (S.D.N.Y. 1972) 266
Fagan v. AmerisourceBergen Corp, 164 Fed.Appx. 37,
   2006 WL 151807 (2d Cir.) 23
Faltings et al. v. International Business Machines Corp., 854 F.2d 1316,
   1988 WL 83316 (4th Cir. 1988) (Unpublished) 82, 83
Fashion Shops of Kentucky, Inc, Abercrombie & Fitch v.,
   363 F. Supp. 2d 952 (S.D. Ohio 2005) 16
Federated Rural Elec. Ins. Corp. v. Kootenai Elec. Co-op, 17 F.3d 1302
   (10th Cir. 1994) 162
Feist Publ'n, Inc. v. Rural Tel. Serv. Co., 499 U.S. 340 (1991) 209
Ferrero U.S.A., Inc. v. Ozark Trading, Inc., 753 F. Supp. 1240 (D.N.J.) 260
Ferrero U.S.A. Inc. v. Ozark Trading, Inc., 952 F.2d 44
   (3d Cir. 1991) 272, 273, 277
Ferry-Morse Seed, Agricultural Servs. Assoc. v., 551 F.2d 1057
   (6th Cir. 1977) 287
First Tech. Safety Sys., Inc. v. Depinet, 11 F.3d 641 (6th Cir. 1993) 167
Fisher v. Dees, 794 F.2d 432 (9th Cir. 1986) 235
Fjeld Mfg., Milwaukee Concrete Studios, Ltd. v., 8 F.3d 441
   (7th Cir. 1993) 163
Flaster Greenberg, P.C., Binns v., 480 F. Supp. 2d 773 (E.D.Pa. 2007) 200, 201
Fleischmann Distilling Corp. v. Maier Brewing Co.,
   386 U.S. 714 (1967) 95, 190
Fonovisa, Inc. v. Cherry Auction, Inc., 76 F.3d 259 (9th Cir. 1996) 33
Ford Motor Co., Chamberlain v., 2003 WL 25751413 slip op. at
   *5 (N.D.Cal. 2003) 290
Form-Eze Systems, Inc., John T. Brady & Co. v., 623 F.2d 261 (2d Cir. 1980) 149
Forry, Inc. v. Neundorfer, Inc., 837 F.2d 259 (6th Cir. 1988) 158
Fournier v. Erickson, 202 F. Supp. 2d 290 (S.D.N.Y. 2002) 212
Frena, Playboy Enters. v., 839 F. Supp. 1552 (M.D. Fla. 1993) 245

Gamut Trading Co. v. U.S. Int'l Trade Com'n, 200 F.3d 775 (Fed. Cir. 1999) 148
Gardner v. Nike, Inc., 279 F.3d 774 (9th Cir. 2002) 229
Gatson's White River Resort v. Rush, 701 F. Supp. 1431 (W.D. Ark. 1988) 286
Gen. Elec. Co. v. Deutz Ag, 270 F.3d 144 (3d Cir. 2001) 93
General Motors, Emich Motors v., 340 U.S. 558 (1951) 156
Gidatex v. Campaniello Imports, Ltd., 82 F. Supp. 2d 119
   (S.D.N.Y. 1999) 135, 137, 138
Giles, United States v., 213 F.3d 1247 (19th Cir. 2000) 154

Golden Quality Ice Cream Co., Inc. v. Deerfield Specialty, 87 F.R.D. 53
  (D.C.Pa. 1980) 157
Goold Elec. Corp., W. Microtechnology, Inc. v., 1993 WL 424244, slip op.
  at *2 (N.D.Ill. 1993) 195
Goss, United States v., 803 F.2d 638 (11th Cir. 1986) 215
Graham Webb International Limited Partnership v. Emporium
  Drug Mart, Inc., 916 F. Supp. 909 (E.D. Ark. 1995) 202, 203, 205, 278, 279
Granada Electronics, Inc., Original Appalachian Artworks, Inc. v.,
  816 F.2d 68 (2d Cir. 1987) 85, 171, 256, 261, 263
Green v. United States, 355 U.S. 184 (1957) 156
Greenwood, California v., 486 U.S. 35 (1988) 140, 141
Grokster, Ltd., MGM Studios Inc. v., 545 U.S. 913 (2005) 231
GTFM, Inc. v. Wal-Mart Stores, Inc., No. 98 Civ. 7724,
  2000 U.S. Dist. LEXIS 3804 (S.D.N.Y. 2000) 182
Guaranty Bank & Trust Co. v. Kaminsky, 356 A.2d 909
  (Conn. Super. 1976) 294

Hampton v. Paramount Pictures Corp., 279 F.2d 100 (9th Cir. 1960) 189, 236
Hanafy, United States v., 124 F. Supp. 2d at 1016 (N.D. Tex. 2000) 153, 154
Hanafy, United States v., 302 F.3d 485 (5th Cir. 2002) 18, 53, 55, 155
Hanson v. Denckla, 357 U.S. 235 (1958) 161
Harper & Row, Publishers, Inc. v. Nation Enter., 471 U.S. 539 (1985) 234
Hasbro, Inc. v. Lanard Toys, Ltd., 858 F.2d 70 (2d Cir. 1988) 171
Haskel Trading, Inc., Monsanto Co. v., 13 F. Supp. 2d 349 (E.D.N.Y. 1998) 154
Hayden Co. of N.Y., Inc. v. Siemens Medical Systems, Inc.,
  879 F.2d 1005 (2d Cir. 1989) 269
Hearst Corp. v. Stark, 639 F. Supp. 970 (N.D. Cal. 1986) 220, 221, 224
Hendrickson v. eBay Inc., 165 F. Supp. 2d 1082 (C.D. Cal. 2001) 33, 303
Herron v. State Farm Mut. Ins. Co., 363 P.2d 310 (Cal. 1961) 196, 204
Hewlett-Packard Co. v. Capital City Micro, Inc, 2006 WL 149034
  (M.D.Tenn. 2006) 127, 128
High-Line Medical Instruments, Summit Technology, Inc. v., 922 F.
  Supp. 299 (C.D. Cal. 1996) 224, 228, 229, 271, 284, 285
Hill, United States v., 171 Fed.Appx. 815 (11th Cir. 2006) 22
Hoffman Co. v. E. I. Du Pont Nemours & Co., 202 Cal. App. 3d 390
  (Cal. Ct. App. 1988) 204
Horn v. District of Columbia, 210 F.R.D. 13 (2002) 157
Howard, Richardson v., 712 F.2d 319 (7th Cir. 1990) 134
HUD, Thomas v., 124 F.3d 1439 (Fed. Cir. 1997) 185
Hustler Magazine v. Falwell, 485 U.S. 46, 52) 204
Hyundai Constr. Equip. U.S.A., Inc. v. Chris Johnson Equip., Inc.,
  2008 WL 4210785, slip op. (N.D. Illinois 2008) 290, 295

Imageline, Inc., Xoom, Inc. v., 323 F.3d 279 (4th Cir. 2003) 211
Imaging Equip. Srvs., Inc., Picker Int'l Corp. v., 931 F. Supp. 18
  (D. Mass. 1995) 228
Indep. Equip. Dealers Ass'n v. EPA, 372 F.3d 420 (2004) 75
Infineon Tech. AG, Inc., Rambus, Inc. v., 222 F.R.D. 280 (E.D. Va. 2004) 180

Inineon Tech. AG, Rambus, Inc. v., 222 F.R.D. 280 (E.D. Va. 2004) 166
In re Adams Golf, Inc., No. 199CV00371 (D. Del. 2008) 69
Intercont'l Parts, Inc. v. Caterpillar, Inc., 631 N.E.2d 1258
 (Ill. App. Ct. 1994)..204
International, Inc. v. Consumer Contacts Ltd., 847 F.2d 1093
 (3d Cir. 1988)...83
International Trade Com'n, Bourdeau Bros., Inc. v., 444 F.3d 1317
 (Fed. Cir. 2006) 4, 147, 148, 285, 286
Interstate Cigar Company, Inc., DEP Corp. v., 622 F.2d 621
 (2d Cir. 1980)... 256, 257
Int'l Collectors Soc'y, Apple Corp. v., 15 F. Supp. 2d 456
 (D.N.J. 1998) 136, 138
Int'l Shoe Co. v. Wash., 326 U.S. 310 (1945)..................................161
Iowa State Univ. Research Found., Inc. v. Am. Broad. Cos., 621 F.2d 57
 (2nd Cir. 1980)..233
Israel v. Wood Dolson Co., 134 N.E.2d 97 (N.Y. 1956)........................192

J. F. Reichert, Inc., Original Appalachian Artworks, Inc. v.,
 658 F. Supp. 458 (E.D. Pa. 1987) 217, 240
Jazzabi v. Allstate Ins. Co., 278 F.3d 979 (9th Cir. 2002).....................158
John Paul Mitchell Systems v. Pete N Larry's Inc., 862 F. Supp. 1020
 (W.D.N.Y. 1994) 15, 279–281
John Paul Mitchell Systems v. Quality King Distributors, Inc., 106 F.
 Supp. 2d 462 (S.D.N.Y. 2000) 195
John Paul Mitchell Systems v. Randalls Food Markets, Inc.,
 S. W. 3d 721 (Tex. App. 2000) 15, 15
Johnson, Buckaloo v., 537 P.2d 865 (Cal. 1975) 193, 200
Johnson Controls, Inc. v. Phoenix Control Sys., Inc. ,
 886 F.2d 1173 (9th Cir. 1989) 210
Johnson Products, Inc. v. Dal International Trading Co.,
 798 F.2d 100 (3d Cir. 1986) 84, 104, 105
Johnson v. Jones, 149 F.3d 494 (6th Cir. 1998)............................212
John T. Brady & Co. v. Form-Eze Systems, Inc., 623 F.2d 261 (2d Cir. 1980) 149
Jones, Elizabeth Lincoln Mercury, Inc. v., 313 Ky. 321 (1950) 186
Jones, Johnson v., 149 F.3d 494 (6th Cir. 1998) 212

Kachmar v. SunGard Data Sys., Inc., 109 F.3d 173 (3d Cir. 1997) 201
Kaminsky, Guaranty Bank & Trust Co. v., 356 A.2d 909
 (Conn. Super. 1976) 294
Katzel, A. Bourjois & Co. v., 260 U.S. 689 (1923).................... 252, 254, 259
Katzel, A. Bourjois & Co. v., 275 F. 539 (2d Cir. 1921) 247–249
KHK Scaffolding Houston Inc., Waco Intern., Inc. v., 278 F.3d 523
 (5th Cir. 2002) 148
Kim, 3 Lab, Inc. v., 2007 WL 2177513 (D.N.J. 2007) 100
Kim, 3 Lab, Inc. v., 2007 WL 2177513 (D.N.J. 2007) 100
King Features Entm't, Inc., United States v., 843 F.2d 394
 (9th Cir. 1988) 235
K Mart Corp. v. Cartier, Inc., 485 U.S. 176 (1988) 250, 252, 254

K Mart Corp. v. Cartier, Inc., 486 U.S. 281 (1988) 226, 249, 285, 286
KNK Tamex Corporation v. Medical-Dental Specialties, Ltd.,
 2000 WL 1470665 (E.D. Pa. 2000) 187, 188
Knowlton v. Allied Van Lines, 900 F.2d 1196 (8th Cir. 1990) 160
Koons, Rogers v., 960 F.2d 301 (2d Cir. 1992) 211
Kootenai Elec. Co-op, Federated Rural Elec. Ins. Corp. v.,
 17 F.3d 1302 (10th Cir. 1994) 162
Kraft Canada Inc., Euro-Excellence Inc. v., 2007 SCC 37 (Can.) 300

Lanard Toys, Ltd., Hasbro, Inc. v., 858 F.2d 70 (2d Cir. 1988) 171
Landis v. N. Am. Co., 299 U.S. 248 (1936) 156
Lanius v. Najman, 472 N.E.2d 170 (Ill. App. Ct. 1984) 193
L'anza Research Intern., Inc., Quality King Distributors, Inc. v.,
 523 U.S. 135 (1998) 225–227, 300
Las Americas Commc'ns, Inc., Bernard v., 84 F.3d 103 (2d Cir. 1995) 185
Lawyers Title Ins. Corp. v. United States Fid. & Guar. Co.,
 122 F.R.D. 567 (1988) 179
LeBlume Import Co., Inc., Coty, Inc. v., 292 F. 264 (S.D.N.Y. 1923) 260
Lefkowitz v. Turley, 414 U.S. 70 (1973) 155
Leonard v. USA Petroleum Corp., 829 F. Supp. 882 (S.D. Tx. 1993) 160
Leonis Navigation Co., Inc., Amoco Egypt Oil Co. v., 1 F.3d 848
 (9th Cir. 1993) 161
Lever Bros. Co. v. United States, 877 F.2d 101 (D.C. Cir. 1989) 255, 277
Lipscher v. LRP Publs., Inc., 266 F.3d 1305 (11th Cir. 2001) 245
Lockheed Info. Mgmt. Sys. Co., Maximus, Inc. v., 493 S.E.2d 375 (Va. 1997) 200
Long Island Jewish Med. Ctr., Estes-El v., 916 F. Supp. 268 (S.D.N.Y. 1995) 156
Longs Drug Stores Corp., Sebastian Intern., Inc. v., 53 F.3d 1073
 (9th Cir. 1995) 283, 284
LRP Publs., Inc., Lipscher v., 266 F.3d 1305 (11th Cir. 2001) 245
Luigino's Inc., Weight Watchers, Int'l, Inc. v., 423 F.3d 137 (2005) 173
Lusk v. Vill. Cold Spring, 475 F. 3d 480 (2d Cir. 2007) 171
Lynn v. Serono Inc, 23, 23

M. Kramer Mfg. Co. v. Andrews, 783 F.2d 421 (4th Cir. 1986);, 215
Maier Brewing Co., Fleischmann Distilling Corp. v., 386 U.S. 714 (1967) . . . 95, 190
MAI Sys. Corp. v. Peak Computer, Inc., 991 F.2d 511 (9th Cir. 1993) 228
Malson, Roth v., 67 Cal. App. 4th 552 (1998) 184
Mamoroneck Ave. Corp. v. 151 East Post Road Corp., 78 N.Y.2d 88 (1991) 187
Mansukhari, Am. Can Co. v., 742 F.2d 314 (7th Cir. 1984) 170
Markowitz, Weil v., 829 F.2d 166 (D.C. Cir. 1987) 156
Martin's Herend Imports v. Diamond & Gem Trading USA,
 112 F.3d 1296 (5th Cir.1997) 168, 260–263, 287
Matrix Essentials, Inc. v. Cosmetic Gallery, Inc., 870 F.
 Supp. 1237 (D.N.J. 1994) 194, 195
Matrix Essentials, Inc. v. Emporium Drug Mart, Inc.,
 988 F.2d 587 (5th Cir. 1993) 268, 269, 277
Matter of Andros Compania Maritima, S.A. (March Rich & Co.),
 579 F.2d 691 (2d Cir. 1978) 149, 149

Maximus, Inc. v. Lockheed Info. Mgmt. Sys. Co.,
   493 S.E.2d 375 (Va. 1997) 200
Mazer v. Stein, 347 U.S. 201 (1954) 51
MCA, Inc. v. Wilson, 677 F.2d 180 (2nd Cir. 1981) 233, 234
McConney, United States v., 728 F. 2d 1195 (9th Cir. 1984) 165
McCurdy Group LLC v. American Biomedical Group, Inc.,
   639 N.W. 2d 455 (N.D. 2002) 179
McKell v. Wash. Mutual, Inc., 142 Cal. App. 4th 1457 (2006) 184
MDY Industries, LLC v. Blizzard Entertainment, Inc., 2008 WL 2757357
   (D. Ariz. July 14, 2008) 231, 232
Medical-Dental Specialties, Ltd., KNK Tamex Corporation v.,
   2000 WL 1470665 (E.D. Pa. 2000) 187, 188
Menendez v. Faber, 345 F. Supp. 527 (S.D.N.Y. 1972) 266
MGM-Pathe Commc'n Co., Subafilms, Ltd. v., 24 F.3d 1088 (9th Cir. 1994) 212
MGM Studios Inc. v. Grokster, Ltd., 545 U.S. 913 (2005) 231
Microsoft v. Compusource Distributors, Inc., 115 F. Supp. 2d 800
   (E.D. Mich. 2000) 21, 189, 236, 237, 240
Midwest Motor Sports v. Arctic Sales, Inc., 347 F.3d 693 (8th Cir. 2003) ... 137, 138
Miller v. California Pac. Med. Ctr., 991 F.2d 536 (9th Cir. 1993) 170
Milwaukee Concrete Studios, Ltd. v. Fjeld Mfg., 8 F.3d 441 (7th Cir. 1993) 163
Mimran ("Polymer I"), Polymer Tech. Corp. v., 37 F.3d 74 (2d Cir. 1994) 172
Minolta Corp, Alan's of Atlanta, Inc. v., 903 F.2d 1414 (11th Cir. 1990) 41, 42
Mishawaka Rubber & Woolen Mfg. Co. v. S.S. Keresge Co.,
   316 U.S. 203 (1942) 263
Monsanto Co. v. Haskel Trading, Inc., 13 F. Supp. 2d 349 (E.D.N.Y. 1998) 154
Montblanc-Simplo GmbH v. Staples, Inc., 172 F. Supp. 2d 231
   (D. Mass. 2001) 238, 239
Monte Carlo Shirt, Inc. v. Daewoo International, Corp................... 267, 267
Morris USA Inc. v. Veles Ltd, 2007 WL 725412 (S.D.N.Y.) 162, 163
M/S Bremen v. Aapata Off-Shore Co., 407 U.S. 1 (1972) 92
Murphy v. Schneider Nat'l, Inc., 362 F.3d 1133 (9th Cir. 2004) 92
M/V Fakredine, Daval Steel Products v., 951 F. 2d 1357 (1991) 181

N. Am. Co., Landis v., 299 U.S. 248 (1936) 156
Najman, Lanius v., 472 N.E.2d 170 (Ill. App. Ct. 1984) 193
Napster, Inc., A&M Records, Inc. v., 239 F.3d 1004 (9th Cir. 2001) 235, 236
National Acceptance Co. v. Bathalter, 705 F.2d 924 (7th Cir. 1983) 155
National Equip. Rental, Ltd. v. Szukhent, 375 U.S. 311 (1964) 160
Nation Enter., Harper & Row, Publishers, Inc. v., 471 U.S. 539 (1985) 234
Nawab, Virgin Enters. Ltd. v., 335 F.3d 141 (2d Cir. 2003) 255
NBC Subsidiary (KCNC-TV), Inc. v. Broad. Info. Serv., Inc., 717 F.
   Supp. 1449 (D.Co. 1988) 211
NEC Electronics v. CAL Circuit Abco, 810 F.2d 1506
   (9th Cir. 1987) 115, 252, 253, 277, 284
Neoge Corp., Edberg v., 17 F. Supp. 2d 104 (D.C. 1998) 162
Netscape Comm'n, Playboy Enter. v., 354 F.3d 1020 (9th Cir. 2004) 245
Neundorfer, Inc., Forry, Inc. v., 837 F.2d 259 (6th Cir. 1988) 158
Neutrogena Corporation v. United States, 1988 WL 166236 (D.S.C.) 223, 224

New City, Inc., Swatch S.A. v., 454 F. Supp. 2d 1245 (S.D. Fla. 2006) 274–276
New York Post Co., Volmar Distribs., Inc. v., 152 F.R.D. 36
  (S.D.N.Y. 1993)) 156
Nike, Inc., Gardner v., 279 F.3d 774 (9th Cir. 2002) 229
Nortel Networks, Inc. v. SMC Electronics, LLC, Case No. 06-CV-00787-RJC
  (W.D. Okl. 2006) 128, 128, 129, 129
Northside Development Corp., Warner-Lambert Co. v.,
  86 F.3d 3 (2d Cir. 1996) 91, 269, 270
Nostalgia Prod. Corp., Pepsico v., 1991 WL 113161 (N.D.Ill.) 18, 277
NY Sound, VAS Indus. v., 2006 WL 1699537 (S.D.N.Y.) 22

Omega S.A. v. Costco Wholesale Corp., 541 F.3d 982
  (9th Cir. Sept. 3, 2008) 19, 20, 227, 300–302
One Stop Micro, Inc., Adobe Systems Inc. v., 84 F. Supp. 2d 1086
  (N.D. Cal. 2000) 230
Oppenheimer Fund, Inc. v. Sanders, 437 U.S. 340 (1978) 180
Original Appalachian Artworks, Inc. v. Granada Electronics, Inc.,
  816 F.2d 68 (2d Cir. 1987) 85, 171, 256, 261, 263
Original Appalachian Artworks, Inc. v. J. F. Reichert, Inc., 658 F. Supp.
  458 (E.D. Pa. 1987) 217, 240
Osawa & Co. v. B&H Photo, 589 F. Supp. 1163 (S.D.N.Y. 1984) 21, 50, 275, 276
Ozark Trading, Inc., Ferrero U.S.A., Inc. v., 753 F. Supp. 1240 (D.N.J.) 260
Ozark Trading, Inc., Ferrero U.S.A. Inc. v., 952 F.2d 44
  (3d Cir. 1991) 272, 273, 277

Pac. Gas & Elec. Co. v. Bear Stearns & Co., 791 P.2d 587 (Cal. 1990) 194
Pall Corp., Porous Media Corp. v., 173 F.3d 1109 (8th Cir. 1999) 287
Panavision Int'l v. Toeppen, 141 F.3d 1316 (9th Cir. 1998) 162
Paramount Pictures Corp., Hampton v., 279 F.2d 100 (9th Cir. 1960) 189, 236
Parbel of Florida, Inc., Alleghany Pharmacal Corp. v., 226 A.D.2d 104
  (N.Y. 1996) 97, 188
Parfums Givenchy, Inc. v. Drug Emporium, Inc., 38 F.3d 477
  (9th Cir. 1994) 16, 210, 221
Peak Computer, Inc., MAI Sys. Corp. v., 991 F.2d 511 (9th Cir. 1993) 228
People v. Superior Court (Shayan), 21 Cal. App. 4th 621 (Cal. Ct. App. 1993) 291
Pepsico v. Nostalgia Prod. Corp., 1991 WL 113161 (N.D.Ill.) 18, 277
Perkins v. Benguet Consol. Mining Co., 342 U.S. 437 (1952) 161
Pete N Larry's Inc., John Paul Mitchell Systems v., 862 F. Supp. 1020
  (W.D.N.Y. 1994) 15, 279–281
Philip Morris Inc. v. Cigarettes for Less, 69 F. Supp. 2d 1181
  (N.D. Cal. 1999) 286
Phoenix Control Sys., Inc., Johnson Controls, Inc. v., 886 F.2d 1173
  (9th Cir. 1989) 210
Phoenix Mining & Mineral, L.L.C. v. Treasury Oil Corp., 2007 WL 951866 at
  *5 (S.D. Tex. 2007) 162
Picker Int'l Corp. v. Imaging Equip. Srvs., Inc., 931 F. Supp. 18
  (D. Mass. 1995) 228
Pike Coal Co., Thompson Coal Co. v., 412 A.2d 466 (PA S.C. 1979) 202

Playboy Enter. v. Netscape Comm'n, 354 F.3d 1020 (9th Cir. 2004) 245
Playboy Enters. v. Frena, 839 F. Supp. 1552 (M.D. Fla. 1993) 245
Polarad Electronics Corp., Polaroid Corp. v., 287 F.2d 492
 (2d Cir. 1961) 256, 281, 282
Polaroid Corp. v. Polarad Electronics Corp., 287 F.2d 492
 (2d Cir. 1961) 256, 281, 282
Polymer Tech. Corp. v. Mimran ("Polymer I"), 37 F.3d 74 (2d Cir. 1994) 172
Pompano Motor Co., Tuckish v., 337 F. Supp. 2d 1313 (S.D. Fla. 2004) 47
Porous Media Corp. v. Pall Corp., 173 F.3d 1109 (8th Cir. 1999) 287
Premier Dental Products Company v. Darby Dental Supply, Inc.,
 794 F.2d 850 (3d Cir. 1986) 258, 260
Premium Tobacco Stores, Inc., R. J. Reynolds Tobacco Co. v.,
 2005 WL 293512 (N.D. Ill. 2005) 240
Premium Tobacco Stores, Inc., R.J. Reynolds Tobacco Co. v.,
 2004 WL 1613563 (N.D. Ill. 2004) 286
President and Commissioners of Princes Anne, Carroll v.,
 393 U.S. 175 (1968) 165
Prestonettes, Inc. v. Coty, 264 U.S. 359 (1924) 154, 248, 283
Prince of Peace Enterprises v. Top Quality Food Market, LLC,
 2007 WL 704171 (S.D.N.Y.) 160
ProCD, Inc. v. Zeinberg, 86 F.3d 1447 (7th Cir. 1996) 229
Procter & Gamble Co., United States v., 356 U.S. 677 (1958) 175
Professional Golfers Association of America v.
 Bankers Life & Casualty Co., 514 F.2d 665 (5th Cir. 1975) 266
P & S Business Machines, Inc. v. Canon USA, Inc., 331 F.3d 804
 (11th Cir. 2003) 92
Publications International, Ty v., 81 F. Supp. 2d 899 (N.D. Ill. 2000) 238
Publ'n Int'l, Ltd., Twin Peaks Prods., Inc. v., 996 F.2d 1366 (2d Cir. 1993) 210
Pulse Commc'n, Inc., DSC Commc'n Corp. v., 170 F.3d 1354
 (Fed. Cir. 1999) 229

Quality King Distributors, Inc., John Paul Mitchell Systems v.,
 106 F. Supp. 2d 462 (S.D.N.Y. 2000) 195
Quality King Distributors, Inc. v. L'anza Research Intern., Inc.,
 523 U.S. 135 (1998) 225–227, 300
Quiksilver Inc. v. Shoe Fantasy, 2005 WL 1274412 (Cal. Ct. App. 2005) 194

R. E. Davis Chem. Corp. v. Diasonics, 826 F.2d 678 (7th Cir. 1987) 195
R. J. Reynolds Tobacco Co. v. Premium Tobacco Stores, Inc.,
 2005 WL 293512 (N.D. Ill. 2005) 240
Railway Exp. Agency Inc. v. Super Scale Models, Ltd.,
 934 F.2d 135 (7th Cir. 1991) 195–197
Rambus, Inc. v. Infineon Tech. AG, Inc., 222 F.R.D. 280 (E.D. Va. 2004) 180
Rambus, Inc. v. Inineon Tech. AG, 222 F.R.D. 280 (E.D. Va. 2004) 166
Red Baron-Franklin Park, Inc. v. Taito Corp.,
 883 F.2d 275 (4th Cir. 1989) 22, 113
Red Baron-Franklin Park, Inc. v. Taito Corporation,
 883 F.2d 275 (4th Cir. 1989) 214

Red Baron-Franklin Park, Inc. v. Taito Corporation,
    883 F.2d 279 (4th Cir. 1989) 215
Reel Fantasy, Inc., DC Comics, Inc. v., 696 F.2d 24 (2nd Cir. 1982) 233
Reid, Cmty. for Creative Non-Violence v., 490 U.S. 730 (1989) 210
Reliance Trading Co., Am. HomeProds v.,
    2000 WL 1263465 (C.D. Cal. 2000) 286
Richardson v. Howard, 712 F.2d 319 (7th Cir. 1990) 134
Rinn Motor Hotels, Superior Motels v., 195 Cal. App. 3d 1032 (1987) 185
R.J. Reynolds Tobacco Co. v. Cigarettes Cheaper!,
    462 F.3d 690 (7th Cir. 2006) 14, 272
R.J. Reynolds Tobacco Co. v. Premium Tobacco Stores, Inc.,
    2004 WL 1613563 (N.D. Ill. 2004) 286
Rogers v. Koons, 960 F.2d 301 (2d Cir. 1992) 211
Roth v. Malson, 67 Cal. App. 4th 552 (1998) 184
Rudzewicz, Burger King Corp. v., 471 U.S. 462 (1985) 161
Rural Tel. Serv. Co., Feist Publ'n, Inc. v., 499 U.S. 340 (1991) 209
Rush, Gatson's White River Resort v., 701 F. Supp. 1431 (W.D. Ark. 1988) 286
Russolillo, Sebastian Int'l, Inc. v., 186 F. Supp. 2d 1055 (C.D.Cal. 2000) 292

Sanders, Oppenheimer Fund, Inc. v., 437 U.S. 340 (1978) 180
San Francisco Arts & Ath. v. United States Olympic Comm.,
    483 U.S. 522 (1987) 244
Santana Prods., Inc. v. Bobrick Washroom Equip.,
    401 F.3d 123 (3d Cir. 2005) 201
Scansteel Serv. Ctr., Inc., Steelvest, Inc. v., 807 S.W.2d 476 (Ky. 1991) 192
Scherer, Apollinaris Co. v., 27 F. 18 (C.C.N.Y. 1886) 21, 246, 247
Schiltgen, Souza v., 1996 WL 241824 (N.D.Cal.) 157
Schmid, Inc. v. Zucker's Gifts, Inc., 766 F. Supp. 118 (S.D.N.Y. 1991) 194
Schneider Nat'l, Inc., Murphy v., 362 F.3d 1133 (9th Cir. 2004) 92
Scorpio, Columbia Broadcasting Systems, Inc. v.,
    569 F. Supp. 47 (E.D. Pa. 1983) 219, 224
Sealed Air Corp. v. U.S. Intern. Trade Com'n, 645 F.2d 976 (C.C.P.A. 1981) 147
Sebastian Intern., Inc. v. Longs Drug Stores Corp.,
    53 F.3d 1073 (9th Cir. 1995) 283, 284
Sebastian International v. Consumer Contacts (PTY) Ltd.,
    847 F.2d 1093 (3d Cir. 1988) 184, 222–224
Sebastian Int'l, Inc. v. Russolillo, 186 F. Supp. 2d 1055 (C.D.Cal. 2000) 292
SEC v. Dresser, 628 F.2d 1368 (D.C. Cir. 1980) 156
Shea v. Emmanuel Coll., 682 N.E.2d 1348 (Mass. 1997) 193
Shell Oil Co. v. Commercial Petroleum, Inc 267, 267, 268, 268,
                                                                269, 269, 271, 271
Shoe Fantasy, Quiksilver Inc. v., 2005 WL 1274412 (Cal. Ct. App. 2005) 194
Shute, Carnival Cruise Lines, Inc. v., 499 U.S. 585 (1991) 92, 163
Siemens Medical Systems, Inc., Hayden Co. of N.Y., Inc. v.,
    879 F.2d 1005 (2d Cir. 1989) 269
SKF USA Inc. v. International Trade Commission 263, 263, 264, 264, 265, 265
Smith, Architects & Contractors Estimating Serv., Inc. v.,
    164 Cal. App. 3d 1001 (1985) 189

Smith v. Dental Products Co., 140 F.2d 140 (7th Cir. 1944) 242
Société Des Produits Nestlé, S.A. v. Casa Helvetia, Inc.,
   982 F.2d 633 (1st Cir. 1992) 18, 255, 260–263, 276, 277
SoftMan Products v. Adobe Systems, 171 F. Supp. 2d 1075 (C.D. Cal. 2001) 230
Sony Corp. of Am. V. Universal City Studios, Inc., 464 U.S. 417 (1984) 233, 233
Souza v. Schiltgen, 1996 WL 241824 (N.D.Cal.) 157
S.S. Keresge Co., Mishawaka Rubber & Woolen Mfg. Co. v.,
   316 U.S. 203 (1942) 263
St. Paul Fire And Marine Insurance Co. v. United States,
   24 Cl.Ct. 513 (1991) 157
Stanford Motor Co. v. Westman, 151 Neb. 850 (1949) 186
Staples, Inc., Montblanc-Simplo GmbH v.,
   172 F. Supp. 2d 231 (D. Mass. 2001) 238, 239
Stargate Software, Adobe Systems v.,
   216 F. Supp. 2d 1051 (N.D. Cal. 2002) 230
Stark, Hearst Corp. v., 639 F. Supp. 970 (N.D. Cal. 1986) 220, 221, 224
State Farm Mut. Ins. Co., Herron v., 363 P.2d 310 (Cal. 1961) 196, 204
Steelvest, Inc. v. Scansteel Serv. Ctr., Inc., 807 S.W.2d 476 (Ky. 1991) 192
Steffens, United States v., 100 U.S. 82 (1879) 244
Stein, Mazer v., 347 U.S. 201 (1954) 51
Stephen Slesinger, Inc. v. Walt Disney Co., 155 Cal.App. 4th 736 (2007) 142
Stewart M. Muller Constr. Co., Inc., Alvord and Swift v.,
   385 N.E.2d 1238 (N.Y. 1978) 193
Stone Forest Indus., Inc. v. United States, 973 F.2d 1548 (Fed. Cir. 1992) 185
Straus, Bobbs-Merrill Co. v., 210 U.S. 339 (1908) 225
Subafilms, Ltd. v. MGM-Pathe Commc'n Co., 24 F.3d 1088 (9th Cir. 1994) 212
Substance, Inc., Chicago Bd. of Educ. v., 354 F.3d 624 (7th Cir. 2003) 234
Summit Technology, Inc. v. High-Line Medical Instruments,
   922 F. Supp. 299 (C.D. Cal. 1996) 224, 228, 229, 271, 284, 285
SunGard Data Sys., Inc., Kachmar v., 109 F.3d 173 (3d Cir. 1997) 201
Sun Line Cruises, Inc., Effron v., 67 F.3d 7 (2nd Cir. 1995) 92
Sup. Ct., Burnham v., 495 U.S. 604 (1990) 160
Superior Court (Shayan), People v., 21 Cal. App. 4th 621
   (Cal. Ct. App. 1993) 291
Superior Motels v. Rinn Motor Hotels, 195 Cal. App. 3d 1032 (1987) 185
Super Scale Models, Ltd., Railway Exp. Agency Inc. v.,
   934 F.2d 135 (7th Cir. 1991) 195–197
Swatch S.A. v. New City, Inc., 454 F. Supp. 2d 1245 (S.D. Fla. 2006) 274–276
Szukhent, National Equip. Rental, Ltd. v., 375 U.S. 311 (1964) 160

Taito Corp., Red Baron-Franklin Park, Inc. v.,
   883 F. 2d 275 (4th Cir. 1989) 22, 113
Taito Corporation, Red Baron-Franklin Park, Inc. v.,
   883 F.2d 275 (4th Cir. 1989) 214
Taito Corporation, Red Baron-Franklin Park, Inc. v.,
   883 F.2d 279 (4th Cir. 1989) 215
This Old Store, Inc., Dell, Inc. v., 2007 WL 2903845, slip op. at 1
   (S.D.Tex. 2007) 202, 205
Thomas v. HUD, 124 F.3d 1439 (Fed. Cir. 1997) 185

Thompson Coal Co. v. Pike Coal Co., 412 A.2d 466 (PA S.C. 1979) 202
3 Lab, Inc. v. Kim, 2007 WL 2177513 (D.N.J. 2007) 100
Time Warner, Inc., Chambers v., 282 F.3d 147 (2d Cir. 2002) 255
Time Warner Entm't Co. v. Does Nos. 1–2, 876 F. Supp. 407 (E.D.N.Y. 1994) . . .168
Toeppen, Panavision Int'l v., 141 F.3d 1316 (9th Cir. 1998) 162
Top Quality Food Market, LLC, Prince of Peace Enterprises v.,
  2007 WL 704171 (S.D.N.Y.) 160
Top Serv. Body Shop, Inc. v. Allstate Ins. Co.,
  582 P.2d 1365 (Or. 1978) 201, 202, 205
Totem Marine Tub & Barge, Inc. v. Alyeska Pipeline Serv. Co.,
  584 P.2d 15 (Alaska 1978) 189
Toyota Motor Sales, U.S.A., Inc., Della Penna v.,
  902 P.2d 740 (Cal. 1995) 200, 203, 205
Treasury Oil Corp., Phoenix Mining & Mineral, L.L.C. v.,
  2007 WL 951866 at *5 (S.D. Tex. 2007) 162
Tuckish v. Pompano Motor Co., 337 F. Supp. 2d 1313 (S.D. Fla. 2004) 47
Turley, Lefkowitz v., 414 U.S. 70 (1973) 155
Twin Peaks Prods., Inc. v. Publ'n Int'l, Ltd., 996 F.2d 1366 (2d Cir. 1993) 210
Ty v. Publications International, 81 F. Supp. 2d 899 (N.D. Ill. 2000) 238

UBS Warburg, LLC, Zubulake v., 217 F.R.D. 309 (S.D.N.Y. 2003) 178
United States, Builders Corp. of Am. v., 148 F. Supp 482 (N.D.Cal. 1957) 199
United States, C3, Inc. v., 4 Cl.Ct 790 (1984) 156
United States, Dowling v., 473 U.S. 207 (1985) 219
United States, Green v., 355 U.S. 184 (1957) 156
United States, Lever Bros. Co. v., 877 F.2d 101 (D.C. Cir. 1989) 255, 277
United States, Neutrogena Corporation v., 1988 WL 166236 (D.S.C.) 223, 224
United States, St. Paul Fire And Marine Insurance Co. v.,
  24 Cl.Ct. 513 (1991) 157
United States, Stone Forest Indus., Inc. v., 973 F.2d 1548 (Fed. Cir. 1992) 185
United States Fid. & Guar. Co., Lawyers Title Ins. Corp. v.,
  122 F.R.D. 567 (1988) 179
United States Olympic Comm., San Francisco Arts & Ath. v.,
  483 U.S. 522 (1987) 244
United States v. Braunstein, 281 F.3d 982 (9th Cir. 2002) 40, 42, 43, 62, 87–89
United States v. Cisneros, 203 F.3d 333 (5th Cir. 2000) 154
United States v. Eight-Nine (89) Bottles of "Eau de Joy,"
  797 F.2d 767 (9th Cir. 1986) 16, 16
United States v. Eighty-Three Rolex Watches, 992 F.2d 508 (5th Cir. 1993) 170
United States v. Giles, 213 F.3d 1247 (19th Cir. 2000) 154
United States v. Goss, 803 F.2d 638 (11th Cir. 1986) 215
United States v. Hanafy, 124 F. Supp. 2d at 1016 (N.D. Tex. 2000) 153, 154
United States v. Hanafy, 302 F.3d 485 (5th Cir. 2002) 18, 53, 55, 155
United States v. Hill, 171 Fed.Appx. 815 (11th Cir. 2006) 22
United States v. King Features Entm't, Inc., 843 F.2d 394 (9th Cir. 1988) 235
United States v. McConney, 728 F. 2d 1195 (9th Cir. 1984) 165
United States v. Procter & Gamble Co., 356 U.S. 677 (1958) 175
United States v. Steffens, 100 U.S. 82 (1879) 244
United States v. Wise, 550 F.2d 1180 (9th Cir. 1977) 231

U.S. Intern. Trade Com'n, Sealed Air Corp. v., 645 F.2d 976 (C.C.P.A. 1981) 147
U.S. Int'l Trade Com'n, Gamut Trading Co. v., 200 F.3d 775 (Fed. Cir. 1999) 148
USA Petroleum Corp., Leonard v., 829 F. Supp. 882 (S.D. Tx. 1993) 160

VAS Indus. v. NY Sound, 2006 WL 1699537 (S.D.N.Y.) 22
Veles Ltd, Morris USA Inc. v., 2007 WL 725412 (S.D.N.Y.) 162, 163
Vernor v. Autodesk, Inc., 555 F. Supp. 2d 1164 (W.D. Wa. 2008) 231, 232
Vill. Cold Spring, Lusk v., 475 F. 3d 480 (2d Cir. 2007) 171
Virgin Enters. Ltd. v. Nawab, 335 F.3d 141 (2d Cir. 2003) 255
Volmar Distribs., Inc. v. New York Post Co., 152 F.R.D. 36 (S.D.N.Y. 1993)) 156

W. Microtechnology, Inc. v. Goold Elec. Corp., 1993 WL 424244, slip op. at
  *2 (N.D.Ill. 1993) 195
Waco Intern., Inc. v. KHK Scaffolding Houston Inc., 278 F.3d 523
  (5th Cir. 2002) 148
Wal-Mart Stores, Inc., No. 98 Civ. 7724, GTFM, Inc. v.,
  2000 U.S. Dist. LEXIS 3804 (S.D.N.Y. 2000) 182
Walt Disney Co., Stephen Slesinger, Inc. v., 155 Cal.App. 4th 736 (2007) 142
Warner-Lambert Co. v. Northside Development Corp.,
  86 F.3d 3 (2d Cir. 1996) 91, 269, 270
Wash., Int'l Shoe Co. v., 326 U.S. 310 (1945) 161
Wash. Mutual, Inc., McKell v., 142 Cal. App. 4th 1457 (2006) 184
Watson, E. Leitz, Inc. v., 152 F. Supp. 631 (D.D.C. 1957) 259
Weight Watchers, Int'l, Inc. v. Luigino's Inc., 423 F.3d 137 (2005) 173
Weil Ceramics & Glass, Inc. v. Dash, 618 F. Supp. 700 (D.N.J. 1985) 260
Weil Ceramics & Glass, Inc. v. Dash, 878 F.2d 659 (3d Cir. 1989) 253, 254, 285
Weil v. Markowitz, 829 F.2d 166 (D.C. Cir. 1987) 156
Western Glove Works Ltd., Blue Bell, Inc. v.,
  816 F. Supp. 236 (S.D.N.Y. 1993) 149, 150
Westman, Stanford Motor Co. v., 151 Neb. 850 (1949) 186
Wilderness Soc'y, Alyeska Pipeline Serv. Co. v., 421 U.S. 240 (1975) 95, 190
Wildlife Express Corp. v. Carol Wright Sales, Inc.,
  18 F.3d 502 (7th Cir. 1994) 211
Wilson, MCA, Inc. v., 677 F.2d 180 (2nd Cir. 1981) 233, 234
Wise, United States v., 550 F.2d 1180 (9th Cir. 1977) 231
Wood Dolson Co., Israel v., 134 N.E.2d 97 (N.Y. 1956) 192
Woodson, World-Wide Volkswagen Corp. v., 444 U.S. 286 (1980) 162
World-Wide Volkswagen Corp. v. Woodson, 444 U.S. 286 (1980) 162

Xoom, Inc. v. Imageline, Inc., 323 F.3d 279 (4th Cir. 2003) 211

Yahoo!, Inc., Anthony v., 421 F. Supp. 2d 1257 (N.D. Cal. 2006) 184

Zeinberg, ProCD, Inc. v., 86 F.3d 1447 (7th Cir. 1996) 229
Ziegman Productions Inc. v. City of Milwaukee,
  496 F. Supp. 965 (D.C. Wis. 1980) 170
Zino Davidoff SA v. CVS Corp., 2007 WL 1933932 (S.D.N.Y. 2007) 91, 172
Zubulake v. UBS Warburg, LLC, 217 F.R.D. 309 (S.D.N.Y. 2003) 178
Zucker's Gifts, Inc., Schmid, Inc. v., 766 F. Supp. 118 (S.D.N.Y. 1991) 194

Index

Abagnale, Frank Jr., 35
Abandonment of copyright, 235–36
Abercrombie and Fitch, 16–17
Adams Golf, 68–70
Adidas, 70
Administrative Procedure Act and ITC investigations, 146
Adobe, 33, 230
Affirmative defenses, 188–89
   copyright infringement claims, 233–37
   intentional interference with contract (IIWC), 197
   intentional interference with prospective economic advantage (IIEA), 204–5
   trademark infringement claims, 282–86
Africa, 24
   South Africa, 83, 184, 222–23
Aggravating circumstances in distribution partner infractions, 99–101
AIDS drugs, 22–24, 116
Airbus, 10
Airline industry. *See* aviation
Akinwade, Tope, 24n85
ALAC, 87–89
Alibaba Web site, 34, 34nn27–28
Alliance for Gray Market and Counterfeit Abatement (AGMA), 73–74
Al Qaeda terrorists and counterfeiting, 59
Alternative dispute resolution, 148–51
Alternative prevention strategies, 115–119
Amazon, 78
American Arbitration Association, 151, 151n28
American Intellectual Property Law Association (AIPLA), 74
AmerisourceBergen Corp. (ABC), 23
Amgen, 23
A&M Records, 235–36
Anemia pharmaceuticals, 23

Anheuser-Busch, 127
Anhui government, 12
Anti-Counterfeiting Group, 17–18
Anti-Gray Market Alliance.
   See KPMG/ Anti-Gray Market Alliance
Antonova, Maria, 305n41
AOL's refusal to cancel service, 48–49
Apollinaris, 246–47
Apple Computer, 42–44
   comeback of, 243
   in India, 309
   iPhones, 114, 116–17
   Latin American distributors of, 62, 87–89
Appliances, 307–8
Arbitration as litigation alternative, 148–51
Arctic Cat, 137–38
Armstrong, Herb, 90
Assignments
   of copyrights, 210
   of trademarks, 257
Association of Leaders in Equipment Distribution, 55–56, 56nn68–69
Association of Service and Computer Dealers International (ASCDI), 34, 35
Aston Martin as valuable brand name, 68
Attorney-client relationship and intentional interference with contract claim, 200–201
Attorneys' fees
   breach of contract claim, 190
   contracts with distribution partners, 95–96, 190
   copyrights, 211–12, 240
Audiovisual works as copyrightable, 209
Audits
   aviation supply lines, 11
   distribution partners' books, 86–90, 131–33
   gray market detection methods, 131–33
   Nike suppliers, 31

Authenticating products, 111–14
Authorized resellers, 45–46
    contracts with supply chain distributors, 84–86
    overcoming supply chain constraints, 63
AutoCAD, 231
Autodesk, 231
Automotive Aftermarket Suppliers Association (AASA), 74
Automotive industry
    and Anhui government, 12
    Daimler-Chrysler, 47–49
    effects of gray market in, 11–13
    General Motors, 11–13, 305
    in Russia, 305–6
    See also Ford Motor Company
Availability of products as benefit, 46
Aviation
    affected industry, 10–11
    erosion of consumer trust, 6
    terrorism detection efforts, 131

Baby food quality, 113
Baby formula counterfeits, 18, 53–55, 113
Balkcom, A. Carter, 304–5nn36–40
Ball bearings, 264–65
Bangalore's knowledge resources, 30
Bangladesh's sweatshops, 31
Barboza, David, 12–13nn17–18, 306n48
Barcodes to track products and components, 109
Barlyn, Suzanne, 30nn6–7
Barnard, Jeff, 18n50
Baseball and steroid use, 125–26
Batch codes and trademark infringement, 262–63, 278, 280
B2B trading networks, 133, 134
Beanie Babies, 238
Bear Sterns, 194
Beatles, 136
Beauty supplies. *See* personal care products
Bednarz, Ann, 109n107
Bed products. *See* mattresses
Beef counterfeits, 18
Benefits of gray market, 60–64
Berlin Wall's fall, 29, 37
Berman, Howard L., 307n50
Berne Convention, 212–13, 212n35, 298–99, 307
Beth, Scott, 63n106, 98n69
Bias of arbitrator, 149

Black market
    airline industry, 11
    automotive industry, 11
    baby formula, 53, 55
    cigarette industry, 13
    commingling with gray market products, 6–7, 53, 55, 153, 170
    decreased trade barriers' effect on, 37–38
    defined, 6
    flea markets, 27–28
    food industry, 18
    globalization's effect on, 28–32
    gray market distinguished, 4
    information technology products, 21
    Internet's effect on, 32–35
    iPhones, 117n5
    Mexico as notorious source of, 301
    pharmaceuticals, 23–24
    tax revenue loses, 56–57
    technology's effect on, 35–37
Blackwell, John Reid, 13n23
Black & White counterfeits, 17
Blizzard Entertainment, 231–32
Blogs used to communicate customer dissatisfaction, 48–49
Blood transfusions and gray market pharmaceuticals, 23–24
Blue Bell, 149–50
Blurring of trademark, 245
Boeing, 10
Bombardier/Learjet, 10
Books. *See* copyrights
Born to Kill gang and counterfeit watches, 60
Bots, 231–32
Bourdeau, 147–48, 285–86
Bourjois, 247–48, 254
Boyle, Edward, 111nn114–15
Brand goodwill generally, 47–49
Brand Name Beds, 273–74
Brand protection purchases, 124–25, 134–40, 170
Brands as focus of gray market's impact, 5–6
Braunstein, 87–89
Breach of contract theory of recovery, 184–90
Bridgestone/Firestone tire recall, 5
Britain's cigarette tax, 59
British Petroleum's investments in Russia, 304
Bromage, C., 148n15
Bruce, Katherine, 60n93
Buckler, Grant, 109n105, 111n114
Burke, Kelly, 23–24

Index

Burros, Marian, 18n47, 53nn50–55
Bush, President George W., 131n1
Business corruption climate in geographically vulnerable locales, 105–6
Business security systems, 106–10
Business-to-business trading networks, 133, 134
Butterfield, Bradley S., 299n14, 307n53

Cabbage Patch dolls, 25, 85, 171–72, 217
California
  cigarette tax, 58
  gray market statutes, 289–92
Cameras
  Minolta, 41–42
  surveillance methods, 107–8
Canada
  cigarette smuggling, 58, 115, 300
  intellectual property laws of, 300–301
  and PT Cruisers, 47
Canal Street market, 27–28
Cancer and gray market pharmaceuticals, 22–24
Capital City Micro, 127–28
Capone, Al, 57
Carney, Scott, 4n4
Car stereo parts, 291–92
Cartier, 72
Cartographic works as copyrightable, 209
Casa Helvetia, 276–77
Caterpillar's investments in Russia, 304
CBS and copyrights in sound recordings, 219–20
CCTV surveillance, 107–8
CDs and technological aids to counterfeiting, 36
Cease and desist correspondence, 174, 236–37
Certification of distribution partners, 80–81
Chain of custody records for food and pharmaceuticals, 108
Chan, Jackie, 28
Channel brand, 72
Chery brand, 12
Children's Hospital of Philadelphia, 129
China
  Alibaba Web site search for products from, 34
  as notorious source of counterfeit and gray market goods, 103
  automotive industry and, 11–13
  counterfeiting software, 60
  film piracy in, 28
  intellectual property laws of, 306–8
  joining WTO, 38
Chinatown, 27–28
Chinatown in New York City, 27–28
CHIP units, 152
Chivas Regal counterfeits, 17
Chocolates, 18, 276–77, 300
Choi, Thomas Y., 46nn24–25
Choice of law provisions in distribution partner contracts, 92–93
Choreographic works as copyrightable, 209
Cigarettes
  effects of gray market in, 13–14, 57–59, 115
  jurisdictional analysis, 162–63
  Reynolds' trademark infringement claim, 272
  state gray market statutes, 289, 295–96
Cigarettes Cheaper!, 272
Ciollli, Anthony, 13–14nn24–26
Circuit boards, 214–16
Cisco
  founding member of Alliance for Gray Market and Counterfeit Abatement (AGMA), 73
  gray market reporting, 140
  software licenses, 232–33
Citrin, James M., 40–41nn3–7
Claus, Dietwalk, 305nn42–43
Clean Air Act, 56
Clifton, Rita
  brand's asset value, 5n13, 31nn10–11, 68nn1–3, 242nn4–6
  costs of monitoring for ethical practices, 31nn10–11
  Internet's effects, 32, 32n15
  power of successful brands, 243n10
  UK's Trade Marks Act, 302n24
Clothing and apparel
  Cartier, 72
  consumer tips for spotting counterfeits, 72
  effects of gray market in, 16–17
  El Greco shoes, 266–67
  intentional interference with contract, 194
  Monte Carlo shirts, 267
  parallel trading, 70
  Ralph Lauren, 222
  Zara, 117–19
Coach brand, 72
Coalition Against Counterfeiting and Piracy (CACP), 55nn64–66, 74

330   Index

Coca-Cola
  brand integrity efforts, 68
  developing economics and gray market goods, 61
  value of brand, 242
Color shifting technology, 112
Commerce Department, 11, 11n10
Commercial Petroleum, 267–68
Compaq Computer Corporation, 187
Compilations as copyrightable, 209
Compliance incentives for distribution partners, 96–99
Component monitoring, 109–10
Compusource, 236–37
Computech International, 186–87
Computer Hacking and Intellectual Property (CHIP) units, 152
Computers
  breach of contract theories, 186–87
  Cisco, 232–33
  Computer Hacking and Intellectual Property (CHIP) units, 152
  contractual requirements for distributors, 82
  electronically stored information (ESI), 175–82
  Latin American distributors of, 87–89
  trademark protection for chips, 252–53
  unusual orders as signs of gray market activity, 126–28
  See also information technology; Internet; software
Connecticut gray market statutes, 289, 293–94
Consequences of gray market, 39–64
Constitutional provisions
  copyright protection, 208
  free speech defense of intentional interference with economic advantage claims, 204
  trademark protection, 244
  See also search and seizure
Construction work
  intentional interference with contract liability, 193
Consumer Contracts, 222
Consumers
  brand trust, 6, 242–43
  California gray market statutes, 290–91
  Connecticut gray market statutes, 293
  education about brand integrity, 72–73
  erosion of trust, 6

health and safety consequences of gray markets, 52–55
product authenticity efforts, 111–14
Contracts
  assignment of trademarks, 257–58
  breach of contract theory of recovery, 184–90
  copyright protection, 218
  with distribution partners, 81–101, 151
  intentional interference with contract, 191–98
  intentional interference with prospective economic advantage, 199–205
  jurisdictional provisions, 160
  work made for hire, 210
Contributory copyright infringement, 231–32, 231n123, 303
Convair airplane, 10–11
Cooper Tire, 12–13
Coors beer, 265–66
COPIAT trademark, 250
Copyrights
  affirmative defenses, 233–37
  alternative litigation strategies, 83
  attorneys' fees, 211–12, 240
  Canadian cases, 300–301
  contract breach remedies compared, 183
  Copyright Act generally, 209
  criminal penalties, 240
  damages, 211–12, 237, 239–40
  destruction of infringing articles, 239, 240
  estoppel defense, 236–37
  fair use defenses, 233–35
  federal jurisdiction, 158
  first sale doctrine and importation rights, 218–33
  importation rights, 216–33
  impoundment and destruction, 239
  infringement generally, 208–9
  injunctions, 238–39
  innocent intent defense, 237
  international agreements, 28
  international protection, 211–13
  originality requirements, 209
  ownership requirements, 209–10
  performance rights, 214–16
  profits, 239–40
  registration, 209–11
  remedies, 237–40
  seizure of infringing goods and instruments, 167–68
  software licenses, 227–33

Index **331**

theories of liability, 208–40
trademark law compared, 213, 248–49
waiver defense, 235–36
See also Berne Convention; Nimmer on Copyright
Copyright Society of America (CSA), 74
Corcoran, James, 82
Corporate records as resource for investigations of potential supply chain partners, 79–80
Corporate subsidiaries and trademark protection, 250–52
Cosmair, 222
Cosmetics. *See* personal care products
Costa-Font, Joan, 60–61*nn*97–101
Costco
 cigarette sales, 58
 decorative figurine sales, 217–18
 Omega watch sales by, 19–20, 227
 Tight Lies golf clubs, 69
Cost of brand protection, 63–64
Cote D'Or chocolates, 300
Cough drops, 270
Counterclaims for wrongful seizure, 168
Counterfeits. *See* black market
Craigslist Web site, 34
Criminal investigations
 of potential supply chain partners, 79
 search and seizure issues, 166–70
Criminal offenses and penalties, 151–57
 copyright infringement claims, 240
 diversion of products in transit, 110–11
 in geographically vulnerable locales, 105–6
 gray market cigarettes, 296
 interference with identification marks, 291
Crutchfield, Lynn G., 112*n*118
Curci, Frank X., 298*n*7, 299*n*13
Customer list security, 110
Customer satisfaction, 47–49
Customs. *See* U.S. Customs Service

Daewoo, 267
Daimler-Chrysler, 47–49
Daly, James, 243*n*8
Damages
 arbitration awards, 149
 breach of contract, 185, 189–90
 contracts with distribution partners, 93–95, 185, 189–90
 copyright infringement, 211–12, 237, 239–40

intentional interference with contract, 192, 196–97
intentional interference with economic advantage, 199–200, 202–3, 205
punitive damages, 192, 197, 205
trademark infringement, 287
Darby Dental Supply, 258–59
Dash, Bernard, 253
Davis, Nicole, 19*n*52
Deere, 147–48, 285–86
Defenses. *See* affirmative defenses
Definitions
 contributory copyright infringement, 231*n*123
 counterfeit mark, 154
 display, 215*n*47
 google, 133*n*6
 gray market, 3, 4
 gray market cigarettes, 295–96
 gray market goods, 294
 MP3, 235*n*143
 perform, 215
 registrant, 257
 tort, 192
 trademark, 244
 waiver, 235
Delivery requests as warning sign of gray market activity, 129
Delivery terms for distribution partners, 98
Demarrais, Kevin, G., 106*n*84, 107*nn*87–88
Dental products, 187–88, 258–60
DEP Corp., 256–57
Designs and fair use doctrine, 234
Destruction of incriminating evidence, 166–67, 173
Destruction of infringing articles and production means, 239, 240, 296
Deterrence value of disciplining infractions, 183
Developing economics and gray market, 61–62
Dey, J., 18*n*43
Diamond & Gem Trading, 260–61
Dickens, Charles, 28
Digital Millennium Copyright Act's safe harbor provision, 33, 303
Dilution of trademark, 244–45
Discipline for distribution partner infractions, 99–101
Disclosure statutes, 289, 293, 294
Discount requests activity as warning sign of gray market activity, 126

Discounts for authorized resellers, 98–99
Discovery in litigation, 159, 175–82
Disney, 142
Display defined, 215n47
Distribution partners
  arbitration clause, 151
  attorneys' fees provisions, 95–96
  audits, 86–90, 131–33
  background research, 78–80
  certification of, 80–81
  choice of law provisions, 92–93
  contracts, 81–101, 151
  damages provisions, 93–95
  delivery terms, 98
  educational efforts concerning brand integrity, 70–72
  guidelines, 84–96
  incentives for compliance, 96–99
  penalties for noncompliance, 99–101
  price monitoring by brand owner, 123–25
  price protection, 98–99
  probation, 99–100
  prohibitions on gray market activities, 83, 84–86
  promises to, 84–96
  qualifying, 78–81
  quality control guidelines, 90–91
  records, 86–89, 132
  return policies, 97–98
  security audits, 90
  selecting, 78–81
  suspension of, 99–100
  technical support and training for, 97
  termination of, 101
  territorial exclusivities, 96–97
  training of, 80–81
  venue selection, 91–92, 106, 164
  warranty support, 97–98
District of Columbia's gray market cigarette statutes, 289, 295–96
Diversion from authorized sales channels as defining gray market, 4
Dobbs, David A., 10–11nn4–9
Dolls, 25, 85, 171–72
Dot.com bust, 29
Double Dragon, 214–16
Dramatic works as copyrightable, 209
Drug Emporium, 221, 268–69, 278–79
Dumpster diving to detect gray market activity, 140–42
Dunn, Patricia, 138–39
Duracell batteries, 40

Duress as affirmative defense to breach of contract claim, 189
Dutta, Devangshu, 117–18nn7–8
DVDs
  as target of gray market activity, 22, 113
  staggered distribution strategies, 116
  technological aids to counterfeiting, 36
Dynamite Enterprises, 222

Eban, Katherine, 124n2
EBay
  AutoCAD software sale, 231
  counterfeit software on, 33, 33nn17–18
  perfume sales, 303
  police Blotter feature, 35
  Verified Rights Owner (VeRO) program, 35
Economic consequences of gray market, 49–52
Economist magazine, 32n16
E-discovery, 176–82
Education
  as prevention strategy, 65–76
  of manufacturing partners as risky, 103
  permissible use of copyrighted material, 216, 233
Eichenwalk, Kurt, 166n6
Electronically stored information (ESI) as subject of discovery, 175–82
Electronic discovery rules, 176–82
Electronic Retailers Association (ERA), 74
Electronics industry
  warranty and service costs, 49–51
  See also computers; information technology; software; telecommunications
Elephant logo, 300
El Greco, 266–67
Employees
  background investigations of potential supply chain partners, 79
  brand integrity education of, 67–70
  health infrastructure in geographically vulnerable locales, 106
  hold notice on electronically stored information (ESI), 180–81
  monitoring, 108–10
  reaction to terminating distribution partner, 101
  sales goals and brand integrity efforts, 67, 70, 132–33
  work made for hire, 210
Engardio, Pete, 37n31

Index **333**

Environmental harm, 55–56
Environmental Protection Agency (EPA) regulations, 56
E.P. Lehmann, 196–97
Epperson, Ron, 74–75nn24–25
ESPE, 258–59
Estoppel defense
  to breach of contract claim, 189
  to copyright infringement claim, 236–37
Ethics codes
  North America Association of Telecommunication Dealers (NATD), 79
  pretext purchasers, 135–36n15, 135–37, 137–38nn28–32
  Web sites, 35
Euro-Excellence, 300
European Union
  counterfeit toys, 24n85
  intellectual property laws, 302–4
  pharmaceutical gray market, 60–61
Evidence
  copyright infringement, 211
  See also discovery in litigation
Exhaustion of rights theory, 302–3
Exxon Mobil's investments in Russia, 304

FAA, 10–11
Fabric, Ltd., 184, 222
Face powder, 247–49
Fair use defense to copyright infringement claim, 233–35
Falkner, James, 110–1nn108–9, 111–13
Faltings, Peter, 82
Fan, Hung, 116n2
FBI and Al Capone, 57n74
Federal Arbitration Act, 149, 149nn17–18
Federal prosecutors, 152–53
FedEx
  and technological improvements, 36
  tracking software, 109
Ferdows, Kasra, 16–17, 117n6, 118–19nn9–12
Ferrari, Vincent, 48
Ferrero, 272–73
Ferretti, Fred, 171n29, 172n32
Fiber-optic cables' effect on communication, 29–30
Fifth Amendment privilege, 155, 156n58
Figurines, 195, 217–18
Film piracy, 28
Fines for distribution partners' infractions, 100–1
Firestone, 5

First Amendment defense of intentional interference with economic advantage claims, 204
First sale doctrine
  and copyright infringement claim, 218–33
  and trademark infringement, 282–84
Fitzgerald, Thomas J., 166–67n7
Fixed price problems, 115–16
Flea markets, 27–28
Focus automobile, 305
Food
  chain of custody records, 108
  effects of gray market on, 17–18
  guidelines for distributors, 91
  infant formula, 18, 53–55, 153–55
Food and Drug Administration (FDA), 18
Forage harvesters, 285–86
Ford Motor Company
  brand name acquisitions, 68
  investment in Russia, 305
  reverse online auctions, 46
Foreign-manufactured goods and copyright protection, 220–21
Forum selection clauses in distribution partner contracts, 91–92, 106, 160
Fourth Amendment issues in dumpster diving, 140–42
47th Street Photo, 250
Fragrances and perfumes
  copyright protection, 221, 222
  Davidoff, 262–63
  eBay sales of, 303
  effects of gray market in, 14–16, 62
  Ralph Lauren, 222
  temporary restraining orders, 172
  trademark protection, 248–49
France
  Bourjois face powder, 247–48
  copyright protection of foreign authors, 213
  Louis Vuitton products, 303–4
Fraud
  in arbitration awards, 149
  as affirmative defense to breach of contract claim, 189
Freedman, Samuel, 30n7
Freeman, Gregory, 57nn75–76, 78–79
Free speech defense of intentional interference with economic advantage claims, 204
Friedman, Thomas L., 3n2, 37, 37n32, 307n52, 308n60

Friendly, Judge Henry, 256
Frivolous prosecution of gray market distributors, 89
Furniss, Todd, 307n53

Gabriel Brothers, 17
Gap, 118
Garmin, 49
Genderson, 265–66
General Electric, 308
General Electric Aircraft Engines, 10
General Motors, 11–13, 305
Geographical exclusivities for distribution partners, 96–97
Geographic vulnerability acknowledgment, 102–6
George, Ricky, 70, 70n17
Ghose, Jayati, 117n5
Gillette, 40–41
Gilson on Trademarks, 245n24
Ginsburg, Justice, 227
Givenchy, 221
Glannon, 157n71
Glen Moray counterfeits, 18
Glider, 231–32
Global Anti-Counterfeiting Group (GACG), 74
Globalization
 gray market effects of, 28–32
 venue selection issues, 91–92
Global positioning systems (GPS), 49
Goebel, 195
Golf clubs, 68–70
Gongloff, Mark, 5n14
Gonzales, Gloria, 119nn20–24
Gonzalez, Alberto, 153n38
Goodgame, Dan, 4n5
Goodwill of product and trademark rights, 257–59
Goodyear, 12–13
Googling to monitor sales, 133–34
Gopal, Chris, 81
Governmental use of copyrighted material, 216
Government relations and brand protection, 75
Graham, Michael R., 74–75nn24–25
Graham Webb, 278–79
Graphics software as gray market aid, 36
Graphic works as copyrightable, 209
Greece and pharmaceutical gray market, 60–61

Green, William, 60n93
Guccci purses, 27–28
Gucci counterfeits, 27–28, 72
Guha, Jishnu, 299n12
Guidelines for distribution partners, 84–96
Gurgaon and knowledge resources, 30
Gutenberg, Johannes, 208

Haier appliances, 307–8
Hair products
 California criminal offense statutes, 292
 salon products, 202–3, 268–69, 277–81, 283–84, 292
 See also personal care products
Halls cough drops, 270
Hangzhou Zhongce Rubber Company, 12
Hannaford-Agor, Paul L., 158n80
Health consequences of gray markets, 52–55, 108n97
Health infrastructure in geographically vulnerable locales, 106
Hearst Corporation, 220–21
Herendi Pocelangyar, 260–62
Hewlett-Packard
 Big Deal pricing program, 127
 founder of Alliance for Gray Market and Counterfeit Abatement (AGMA), 73–74
 pretextual investigations, 138–39
 production outsourcing, 119
Hezbollah terrorists and counterfeiting, 59
High-Line Medical Instruments, 271, 284
H&M, 118
Hoffman, William, 110n110
Holmes, Justice, 248
Holographic imaging, 112, 292
Home security systems, 106–10
Honingsbaum, Mark, 14–15nn29–32, 62n105
Honorable resellers, 45–46
Hopkins, David M., 4n11
 Berne Convention, 307n51
 China's Quality Brands Protection Committee, 307n54
 DVDs, 22n70
 eBay and counterfeit software, 33nn17–18
 invention costs, 51–52nn48–49
 Mexican Institute of Industrial Property, 301n21
 online tips for spotting counterfeit goods, 72n18

Paul Mitchell products, 15n34
Serostim, 24n82
warranty service on illegitimate products, 49n36
Horwitz, Sari, 59n92
Howe, Kenneth, 13nn19–20, 58nn80–84
HP. *See* Hewlett-Packard
Hunter, Michelle, 107n88

IACC White Paper, 10n3
IBM computer distributors, 82
Implied authority to import copyrighted goods, 217–18
Importation rights under copyright law, 216–33
Impoundment of copyright infringing articles and production means, 239
IMPREGUM, 258–60
Independent Equipment Dealers Association (IEDA), 56
India
  intellectual property laws of, 308–9
  knowledge resources, 30
Inditex, 117–19
Industry alliances' educational efforts, 73–75
Infant formula, 18, 53–55, 153–55
Informant use to detect gray market activity, 140
Information technology (IT)
  discovery of electronically stored information (ESI), 175–82
  gray market effects on generally, 21–22
  losses to gray market, 3
  See also computers; Internet; software
Infringement. *See* copyrights; trademarks
Injunctions
  arbitrator's authority to order, 149–50
  copyright infringement, 223–24, 238–39
  intentional interference with contract claim, 198
  intentional interference with economic advantage claims, 205
  New York gray market statutes, 295
  preliminary remedies, 170–73
  trademark infringement, 286
Innocent intent defense to copyright infringement claims, 237
Installation guidelines for distributors, 91
Instruction manuals and fair use doctrine, 234
Insurance
  for intellectual property protection, 119

intentional interference with economic advantage claims and, 201–2
Intaglio printing, 112
Intellectual property
  Canadian laws, 300–301
  Chinese laws, 306–8
  European Union laws, 302–4
  Indian laws, 308–9
  insurance protection, 119
  international law concerning, 298–99
  Mexican laws, 301
  Russian laws, 304–6
  See also copyright; trademarks
Intellectual Property Owners Association (IPO), 74
Intentional interference with contract (IIWC), 191–98
  compared with intentional interference with prospective economic advantage, 193, 200
Intentional interference with prospective economic advantage (IIEA), 199–205
  compared with intentional interference with contract, 193, 200
Interbrand, 307
Internal distribution prevention strategy, 117–119
International protection
  for copyrights, 211–13
  for intellectual property generally, 297–309
International Trade Commission (ITC)
  as litigation alternative, 145–48
  SKF ball bearings, 264–65
International Trademark Association (ITA), 74, 134n9
  exhaustion of rights theory, 302, 302n25, 303, 303n28
  and gray market laws, 299, 299n11
  pretext investigations, 139
International Traders, 220
Internet
  cigarette sales via, 13–14, 58
  effect on gray market generally, 27–38
  jewelry industry and, 19–20
  jurisdiction in context of, 161–62
  monitoring to detect gray market activity, 133–34
  See also eBay
Interpol, 32n14
Interstate Cigar Company, 256–57
Inventory monitoring, 108–10

Investigations
  brand protection purchases, 134–40
  costs of gray market protection, 63
  intentional interference with contract as tool for, 194
  ITC, 146–48
  of potential supply chain partners, 78–80
  search and seizure issues, 166–70
IOffer Web site, 34
IP. *See* intellectual property
IPhones, 114, 116–17
IPods in India, 309
Italy's copyright protection for American authors, 213

Jade, 279–80
Jaguar as valuable brand name, 68
Jalyn Corp., 253–54
Jeans, 149–50
Jewelry, 18–20
John Deere, 147–48
Johnnie Walker Blue Label counterfeits, 17
Jones, Benjamin, 112n121
Joseph, Gehard, 28n3
Joshi, Pradnya, 33n24
Judges, state vs. federal comparison, 158
Juhasz, Judit and Frank, 261–62
Jurisdiction
  arbitrators', 150
  globalization and, 38
  ITC investigations, 147
  litigation strategies, 157–164
  state or federal court, 157–59
Jury trial differences in state and federal court, 158
Justice Department hotline, 75
Justice systems in geographically vulnerable locales, 106
Justification defense to intentional interference with contract claim, 197

Kahney, Leander, 243n9
Kanavos, Panos, 60–61nn97–101, 61
Kessler, Michelle, 35nn29–30, 49nn37–40
Key personnel of potential supply chain partners, 79
Kilts, John, 40–41
K Mart, 250
Knight, Rebecca, 3n1
KNK Medical-Dental Specialties, 187–88
Knock 'n talks, 173
Knowledge of infringement, 236–37

Knowledge resources, 30
Kopczynski, Mary, 15, 299nn12
Korolyov, Igor, 306n45
Kosick, Lawrence, 19
KPMG/ Anti-Gray Market Alliance
  audits of distributors' books, 87n30, 132n2
  contractual requirements for distributors, 82, 82nn7–9, 87n30
  IT manufacturers' loss to gray market, 3n3, 21n63
  quality control responsibility, 49n41
  relative speed of procuring products through gray market, 98n68
  sourcing from gray market, 46, 46n23
Kraft, 300
Krebs, Michelle, 305n44
Kriesberg, Louis, 20n59
Kwon, Michael, 13n22

Labels
  and fair use doctrine, 234
  technological aids to counterfeiting, 36
Lacoste, 70
LaFountain, R., 148n15
Laguna Beach police, 140–41
Land Rover as valuable brand name, 68
Lanham Act, 154–55, 244, 254–82
L'anza, 225–26
Laphroaig counterfeits, 18
Laser printers as gray market aid, 36
Laser systems, 224, 271, 284
Lee, Hau L., 119nn18–19
Lee jeans, 149–50
Legal profession outsourcing to India, 30
Lemon laws and Canadian PT Cruisers, 47
Lennon, John, 136
Lewis, Michael A., 117n6
Lexus, 203–4
Licenses and copyrights, 227–33
Liker, Jeffrey K., 46nn24–25
Limits on purchases to prevent gray market activity, 114
Lin, Anthony, 307–8nn55–57
Lincoln automobiles, 186
Liquidated damages clauses in distribution partner contracts, 93–95
Literary works as copyrightable, 209
Litigation
  alternatives, 145–148
  civil litigation, 151–157
  costs of gray market protection, 63–64

criminal litigation, 151–157
hold notice on electronically stored information (ESI), 180–81
initial strategies, 145–164
jurisdiction, 159–164
preliminary remedies, 165–74
state or federal court, 157–159
venue, 159–164
See also discovery in litigation
Lladro, 253–54
Locke, John, 51
Longs Drugs, 283–84
Lord, Richard A., 232n124
Los Angeles tax revenue lost, 57
Louis Vuitton goods, 303–4
Lubove, Seth, 59nn89–91
Lupron, 22–24
Luxury goods, 261–62, 303, 307

Mach3 razors, 40
Machuca, Jose A.D., 117n6
Madrid system of trademark protection, 299, 299nn9–10
Malawi sweatshops, 31
Malaysian gray market steel industry, 21–22
Maltbie, John, 74–75nn24–25
Mamiya cameras, 50–51
Management and brand integrity education, 67–70
Manson counterfeit movie, 33, 303
MarkMonitor, 134, 134n8
Markoff, John, 243n7
Marlboro, 13–14, 162–63
Martell counterfeits, 18
Martin, Andrew, 12–13nn17–18, 306n48
Martin's Herend Imports, 260–62
Material difference as trademark infringement test, 260–82
Matrix hair products, 268–69
Mattresses, 273–74
  signatures on distribution contracts, 86
  training distribution partners, 80–81
McDonalds in developing economics, 61
McGregor, Richard, 12nn13–15
MDY, 231–32
Media outlets for brand integrity protection efforts, 76
Medical equipment, 224, 228–29, 271
  Siemens, 269
Merck & Co. efforts to combat gray market pharmaceuticals, 55

Metadata, 179
Mexican Institute of Industrial Property, 301
Mexico, 301
Michigan's gray market cigarette statutes, 289, 295–96
Microsoft
  anti-piracy hotline, 140, 140n40
  and Compuserve, 21
  and estoppel defense, 236–37
  value of brand, 242
Mineral water, 246–47
Minimum contacts for jurisdiction, 161–63
Minolta, 41–42
Mistake as affirmative defense to breach of contract claim, 189
Mitchell, Senator George J., 125–26nn4–5
Mitigating circumstances in distribution partner infractions, 99–101
Montblanc pens, 238–39
Monte Carlo shirts, 267
Motion Picture Association of America (MPAA), 116nn3–4
  pretext purchase investigations, 139–40
  staggered distribution strategies, 116
Motor oil, 267–68
Motorola's investments in Russia, 304
MP3, 235–36, 235n143
Mumbai's knowledge resources, 30
Music
  copyrightable works, 209
  equipment as target of gray market activity, 22
  instruments' warranty service, 72–73
  pretext purchase investigations, 139–40

NAFTA, 37–38, 301
Naím, Moisés, 12n16, 27n1, 39, 39n1, 57n77
Nanotechnology, 112
Napolitano, Maida, 108n99
NATD. *See* North America Association of Telecommunication Dealers (NATD)
National Intellectual Property Law Enforcement Coordination Council (NIPLECC), 151–52, 152nn31–34
Natural resources, gray market effects on, 21–22
Navy's Mine Warfare Training Center, 90
NEC, 252–53
Neff, Thomas J., 40–41nn3–7
Nehila, Heather, 213n37
Nestlé chocolates, 276–77

Quality Brands Protection Committee (QBPC), 74
Quality controls
  guidelines for distribution partners, 90–91
  preventive strategy, 65–66
  trademark infringement issues, 265–71
Quality King, 104–5, 196, 225, 270
Quantifying damages
  in copyright infringement cases, 239–40
  in distribution partner disputes, 93–95
  in trademark infringement cases, 287
Quebec's cigarette tax, 58

Radio-frequency identification (RFID) to track products and components, 109
Raftery, W., 148n15
Railway Express Agency (REA), 196–97
Rainbow Music, 220
Ralph Lauren, 222
Randalls, 279–80
Raw materials
  limitation effects in automotive industry, 12–13
  monitoring, 109–10
Records
  distribution partners', 86–89, 132
  of investigations of potential supply chain partners, 79–80
  See also audits
Red Baron, 214–16
Red flags of gray market activity, 123–29
Regan, Ronald W., 131
Registration
  of copyright, 209–11
  of trademark, 255
Reichert, J. F., 217
Rejected supply chain partners, 80
Religious use of copyrighted material, 216
Remy Martin counterfeits, 18
Research and development costs, 51–52
Return policies, 97–98
Revenue
  increase in gray and black markets, 32
  See also tax revenue
Reverse online auctions' effect, 46
Reverse palming off, 245
Revised Uniform Arbitration Act, 150n23
Reynolds Tobacco, 272
Ripping software, 235n143
Rippling effect of gray markets, 39–64
Roberts, Dexter, 37n31
Rohwer, Claude D., 190n33

Rolex watches, 170n19
Rolls-Royce aircraft, 10
Rotella, 267–68
Royal Crown counterfeits, 17
Russia
  intellectual property laws of, 304–6
  organized crime and counterfeiting, 59–60
Ruston, Gerard, 242nn1–2

Sachs, Jeffrey, 31, 31nn12–13, 308n59
Sales channels and definition of gray market, 4–5
Sales goals and brand integrity efforts, 67, 70, 132–33
Sales records of distribution partners, 86–89, 132
Salon products, 202–3, 268–69, 277–81, 283–84, 292
Samghabadi, Raji, 4n5
Samsung, 308
Satellite services as target of gray market activity, 22
Saturn, 98
Saudi Arabia, gray marketing in, 62, 128
Saxlehner, Andreas, 246–47
Scanners as gray market aid, 36
Schaber, Gordon D., 190n33
Schauffler, R., 148n15
Scherer, 246–47
Schmid, 195
Scholarly use of copyrighted material, 216, 233
Schultz, John D., 108n97
Schwarzenegger, Arnold, 28
Schwarzer, 158n83, 161n100, 164n119
Scorpio Music Distributors, 220
Scotch whiskey counterfeits, 17–18
Sculptural works as copyrightable, 209
Search and seizure
  dumpster diving and, 140–42
  preliminary remedies, 165, 166–70
Seattle and WTO conference, 30
Sebastian, 83, 184, 222–23, 283–84
Section 337 investigations, 146–48
Security
  audits of distribution partners, 90
  costs of gray market protection, 63
  of supply chain, 106–14
Security Software, 82
Sedona Conference, 176–77n6
Self-incrimination privilege, 155, 156n58
Selig, Alan H. "Bud," 125
Serial numbers

Networking technologies, 232–33
Neupogen, 22–24
Neutrogena, 223–24
New City, 275–76
Newman, Matthew, 60nn95–96
New York City's Chinatown, 27–28
New York gray market statutes, 289, 294–96
Nicherson, Colin, 58nn85–88
Nike, 30, 70
Nikon warranty service, 49
Nilson, Thorsten H., 47n32
Nimmer on Copyright
  damages calculation, 240n166
  estoppel defense, 236n146
  importation rights, 221n71
  innocent intent defense, 237n150
  international protection, 213nn38–40
Nortel
  founding member of Alliance for Gray Market and Counterfeit Abatement (AGMA), 74
  gray market reporting, 140, 140n41
  warranty exchange requests, 128–29
North America Association of Telecommunication Dealers (NATD), 34, 35
  investigating potential supply chain partners via Web site, 79
  member trading, 134n7
  monitoring sales of products via Web site, 133–34
North American Free Trade Agreement (NAFTA), 37–38, 301
Novelty and copyright law, 209
Nuisance of gray market, 4

Oldenburg, Don, 24n81
Olson, Bradley J., 74–75nn24–25
Omega watches, 19–20, 227
Online Channel Protection (OCP) software, 134
On-site security, 106–10
On-site visit of potential supply chain partners, 79–80
Ophthalmological equipment, 224, 228–29, 271, 284
Oral-B toothbrushes, 40
Order activity as warning sign of gray market activity, 125–27
Organized crime and counterfeit goods, 59–60
Original Appalachian Artworks, Inc., 25, 85, 217

Orlek, Joy, 109n102
Ortega, Amancio, 118
Osawa photographic equipment, 21–22, 50–51
Ozark Trading, 272–73

Packaging guidelines for distributors, 91
Painter, Steve, 109nn103–6
Palming off as trademark infringement, 245
Pantomimic works as copyrightable, 209
Parallel importation, 223, 226, 250
Parallel trading, 70
Parfums Givenchy, 221
Partner relationships imperiled, 44–46
Passariello, Christina, 303n32
Patents' novelty requirement, 209
Paul Mitchell, 15–16, 15n33, 196, 279–81
PayPal and technological improvements, 36
P&E, 127–28
Pears soap, 256–57
Penalties
  New York gray market statutes, 295
  for noncompliance by distribution partners, 99–101
  See also criminal offenses and penalties; punitive damages
Pens, 238–39
People as key to secure distribution channel, 78
Performance rights under copyright law, 214–16
Perfumes. See fragrances and perfumes
Perishables and distribution guidelines, 91
Personal care products
  California criminal offense statutes, 292
  copyright protection, 222–23, 225, 228–29
  Davidoff fragrances, 262–63
  eBay sales of, 303
  effects of gray market in, 14–16
  intentional interference with prospective economic advantage, 202–3
  Matrix hair products, 268–69
  Pears soap, 256–57
  Ralph Lauren, 222
  salon products, 202–3, 268–69, 277–81, 283–84, 292
  Sebastian, 283–84
  trademark protection, 247–49
  See also fragrances and perfumes; hair products; toothbrushes
Personal jurisdiction, 159–64

Perugina chocolates, 276–77
Pets.com and dot.com bust, 29
Pharmaceuticals
  chain of custody records, 108
  China as primary source of counterfeits, 103
  Congressional hearings on smuggling, 153n39
  consumer health and safety issues with counterfeits, 55
  erosion of consumer trust, 6
  EU gray market, 60–61
  gray market effects on, 22–24
  guidelines for distributors, 91
  pricing discrepancies, 116
  research and development costs, 51, 116
Philip Morris, 13–14, 162–63
Photographic equipment, 21–22, 49–51
Pictorial works as copyrightable, 209
Place of business
  forum selection clauses in distribution partner contracts, 92, 100, 106, 160
  investigation of potential supply chain partners, 79–80
PLD, 262–63
Poaching talent, 78
Point-of-sale reports, 132
Poland, 84, 104–5
Polaroid factors for trademark confusion, 256, 281–82
Police Blotter feature of eBay, 35
Political systems in geographically vulnerable locales, 106
Porcelain figurines and products, 195, 217–18, 253, 260–61
Porsche, 242
Post, Richard S. and Penelope N.
  Chinese legal system, 306n49, 308n58
  Global Brand Integrity Management, 9, 9n1, 44n21, 70n16, 102–3
  software piracy in Vietnam, 102–3
Postage stamps of The Beatles, 136
Postal Appropriations Act, 151n29
Potter's mark, 242
Power purchases and intentional interference with contract (IIWC), 194
Pratt & Whitney, 10
Preferred pricing for authorized resellers, 100–1
Prejudgment interest in copyright infringement cases, 240
Premier Dental Products, 258–60
Preregistration rule for copyrights, 211

Preservation of electronically stored information (ESI), 178–82
Presumption of confusion in trademark infringement cases, 260
Pretext purchasers, 134–40
Preventive strategies, 65–119
  alternative strategies, 115–119
  education, 65–76
  insurance, 119
  internal distribution, 117–119
  staggered distribution, 116–117
  troubleshooting supply chain vulnerabilities, 77–114
  worldwide pricing, 115–116
Price
  arbitrage generally, 36, 40, 104–5, 236
  monitoring, 123–25
  protection for distribution partners, 98–101
  strategies for preventing gray market activity, 98–101, 115–16
  warning signs of gray market activity, 123–25
Principal place of business concept and globalization, 38
Printing press invention, 208
Prius, 242
Privacy issues in investigations, 139, 140–42
Private use of copyrighted material, 216
Proactive strategies. See preventive strategies
Probation for distribution partners, 99–100
Production costs in geographically vulnerable locales, 105–6
Product security, 111–14
Profits
  as trademark infringement damages, 287
  and copyright infringement remedies, 239–40
Promises to distribution partners, 84–96
Prosser on Trots, 204n37
PT Cruiser, 47–49
Public Health Security and Bioterrorism Preparedness and Response Act, 108n97
Puerto Rico, 276–77
Punitive damages
  intentional interference with contract, 192, 197
  intentional interference with economic advantage, 205

Quaker brand, 242
Qualifying distribution partners, 78–81

California criminal offense of interference
  with, 291
and trademark infringement, 278

Serostim, 22–24
Service costs, 49–51
Service of process to acquire
  jurisdiction, 160
Shanghai Automotive Industry Corporation
  (SAIC), 12
Shanghai government, 12
Shefsky, Professor Lloyd, 3
Shell Oil, 267–68
Shipping guidelines for distributors, 91
Shoes, 266–67
Shoe World, 266–67
Siemens, 269
Signatures on distribution channel contracts,
  85–86
Sinclair, Upton, 132n3
Sisario, Ben, 28n2
SKF Manufacturing, 264–65
Slatalia, Michelle, 124n1
SMC Electronics, 128–29
Snowmobiles, 137–38
Soames, Emma, 118n15
Soap products, 256–57
Social consequences of gray market, 52–60
Soda counterfeits, 18
SoftMan, 230
Software
  Adobe, 33, 230
  AutoCAD, 231
  breach of contract theories, 186–87
  eBay offerings of counterfeit
    software, 33
  India, 308
  licenses and copyrights, 227–33
  Napster, 235–36
  See also computers; information
    technology; Microsoft
Sony warranty service, 49
Sorkin, Andrew Ross, 29n5
Sound recordings
  as copyrightable, 209
  Napster software, 235–36
South Africa, 83, 184, 222–23
Soviet Union breakup and gray market, 29
  See also Russia
Spain
  benefits of pharmaceutical gray market,
    60–61
  Cabbage Patch dolls, 85

Lladro Corp., 253–54
Zara brand, 117–19
Spikes in orders as warning sign of gray
  market activity, 125–26
Sports apparel and parallel trading, 70
Staggered distribution prevention strategy,
  116–117
Staples, 238–39
Stark Corporation, 220–21
State law, 289–96
Statute of Anne, 208, 208n1
Stay of civil proceedings, 156
Steel, gray market effects on, 21–22
Stephen Slesinger, Inc., 142
Stern, Willy, 10n2
Steroid use by baseball players, 125–26
Stevens, Justice, 226
Stolichnaya vodka, 17, 18
Storage guidelines for distributors, 91
Strickland, S., 148n15
Stross, Randall, 48nn33–35
Stuart, John, 242
Subsidiary corporations and trademark
  protection, 250–52
Successive corporate names as resource for
  investigations of potential supply chain
  partners, 79
Summit Technology, 224, 228–29,
  271, 284
Supply chain
  acknowledging geographic vulnerabilities,
    102–6
  on-site security, 106–10
  product security, 111–14
  security, 106–14
  tightening, 102–14
  transit security, 110–1
  troubleshooting vulnerabilities, 77–114
Suspension of distribution partners,
  99–100
Swatch products, 274–76
Sweatshops and Nike, 30, 31
Sweden's copyright protection for American
  authors, 213

Tacit approval of unauthorized
  exportation, 62
Taito Corp., 214–16
Tamex Corporation, 187–88
Tap Pharmaceuticals, 22
Tariff Act of 1930, 146
Tarnishment of trademark, 244–45
Tashima, 158n83, 161n100, 164n119

Tax revenue
 black market's effect on, 56–59
 cigarette gray market's effect on, 13–14, 56–59
 India's import taxes, 309
Taylor, Ned, 19
Technical support and training for distribution partners, 97
Technology
 as gray market aid, 35–37
 See also information technology (IT)
Telecommunications
 iPhones, 114, 116–17
 See also Internet; North America Association of Telecommunication Dealers (NATD)
Temporary restraining orders, 165, 167n8, 170–73
Tempur-Pedic, 80–81, 86, 273–74
Tenereillo, Pete, 107–8nn93–96
Teran, Horacio, 297n1
Terminated supply chain partners, 80
Termination of distribution partners, 101
Territorial exclusivities for distribution partners, 96–97
Terrorism
 and counterfeiting, 59–60, 60n94
 detection efforts, 131
Terry, Lisa, 107n91, 108nn98–99, 109nn102–3
The Beatles, 136
Thiel, Art, 30n8
Thilmany, Jean, 109nn100–1
Thompson, Stuart, 21n61
3Com as founding member of Alliance for Gray Market and Counterfeit Abatement (AGMA), 73
3-D Marketing Services, 184, 222–23
Tic Tacs, 18, 273
Tight Lies golf clubs, 68–70
Timber gray market, 22
Tires
 Bridgestone/Firestone tire recall, 5
 raw material limitation effects, 12–13
Tobacco
 settlement's gray market effect, 13–14
 See also cigarettes
Toblerone chocolates, 300
Toothbrushes
 Oral-B, 40
 oral contract with distributor of, 84, 104–5

Torts
 intentional interference with contract (IIWC), 191–98
 intentional interference with prospective economic advantage (IIEA), 199–205
Toy industry, 24–25
Toyota, 203–4
Tracking software, 109
Trade associations
 as resource for investigations of potential supply chain partners, 79
 See also specific trade associations
Trade barrier removal, 37–38
Trade loading by Gillette, 41
Trademark industry lobbying, 75
Trademark Protection Acts, 244
Trademarks, 242–87
 affirmative defenses, 282–86
 aggregate differences and infringement, 276–77
 artistic goods and material difference, 260–63
 authorized use exception, 250, 251
 causes of action, 244–45
 common control exception, 249–50, 251–52
 contract breach remedies compared, 183
 copyright distinguished, 248–49
 damages, 287
 definition of gray market, 4
 early gray market cases, 246–49
 European laws, 302–304
 federal jurisdiction, 158
 first sale doctrine, 282–84
 importance of, 242–44
 ingredient differences, 272–73
 injunctions for infringement, 286
 international registry, 298–99
 Lanham Act, 154–55, 244, 254–82
 likelihood of confusion, 245, 260–82
 material difference in goods, 260–82
 post-sale services and material difference, 263–65
 quality controls and material difference, 265–71
 registration of, 255
 remedies for infringement, 286–87
 Salon cases, 277–81
 seizure of infringing goods and marks, 167
 tampering with packaging, 218
 Tariff Act and gray market, 249–54

technological aids to counterfeiting, 36
warranty protection, 273–76
Trade Related Aspects of Intellectual Property (TRIPS) Agreement, 303, 303n29, 309
Trade secret security, 110
Training distribution partners, 80–81
Transit security through supply chain, 110–1
Transportation improvements' effects, 36
Treasury/Postal Appropriations Act, 151n29
Treble damages for trademark infringement, 287
TRIPS agreement, 303, 303n29, 309
Trout, Jack, 5n15
Truman, President and gray market steel industry, 21
Ty, 238
Tynan, Daniel, 90n41

UK. *See* United Kingdom
Unanimity rule for jury verdicts, 158
Unannounced visits of potential supply chain partners, 80
Undue influence as affirmative defense to breach of contract claim, 189
Unfair trade practices
    California gray market statutes, 290–91, 292
    Connecticut gray market statutes, 293–94
    International Trade Commission, 146
    New York gray market statutes, 295
    palming off, 245
Unilateral mistake as affirmative defense to breach of contract claim, 189
Unilever, 256–57
Unisys, 81
United Arab Emirates as market for gray market perfumes, 62
United Kingdom
    cigarette tax, 59
    Trade Marks Act, 302
United States Supreme Court
    first sale doctrine and importation rights, 224–27
    gray market defined, 4
    intellectual property protection, 51
    trademark infringement, 248–49
    trademark statutes, 244, 249, 251
    trash searches, 141–42
University of Maine, 112n122

UPC codes to track products and components, 109
UPS
    and technological improvements, 36
    tracking software, 109
U.S. Attorneys' CHIP units, 152
U.S. Customs Service
    and brand protection, 75
    and copyright protection, 212
    trademark importation regulations, 249–52
U.S. Embassy in Mexico, 301, 301n22
U.S. Trade Representative and Russian laws, 304, 304nn34–35

Venezuela and sale of Perugina chocolates, 276–77
Venue
    contractual provision with distribution partners, 91–92, 106, 164
    globalization and, 38
    litigation strategies, 163–64
Verified Rights Owner (VeRO) program on eBay, 35
Vernor, 231
Vesilind, Emili, 118n14
ViaLuxe, 19–20
Vicor Music, 220
Video games
    as target of gray market activity, 22
    copyright law, 214–16
Video surveillance, 107–8
Vietnam
    counterfeit watches, 60
    software piracy in, 102–3
Virginia Slims, 162–63
Vodka counterfeits, 17
Volvo as valuable brand name, 68
Vuitton, 303–4
Vulnerabilities
    acknowledging geographic vulnerabilities, 102–6
    troubleshooting supply chain vulnerabilities, 77–114

Wagstaffe, 158n83, 161n100, 164n119
Waiver
    breach of contract claim, 189
    copyright infringement claims, 235–36
    trademark infringement claims, 275–76
Walker, Leslie, 33n24
Wal-Mart, 78
Walt Disney Co., 142

Warner-Lambert, 270
Warning signs of gray market activity, 123–29
Warranties
  California gray market statutes, 289–91
  claims, 49–51
  Connecticut gray market statutes, 293–94
  exchange requests as warning sign of gray market activity, 128–29
  incentives for distribution partners, 97–98
  New York gray market statutes, 294
  product security and, 111–14
  Swatch products, 275–76
  trademark infringement issues, 273–76
  Yamaha's gray market policy statement, 72–73
Watches, 18–20, 170n19, 227, 274–76
Water's gray market, 22
Web sites. *See* Internet
Webvan and dot.com bust, 29
Weil Ceramics and Glass, 253–54
Western Glove, 149–50
Wicker, Dave, 112nn119–20
Williston on Contracts, 232n124
Winston cigarettes, 272
Wired magazine, 243
Withers, Kenneth J., 176n5

Worker safety infrastructure in geographically vulnerable locales, 106
Work made for hire, 210
Workstation audits, 90
World Health Organization (WHO) and counterfeit pharmaceuticals, 55n64
World Intellectual Property Organization (WIPO), 212n36, 298–99
World of Warcraft, 231–32
World Trade Organization (WTO)
  China's joining, 307
  established, 38
  Seattle conference in 1999, 30
Worldwide pricing as prevention strategy, 115–116
WoW game, 231–32
WowGlider, 231–32
Wrangler jeans, 149–50

Yamaha's warranty service on counterfeit goods, 72–73

Zamiska, Nicholas, 306n47
Zara, 117–19
Zehren, Charles V., 33n24
Zimmerman, Craig, 233n126
Zudker's Gifts, 195